D0085224

The Bloomsbury Group

a reference guide

A
Reference
Guide
to
Literature

Michael Begnal
Editor

The Bloomsbury Group

a reference guide

LAWRENCE W. MARKERT

G.K.HALL &CO.
70 LINCOLN STREET, BOSTON, MASS.

PR
478
.B46
M37
1990

All rights reserved.
Copyright 1990 by Lawrence. W. Markert

Library of Congress Cataloging-in-Publication Data

Markert, Lawrence W. (Lawrence Wayne), 1946-
The Bloomsbury group: a reference guide / Lawrence Wayne Markert.
p. cm. -- (A Reference guide to literature)
ISBN 0-8161-8936-6
1. English literature--20th century--History and criticism--Bibliography.
2. Bloomsbury group--Bibliography. I. Title. II. Series.
Z2013.M37 1989
[PR478.B46]
016.8209'00912--dc20   89-24408   CIP

This publication is printed on permanent/durable acid-free paper
MANUFACTURED IN THE UNITED STATES OF AMERICA

20358413

Contents

The Author

Lawrence W. Markert is the dean of the Yale Gordon College of Liberal Arts at the University of Baltimore. After completing his B.A. at the University of Baltimore and M.A. in the Writing Seminars at The Johns Hopkins University, Dr. Markert went on to complete his B.Phil. and D.Phil. at Oxford University. He is the author of various articles on late nineteenth- and twentieth-century literature and culture, as well as of several books, including *Arthur Symons: Critic of the Seven Arts* (UMI) and *Riddle and Incest: Poems* (New Poets Series). He also edited, with Carol Peirce, *On Miracle Ground II: Second International Lawrence Durrell Conference Proceedings* (*Deus Loci* and the University of Baltimore Monograph Series). *Arthur Symons: A Bibliography*, which he completed along with Karl Beckson, Ian Fletcher, and John Stokes, is due out shortly from ELT Press.

Preface

Bloomsbury: A Reference Guide provides students and scholars with a list of major works about this important group of British intellectuals, writers, and artists. As the index indicates, another checklist on Bloomsbury exists, The Bloomsbury Group: A Selective Bibliography (1978) by Rae Gallant Robbins, as do checklists on individual authors. However, this reference guide is the first annotated, comprehensive bibliography of secondary sources on the Bloomsbury Group as a whole.

The amount of written material about Bloomsbury and Bloomsbury figures which has been published is immense. It would be impossible to find and describe all that has appeared in print which relates to this group. Some selectivity, therefore, was necessary in preparing this guide. Part of the selection of materials to included involved deciding on who should be encompassed in the Group. S.P. Rosenbaum in The Bloomsbury Group: A Collection of Memoirs, Commentary and Criticism (1975) offers the best and most complete discussion of Bloomsbury membership. He begins by accepting Leonard Woolf's explanation that the original group, "Old Bloomsbury," should be defined by the original membership of the Memoir Club, which was formed in 1920 and was comprised of thirteen members who met to read memoirs, dine, and socialize. They were Virginia and Leonard Woolf, Vanessa and Clive Bell, Molly and Desmond MacCarthy, Adrian Stephen, Lytton Strachey, John Maynard Keynes, Duncan Grant, E.M. Forster, Saxon Sydney Turner, and Roger Fry. There is, however, room for some expansion of this list, as well as some argument with the names included in it. Quentin Bell in Bloomsbury (1968) states, for example, that Adrian Stephen was not a member of the Memoir Club, whereas Sydney Waterlow was.

Rosenbaum goes on to declare that this is a minimal list. Many others moved in and out of Bloomsbury over the years:

Edwardian Bloomsbury appears to have included, in addition

to the original thirteen, H.T.J. Norton, Gerald Shove, Sydney Waterlow, and innumerable Stracheys, especially James and Marjorie. During the First World War other members were added, including David Garnett, Francis Birrell, Mary St. John Hutchinson, Karin Costelloe, Barbara Hiles, Arthur Waley, Alix Sargent-Florence, Dora Carrington, Dorothy Brett, Mark Gertler, and Ralph Partridge. In the twenties and thirties many other figures became associated with the group, including Raymond Mortimer, George Rylands, Angus Davidson, Stephen Tomlin, Frances Marshall, Roger Stenhouse, and Lydia Lopokova. The Bell children, Julian, Quentin, and Angelica, should be added to this group, along with John Lehmann and Jane Bussy.

Rosenbaum stops short, though, in the comprehensiveness of his list. He does not include Lady Ottoline Morrell, T.S. Eliot, Bertrand Russell, Vita Sackville-West, Harold Nicolson, or the three Sitwells, Edith, Osbert, and Sacheveral. These figures also moved in and out of Bloomsbury, as did D.H. Lawrence.

The broadest definition possible of the membership of Bloomsbury is used for the purposes of this research guide, which includes all the names mentioned above. Only material that actually deals with these various figures in relation to Bloomsbury, however, is included and discussed.

Another aspect of the selection of the listings in this guide involves the range of activities in which Bloomsbury figures were involved. Some were painters. Others were critics, biographers, or economists. And others were novelists. This research guide gives an extensive sense of the range of activities and disciplines that occupied the members of Bloomsbury. It also includes articles and reviews that deal with the major events in Bloomsbury's history, such as the early days at Cambridge University and the Apostles, the two Post-impressionist exhibitions, and pacifism during World War I.

Finally, the selection of items included in this guide is designed to give an overall sense of the range of commentaries that has appeared on Bloomsbury. Obviously it includes the commentary by those who were drawn to Bloomsbury and those who were repelled. It also includes commentary or references that have appeared in memoirs, more substantial analyses in critical articles, as well as some reviews and commentary that are provocative if somewhat minor.

Inevitably, some commentary on Bloomsbury that may be significant may not be included in this guide. Some that is *insignificant* is certainly included. As more work appears, this guide will need to be brought up to date. I hope, therefore, that as students and scholars use this guide they will feel free to offer suggestions and corrections about articles and commentaries that should be included.

Compiling a bibliography about such a large number of people from such diverse backgrounds has required the assistance of various libraries, not to mention the dedication of two excellent graduate students. I am very much indebted to the Inter-Library Loan Department of the Milton Eisenhower Library of The Johns Hopkins University and the University of Baltimore Library staff. Two graduate students, Susan S. Flanigan and Andrea Markowitz, worked long hours and helped track down innumerable items. Susan, especially, I thank for many tedious hours of work.

Introduction

Stephen Spender in his autobiography *World within World* (1951) characterizes well the range of responses to Bloomsbury: "Bloomsbury has been derided by some people and has attracted the snobbish admiration of others: but I think it was the most constructive and creative influence on English taste between the two wars." E.M. Forster, in 1929, wrote that Bloomsbury was "the only genuine *movement* in English civilization" (1956). The debate over the literary history of Bloomsbury follows along these lines, questioning whether the Group actually existed and, even if it did, whether the it warrants serious study, as well as evaluating the reach of activities of the various members. Spender's and Forster's comments suggest that the influence of Bloomsbury extended into many aspects of British civilization. Some members were involved in fiction, biography, economics, painting, and the decorative arts; others were practitioners of literary, social, and art criticism; and still others became active in publishing and journalism.

Commentary on the Bloomsbury Group from the beginning addresses the issue of its social and cultural importance. Some early critics, such as Frank Swinnerton, Dmitri Mirsky, and F.R. and Q.D. Leavis, antagonistically dismissed Bloomsbury. Swinnerton in *The Georgian Literary Scene* (1934) states that the Group is "intellectually Royalist--royalist, you understand, to itself." Mirsky in *The Intelligentsia of Great Britain* (1935) describes Bloomsbury's liberalism as "thin-skinned humanism for enlightened and sensitive members of the capitalist class." The Leavises and their followers, particularly in their journal *Scrutiny*, describe Bloomsbury as "insulated by class" (1936).

Part of the negative reaction to Bloomsbury is based on controversial social and cultural activities of the Group. One of the first major events in the history of Bloomsbury was the Post-impressionist Exhibition of 1910, followed by the one in 1912, both organized by Roger Fry. The attitude of the general public to these events overflowed into the attitude towards Bloomsbury. Desmond MacCarthy served as secretary for the first exhibition, and Leonard Woolf served as secretary for the second, which included several paintings by Bloomsbury artists, including Vanessa Bell and Duncan Grant. Frank Reynolds's sketches in the *Illustrated London News* depict the confused and outraged faces of the those who attended the first exhibition (1910.9). Ian Dunlop in *The Shock of the New: Seven Historic Exhibitions of Modern Art* (1972) evaluates the nature of the public reaction and the importance of these events in the history of art and in the history of Bloomsbury.

Fry followed these events by establishing the Omega Workshops, which brought additional figures into the Bloomsbury fold, often with additional negative results (1911.15). Wyndham Lewis, for example, was involved in Omega and finally rejected Fry over a controversy with the commission for the Ideal Home Exhibition. Lewis then began his own campaign against Bloomsbury (Bell 1964.6). The Omega Workshops, however, gave other artists, such as Duncan Grant and Vanessa Bell, the opportunity to apply post-impressionist aesthetics to the decorative arts. The impact of this remained with them throughout their lives and showed up tangibly in Vanessa Bell's home in the country, Charleston. A considerable amount of recent criticism, some associated with the restoration of Charleston, deals with Omega and the decorative arts (1985.16).

Bloomsbury artists have become a popular ground for discussion, as has the interaction of the verbal and visual arts. The commentary on various exhibitions and the narrative in exhibition catalogs give some details of the work of these artists. Quentin Bell, in "Bloomsbury and the Arts in the Early Twentieth Century" (1964), describes Bloomsbury aesthetics as a revolt against Victorian aesthetics. Two biographical studies, *Vanessa Bell* by Frances Spalding (1975) and *Duncan Grant* by Douglas Blair Turnbaugh (1987), also discuss this connection. More recently, Diane Filby Gillespie's *The Sisters' Arts: The Writing and Painting of Virginia Woolf and Vanessa Bell* (1988) evaluates the inter-relation of the creative theory and expression of these sisters.

Was there really a Bloomsbury Group and who belonged to it? Several studies comment on this issue, including some by Bloomsbury figures themselves. Clive Bell in "Who is Bloomsbury?" (1954) and Leonard Woolf in *Beginning Again: An Autobiography of the Years 1911-1918* (1964) have commented on the membership. More recent studies have also dealt with this problem, including S.P. Rosenbaum, perhaps the foremost Bloomsbury scholar, in his introduction to *The Bloomsbury Group: A Collection of Memoirs, Commentary and Criticism* (1975) and Leon Edel in *Bloomsbury: The House of Lions* (1979). Quentin Bell, a member of the second generation of Bloomsbury, published his own study, *Bloomsbury* (1968). He suggests that the world was in need of "Bloomsbury liberation" and gives his sense of the membership.

The question of who actually belonged to Bloomsbury and who were merely associated continues to draw commentary. S.P. Rosenbaum gives one of the most liberal definitions of membership in *The Bloomsbury Group: A Collection of Memoirs, Commentary and Criticism* (1975), although he stops short of including such figures as Lady Ottoline Morrell, Bertrand Russell, and Vita Sackville-West. Quentin Bell in *Bloomsbury* (1968) offers his own list of members, as does Leonard Woolf in *Beginning Again: An Autobiography of the Years 1911 to 1918* (1964).

Related to the question of who belonged to Bloomsbury is the question of its origin. Most commentary, by both critics and by the members of Bloomsbury, place the beginnings at Cambridge University where many of the members first met, particularly Leonard Woolf, Thoby Stephen, Lytton Strachey, John Maynard Keynes, and Clive Bell. It was at Cambridge that the society or group spirit was born. As students these figures formed the Midnight Society, a reading and discussion group, and all but Bell were elected to the elite Apostles, properly known as the Cambridge Conversazione Society (Deacon 1985.11). Other figures who belonged to this society just prior to or during this period were Roger Fry, G.E. Moore, Bertrand Russell, E.M. Forster, David Garnett, Duncan Grant, and Desmond MacCarthy. It was through the associations of this society that much of the philosophy of G.E. Moore, which was so central to Bloomsbury, took shape, and that the relationships that were to form Bloomsbury began. Irma Rantavaara's *Virginia Woolf and Bloomsbury* (1953) and J.K. Johnston's *The Bloomsbury Group: A Study of E.M. Forster, Lytton Strachey, Virginia Woolf and Their Circle* were the first major studies to look at the connection between Moore's philosophy and Bloomsbury. Tom Regan's *Bloomsbury's Prophet: G.E. Moore and the Development of Moral Philosophy* (1987) is a recent study which makes this same connection.

There is another aspect of Cambridge, though, that must be taken into account, that of Leslie Stephen, father to Thoby, Adrian, Virginia and Vanessa. His intellectual tradition was passed on through his children and also influenced the attitudes of Bloomsbury, both adversely and positively.

Recently, S.P. Rosenbaum evaluates this aspect of the origins of Bloomsbury in his full-length study, *Victorian Bloomsbury: The Early Literary History of Bloomsbury* (1987).

The name *Bloomsbury* came with the relocation of the Stephen children following Leslie Stephen's death in 1904. 46 Gordon Square, Bloomsbury, became the seat of operation for both them and their Cambridge friends. This move, in itself, was a major event. It helped promote the tone of freedom and revolt against convention that became central to Bloomsbury. Many studies of Virginia Woolf, such as the early biographical study by Aileen Pippett, *The Moth and the Star: A Biography of Virginia Woolf*, point to this change as decisive.

World War I was the first major social-political event for Bloomsbury. Like all aspects of British culture Bloomsbury never fully recovered from the turmoil created by the war. Many of its members were actively involved in reaction against the war. Leonard Woolf, Lytton Strachey, Duncan Grant, and David Garnett were involved in the pacifist movement. It was during this period also that Bertrand Russell's association with the Group took shape, as did D.H. Lawrence's and Lady Ottoline Morrell's. David Garnett describes the association of some members during this period in "Keynes, Strachey and Virginia Woolf and 1917" (1955). Alan Wood's *Bertrand Russell: The Passionate Skeptic* (1957) describes Bloomsbury and Garsington Manor, Lady Ottoline Morrell's country home, and English pacifism. There are as well some studies which relate the war to the changing aesthetic of these figures, such as J.K. Johnston's "World War I and the Novels of Virginia Woolf" (1968).

There are other events fundamental to the history of Bloomsbury that occurred during or just after World War I. The Bells and the Woolfs established homes outside of London during the war. Some moved to farming areas in order to perform alternative service. Lady Ottoline Morrell's Garsington formed a parallel community where many Bloomsbury figures spent weekends.

Also during the war, in 1917, Leonard and Virginia Woolf established the Hogarth Press, which became the hub of much activity and brought together many artists and other figures who worked for the press, including John Lehmann. The press published T.S. Eliot's *The Waste Land*, among other works by some of the great writers of the period. Leonard Woolf's "How the Hogarth Press Began" (1964) describes its origin. Other memoirs give alternative perspectives. Richard Kennedy's *A Boy at the Hogarth Press* (1972) gives a critical portrait of Leonard Woolf as an employer. John Lehmann's *Thrown to the Woolfs* (1978) gives his bittersweet memories of his association with Hogarth. In 1924 the press began to publish the collected works of Sigmund Freud, edited by Alix and James Strachey. A recent edition of the letters of these two, *Bloomsbury-Freud: The Letters of James and Alix Strachey*, including an introduction by Perry Meisel and Walter Kenrick, gives the history of this aspect of Bloomsbury (1985).

The real activities of Bloomsbury ended with the death of Virginia Woolf in 1941, during the early years of World War II. Many of original group, however, lived well beyond the war, and the last meeting of the Memoir Club was in 1956. By this time, though, Bloomsbury was entirely backward looking. Memoirs and diaries had replaced fiction and art criticism. Leonard Woolf's autobiography began to appear in 1960 with *Sowing* and was followed by four more volumes. John Lehmann published *The Whispering Gallery: Autobiography I* and "Working With Virginia Woolf" (1955) and *I Am My Brother: Autobiography II* (1960). Lady Ottoline Morrell's *Ottoline at Garsington: Memoirs 1915-1918* (1974) describes the various Bloomsbury figures who visited her country manor outside of Oxford. *The Diary of Virginia Woolf* (1977) gives detailed and personal commentary on the developing attitude towards Bloomsbury, as well as insights into various Bloomsbury figures and relationships.

Works also began to appear that related to the figures in the second generation of Bloomsbury. Peter Stansky and William Abrahams published *Journey to the Frontier: Julian Bell and John Cornford* (1966), which deals with Julian Bell's Bloomsbury childhood. More recently, Angelic Garnett describes her somewhat bitter experiences in *Deceived With Kindness* (1984).

The variety of responses to the Bloomsbury Group is due in part to the variety of critical commentary that has been published. Over the years much that has appeared on Bloomsbury deals more with gossip than with real critical attention to the figures and the works they produced. The open and homosexual relationships have created some sensation. This phenomenon is in part due to the proliferation of diaries and memoirs associated with the Group. Several studies, however, try to deal seriously with the complexity of the relationships that made up much of Bloomsbury. Nigel Nicolson's *Portrait of a Marriage* (1973) deals fully and honestly with the marriage of Vita Sackville-West and Harold Nicolson, as well as with the relationship between Sackville-West and Virginia Woolf, which became a part of Bloomsbury in the 1920s. And George Spater and Ian Parsons published *A Marriage of True Minds: An Intimate Portrait of Leonard and Virginia Woolf* in 1978. Studies such as David Gadd's *Loving Friends: A Portrait of Bloomsbury* (1974) tend to promote the less serious, more gossipy approach.

Another aspect of the study of Bloomsbury, related to the study of the relationships that were central to the Group, involves the biographical studies of the various members. Virginia Woolf has inspired several accounts, including one by her nephew, Quentin Bell (1972), but perhaps the most provocative account that drew on itself much negative Bloomsbury commentary is Michael Holroyd's massive *Lytton Strachey* (1967). Much that brings John Maynard Keynes into Bloomsbury is biographical, beginning with Roy Harrod's *John Maynard Keynes* (1951), which does not, however, take into account Keynes's homosexuality as a part of his association with Bloomsbury as fully as subsequent studies. More recently, for example, Robert Skidelsky's *John Maynard Keynes*, vol. 1, *Hopes Betrayed: 1883-1920* deals much more extensively with the relationship between Keynes's private life and his economic theory.

These studies of the Bloomsbury Group, along with the many others included in this research guide, show that the nature and importance of this aspect of British culture is worthy of serious study. Numerous directions and possibilities remain unexplored. A recent conference in London that was advertised in the *London Review of Books* demonstrates the range of current interests and suggests some future directions:

> **Bloomsbury and Beyond**: Series of events reappraising the Bloomsbury myth, including "Art and Psychoanalysis," Peter Fuller's lecture, introduced by Charles Rycroft, about the relationship between the emergent psychoanalytic movement and the Hogarth Press (Friday 3 March at 7:30 p.m.) and "Post-Impressionism, Pure and Applied," a debate about Bloomsbury artists and critics, with Rosemary Hill, Judith Collins, Richard Cork and Frances Spalding (Friday 10 March at 7:30 p.m.).

Writings about the Bloomsbury Group, 1905-1989

1905

1   [STEPHEN, JULIAN THOBY.] "The Cambridge Muse."
Cambridge Review 27 (19 October):8.
    Review by Thoby Stephen, Virginia Woolf and Vanessa Bell's brother, of a collection of poems by various Bloomsbury figures, who were then students at Cambridge. Basis of article by S.P. Rosenbaum. (See 1984.57).

2   ____. "Euphrosyne." *Cambridge Review* 27 (2 November):49.
    Review of poems by Bloomsbury figures by their friend, Thoby Stephen. Basis of article by S.P. Rosenbaum. (See 1984.57).

1906

1   BROOKFIELD, FRANCES M. *The Cambridge "Apostles."* London: Pittman; New York: Charles Scribner's Sons. Reprint. New York: AMS Press, 1973.
    Gives background of Apostles and some selections of letters of various famous members, including Tennyson, Hallam, etc. Nothing specific on Bloomsbury. Helps to understand this aspect of the Group's background.

2   MAITLAND, FREDERIC WILLIAM. *The Life and Letters of Leslie Stephen*. London: Duckworth, 510 pp.
    Early study of Leslie Stephen. Gives intellectual and social background of Stephen children, who formed the center of Bloomsbury. Includes a section (pp. 474-76), "Impressions of Sir Leslie Stephen by One of His Daughters" (i.e. Virginia Stephen).

1910

1   BELL, CLIVE. Review of *Howard's End*, by E.M. Forster.
     Athenaeum 2 (3 December):696.
          Unsigned review that comments on the best in civilization: "The
     Schlegels are clever, sensitive, refined; they have a feeling for beauty
     and truth, a sense of justice and of proportion; they stand for what is
     best in modern civilization."

2   BINYON, LAURENCE. "Post-Impressionists." *Saturday Review*
     110:609-10.
          Early reaction to the post impressionist exhibition organized by
     Roger Fry. The reactions to this event set the tone for the reaction to
     the Bloomsbury Group in general.

3   "By Men Who Think the Impressionists Too Naturalistic:
     Attractions of All Societies: Works by Post-Impressionists."
     Illustrated London News (November 26):824-5.
          Photographs of various paintings in the first Post-impressionist
     exhibition. Gives good sense of the reaction to the exhibition.

4   "French Post-Impressionists at the Grafton Gallery." *Connoisseur* 28
     (December):315-16.
          Negative review of the exhibition, which was "largely filled with
     the works of extremists." These artists have "gone back to the most
     simple and primitive forms of expression, those of children and savage
     races. The result is the negation of art." No mention of Fry or
     Bloomsbury, but gives good sense of reaction to the exhibition Fry
     organized.

5   H., S. "The Grafton Gallery." *Spectator* 105 (12 November):797-98.
          Antagonistic review. "Post-impressionism apparently consists in
     forgetting all past art, and attempting to see the world as it appears to
     a child when it first begins to draw."

6   HIND, C. LEWIS. "The New Impressionism." *English Review*
     (December):78-89.
          Parts reprinted in *The Post Impressionists*. (See 1911.6).

7   HOLMES, C.J. *Notes on the Post-Impressionist Painters: Grafton Galleries, 1910-11*. London: Philip Lee Warner.
     Reaction to the exhibition Fry organized: "In surveying the exhibition as a whole, two or three facts assume particular prominence. In the first place it is undeniable that the effect of the collection is stimulating, even if we cannot at the moment diagnose the exact source of the stimulus." Gives overview of Post-impressionist aesthetic.

8   "Manet and the Post-Impressionists." *Athenaeum* (12 November):598-99.
     Sees work as opposition to established standards of "truth, morals, and aesthetics." Balanced review, opposed, however, to the view that "what is most attractive about these painters is that their acceptance would seem to imply a wiping-out of our whole system of aesthetics--a cleaning of the slate and a fresh start." Nothing specific on Fry or Bloomsbury. Sets tone for evaluation of the exhibition Fry organized.

9   "Post-Impressionist Paintings." *Times* (London) (7 November):12.
     "It [Post-impressionist art] professes to simplify, and to gain simplicity it throws away all that the long developed skill of past artists had acquired and bequeathed. It begins all over again and stops where a child would stop. . . ."

10   REYNOLDS, FRANK. "Post-Impressionist Expressions--Sketches." *Illustrated London News* (December):883.
     Illustrations of people at the Grafton Galleries for the first post-impressionist exhibition, depicting faces and attitudes of bewilderment.

11   RUTTER, FRANK. "Post Impressionist." *Sunday Times* (London) (15 November):14.
     Brief review stating that the Post-Impressionists "take an unorthodox view of form."

12   SICKERT, WALTER. "Post-Impressionists." *New Age* (2 June):23-29.
     Mostly negative reaction to the Post-impressionist exhibition organized by Roger Fry. (See 1911.9).

1911

1   BELL, CLIVE. "The Decorations at the Borough Polytechnique." *Athenaeum* (23 September):366.

      Positive commentary on the art of Roger Fry, Duncan Grant, and others associated with this project: "At the Borough Polytechnique one cannot help recalling the communal art of the great ages."

2   _____. Review of *Notes on the Post-Impressionist Painters, Grafton Galleries, 1910-11*, by C.J. Holmes. *Athenaeum* (7 January):19-20.

      Favorable opinion of book dealing with Post-impressionists and the reactions to the exhibition Roger Fry organized. Painters should not continue to "show their cleverness by creating illusions of reality."

3   _____. Review of *The Post-Impressionists*, by C. Lewis Hind. *Athenaeum* (8 July):51.

      Comments on critics troubled by the Post-impressionist exhibition; they have grown too used to materialist art rather than works that "express the spiritual significance of things."

4   CLUTTON-BROCK, A. "The Post-Impressionists." *Burlington Magazine* 18 (January):216-19.

      Does not mention Fry, but this is a commentary on the Post-impressionist exhibition. Compares throughout the work of Post-impressionists to poetry: "The better their pictures are, the more they look as if anyone could have painted them who had had the luck to conceive them; in fact, they look just as easy as the lyrical poems of Wordsworth or Blake."

5   FRY, ROGER. "Post-Impressionism." *Fortnightly Review* 89 (May):856-67.

      Article based on a lecture delivered at the Grafton Gallery, at the close of the Post-impressionist exhibition. Explains post-impressionism as an attempt to "discover the visual language of the imagination." Aim of this art is to "speak directly to the imagination through images created, not because of their likeness to external nature, but because of the fitness to appeal to the imaginative and contemplative life."

6   HIND, CHARLES LEWIS. *The Post-Impressionists*. London:
    Methuen. Reprint. Freeport, N. Y.: Books for Libraries Press,
    1969.
       Early discussion of post-impressionism which had become a
    novelty in England: "to some it is a re-birth of vision and feeling, to
    others the foul fruit of a horrid egotism." Post-impressionism opened
    avenues.

7   MacCARTHY, DESMOND. "Post-Impressionist Frescoes." *Eye
    Witness* (9 November):661-62.
       Commentary on the frescoes painted in the Borough Polytechnic
    by Duncan Grant, Roger Fry, and others: "Of the seven frescoes, Mr.
    Duncan Grant's bathers is certainly the best. The rhythm and vitality
    of the figures, the streaming wavy lines which symbolize the water,
    show how near an artist can get to suggesting reality by a convention
    which makes no attempt to represent it." This art is appropriate for an
    educational institution because it should provoke thought, breaks
    conventions.

8   SARGENT, JOHN S. "Letter to the Editor." *Nation* (7 January):65.
       Reaction to Roger Fry's article "A Postscript on Post-
    Impressionism" in which Fry mentions Sargent as a supporter of the
    Grafton exhibition. Sargent states that he is "absolutely skeptical as to
    their having any claim whatever to being works of art." Fry's response
    to this letter was published on 14 January 1911.

9   SICKERT, WALTER. "Post-Impressionists." *Fortnightly Review* 89
    (2 January):79-89.
       Negative commentary by one of England most distinguished
    painters on most aspects of the first Post-impressionist exhibition
    organized by Roger Fry. The overall attitude relates to the public
    reaction to Bloomsbury art.

1912

1   MacCARTHY, DESMOND. "Kant and Post-Impressionism." *Eye
    Witness* (10 October):533-34.
       Article comparing aesthetic theories of Kant to commentary on
    the second Post-impressionist exhibition by Roger Fry and Clive Bell:
    "It is not my purpose here to criticize the pictures, but to review the

preface, or rather these prefaces, for there are three, one by Mr. Fry, one by Mr. Clive Bell, and one by M. Anrep." Focuses on the problem of aesthetic merit in relation to representation. Bell's "significant form" is what Kant meant by "free beauty." Finally points out that a picture has to combine "secondary" or "romantic" beauty with what Fry calls "classic" beauty.

2   MacCOLL, D.S. "Year of Post-Impressionism." *Nineteenth Century* 71 (February):285-302.
       Overview article on the Post-impressionist controversy. Deals with Fry's various commentaries, including the lecture he gave at the end of the Post-impressionist exhibition. Agrees with Fry on many points. Also discusses the paintings of Fry and Duncan Grant. Focuses on the confusion of terms, *Classic* and *Romantic*: The school, in a word, renders their emotions about objects rather than the objects themselves, and Fry makes it the definition of all drawing that it distorts the object. Personal feeling, then, is the note of the movement, and the 'Post-Impressionists,' therefore, are not classic at all but extreme Romantics." Reprinted in *What is Art?* (New York: Harcort Brace, 1931).

1913

1   B., M.M. "Post-Impressionist Furniture." *Daily News and Leader* (7 August):3.
       Positive review of opening of the Omega Workshops: "Mr. Fry is trying to bring a 'spirit of fun' into our sedate homes." The showrooms had "a curiously exhilarating effect."

2   BELL, CLIVE. "Mr. Roger Fry's Criticism." *Nation* 12 (22 February):853-54.
       Letter to the editor in response to George Bernard Shaw's letter about a Roger Fry article. Describes Bloomsbury aesthetics. Describes "official art" and "aesthetic art."

3   ____. "Mr. Shaw and Mr. Fry." *Nation* 12 (8 March):928.
       Another letter to the editor, part of the critical exchange between George Bernard Shaw and Roger Fry about Bloomsbury aesthetics. Comments on the two views of art, "official" and "aesthetic."

Refers to G.E. Moore as the source: "Good drawing is ethically valuable, because it is a means to a good state of mind."

4   _____. "The New Post Impressionist Show." *Nation* (25 October):172-73.
     Commentary on exhibition organized by Frank Rutter, "Post-Impressionist and Futurist Exhibition," which included works by Cezanne and Wyndham Lewis. Expresses concern over the direction of English Post-impressionist painters: "Too many of the English Post-Impressionists are coming to regard certain simplifications, schematizations, and tricks of drawing, not as means of expression and creation, but as ends in themselves, not as instruments but as party favors." Reprinted as "English Post-Impressionists" in *Pot-Boilers*. (See 1918).

5   _____. "Post-Impressionism Again." *Nation* (29 March):1060-61.
     Uses praise for the pictures of children as a means of describing "The Grafton Group," which is exhibiting at the Alpine Club and includes Vanessa Bell, Frederick Etchells, Roger Fry, Duncan Grant, and Wyndham Lewis. States that "Post-Impressionism is not anarchic; it is indeed in spirit a protest against the anarchy which naturalism, impressionism, symbolism, romanticism, and anecdotic painting have all helped to introduce in modern art."

6   _____. "Post-Impressionism and Aesthetics." *Burlington Magazine* 22 (January):226-30.
     Article describing "significant form" based upon the negative reaction to the Post-impressionist exhibitions. "What quality is shared by all works that stir our aesthetic emotions? . . . Only one answer seems possible--significant form. In each, form and relations of forms stir our aesthetic emotions."

7   "Cezanne and the Post-Impressionists." *Times* (London) (8 January):10.
     Review focusing on Cezanne's water-colors: "But Cezanne's designs, however abstract, were always conceived in three dimensions; his music was the music of masses, not of lines or of flat spaces. That is what makes his art original and at the same time difficult."

8   CLIFFORD, H. "Mankind and the Jungle." *Blackwood's Edinburgh Magazine* 193 (June):844-51.
     Early review of Leonard Woolf's *The Village in the Jungle*.

9   "The Grafton Group." *Athenaeum* (22 March):339.
     Review of the Grafton Group at the Alpine Club Galleries, which included work by Duncan Grant, Roger Fry, and Wyndham Lewis.

10   "Inspired by Post-Impressionism." *Illustrated London News*, Ladies Supplement (25 October):iv.
     Photographs of a room designed by Roger Fry. The caption reads: "A Room designed by Roger Fry, where everything, even the furniture and ornaments, is cubist."

11   M., E. "The Omega Workshops." *Illustrated London News* (13 September):408.
     Commentary that focuses on one of the Omega Workshops screens: "The screen is 'anti-tradition." The fabrics are an assault upon the "rule of garlands and festoons, upon the sovereignty of the repeating pattern."

12   ____. "The Omega Workshops." *Illustrated London News* (27 December):1100.
     Commentary on the Omega Workshops as a part of "Art Notes": "Mr. Roger Fry is for the art that is at the heart of the barbarous Britisher; he is for real artistic invention in the things of daily life."

13   "Mr. Roger Fry on Principles of Design." *Connoisseur* (May):1.
     Comments on Roger Fry's Post-impressionist aesthetics and formalism.

14   "A New Venture in Art--Exhibition at the Omega Workshops." *Times* (London) (9 July):4
     Commentary on the Omega Workshops Exhibition, including Roger Fry's watercolors. Defines Fry's work in relation to his association with Post-impressionist aesthetics. Also comments on Duncan Grant and Wyndham Lewis, as well as on the various domestic articles on display: "They all follow Post-Impressionist principles that the representation of real objects, whenever practiced, is used as a motive of design and not to remind us of the realities represented."

15 "The Omega Workshops." *Times* (London) (10 December):13.
    Anyone who goes to the Omega Workshops Exhibitions and
forgets about such words as "Post-impressionists and futurist and their
horrid associations will find many things that are simply pleasant to the
eye." Most of the objects and patterns use abstract form.

16 SHAW, GEORGE BERNARD. "Mr. Roger Fry's Criticism."
    Nation 12 (15 February):817-18.
    Letter to the editor in response to the controversy over the Post-
impression exhibitions: "The Post-impressionists, stumbling over newly
broken ground, naturally give Alma-Tadema little credit for keeping his
balance so perfectly on the asphalt." Admires the technical
accomplishments of the artist.

17 _____. "Mr. Roger Fry's Criticism." *Nation* 12 (1 March):888-89.
    Another letter to the editor about the Post-impressionist
aesthetic. Comments on both Fry's and Bell's responses. Suggests there
is no such distinction between "academic drawing" and "aesthetic art."
Offers support for Fry's projects, finally.

1914

1 "Art and Reality." *Times* (London) (8 May):4.
    Deals with the Post-impressionist aesthetic and representational
art, based upon a review of exhibition at the Piccadilly Gallery, which
included paintings by Roger Fry, Wyndham Lewis, and Mark Gertler.

2 DAVIES, RANDALL. "The Grafton Group." *New Statesman* (10
    January):436-37.
    Discusses various works by Duncan Grant, Vanessa Bell, and
Roger Fry. Compared to Bell and Grant, "Roger Fry's landscapes
appear positively archaic." Sees the group as holding the future of art
in their hands.

3 _____. "The Omega Workshops." *New Statesman* (27 January):501-
    2.
    The Omega Workshops is a sign of the "revolt against the
soulless machine-made articles that were turned out of the factories in
the Victorian era." The "Omega designs are too violent a shock."

4   FRY, ROGER. "Art." *Nation* (7 March):937-39.
        Review of Clive Bell's *Art* in which Fry questions some aspects
of Bell's theory of significant form. He wishes that Bell had extended
his theory and "taken literature (in so far as it is an art) into fuller
consideration, for I feel confident that great poetry arouses aesthetic
emotions of a similar kind to painting and architecture."

5   "The Grafton Group at the Alpine Gallery." *Athenaeum* (10
    January):70.
        "Mrs. Clive Bell, Mr. Roger Fry, and Mr. Duncan Grant, being
alone named under this heading on the outside of the catalogue, we
must assume them to be now the sole members of the Group, and the
works of other exhibitors either that of well-meaning aspirants or
illustrious set there for our delight and edification."

6   HULME, T.E. "Modern Art I--The Grafton Group." *New Age* (15
    January):341-42.
        Commentary on the Grafton Group exhibition, which included
paintings by Vanessa Bell, Duncan Grant, and Roger Fry.

7   WOOLF, LEONARD. *The Wise Virgins: A Story of Words, Opinions
    and a Few Emotions*. London: Edward Arnold, 336 pp.
        Leonard Woolf's autobiographical novel based upon his early
association with Virginia and Vanessa Stephen and other Bloomsbury
figures. Gives good picture of Leonard's early reaction to the
Bloomsbury milieu. Leonard destroyed most copies not long after its
publication.

1915

1   AITKEN, CHARLES. "On Art and Aesthetics." *Burlington
    Magazine* 26 (February):194-96.
        Review-article on Clive Bell's *Art,* which focuses on the concept
of significant form. Deals somewhat with the relationship between
Bell's thought and Roger Fry: "Unfortunately, as it seems to me, the
author is resolved to separate art from life and ethics, and also to
underrate the human element."

2   FORSTER, E.M. Review of *The Voyage Out*, by Virginia Woolf.
     Daily News and Leader (8 April):7.
         "And perhaps the first comment to make about *The Voyage Out*
     is that it is absolutely unafraid, and that its courage springs, not from
     naivete, but from education."

3   "Mr. Roger Fry's Art: Composition in Three Dimensions." *Times*
     (London) (11 November):11.
         Looking at Fry's paintings, one can forget about the
     controversies of art criticism associated with him: "Mr. Fry may talk
     sometimes as if reality were nothing to him but a pretext or
     provocation to abstract design; but, in practice, he wins his greatest
     successes when he is immediately inspired by reality."

4   P., G. "A Monthly Chronicle--Omega Workshops." *Burlington
     Magazine* (November):80.
         Deals with the Omega Workshops' movement into literary
     publications and illustrations. The ideal is to create a publication in
     which page and illustration form a harmony with the literary idea.

5   SICKERT, WALTER. "A Monthly Chronicle: Roger Fry."
     Burlington Magazine (December):117-18.
         Negative review of Fry's paintings, based upon a negative
     reaction to Post-impressionism.

1916

1   BELL, CLIVE. "Modern Art." *Times* (London) (11 February):9.
         Includes some commentary on the Post-impressionist aesthetic,
     along with a discussion of the work of Spencer Frederick Gore. A
     separate section describes the Omega Workshops, along with the
     paintings of Vanessa Bell. Suggests that the method of the painters is
     more than "an absurd scribbling with paint."

2   CANNAN, GILBERT. *Mendel.* London: T. Fisher Unwin, 429 pp.
         Story of Mark Gertler's early life, including relationship with
     Dora Carrington. Carrington, who was a pupil of Gertler's at the
     Slade School of Art, is the novel's heroine. Involves considerable
     commentary on Bloomsbury in fictional context.

3   PHILLIPS, CLAUDE. "Roger Fry Exhibition." *Daily Telegraph* (16 November):3.
        Review of paintings by Roger Fry.

1917

1   MARRIOTT, CHARLES. "The New Movement in Art." *Land and Water* 18 (18 October):19-20.
        Commentary of exhibition organized by Roger Fry under the title, "The New Movement in Art." Most of the problems "about the new movement, about art in general, indeed, are caused by regarding art as an isolated phenomenon, beginning in the studio and ending in the exhibition, without any very close connection with the rest of life." Describes specific works by Duncan Grant and other Bloomsbury artists.

2   S., R. "The New Movement in Art." *Burlington Magazine* 31 (November):202.
        Review of exhibition held at Mansard Gallery for which the paintings were selected by Roger Fry. Includes paintings by Mark Gertler, Duncan Grant, Vanessa Bell. Sees them as realists in the tradition of Cezanne.

3   "A Visit to the Omega Workshops--Mr. Roger Fry on Modern Design and Applied Art." *Drawing and Design* (August):76-77.
        Commentary on the work of the Omega Workshops, which includes material on Fry's theory of the applied arts.

1918

1   BELL, CLIVE. *Pot-Boilers*. London: Chatto & Windus, 256 pp.
        Includes "The New Post-Impressionist Show" and other review articles that relate to Bloomsbury activities.

2   "Exhibition of Modern Paintings and Drawings at the Omega Workshops." *Burlington Magazine* 33 (December):233.
        Brief review of Omega painters, including Fry, Vanessa Bell, Duncan Grant, Mark Gertler, and Nina Hamnett: "The Omega Workshops have for some time past become a focus for certain artists

who take a leading part in the development of the modern movement in London."

1919

1 BELL, CLIVE. "Significant Form." *Burlington Magazine* 34 (June):257.
   Letter to the editor about D.S. MacColl's comment that Bell deals with "insignificant form."

2 FORSTER, E.M. "Visions." *Daily News* (31 July):2.
   Review of "Kew Gardens," by Virginia Woolf. Emphasizes the visual aspect of Woolf's work: "A vision has nothing to do either with unreality or with edification. It is merely something that has been seen, and in this sense Mrs. Woolf's two stories are visions." Also comments on Hogarth Press, which issued the text.

3 FRY, ROGER. "Modern French Art at the Mansard Gallery." *Athenaeum* (8 August):723-24.
   Comments in passing on the work of Virginia Woolf in which he compares her writing to contemporary painting.

4 "Look Here." *Sketch* (9 July):39.
   Commentary on the closing of the Omega Workshops.

5 MacCOLL, D.S. "Mr. Fry and Drawing--I." *Burlington Magazine* 34 (May):203-6.
   First of three lengthy letters to the editor in response to Fry's article on modern drawing. Argues against Fry's view that of the two basic elements in art, "significance" and "beauty," significance is the least important. Focuses on draftsmanship. Relates these issues to Clive Bell's "significant form."

6 _____. "Mr. Fry and Drawing--II." *Burlington Magazine* 34 (June):254-56.
   Second letter in the series, which argues with Fry's distinction between "calligraphy" and "structure," for the middle field is left out "from which springs all richness and subtlety of invention and discovery in design itself."

7   ____. "Mr. Fry and Drawing--III." *Burlington Magazine* 35
     (July):42-46.
         Third letter to the editor, dealing with Fry as artist, which deals
with concern with pure abstract design. Includes discussion of Wyndham
Lewis and Clive Bell and the "canon of form."

1920

1   BELL, CLIVE. "Duncan Grant." *Athenaeum* (6 February):182-83.
         Discussion of Duncan Grant in which Bell compares him to
Gainsbourgh and identifies his debt to Cezanne: "My notion is that
Duncan Grant often starts from some mixed motif which, as he labours
to reduce it to form and colour, he cuts, chips and knocks about till
you would suppose that he must have quite whittled the alloy away."
Reprinted as "Duncan Grant: A Great Modern English Painter" in *Arts
and Decorations* 13 (September 1920):246, and in *Since Cézanne* (New
York: Harcourt Brace, 1935).

2   ____. "Mr. Fry's Pictures." *New Statesman* 15 (19 June):307-08.
         Review of Fry's paintings at the Independent Gallery in Grafton
Street. Comments on the influence of Fry as art critic on Fry as
painter: "Mr. Fry does not paint like a school-master, but he does
paint like a critic." Concludes that his painting and criticism are of
equal value.

3   FRY, ROGER. "Mr. Duncan Grant's Pictures at Patterson's
     Gallery." *New Statesman* 14 (21 February):586-87.
         Review of Duncan Grant's first major show: "Mr. Duncan
Grant's work has never before been seen in mass." Comments on
Grant's use of colour and on his overall artistic development.

1921

1   BELL, CLIVE. "Mr. Fry's Criticism." *New Statesman* 16 (8
     January):422-23.
         Review of Roger Fry's *Vision and Design*. Describes Fry's
abilities to identify the "aesthetic key" to paintings: "It is easy to say
that Mr. Fry's supreme gift, as a critic, is a power of infecting others

with his own enthusiasm; difficulty begins when one tries to explain how he does it."

2   CANNAN, GILBERT. *Pugs and Peacocks*. London: Hutchinson, 288 pp.
      Fictional account of various Bloomsbury activities. Deals primarily with Bertrand Russell, Lady Ottoline Morrell, and Bloomsbury at Garsington.

3   CRAVEN, THOMAS JEWELL. "Mr. Roger Fry and the Artistic Vision." *Dial* 71:101-6.
      Commentary on Roger Fry's aesthetic, with special attention to the development of abstractionist ideals.

4   DREY, O.R. "Emotional Aesthetics." *Tyro* 1 (April):15.
      Includes negative commentary on the aesthetic approach of Roger Fry. Follows the lead of Wyndham Lewis and his conflict with Fry.

5   HOLMES, C.J. "Vision and Design." *Burlington Magazine* 38 (February):82-84.
      Review on Roger Fry's *Vision and Design*, which expresses concern over the separation of design from content. Based more upon a reaction to Fry and the Post-impressionist.

6   HUXLEY, ALDUS. *Crome Yellow*. London: Chatto & Windus. New York: George H. Doran, 1922, 307 pp.
      The setting is Philip and Lady Ottoline Morrell's country home, Garsington Manor. Both, along with Mark Gertler, Dorothy Brett, and other figures associated with Bloomsbury, are caricatured in the novel.

7   MacCARTHY, DESMOND. Review of *Monday or Tuesday*, by Virginia Woolf. *New Statesman* (9 April):18.
      Comments on Virginia and Leonard Woolf and the value of the Hogarth Press: "The Hogarth Press is a small, out-of-the-way tree which grows at Richmond and bears from time to time peculiar fruit." The inner life "seems to her incomparably the more vivid and real."

1922

1   BELL, CLIVE. *After Cezanne*. New York: Harcourt Brace &
    World, 230 pp.
        Collection of essays published in various periodicals. Includes
    "Duncan Grant" (pp. 105-12) and "Since Cezanne" (pp. 1-39), which
    comment on the Bloomsbury artists. Suggests that the work of Mark
    Gertler, Vanessa Bell, and Duncan Grant is generating interest because
    of their connection with Post-impressionists.

2   MORTIMER, RAYMOND. "Mr. Strachey's Past." *Dial* 73
    (September):338-42.
        Review of *Books and Characters*, by Strachey. Identifies qualities
    of Strachey's work, including "the startling vividity with which he paints
    his personages, . . . his attitude of ironic detachment, . . . the expert
    eye of a theatrical producer for dramatic effect."

3   ORANGE, A.R. "Mr. Bell's Pot." In *Readers and Writers*. New
    York: Alfred A. Knopf. London: Allen & Unwin, pp. 52-54.
        Negative commentary on Clive Bell's collection of essays *Pot
    Boilers*. Argues against Bell's Bohemian conception of art and his
    "Kensington Olympianism." Focuses on Bell in relation to World War
    I.

4   RASCOE, BURTON. "Art and Clive Bell." *Reviewer* 3, no. 3
    (June):487-95.
        Commentary on the aesthetic theories of Clive Bell, with some
    attention to the relationship between Bell and Roger Fry.

5   SICKERT, WALTER. "Vanessa Bell." *Burlington Magazine* 41
    (July):33-24.
        Review of Bell's painting, suggesting that women painters have
    an advantage: "Woman, then (and this is no toast), has this unsporting
    advantage over man, in her work, that she is generally free from the
    more piffling forms of dissipation, in which the lords of creation tend to
    waste a portion of their valuable time and energy."

1923

1   BELL, CLIVE. "Lytton Strachey." *New Statesman* 21 (4

August):496-97.

Reprinted and enlarged as "Recollections of Lytton Strachey." *Cornhill Magazine* 165 (Winter 1950):1-12. Collected in *Old Friends: Personal Recollections*. (See 1956.1).

2   FRY, ROGER. Introduction to *Living Painters: Duncan Grant*. Richmond: Leonard and Virginia Woolf. Reprint 1930, xi pp., 24 pl.

Duncan Grant is related implicitly to Bloomsbury through Fry's discussion of the "personality of his work." It is natural, spontaneous, and joyful. Also discusses his decorative work: "It is indeed greatly to be regretted that so rare a talent as Duncan Grant shows for all kinds of decorative design can find so little outlet in our modern life."

3   MIRSKY, DMITRI. "Mr. Lytton Strachey." *London Mercury* 8 (June):175-31.

Commentary by one of Bloomsbury's critics. Deals with Strachey's relationship with John Maynard Keynes. Reprinted in *Living Age* no. 308 (21 July):126-31.

1924

1   BELL, CLIVE. "Virginia Woolf." *Dial* 77 (December):451-65.

Deals with the painterly qualities of Woolf's work, which relates to his theory of "significant form": "In her reviews, as in her purely imaginative writings, she depended on that familiar impressionist method of hers." Suggest that "a first rate literary artist can never really be like a painter; for it is out of words that the literary arts have to create the forms that are to clothe their visions, and words carry a significance altogether different from the significance of lines and colours."

2   CANNAN, GILBERT. *The House of Prophecy*. London: Thornton Butterworth, 320 pp.

Fictional account that deals with various Bloomsbury activities. Focuses on Lady Ottoline Morrell's world at Garsington Manor, as well as the involvement of Bertrand Russell and other Bloomsbury figures.

1925

1   HUGHES, RICHARD. "A Day in London Life." *Saturday Review of Literature* (16 May):755.
       Review of *Mrs. Dalloway*, by Virginia Woolf. Compares the novel to the painting of Cezanne: "As well as the power of brilliant evocation she has the creative faculty of form which differs from what is ordinarily called construction in the same way that life differs from mechanism: the same quality as Cezanne."

2   LAVER, JAMES. *Portraits in Oil and Vinegar.* New York: Lincoln MacVeagh; Dial Press, 147 pp.
       Includes personal commentary on Roger Fry and his activities during the period of the Post-impressionists exhibitions.

1926

1   FORSTER, E.M. "The Novels of Virginia Woolf." *Yale Review* 15, 3 (April):505-14.
       Woolf has made a definite contribution to the novelist's art. She is not an "impressionistic writer, with little feeling for form and none for actuality." Reviews her novels in order. Reprinted as "The Early Novels of Virginia Woolf" in *Abinger Harvest* London: Edward Arnold, 1936.

2   FRY, ROGER. "Vanessa Bell." *Vogue* (Early February):33-35, 78.
       Commentary on the paintings and life of Vanessa Bell. Deals with her relationship with other Bloomsbury figures, as well with formal qualities of her painting and crafts work.

3   MUIR, EDWIN. *Transition: Essays on Contemporary Literature.* New York: Viking Press, 346 pp.
       Includes essays on Lytton Strachey and Virginia Woolf in relation to trends in modern literature.

4   PARKER, DeWITT. *The Analysis of Art.* New Haven: Yale University Press, 190 pp.
       General consideration of artistic analysis, with discussions of aesthetic form, design, and the function of art. Draws heavily upon the work of Clive Bell and Rover Fry, and includes some commentary on

the combined writings of these two Bloomsbury figures in relation to aesthetic theory.

1927

1   BLANCHE, J.-E. "An Interview with Virginia Woolf." *Les Nouvelles Littéraires* (13 August):1-2.
    Gives an impression of the Bloomsbury world of which Virginia Woolf was a part: "The small circle of Bloomsbury Intelligentsia protects the delicate health of its captive from a public curiosity which fashion increases from year to year, in America as well as in England."

2   BURDETT, OSBERT. "The Sitwells." *London Mercury* 15 (March):515-25.
    Commentary on the literary scene in Georgian England, including the work of the Sitwells. Involves some discussion of Bloomsbury and Bloomsbury-related figures.

3   DAVIS, ROBERT TYLER. "Mr. Bell and Mr. Fry." *Hound & Horn* 1, no. 1 (Summer):18-22.
    Describes the connection between the aesthetics of Clive Bell and Roger Fry.

4   FORSTER, E.M. *Aspects of the Novel.* London: Edward Arnold. 153 pp.
    Compares Virginia Woolf to Laurence Sterne. They are both "fantasists": "They start with a little object, take a flutter from it, and settle on it again."

5   FRANK SWINNERTON [Simon Pure]. "The Londoner." *Bookman* 65, no. 4 (June):456-58.
    Negative commentary on Bloomsbury based upon a critical assessment of articles by Lytton Strachey and Virginia Woolf in *Nation*: "Mrs. Woolf and Mr. Strachey are intellectuals. They are paragons of taste. And, like most of their kind, they are lacking in sensibility." This is the world of Bloomsbury.

1928

1   MacCARTHY, DESMOND. "Modern Biography." *Life and Letters*
    1, no. 2 (July):136-40.
        MacCarthy suggests that Strachey's influence on biographical
    technique has some negative characteristics. Ever since *Eminent
    Victorians*, biographers have attempted to "arrest our attention by their
    opening sentence and to stuff every subsequent page with picturesque
    details."

2   ____. "Phantasmagoria." *Sunday Times* (London) (14 October):10.
        Review of *Orlando* by Virginia Woolf. Gives overview of her
    work, identifying *Orlando* as one of her best books.

3   MORTIMER, RAYMOND. "London Letter." *Dial* 89
    (February):238-40.
        Open letter describing some aspects of the Bloomsbury Group
    based upon his experiences: "But the group was always an oligarchy--
    fierce mutual criticism was the breath of its existence." Does not think
    he can offer a full definition of the Bloomsbury spirit: "But I would
    place first a belief in Reason, and a conviction that the pursuit of
    Truth and a contemplation of Beauty are the most important of human
    activities."

4   ____. "Mr. Strachey's New Book." *Nation and Athenaeum* 44
    (November):295.
        Review of Strachey's *Elizabeth and Essex*. Sees Strachey as a
    Romantic, as especially revealed in this book: "The book is designed
    and executed as a picturesque tragedy."

5   NICOLSON, HAROLD. *The Development of English Biography*.
    New York: Harcourt, Brace, pp. 148-54.
        Commentary on Strachey's biographical method by one of the
    later Bloomsbury members. Strachey's work is based upon "a fervent
    belief in intellectual honesty" and on "a calm conviction that thought
    and reason are in fact the most important elements in human nature."
    Cannot, finally, call Strachey's work "pure biography."

6   SWINNERTON, FRANK. *A London Bookman*. London: Secker &
    Warburg, 210 pp.
        Includes negative commentary on Bloomsbury: "Just as it seems

to me that this group suffers from intellectual inbreeding, so I feel that it has no relation whatever to the normal life of the community. Before one can appeal to a member of this group, one must be, above everything else, strange. One must be bizarre. One must be exotic."

7   WOOLF, VIRGINIA. Preface to *Orlando*. New York: Harcourt, Brace, pp. 11-14.
      Acknowledges various Bloomsbury figures as important to Woolf's artistic development, including Saxon Sydney-Turner, Lydia Lopokova, and Lady Ottoline Morrell. The list is extensive.

1929

1   BAYES, W. "Mr. Duncan Grant." *Saturday Review* 147 (23 February):245-46.
      Commentary on the painting of Duncan Grant, which connects him to the Omega Workshops and other Bloomsbury artists.

2   EARP, T.W. "Mr. Duncan Grant." *New Statesman* 32 (23 February):633.
      Review of Duncan Grant's work at the Paul Guillaume Gallery. Grant's reputation among connoisseurs is good, but the general public is not aware of his work.

3   HUDGSON, S. "Mr. J.M. Keynes." In *Portraits and Reflections*. New York: Dutton, pp. 152-57.
      Personal comments on John Maynard Keynes, which makes some connection between Keynes and his Bloomsbury friends, many of whom he met at Cambridge.

4   MORTIMER, RAYMOND. "Mrs. Woolf and Mr. Strachey." *Bookman* 68 (February):625-29.
      Sees *Elizabeth and Essex* and *Orlando* as the most remarkable books of the autumn season: "Both Mrs. Woolf and Mr. Strachey are firebrands: she has revolutionized fiction and he, biography." Deals with the life and work of each, describing as well some aspects of the development of the Hogarth Press. Finally, they have in common "a quality of inherited culture."

5   SACKVILLE-WEST, VITA. Review of *A Room of One's Own*.
    Listener (6 November):620.
        Comments on Woolf's message to women, as well as to men:
"The burden of Mrs. Woolf's exhortation to women is that they should
be themselves, and should exploit their own particular gifts instead of
trying to emulate the gifts proper to the masculine mind."

6   SICKERT, R. "Duncan Grant." *Nation* 44 (16 February):687.
        Brief commentary on the work of Duncan Grant. Relates him
somewhat to other Bloomsbury artists.

7   SMYTH, CHARLES. "A Note on Historical Biography and Mr.
    Strachey." *Criterion* 8 (July):658.
        Discussion of the qualities necessary in good history and good
biography, which include selectivity, quality prose style, and a sense of
humor. Identifies Strachey as the idol of "the Bright Young Men who
have somehow made a corner in contemporary criticism."

8   THURSTON, MARJORIE. "The Development of Lytton Strachey's
    Biographical Method." Ph.D. dissertation, University of Chicago, 235
    pp.
        Early critical study of Lytton Strachey. Deals with the intellectual
milieu from which Strachey came, including his Cambridge associates
and Bloomsbury friends.

1930

1   FURST, H. "Vanessa Bell: Recent Paintings at the London Artist's
    Association." *Apollo* 11 (March):224.
        Review of paintings by Vanessa Bell. Brief commentary on her
artistic association with other Bloomsbury figures.

2   WOOLF, VIRGINIA. Introduction to *Vanessa Bell: Recent Paintings*.
    Exhibition Catalog. London: London Artists' Association; Cooling
    Galleries.
        Describes the unique fact that a woman is showing pictures: "It
is Mrs. Bell who is determined that we shall not loll about juggling with
pretty words or dallying with delicious sensations. There is something
compromising about her art."

1931

1   CAMPBELL, ROY. *The Georgiand: A Satirical Fantasy in Verse.*
     London: Boriswood, 64 pp.
         Narrative poem that satirizes Bloomsbury and individual
     Bloomsbury figures.

2   EARP, T.W. "Mr. Roger Fry." *New Statesman* 36 (21
     February):585-86.
         Review of Roger Fry paintings at the Cooling Galleries: "In the
     earlier work there are traces of the influence of Whistler, Richard
     Wilson, and the first revelation of post-impressionism narrowing down
     to a deep admiration of Cézanne."

3   GARNETT, DAVID. Foreword to *Duncan Grant: Recent Paintings.*
     Exhibition Catalog. London: Cooling Galleries.
         Comments on Grant's connection with the Omega Workshops
     and other Bloomsbury artists, such as Vanessa Bell.

4   MacCARTHY, DESMOND. *Portraits.* London: Putnam. New
     York: Macmillan, 1932. Reprint. New York: Oxford University
     Press, 1954. Freeport: Books for Libraries, 1972.
         Includes commentary on Henry James's influence on Lytton
     Strachey's Cambridge and the carryover to Bloomsbury in general:
     "We were not much interested in politics. Abstract speculation was
     much more absorbing. Philosophy was much more interesting to us than
     public causes. The wave of Fabian socialism, which affected some of
     Lytton Strachey's younger contemporaries like Rupert Brooke, had not
     reached Cambridge in my time." Strachey fixed attention on emotions
     and the relationships between human beings.

5   MacCOLL, D.S. *Confessions of a Keeper and Other Papers.* New
     York: Macmillan, 235 pp.
         Includes commentary on the Post-impressionist exhibitions that
     Roger Fry organized, including reactions of the general public. Relates
     the reactions to Bloomsbury in general.

6   MORTIMER, RAYMOND. "Grant: Exhibition at 92 Bond Street."
     Architectural Review 69 (June):218.
         Commentary on Duncan Grant exhibition by one of his
     Bloomsbury friends.

7   NICOLSON, HAROLD. Review of *The Waves*, by Virginia Woolf. *Action* (8 October):8.

      This novel will cause a sensation because Woolf has carried the internal monologue "a stage further than was dreamt of even by Joyce." Woolf's aim is "to convey the half-lights of human experience and the fluid edges of personal identity."

8   ____. "The Writing of Virginia Woolf." *Listener* (18 November):864.

      Discussion of Woolf's work by Vita Sackville-West's husband and a related Bloomsbury figure.

1932

1   HAMNETT, NINA. *Laughing Torso: Reminiscences of Nina Hamnett*. London: Constable; New York: Ray Long and Richard R. Smith, 326 pp.

      Includes personal accounts of various Bloomsbury figures, including, in particular, Roger Fry, for whom Hamnett worked during the Omega Workshops days. Also comments on the Sitwells.

2   MacCARTHY, DESMOND. "Lytton Strachey as a Biographer." *Life and Letters* 8 (March):90-102.

      Argues that Strachey's real importance was not in his reaction against the Victorian Age but in his artistry as a biographer: "To Lytton Strachey biography was interpretation, and therefore the record, not only of facts, but of the biographer's deepest response to them." His work shows that in history an interest in human nature and character should be most important.

3   ROTHENSTEIN, JOHN. *Men and Memories: Recollections of William Rothenstein, 1900-1922*. New York: Coward-Mcann, 395 pp.

      Includes a considerable amount of commentary on Roger Fry, especially in relation to the Post-impressionist exhibition. Fry became the central figure to a group of young English painters: "Fry is symbolic of his time, a time when opinions seem of supreme importance."

4   SHEEAN, VINCENT. "Lytton Strachey: Cambridge and
      Bloomsbury." *New Republic* 70 (February 17):19-20.
          A response to Strachey's recent death. Overview of his life and
the formation of Bloomsbury during World War I. Identifies the
"particular thing called 'Bloomsbury' in contemporary English letters
and art" as related to G.E. Moore. The highest good is found in
"personal affection" and "aesthetic enjoyment."

5   WILSON, EDMUND. "Lytton Strachey." *New Republic* 72 (2
      September):146-48.
          Lytton Strachey's "chief mission, of course, was to take down
once for all the pretensions of the Victorian Age to moral superiority."
In *Elizabeth and Essex* we "become disagreeably aware of the high-
voiced old Bloomsbury gossip gloating over the scandals of the past as
he ferrets them out in his library." Also printed in *New Statesman* 4
(24 September):344-45, and in *The Shores of Light* (New York: Farrar,
Strauss & Young, 1952), pp. 551-56.

6   WOOLF, LEONARD. "Lytton Strachey." *New Statesman and
      Nation* 3 (30 January):118-19.
          The most important thing about Strachey's work is "that his
writings came so directly from himself, from the very core of his
character." Comments on his time at Cambridge with Strachey. "He
became a prose writer partly because his verse never came up to the
standard which he himself demanded of poetry, and partly because the
immense influence which Professor G.E. Moore and *Principia Ethica*
exercised upon him, as upon so many of his contemporaries, turned his
mind in other directions." Strachey's character is a combination of
contradictory qualities. "He was an iconoclast who loved traditions," a
cynic and a romantic.

1933

1   BARNES, T.R. "Lytton Strachey." *Scrutiny* 2 (December):301-3.
          Review of Strachey's *Characters and Commentaries*. Comments
on Strachey's "snobbery and querulous inferiority feelings." Thinks he
is a negative influence on English letters: "He set a tone which still
dominates certain areas of the highbrow world--e.g. that part of
Bloomsbury which has a well-known annex in Cambridge." Sees

Virginia Woolf's last work as poor and the result of this negative
influence.

2   BRETT, DOROTHY. *Lawrence and Brett: A Friendship.*
     Philadelphia: Lippincott, 301 pp.
         The opening chapter, "London," describes Lawrence's first
     meeting with Brett and the relationship that developed within the
     context of the intellectual life in London during and after World War I.
     Brett at this time was close friends with Dora Carrington and Mark
     Gertler, as well as with Katherine Mansfield. The bulk of the book
     deals with Brett and Lawrence once they had left London for New
     Mexico.

3   CLARK, KENNETH. "Drawings by Duncan Grant at Agnew's."
     New Statesman and Nation (17 June):790.
         Comments on Duncan Grant's use of color and on his pastels:
     "Mr. Clive Bell once compared his imagination to that of the more
     lyrical Elizabethan dramatists. Like them, he is much concerned with
     the sensuous world of Paganism and earthy adventures of amorous
     gods."

1934

1   BELL, CLIVE. "Duncan Grant." *New Statesman and Nation* 7 (19
     May):763-64.
         Commentary on exhibition at the Lefevre Galleries. Compares
     Grant's work to Vanessa Bell's, suggesting that before this exhibition
     they were similar: "Duncan Grant has deliberately called the intellect
     into play." Identifies Constable and Cézanne as influences.

2   FORSTER, E.M. *Goldsworthy Lowes Dickinson*. London: Edward
     Arnold, 397 pp.
         Comments briefly on G.E. Moore's influence at Cambridge.
     Mentions other members of the Bloomsbury Group who were at
     Cambridge during this period.

3   ____. "Roger Fry." *London Mercury* 30 (October):495-96.
         Obituary notice: "He was charming, polite, courageous, and gay
     in his private life; he was generous and energetic; he was always
     helping people, especially the young and the obscure." He "rejected

authority, mistrusted intuition." Reprinted as "Roger Fry: An Obituary Note" in *Abinger Harvest* (London: Edward Arnold, 1936).

4   HOLMES, SIR CHARLES J. "Roger Fry and *The Burlington*." *Burlington Magazine* 65 (October):145-46.
   Brief commentary on Fry's efforts in the establishment of the *Burlington Magazine*. Mentions the 1918 purchase of paintings for National Collection, which were purchased by the Treasury through Keynes's influence.

5   LEWIS, WYNDHAM. Letter to the Editor. *Spectator* (2 November):578.
   Response to Stephen Spender's review of *Men Without Art* and Spender's defense of Virginia Woolf.

6   ____. "Roger Fry." *New Statesman and Nation* 8 (22 September):356-57.
   Describes personal reaction to Fry's thought as an art critic, identifying candor as necessary for "arriving at a true judgment or disentangling a mutual predicament, a quality so valuable in personal relations and so necessary to the intellectual life."

7   ____. "Virginia Woolf." In *Men Without Art*. London: Williams Press, pp. 158-71.
   Attacks Virginia Woolf and Bloomsbury: "I am ready to agree that the intrinsic literary importance of Virginia Woolf has been exaggerated by her friends." She has "crystallized for us, in her critical essays, what is in fact *the feminine*--as distinguished from the feminist-- standpoint."

8   MacCARTHY, DESMOND. "Roger Fry as a Critic." *New Statesman and Nation* 8 (15 September):324-25.
   Art criticism requires various qualities, which Fry possessed to a rare degree: "sincerity is self-observation, intensity of feeling, the gift of intellectual analysis, wide aesthetic experience and enthusiastic curiosity."

9   MacCOLL, D.S. "Note on Roger Fry." *Burlington Magazine* 65 (September):23-25.
   Gives background to Fry and his aesthetic, as well as some

personal reactions to Fry. Identifies the trends in Fry's thought, including some aspects of the Bloomsbury influence.

10   MORTIMER, RAYMOND. "Saucers and Socialism." *New Statesman and Nation* 27 (27 October):585-86.
         Commentary on industrial design, particularly in relation to the Ideal Home Exhibition. The results in home furnishing designs as a result of commissions to thirty or more artists are "amazingly good." Vanessa Bell's and Duncan Grant's designs are singled out for design.

11   ROWDON, JOHN. *This Book about Painting deals with the Work of Duncan Grant from the Point of View of John Rowdon.* London: H.J.W. Marks, 35 pp.
         Commentary on the painting of Duncan Grant. Includes some allusions to other Bloomsbury painters.

12   SANDLER, MICHAEL E. "Roger Fry: An Appreciation." *Life & Letters* 11, no. 58 (October):14-20.
         Describes influence Roger Fry and C.J. Holmes have had on his sense of "the design of pictures and the significance of art." Fry's Quaker background has instilled "sincerity of vision, integrity of mind, fearlessness, devotion to honesty in judgment and in utterance." Describes the importance of Fry's organization of the Post-impressionist xhibitions and the Omega Workshops.

13   SPENDER, STEPHEN. Review of *Men without Art*, by Wyndham Lewis. *Spectator* (19 October):574, 576.
         Defends Virginia Woolf against Lewis's anti-Bloomsbury attacks: "Why should Mrs. Woolf seem to suffocate Mr. Lewis?" The book lacks true critical perspective.

14   SWINNERTON, FRANK. "Bloomsbury." In *The Georgian Literary Scene.* New York: Farrar & Rinehart, pp. 339-77.
         Chapter 13, "Bloomsbury: Bertrand Russell, Roger Fry and Clive Bell, Lytton Strachey, Women, Virginia Woolf." Lengthy, antagonistic evaluation of Bloomsbury. Feels the group was comprised of "ill-mannered and pretentious dilettanti." The Group was "politically Left, and only intellectually Royalist--royalist, you understand, to itself." Describes the history of Bloomsbury, "how I think Bloomsbury came into being, and how in the War-time and immediately after the War it found its opportunity for taking the town." Sections on individual

figures are often equally critical. Russell relies on facts, "but for some people, such as myself, to whom logic is the enemy of truth, Russell is an unconvincing pleader." Less disparaging of Clive Bell and Roger Fry, although their association with Bloomsbury still condemns them. Lytton Strachey, however, is too bookish: "He was a bookworm and a talker with bookworms, a male bluestocking." Identifies Philip Guedalla as an imitator of Strachey and Bloomsbury aesthetics. Discusses development of women's movement and of women's education in relation to World War I as leading directly to the work of Virginia Woolf. Her novels seem "very clever, very ingenious, but on the whole creatively unimportant." Her success is due to educational snobbery.

1935

1   BELL, CLIVE. "Art in 1910." *New Statesman and Nation* 9 (4 May):632-35.
    Commentary on the state of art in England prior to the first Post-impressionist exhibition in 1910: "The New English Art Club stood for what was then modern and intelligent in England. For the most part its members derived inspiration, directly or indirectly, from the Impressionists: they were followers of followers of the masters."

2   BELL, JULIAN, ed. *We Did Not Fight: Experiences of War Resisters*. London: Cobden-Sanderson, 392 pp.
    Includes some commentary on the Bloomsbury figures who were involved in the pacifist movement during World War I.

3   BOAS, GUY. *Lytton Strachey*. London: English Association. An English Association Pamphlet. London: Oxford University Press, 32 pp.
    General discussion of the life and work of Lytton Strachey. Gives some detailed references to his affiliation with Bloomsbury.

4   MIRSKY, DMITRI. "The Highbrows: Bloomsbury." In *The Intelligentsia of Great Britain*. Translated by Alec Brown. London: Victor Gollancz, pp. 111-20.
    Negative commentary on Bloomsbury ideals, giving the history of Bloomsbury's origins in Cambridge: "The basic trait of Bloomsbury is a mixture of philosophical rationalism, political rationalism, estheticism, and a cult of individuality." Bloomsbury's liberalism can be defined as

"thin-skinned humanism for enlightened and sensitive members of the capitalist class." Virginia Woolf is the "principle literary expression of Bloomsbury."

5   MYERS, L.H. *The Root and the Flower*. London: Jonathan Cape. 583 pp.
       Novelistic account of Bloomsbury activities, which satirizes Bloomsbury.

6   ROBERTS, R. ELLIS. "The Georgian Authors: Gaps in Mr. Swinnerton's Picture." *Sunday Times* (London) (14 April):17.
       Defends Virginia Woolf and Bloomsbury, suggesting that Woolf is the most original mind that has written novels in the last 20 years.

7   WOOLF, VIRGINIA. Introduction to *Roger Fry: Memorial Exhibition*. Exhibition Catalogue. Bristol: Bristol Museum and Art Gallery.
       Reprinted in *The Moment and Other Essays*. (See 1947.10).

1936

1   GARNETT, DAVID. "Books in General." *New Statesman and Nation* 11 (21 March):459.
       Review of E.M. Forster's *Abinger Harvest*. Compares Forster to Lowes Dickinson, Roger Fry, and Lytton Strachey in relation to World War I and current world violence and Fascism. These figures have in common a belief in reason and a mistrust of intuition.

2   HENDERSON, PHILIP. "Bloomsbury: Virginia Woolf, E.M. Forster." In *The Novel Today: Studies in Contemporary Attitudes*. London: John Lane; Bodley Head, pp. 87-96.
       Woolf's novels depict "a drawing-room world liable to be shattered as soon as its doors and windows are thrown open to the rumors of a greater and more turbulent life outside." Civilization as Woolf defines it can be drawn from Clive Bell's *Civilization*: "The only really civilized epochs in history were the age of Pericles in Athens, the Italian Renaissance, and eighteenth-century France, where culture was the expression of the lives of an enlightened leisure class." Forster deals with this issue, even in *A Passage to India*, "in which Bloomsbury may be seen making a temporary excursus from its ivory tower."

3   HOLMES, C.J. *Self and Partners (Mostly Self)*. London: Constable.
New York: Macmillan, 187 pp.
    Autobiographical account, which includes commentary on Roger
Fry and on the Post-impressionist exhibitions.

4   JONES, E.B.C. "Virginia Woolf and E.M. Forster." In *The English
Novelist*. Edited by Derek Verschoyle. London: Chatto & Windus,
pp. 261-63.
    Commentary on the exchange of ideas between Virginia Woolf
and E.M. Forster. Deals somewhat with the Bloomsbury context in
which the aesthetic ideals of these two writers developed.

5   STEPHEN, ADRIAN. *The "Dreadnought" Hoax*. London: Leonard
and Virginia Woolf. Reprinted with introduction by Quentin Bell.
London: Chatto & Windus; Hogarth Press, 1983, 61 pp.
    Account of Horace de Vere Cole's hoax of the Royal Navy
when he visited the fleet dressed as the uncle of the Sultan of
Zanzibar. His entourage included Duncan Grant, Adrian Stephen, and
Virginia Woolf. Quentin Bell states in his introduction that the hoax
was the source of endless merriment and some indignation. This
incident in part is responsible for the Bloomsbury reputation for
frivolity.

1937

1   BLANCHE, JACQUES-EMILE. *Portraits of a Life-Time*. London:
J.M. Dent, 316 pp.
    Autobiographical account, which includes some commentary on
Blanche's early association with Bloomsbury figures.

2   COMPTON-RICKETT, ARTHUR. *Portraits and Personalities*.
London: J.M. Dent, 177 pp.
    Includes personal commentary on Lytton Strachey and the
Bloomsbury milieu.

3   GARNETT, DAVID. Review of *The Years*, by Virginia Woolf. *New
Statesman and Nation* (20 March):481.
    The main business of life "is not what stimulates Mrs. Woolf's
imagination; it is not what she feels impelled to tell us about."
Comments on the "enchanted" world she is able to create.

4   HANNAY, HOWARD. *Roger Fry and Other Essays*. London:
     George Allen & Unwin, pp. 15-51.
         Article on Roger Fry deals with his importance in relation to the
     two Post-impressionist exhibitions. Also describes the founding of the
     Omega Workshops and some aspects of Fry's association with
     Bloomsbury, especially Clive Bell.

5   JOHNSON, EDGAR. *One Mighty Torrent*. New York: Stackpole,
     128 pp.
         Includes commentary on Lytton Strachey in relation to the social
     and cultural changes of the time.

6   LEWIS, WYNDHAM. *Blasting and Bombardiering*. London: Eyre
     and Spottiswoode. Rev. ed. with a preface by Anne Wyndham
     Lewis. Berkeley: University of California Press, 1967, 343 pp.
         Deals in part with Lewis's activities during the time he was
     associated with Omega and Bloomsbury. He comments on how "how
     the richest society in the world reacts to its lions, and how its lions
     react for the most part to this society." This society includes Lady
     Ottoline Morrell, "a *grande dame* of Bloomsbury."

7   MacCARTHY, DESMOND. "Duncan Grant." *New Statesman and
     Nation* 14 (20 November):833-34.
         Review of works by Duncan Grant on display at the Agnew's
     Gallery, including the panels he designed for the *Queen Mary* for the
     Cunard Lines, which were rejected: "I do not think it likely that the
     Cunard Company will have found as good an artist as Mr. Duncan
     Grant to take his place, but they will have had no difficulty, I expect, in
     finding one who can produce decorations more in harmony with costly
     fittings."

8   ____. *Leslie Stephen*. Cambridge: Cambridge University Press.
     Reprint. Folcroft, Pa.: Folcroft Press, 1969, 47 pp.
         Lecture on Leslie Stephen that mentions Virginia Woolf. States
     that Stephen is a non aesthetic critic. Led to argument with F.R.
     Leavis. Representative of Bloomsbury point of view.

9   MELLERS, W.H. "Mrs. Woolf and Life." *Scrutiny* 6, no. 1
     (June):71-75.
         Review of Woolf's *The Years*, compared negatively to *To the
     Lighthouse*. *The Years* is more like *The Waves*, in which her attitude is

more like "that of the undergraduate- or Bloomsbury-poet." The novel is "a document of purposelessness." Finally, her work only "enforces the feeling of weakness and sterility." Reprinted in *The Importance of Scrutiny*, pp. 376-79. (See 1948.20).

10 TROY, WILLIAM. "Virginia Woolf: The Novel of Sensibility." In *Literary Opinion in America*. Edited by Morton Zabel. New York: Harper, pp. 340-58.
    Deals with the influence of Henri Bergson and Proust on Woolf's novel of sensibility. Relates to Bloomsbury aesthetic ideals.

1938

1 BELL, JULIAN. *Essays, Poems and Letters*. Edited by Quentin Bell. London: Hogarth Press, 396 pp.
    Includes various articles and letters that relate to Bloomsbury and Julian Bell's association with the Group. Includes the perspective of a second-generation Bloomsbury figure.

2 IYENGAR, K.R. SRINIVASA. *Lytton Strachey: A Critical Study*. London: Chatto & Windus. Reprint. Port Washington, N. Y.: Kennikat Press, 1967, 208 pp.
    "I have tried to state the facts concerning Strachey, both as a man and as a 'classic,' as I understand them, nothing extenuated nor aught set down in malice." Describes his Bloomsbury background, particularly in relation to the negative criticism of the Group: "Bloomsbury! The epithet was being flung at him and his friends."

3 LEAVIS, Q.D. "Caterpillars of the Commonwealth Unite." *Scrutiny* 7 (September):203-16.
    Review of *Three Guineas*, by Virginia Woolf. Objects to the notion of class in Woolf's book: "Woolf is not living in the contemporary world; almost the first thing we notice is that the author of *Three Guineas* is quite insulated by class."

4 MacCARTHY, DESMOND. Review of Rose Macauley's *The Writings of E.M. Forster*. *Sunday Times* (London) (15 May):18.
    Commentary on this critical study and on Forster: "Mr. Forster's peculiar balance of qualities is more often found in woman than in man; and if I could be confident of not being misunderstood by those

who are pleased to consider intellect a masculine specialty, I would add that his point of view, both as a critic and a creator, is feminine rather than masculine."

1939

1   BELL, CLIVE. "Roger Fry's Last Lectures." *New Statesman and Nation* 18 (21 October):564.
Review of Roger Fry's *Last Lectures*, edited by Sir Kenneth Clark. Argues with some of Clark's observations, in the introduction, about Fry's theories, especially Fry's view of Greek art: "He declines to swallow Greek art whole." Clark's criticism show that "symptoms of a strange museum malady still exist."

2   BLANCHE, JACQUES-EMILE. *More Portraits of a Life-Time, 1918-1938*. Translated and edited by Walter Clement. London: J.M. Dent, 330 pp.
Memoirs that include commentary on Blanche's connection to various Bloomsbury figures, especially Virginia Woolf and Roger Fry. Also discusses Francis Birrell: "Francis and I had friends in common in Chelsea and in Bloomsbury, and we both knew Roger Fry."

3   CLARKE, KENNETH. Introduction to *Last Lectures*, by Roger Fry. London: Hogarth Press, pp. ix-xxix.
Commentary on the art criticism of Roger Fry with references to his Bloomsbury associations: "In so far as taste can be changed by one man, it was changed by Roger Fry." Fry's mind was "invincibly experimental." Post-impressionism solidified Fry's conviction that the literary element in painting was insignificant.

4   ROTHENSTEIN, WILLIAM. *Since Fifty: Men and Memories, 1922-1938*. London: Faber & Faber Limited, 278 pp.
Memoirs of the age, which includes commentary on T.E. Lawrence, D.H. Lawrence, Wyndham Lewis, and Roger Fry. Discussion of Fry relates to Lewis, the Post-impressionists, and significant form: "Fry had an infectious enthusiasm; but he was disingenuous and was too closely associated with a group of artists whose interests he was eager to advance."

5   SMITH, JANET ADAM. "The Limitations of Bloomsbury."
     London Mercury (January):216-17.
         Highly disparaging review of *Julian Bell: Essays, Poems and
Letters*. Argues against the equivocal nature of Bell's views on war,
socialism, and the "whole set of ideas and values that are commonly
called Bloomsbury."

6   WOOLF, VIRGINIA. "The Art of Biography." *Atlantic Monthly* 163
     (April):506-10.
         The figure of Lytton Strachey is important in the history of
biography, although she finds fault in his work. His work suggests
"many possible answer to the questions whether biography is an art,
and if not why it fails." Reprinted in *The Death of the Moth and Other
Essays*. (See 1942.9).

1940

1   BEERBOHM, MAX. "Tale of Two Sections: Bloomsbury and
     Bayswater." *Living Age* 349 (October):155-58.
         Gives history of Bloomsbury area prior to the association with
the Bloomsbury Group. Since 1918 Bloomsbury "has become an
intellectual center--or, as it would call itself (for it is very Russian in its
leanings), a focus of the intelligentsia." Discusses tradition and revolt in
art and literature in the context of Bloomsbury.

2   FORSTER, E.M. Review of *Roger Fry*, by Virginia Woolf. *New
     Statesman and Nation* (10 August):140-41.
         Suggests that "Fry epitomized a way of life which has failed.
Barbarians are prim, as he discovered." Relates this attitude to the
failure of the Omega Workshops and to the interest in Cézanne.

3   READ, HERBERT. Review of *Roger Fry*, by Virginia Woolf.
     Spectator (2 August):124.
         Suggests that the limitations in this biography are "those of an
inside view." Woolf, too, belonged to Bloomsbury, which had been
nourished at Cambridge: "But no less certainly it could never be
identified with a true sense of reality. It turned with a shudder from the
threatening advance of what it would call 'the herd'."

4   WOOLF, VIRGINIA. *Roger Fry: A Biography*. London: Hogarth
     Press; New York: Harcourt Brace Jovanovich, 307 pp.
         Personalized biographical study by Woolf, including many
references to other Bloomsbury figures and specific chapters on "The
Post-impressionists" and "The Omega." The Post-impressionist
exhibitions had important results in Fry's life: "Roger Fry may have
sacrificed his reputation with the cultivated; but he had made it with
the young." Woolf suggests that in the Omega Workshops was a link
that brought the public and the artist together. The war "broke into
many of the lives that Roger Fry lived simultaneously. It was no longer
possible to believe that the world generally was becoming more
civilized."

1941

1   "The Eclipse of the Highbrow." *Times* (London) (25 March):15.
         Deals with a book of reflections by Lord Elton, which comments
on the passing of an era. Includes some commentary on Bloomsbury.

2   ELIOT, T.S. "Virginia Woolf." *Horizon* 3 (May):313-16.
         Admiring commentary on Virginia Woolf following her death
which places her somewhat in the Bloomsbury milieu. Suggests that
Bloomsbury, "without Virginia Woolf at the center of it," would have
"formless or marginal." Defines art in relation to the upper-class status
of this group: "With the death of Virginia Woolf, a whole pattern of
culture is broken; she may be, from one point of view, only a symbol of
it; but she would not be the symbol if she had not been, more than
anyone in her time, the maintainer of it."

3   "End of an Epoch." *Times Literary Supplement* (London) (12
     April):179.
         Obituary of Virginia Woolf that states that it was "by unkindly
fate and a geographic accident that Mrs. Woolf became associated with
a set and a propaganda; and Bloomsbury itself, with its look of solid
well-being and respectability, deserves better than that its name should
become a synonym used in anger or derision." Tries to differentiate
between the negatives associated with Bloomsbury and the admirable
qualities of Woolf's work.

4 F., H.G. "Roger Fry: A Biography." *Connoisseur* 107 (February):84-85.

Considers Virginia Woolf's biography of Fry as an *eulogium*. Feels that Fry's influence is over-rated and "will eventually disappear." Comments negatively on Fry's aesthetic theories: "Over and over again, Fry's sophistries are unwittingly exposed in Woolf's pages."

5 GARNETT, DAVID. "Virginia Woolf." *New Statesman and Nation* 21 (12 April):386.

Obituary, with personal recollections: "She herself had the changing, easily startled moods of a thoroughbred racehorse. She was aristocratic in appearance but unconscious and unaware of her own dignity." Comments on the depiction of men and women in Woolf's book and on her heritage as the daughter of Leslie Stephen.

6 GRANT, DUNCAN. "Virginia Woolf." *Horizon* 3 (June):402-6.

Personal account of Grant's relationship with Virginia Woolf. Deals with the early days of Bloomsbury at 29 Fitzroy Square: "About ten o'clock in the evening people used to appear and continue to come at intervals till twelve o'clock at night, and it was seldom that the last guest left before two or three in the morning." Gives details of the Bloomsbury aesthetic that developed out of the teachings of G.E. Moore. Reprinted in *The Golden Horizon,* ed. Cyril Connolly (London: Weidersfeld & Nicholson, 1953, pp. 390-94).

7 ISHERWOOD, CHRISTOPHER. "Virginia Woolf." *Decision* 1, no. 5 (May):36-38.

Comment of Woolf and the Bloomsbury group occasioned by Woolf's death. Bloomsbury "wasn't a group at all, in the self-conscious sense, but a kind of clan; one of those natural families" of a few sensitive and imaginative people. "Artistic integrity was the family religion."

8 MacCARTHY, DESMOND. "Virginia Woolf." *Sunday Times* (London) (6 April):8.

Commentary on the death of Virginia Woolf by one of her close Bloomsbury associates.

9 MACAULAY, ROSE. "Virginia Woolf." *Horizon* 3 (May):316-18.

Memories of Virginia Woolf, which include commentary on Bloomsbury conversations and attitudes: "How to recapture or convey talk? That throaty, deepish, wholly attractive voice." Quotes Woolf as saying "all this rubbish about Bloomsbury. . . . I don't feel Bloomsbury."

10   PEVSNER, NIKOLAUS. "Omega Workshops." *Architectural Review* 90 (August):45-48.
   Early, important article on Roger Fry and the Omega Workshops. Connects the Omega aesthetic to Post-impressionism and to Bloomsbury.

11   PLOMER, WILLIAM. "Virginia Woolf." *Horizon* 3 (May):323-27.
   Memory of Virginia Woolf, which includes some commentary on Lady Ottoline Morrell and other Bloomsbury figures: "Both had an insatiable curiosity about their fellow-creatures, and both loved to gossip (in no disparaging sense of the word) and a capacity to be amused or astonished which goes with that virtue."

12   SACKVILLE-WEST, VITA. "Virginia Woolf." *Horizon* 3 (May):318-23.
   Admiring commentary on Virginia Woolf in the form of a letter. Identifies Arnold Bennett as the person who labeled her "Queen of Bloomsbury" and "Queen of the Highbrows."

1942

1   BURNHAM, DAVID. "The Invalid Lady of Bloomsbury." *Commonweal* 36 (October 2):567-68.
   Review-article of Virginia Woolf's *The Death of the Moth*, David Daiches's *Virginia Woolf*, and E.M. Forster's *Virginia Woolf*. Identifies Woolf in relation to unpublished letter to the editor of the *New Statesmen* published in *The Death of the Moth* in which she describes herself as highbrow and Bloomsbury. Daiches and Forster use "intellectual snob." Concludes that "the enemy of our civilization is not the highbrow but the highbrow's jealous enemy, the middlebrow--compromiser, appeaser, opportunist."

2   CLEMENS, CYRIL. *Lytton Strachey*. International Mark Twain Society, Biographical Series, no. 11. Webster Groves, Mo., London: T.W. Laurie, 19 pp.
   General commentary on Strachey. Includes some references to his Cambridge associations and to his connection with Bloomsbury.

Includes foreword by Andre Maurois and a brief pedigree by Sir
Charles Strachey.

3   DAICHES, DAVID. *Virginia Woolf*. New York: New Directions.
    Rev. ed. New York: New Directions, 1962, 163 pp.
        Early section, "Mainly Biographical," describes Woolf in relation
    to her Bloomsbury surroundings. Bloomsbury did not exist, and the
    term "Bloomsbury" in "this connection is a distortion founded on a
    topographic accident."

4   FORSTER, E.M. "The Art of Virginia Woolf." *Atlantic Monthly*
    (September):82-90.
        Reprinted in *Two Cheers for Democracy*. (See 1951.5)

5   _____. *Virginia Woolf*. Cambridge: Cambridge University Press.
    New York: Harcourt, Brace, 37 pp.
        Delivered as the Rede Lecture, Cambridge: "As soon as we
    dismiss the legend of the Invalid Lady of Bloomsbury, so guilelessly
    accepted by Arnold Bennett, we find ourselves in a bewildering world
    where there are few headlines." Her work is rich and complex, difficult
    to sum up. Describes the development of her feminism. Disliked
    "mateyness" and the "crowd." Also hated the popular press, the
    middlemen who interpret the crowd: "These middlemen form after all
    a very small clique--larger than the Bloomsbury they so tirelessly
    denounce, but a mere drop in the ocean of humanity." Reprinted in
    Two Cheers for Democracy. (See 1951.5).

6   LEAVIS, F.R. "After *To the Lighthouse*." *Scrutiny* 10, no. 3
    (January):295-98.
        Antagonistic review that states that *To the Lighthouse* is Woolf's
    only good novel. Her work shuts out experience in favor of "something
    closely akin to a sophisticated aestheticism." Associates her writing with
    the Bloomsbury milieu.

7   MELLERS, W.H. "Virginia Woolf: The Last Phase." *Kenyon
    Review* 4 (Winter):381-87.
        Same article as 1937.9 with minor revisions. Assessment of
    Woolf's later works. Comments on her "femininity, which quality seems
    to go hand and hand with the curiously tepid Bloomsbury prose into
    which she has always, in unguarded moments, been inclined to trickle."

8 MORTIMER, RAYMOND. *Channel Packet*. London: Hogarth Press, 216 pp.

Includes personal commentary on various Bloomsbury figures and with the Bloomsbury milieu. Separate section (pp. 27-32) is devoted to Virginia Woolf.

9 WOOLF, VIRGINIA. *The Death of the Moth and Other Essays*. Edited by Leonard Woolf. London: Hogarth Press; New York: Harcourt, Brace. 160 pp.

Includes essays on various Bloomsbury figures, such as E.M. Forster and Lytton Strachey.

1943

1 BEERBOHM, MAX. *Lytton Strachey*. Cambridge: Cambridge University Press; New York: Alfred A. Knopf, 26 pp.

Brief commentary on Strachey, with some minor references to Bloomsbury.

2 TORIEN, B.J. *A Bibliography of Virginia Woolf, 1882-1941*. Cape Town: Stone Press, 37 pp.

Earliest checklist of Virginia Woolf criticism. Gives abstracts from articles and reviews, some of which relate to Bloomsbury.

1944

1 LEAVIS, F.R. "Meet Mr. Forster." *Scrutiny* 12 (Autumn):308-9.

Negative commentary on Strachey and Bloomsbury, which was typical of *Scrutiny* at this time.

2 MORTIMER, RAYMOND. Introduction to *Duncan Grant*. Harmondsworth: Penguin Books. pp. vi-xi.

Mortimer places Grant in the Bloomsbury setting, suggesting that Grant's environment affected him greatly. Also tries to distinguish between the painting of Grant and that of Vanessa Bell: "Fry, already well known both as a painter and an expert authority on the Old Masters, was a fascinating and invaluable companion for Duncan Grant, but the whole Bloomsbury group gave him an environment different from that of most young painters." Relates him clearly to the Post-impressionists.

3   TRILLING, LIONEL. *E.M. Forster: A Study*. London: Hogarth Press, 164 pp.
    Early, important study of Forster. Makes some connections between Forster's work and his association with Virginia Woolf and other Bloomsbury figures.

1945

1   CHAPMAN, RONALD. *The Laurel and The Thorn, A Study of G.F. Watts*. London: Faber & Faber, 187 pp.
    Includes commentary on *Freshwater*, the play Virginia Woolf wrote for Angelica Bell's birthday.

2   GAUNT, WILLIAM. "Threshold of a New Age." In *Aesthetic Adventures*. London: Jonathan Cape; New York: Harcourt, Brace, pp. 236-56.
    Suggests that the history of Roger Fry reflects a "cynical reversion of the whole Victorian creed." The Post-impressionists presented a "doctrine of Art for Art's sake brought up to date. There was the characteristic reversal of importance as between nature and art."

3   GOLDRING, DOUGLAS. *The Nineteen Twenties: A General Survey and Some Personal Memories*. London: Nicholson and Watson, 266 pp.
    Includes personal commentary on the influence of Bloomsbury on the cultural climate of Britain during the 1920s.

4   HOFFMAN, FREDERICK J. *Freudianism and the Literary Mind*. Baton Rouge: Louisiana State University Press, 346 pp.
    Deals somewhat with the influence of Freud and the importance of Bloomsbury in the introduction of Freud to British culture.

5   HOGAN, J.P. "Virginia Woolf." *Adelphi* (July-September):191-92.
    Early study that relates Woolf to her cultural circumstances, including Bloomsbury.

6   MacCARTHY, DESMOND. "The Art-Quake of 1910." *Listener* (1 February):625-28.

Deals with the impact of Roger Fry and the Post-impressionist exhibitions. MacCarthy served as secretary for the first exhibition.

7   READ, HERBERT. "Roger Fry." In *A Coat of Many Colours: Occasional Essays*. London: George Routledge, pp. 282-91.

Gives a detailed evaluation of Fry and his work in relation to Bloomsbury and its intellectual and social ideals: "It was an *elite*--of birth no less than of education; its leading members were sons and daughters of eminent Victorians, and they had passed through one or other of our public schools."

8   SMITH, LOGAN PEARSALL. "Tavistock Square." *Orion: A Miscellany* 2:73-86.

Describes his "curious kind of relationship with Virginia Woolf."

9   WOOLF, LEONARD. "The Belief of Keynes." *Listener* (9 June):824.

Review of Keynes's *Two Memoirs. Dr. Melchior: A Defeated Enemy and My Early Beliefs*. "The second paper is more private and more intimate. To me personally it recalls with astonishing clearness the intellectual atmosphere of youth which I share with Keynes at Cambridge." Focuses on reason as central to Bloomsbury: "He was right in this, because the sordid and savage story of history has been written by man's irrationality, and the thin precarious crust of civilization which has from time to time been built over the bloody mess has always been built by reason."

1946

1   ROBERTS, JOHN HAWLEY. "Vision and Design in Virginia Woolf." *PMLA* 61 (September):835-47.

Thorough analysis of some aspects of Roger Fry's influence on Virginia Woolf's fiction, with commentary on "Mr. Bennett and Mrs. Brown" in relation to various Fry essays: "I believe that an understanding of Fry's theories will illuminate one's reading of Virginia Woolf, particularly *Mrs. Dalloway* and *To the Lighthouse*." Woolf followed Fry's lead in flinging "representation to the winds, and along with it, the established notion of plot." Discusses both texts in relation to Fry's artistic theories.

2   SITWELL, OSBERT. *The Scarlet Tree.* Boston: Little, Brown, pp. 320-22.
    Autobiographical account that briefly describes his association with various Bloomsbury figures.

1947

1   BUERMEYER, LAURENCE. "The Esthetics of Roger Fry." In *Art and Education.* Edited by John Dewey, Albert C. Barnes, Laurence Buermeyer, Mary Mullen, and Violette de Mazia. Merion, Pa.: Barnes Foundation Press, pp. 232-46.
    Deals with the connection between aesthetics and human perception. Fry's theories are defective because he lacks a basic understanding of human psychology. Describes various aspects of Fry's theories that were influenced by Clive Bell, including Bell's concept of significant form.

2   CHAMBERS, R.L. *The Novels of Virginia Woolf.* Edinburgh: Oliver & Boyd; New York: Russell & Russell, 102 pp.
    Early study of Virginia Woolf that includes some commentary on the development of her role as a writer within the Bloomsbury context. Reissued in 1955.

3   ISHERWOOD, CHRISTOPHER. *Lions and Shadows: An Education on the Twenties.* Norfolk, Conn.: New Directions, 228 pp.
    Includes personalized account of his association with Hogarth Press and Bloomsbury during the 1920s.

4   LEAVIS, Q.D. "Henry Sidgwick's Cambridge." *Scrutiny* (December):3-11.
    Gives background to the Cambridge world that Lytton Strachey, Leonard Woolf, and other Bloomsbury figures inherited.

5   ROBINSON, E.A.G. *J.M. Keynes, 1883-1946.* Cambridge: Cambridge University Press, 73 pp.
    Early study which somewhat relates Keynes to his Bloomsbury

association at Cambridge and after. Deals with his membership in the Apostles.

6 _____. "John Maynard Keynes, 1883-1946." *Economic Journal* (March):38-42.
      Gives some attention to the influence on Keynes's thought of his days at Cambridge with Leonard Woolf, Lytton Strachey, and other Bloomsbury figures, as well as his connection to Bloomsbury after coming down from Cambridge.

7 RUSSELL, JOHN. "Lytton Strachey." *Horizon* 15 (February):91-116.
      Thorough, admiring evaluation of Strachey's work. No specific mention of Bloomsbury in this assessment. Comments on his technique as biographer, which his followers could never recapture: "the reproduction of the *glissade* of the unconscious mind." Virginia Woolf "skillfully grafted" this procedure "onto the rude structure of the novel of incident."

8 SICKERT, WALTER. *A Free House*. Edited by Osbert Sitwell. London: Macmillan, 281 pp.
      Deals with Sickert's reaction to the Post-impressionist exhibition and to Roger Fry, as well as the art that Post-impressionism inspired in England during the early years of the twentieth century.

9 TINDALL, WILLIAM YORK. *Forces in Modern British Literature*. New York: Viking Press, 186 pp.
      Extensive material on Virginia Woolf, E.M. Forster, and Lytton Strachey. Often relates their work to the Bloomsbury background. Sees Forster as master of Bloomsbury prose. Comments on Strachey's theory of biography: "The improvement of biography in our own time is largely Strachey's affair."

10 WOOLF, VIRGINIA. *The Moment and Other Essays*. London: Hogarth Press. Reprint. New York: Harcourt Brace, 1948, 191 pp.
      Includes various essays that relate to Bloomsbury and Bloomsbury aesthetics. The essay on Roger Fry (pp. 83-88) is the text of an address Woolf gave at the Roger Fry Memorial Exhibition at the Bristol Museum and Art Gallery in 1935.

1948

1   BECK, WARREN. "For Virginia Woolf." In *Forms of Modern Fiction*, edited by William Van O'Connor. Minneapolis and London: University of Minnesota Press, pp. 343-53.

Evaluates Woolf's introspectiveness, suggesting that she does "interrelate subjective individualism and the social order." Shows the connection between these aspects of her fiction and her background, including the influence of Bloomsbury intellectual ideals.

2   BENTLEY, ERIC, ed. *The Importance of Scrutiny: Selections from Scrutiny: A Quarterly Review, 1932-1948.* New York: George W. Stewart, 444 pp.

Includes most of the essays and articles that relate to the quarrel the Leavises had with Bloomsbury and various Bloomsbury figures.

3   "'Bloomsbury' and Beyond." *Times Literary Supplement* (London) (17 July):401.

Commentary on lecture, "'Bloomsbury' and Beyond in the Eighteen-nineties," given by Conal O'Riordan at the Royal Society for Literature. Points out that Bloomsbury in the nineties was not the same as became popular during the 1920s. Sees one ground for comparison of the two periods: "Both periods had their purely arbitrary tendencies. One said art existed only for itself; the later that it was dead, that art was once fairly good and had gone, and would come again only when men had developed new senses." Criticizes further Bloomsbury for its fetish of obscurity, but it has now faded away as a movement.

4   BROWN, E.K. "The Revival of E.M. Forster." In *Forms of Modern Fiction*, edited by William Van O'Connor. Minneapolis and London: University of Minnesota Press, pp. 161-74.

Commentary of the fiction of E.M. Forster, which gives special attention to some of the connections between his work and the fiction of Virginia Woolf.

5   GODFREY, F.M. "Rebirth of an Aesthetic Ideal: An Essay on Three Masters of Art Appreciation: Pater, Wilde, and Fry." *Studio International* 135 (October):150-51, 182-85.

Deals with the pure aesthetic in relation to these figures.

Includes some mention of the relationship between Clive Bell and
Roger Fry.

6   HOUGH, GRAHAM. "Ruskin and Roger Fry: Two Aesthetic
     Theories." *Cambridge Journal* 1 (1947-48):14-27.
          Deals extensively with the development of Roger Fry's aesthetic,
     including some brief commentary on the connection of Clive Bell's
     writing and Roger Fry's thought.

7   JEWKES, JOHN. *Ordeal by Planning.* New York: Macmillan. 210
     pp.
          A passage from this text (pp. 27-29) is quoted by Quentin Bell
     in *Bloomsbury*. Deals primarily with the intelligentsia in Britain, with
     specific reference to Bloomsbury. The book deals with urban planning
     and gives an interesting context for the evaluation of Bloomsbury.

8   MORTIMER, RAYMOND. Introduction to *Duncan Grant*.
     Harmondsworth: Penguin Books, pp. 1-16.
          Commentary by member of the Bloomsbury Group on one of
     the most significant of the Bloomsbury painters. Describes his
     association with Roger Fry and Vanessa Bell.

9   SITWELL, OSBERT. *Great Morning.* Boston: Little Brown, 218 pp.
          Autobiographical account that includes some commentary on
     Sitwell's Bloomsbury associations.

10   _____. *Laughter in the Next Room.* London: Macmillan. Boston:
     Little Brown, 219 pp.
          Autobiographical account beginning with the end of World War
     One. At the Adelphi he comments on Bloomsbury: "Here, in these
     rooms, was gathered the *elite* of the intellectual and artistic world, the
     dark flower of Bloomsbury." Sets out to describe what the Group
     stood for: "The outlook, natural in the grand exemplars, and acquired
     by their followers, was one of great tolerance: surprise was never shown
     at any human idiosyncrasy." In these days Bloomsbury was "austere,
     with a degree of Quaker earnestness latent in it."

11   STRACHEY, OLIVER. "'Bloomsbury' and Beyond." *Times Literary
     Supplement* (London) (31 July):429.
          Letter to the editor in response to "'Bloomsbury' and Beyond"
     editorial in 17 July 1948 issue of the *Supplement* (see 1948.1). States

that editor must have had in mind some other group: "How could *The Times Literary Supplement* accuse this group, or any member of it, of passionate rejection of anything approaching enjoyment in art?" Editor comments that there does seem to be some confusion: "A clear distinction must be made between those distinguished writers and painters who lived--in some cases still live--in Bloomsbury, and the rank and file of nonentities who, for nearly twenty years attached to themselves what reflected glory they might from the luminaries of W.C.1."

12   WARSHOW, ROBERT. "A View of Sir Osbert Sitwell." *Partisan Review* 15, no. 2:1364-68.
        Overview of Sitwell's work. Sees his work as an opposition to "stuffy middle-class pretentiousness and Bloomsbury clique-forming which he felt were draining the life from the English literature of the time."

1949

1   BOWEN, ELIZABETH. "The Achievement of Virginia Woolf." *New York Times Book Review* (26 January):1-21.
        Reprinted in Bowen, *Collected Impressions.* (See 1950.1).

2   BUSSY, DOROTHY ["OLIVIA"]. *Olivia.* London: Hogarth Press; New York: William Sloan Associates, 109 pp.
        Autobiographical account of Dorothy Bussy's experiences in and out of the Bloomsbury circle. Includes commentary on her association with the Stracheys and with Cambridge, which was still dominated by the Bloomsbury ideal.

3   CECIL, LORD DAVID. "E.M. Forster." *Atlantic Monthly* 183 (January):60-65.
        Examination of E.M. Forster's writing style, minor references that compare Forster to Virginia Woolf.

4   _____. "Lytton Strachey." In *Dictionary of National Biography: 1931-1940.* London: Oxford University Press, pp. 897-98.
        Gives overview of Strachey's life and accomplishments, with commentary on his Bloomsbury affiliation that began during his years at Cambridge: "Strachey was a conspicuous figure wherever he appeared,

with his wit and his silence, his tall, emaciated figure, and his red beard."

5   "A Change of Vision." *Times Literary Supplement* (London) (17 June):1-3.
     Deals with changing aesthetics during the twentieth century, particularly the movement from impressionism to Post-impressionism. Ties Bloomsbury to this "change of vision."

6   "In the Middle of the Channel." *Times Literary Supplement* (17 June):15-16.
     Review of various texts by Lytton Strachey. Includes negative commentary on Bloomsbury: "For those too young to have known it, the Bloomsbury world is like the memory of a legendary great-aunt; a clever, witty, rather scandalous great-aunt, who was a brilliant pianist, scholar, needlewoman, who could read six languages and make sauces, who collected epigrams and china and daringly turned her back on charity and good works."

7   *John Maynard Keynes, 1883-1946; Fellow and Bursar*, A Memoir Prepared by Direction of the Council of Kings College, Cambridge. Not seen.

8   KEYNES, JOHN MAYNARD. *Two Memoirs: Dr. Melchior, a Defeated Enemy, and My Early Beliefs*. Introduction by David Garnett. London: Rupert Hart-Davis; New York: August M. Kelley, 186 pp.
     Includes some of Keynes's autobiographical articles. "My Early Beliefs," which deals with G.E. Moore and the origins of Bloomsbury in Cambridge, was first presented to the Memoir Club.

1950

1   BATES, H.E. *Edward Garnett*. London: Max Parrish, 87 pp.
     Biographical study that includes some commentary on David Garnett and his Bloomsbury association.

2   BELL, CLIVE. "How England Met Modern Art." *Artnews* 49 (October):24-27, 61.
     Commentary on the negative reactions to the Post-impressionist

aesthetic and to the exhibitions of 1910 and 1912: "How did the public take it? The howls of rage and the shrieks of venomous laughter emitted by the cultivated public no less fiercely than by the general have become historic almost--a byword and a warning." But both exhibitions were a huge success in terms of attendance and in the discussions they raised: "The effect of these two exhibitions on the more thoughtful part of the British public was considerable. Art began to be taken seriously." Still laments belief that "art is something to be found only in museums" and is "a branch of welfare work."

3   ____. "Reflections on Lytton Strachey." *Cornhill* 165 (Winter):11-21.
     Reprinted in *Old Friends: Personal Recollections.* (See 1956.1).

4   BOWEN, ELIZABETH. *Collected Impressions.* New York: Alfred
     A. Knopf, 269 pp.
     Includes commentary on Virginia Woolf (pp. 78-82) based upon
a review of *Virginia Woolf*, by Bernard Blackstone. Deals with the
charge that her works was remote, unworldly, which relates to the
Bloomsbury milieu.

5   GORDON, EDWARD and A.F.L. DEESON. *The Book of
     Bloomsbury.* London: Edward Gordon, 224 pp.
     Travel book that includes some commentary on Bloomsbury's
literary significance.

6   LEWIS, PERCY WYNDHAM. *Rude Assignment: An Intellectual
     Autobiography.* London: Hutchinson. Reprint. Edited by Toby
     Foshay. Santa Barbara: Black Sparrow Press, 1984, 387 pp.
     Mentions the sale of one of his paintings through Bloomsbury's
influence, in particular Clive Bell, to the Contemporary Art Society.
Gives text of letter from Roger Fry to Lewis. Deals with his days with
the Omega Workshops. Identifies that "certain transactions of a
disagreeable nature caused me to sever my connection with the
Omega," but he does not elaborate.

7   NEWTON, ERIC. "Personal Flavor." In *In My View.* London:
     Longmans, Green, pp. 69-72.
     Includes commentary on Duncan Grant and the impact of
Bloomsbury on his artistic development.

8   SAVAGE, D.S. "Virginia Woolf." In *The Withered Branch: Six Studies in the Modern Novel*. London: Eyre & Spottiswoode, pp. 70-105.

Virginia Woolf's development as a novelist was somewhat dependent on the Bloomsbury aesthetics to which she was exposed.

9   SITWELL, OSBERT. *Noble Essences*. London: Macmillan; Boston: Little, Brown, 323 pp.

Autobiographical account, which includes some commentary on his Bloomsbury association.

10   WILSON, ANGUS. "Sense and Sensibility in Recent Writing." *Listener* 44 (24 August):279-80.

Overview of Virginia Woolf's work, with some comparisons to other Bloomsbury figures, including Roger Fry, Lytton Strachey, Clive Bell, and David Garnett. Defines the "esoteric radiance" of the age, referring to Keynes's memoir, as "the good talk, the civilized companionship, the exaltation of states of mind as the highest value. It was, he says, a purer, sweeter air by far than Freud *cum* Marx." Also discusses the limitations of Woolf's novels, "a basic failure of the imagination towards the outside world."

11   WOOLF, VIRGINIA. *The Captain's Death Bed and Other Essays*. Edited by Leonard Woolf. London: Hogarth Press, 224 pp.

Includes essays that relate to Bloomsbury, including "Leslie Stephen" and "Walter Sickert."

1951

1   ANNAN, NOEL. *Leslie Stephen: His Thought and Character in Relation to His Time*. London: MacGibbon and Kee. Reprint. Cambridge: Harvard University Press, 1952, 270 pp.

Originally published in 1938. Early commentary on Bloomsbury Group. "Bloomsbury, like Clapham, was a coterie. It was exclusive and clannish." Bloomsbury's creed was that "worldly values were grotesquely stupid and wicked." Continues with comparison to Clapham Sect. Summarizes Vanessa Bell's "Old Bloomsbury." The Group is more fully dealt with in *Leslie Stephen: The Godless Victorian*. (See 1984.5.)

2   _____. "The Twenties." *Listener* 45 (8 February):678.
     Brief commentary on Bloomsbury and G.E. Moore in relation to
the nineteen-twenties.

3   BANTOCK, G.H. "John Maynard Keynes." *Listener* (3 May):721.
     Comments on G.E. Moore in relation to Keynes and the
Bloomsbury Group.

4   _____. "The Private Heaven of the Twenties." *Listener* 45 (15
     March):418-19.
     The intellectual character of the twenties, of the post-war world,
is defined by a belief in the private world: "The intellectuals of the
post-war world, then, were profoundly interested in the states of their
own minds. Their values were aesthetic rather than moral or ethical."
Bloomsbury figures significantly, formed a "dominating motif for the
nineteen-twenties." Discusses Freud and the notion of "no taboos" in
relation to Bloomsbury.

5   FORSTER, E.M. *Two Cheers for Democracy*. London: Edward
     Arnold; New York: Harcourt, Brace, 371 pp.
     Includes some essays that discuss various Bloomsbury figures.

6   GARNETT, DAVID. "The Importance of Keynes--and the
     Greatness." *New Republic* 124 (7 May):14-20.
     Review of R.F. Harrod's *The Life of John Maynard Keynes* and
Florence Ada Keynes's *Gathering Up the Threads*. Thinks Harrod's life
of Keynes "a great book," even with some inaccuracies and "irritating
mannerisms." Gives overview of Keynes from Eton, through Cambridge
and G.E. Moore's influence, to "Old Bloomsbury." States that Harrod
conveys a "false impression by seeming to attribute to Keynes an
intellectual primacy among them [Old Bloomsbury]." Keynes was not
"look up to or regarded in any ways as its intellectual leader."

7   HARROD, SIR ROY F. *The Life of John Maynard Keynes*.
     London: Macmillan; New York: Harcourt Brace and Jovanovich.
     674 pp. Reprint. New York: St. Martin's Press, 1965.
     First biographic study of Keynes. Chapter 5, "Bloomsbury" (pp.
172-94), deals specifically with Keynes in relation to Bloomsbury. States
that Lytton Strachey and the Stephen sisters form the essential coterie:
"In Vanessa and Virginia he found two women who were Apostles to
the finger-tips." Suggests that Keynes was a part of the innermost

circle of Bloomsbury, even though his life was more littered up "with the transactions of business and he had at times fairly close dealings with the great, whom Bloomsbury despised." Emphasizes the Cambridge background of the group. Bloomsbury set out to achieve a way of life: "the Cambridge ideals of unworldliness, pursuit of truth and other absolute values, were carried forward, and the group of friends attempted, in ways admittedly imperfect, to pursue them."

8   LEAVIS, F.R. "Keynes, Spender and Currency Values." *Scrutiny* 18 (June):50-56.
     Review of Stephen Spender's *World Within World* and R.F. Harrod's *The Life of John Maynard Keynes*. Antagonistic account of Spender and Keynes, tieing them to the failings of literary culture in general. Focuses on Bloomsbury and the "social-personal" club spirit. Keynes "promoted in enormously influential ways the habit of substituting the social-personal values for the relevant ones." He, in turn, "helped substantially to bring about the state of things revealed in Mr. Spender's autobiography."

9   NICOLSON, BENEDICT. "Post-Impressionism and Roger Fry." *Burlington Magazine* 93 (January):11-15.
     Forty years since the first Post-impressionist exhibition: "The time has come to commemorate it, to treat it academically as a major incident in the history of taste, to assess its merits and shortcomings, to compare it with the second show held two years later when, contemptuous of the scandal that the first caused, encouraged by the esteem in which a few quarters it had been held, the organizers moved forwards from the old masters to a closer examination of the contemporary movement." England was behind in "recognizing what was vital in modern art." Gives details of the two exhibitions, listing many of the works included. In the second show the "emphasis was shifted to the contemporary movement." Significant form was a much too rigid doctrine that would have led to pure abstraction: "Later Fry turned away from abstraction, seeing in it a denial of artistic sensibility."

10   PRYCE-JONES, ALAN. "The Frightening Pundits of Bloomsbury." *Listener* 45 (1 March):345-46.
     Personalized commentary on Bloomsbury, which tries to recapture the effect of the scintillating intellectual virtuosity of the Bloomsbury conversationalists.

11 SANDERS, CHARLES RICHARD. "Lytton Strachey's Conception
    of Biography." *PMLA* 66, no. 4 (June):301.
    In-depth study of the development of Strachey's biographical
method, which includes a discussion of the tradition with which he
found fault. Biography should be based upon fact, "it should be art,
with judicious selection, good structure, and good style." The
development of his conception of biography relates somewhat to his
Bloomsbury ideals. Incorporated in *Lytton Strachey: His Mind and His
Art.* (See 1957.16).

12 SPENDER, STEPHEN. *World within World.* London: Faber and
    Faber, 364 pp.
    Autobiographical account that states that "Bloomsbury has been
derided by some people and has attracted the snobbish admiration of
others: but I think it was the most constructive and creative influence
on English taste between the two wars." Suggests that E.M. Forster
and T.S. Eliot are associated with the group. Describes the French
influence, in both painting and literature. Bloomsbury "was like the last
kick of an enlightened aristocratic tradition."

13 WOOLF, LEONARD. Review of *The Life of John Maynard Keynes*,
    by R.F. Harrod. *Listener* (25 January):28.
    Briefly mentions Bloomsbury. Sees the biography as flawed
because of Harrod's literary style, "which oscillates between
inappropriate intimacy and strings of rhetorical questions."

1952

1   BELL, CLIVE. "Roger Fry (1866-1934)." *Cornhill Magazine* 166
    (Autumn):180-97.
    Reprinted in *Old Friends: Personal Recollections.* See 1956.1.

2   GERNSHEIM, HELMUT and ALISON. *Those Impossible English.*
    Introduction by Quentin Bell. London: Weidenfeld & Nicolson.
    164 pp.
    Gives cultural background to Bloomsbury world.

3   JOHNSTONE, J.K. "The Philosophical Background and the Works
    of Art of the Group Known as 'Bloomsbury.'" Ph.D. dissertation,
    University of Leeds.

Published as *The Bloomsbury Group: A Study of E. M. Forster, Lytton Strachey, Virginia Woolf, and their Circle.* (See 1954.9).

4   LEAVIS, F.R. *The Common Pursuit.* London: Chatto & Windus, 307 pp.
    Several essays in this collection, drawn from *Scrutiny*, are relevant to Bloomsbury. "Keynes, Lawrence and Cambridge" (pp. 255-60) evaluates the repugnance D.H. Lawrence felt toward Garnett's Cambridge Friends and the "Cambridge-Bloomsbury milieu in general." Also discusses and dismisses other explanations, such as Garnett's that Lawrence was jealous: "One can readily imagine how the incontinently flippant talk and the shiny complacency, snub-proof in its obtuse completeness, infuriated him." It was not that he was inexperienced as Keynes suggests. He hated the triviality of this group, which Leavis contrasts to the Cambridge of Sidgwick, Leslie Stephen, and Maitland. "E.M. Forster" (pp. 261-77) states that Forster's writings are "Bloomsbury in the valuations they accept (in spite of the showings of real critical perception), in the assumptions they innocently express, and in the prevailing ethos."

5   LEHMANN, JOHN. *Edith Sitwell.* London: Longmans, Green, 40 pp.
    Early study of Edith Sitwell by one of the second generation Bloomsbury figures. Involves mostly analytical evaluation of her work but includes some commentary that relates to her association with Bloomsbury.

6   ____. *The Open Night.* London: Longmans, Green. New York: Harcourt, Brace, 56 pp.
    Contains an appreciation of Virginia Woolf by one of her Bloomsbury friends and manager of the Hogarth Press.

7   MacCARTHY, DESMOND. Introduction to *Roger Fry: Paintings and Drawings.* Exhibition Catalog. London: Arts Council.
    Commentary on Fry by a close Bloomsbury associate. Gives details about his work and his connection with Bloomsbury.

8   ROSS, ROBERT. *Friend of Friends: Art Critic Letters and Extracts from Articles.* Edited by Margery Ross. London: Jonathan Cape, 367 pp.
    Includes commentary on the Post-impressionist exhibition, the

Omega Workshops, and other related Bloomsbury activities. Deals with the various artists who moved in and out of Bloomsbury.

9   ROTHENSTEIN, JOHN. *Modern English Painters: Sickert to Smith*. London: Eyre & Spottiswood, 256 pp.
    Deals also with Bloomsbury hostility. Relates to his father's relationship with Roger Fry. Includes negative commentary on Bloomsbury in relation to Wyndham Lewis and Duncan Grant. The revised edition eliminates the most antagonistic material. Describes Lewis's early clash with Roger Fry, the Omega Workshops, and Bloomsbury, stating that because of the "pervasiveness of 'Bloomsbury' influence his activities were therefore ignored often." The chapter on Duncan Grant deals specifically with Rothenstein's sense of "Bloomsbury hostility": "Duncan Grant is not a good hater, and he took no part that I know of in the Bloomsbury vendetta against my father, who was I believe, one of the first artists to give him encouragement." This text was reissued at various times in several volumes.

10 RUSSELL, BERTRAND. "Portraits from Memory--II." *Listener* 48 (17 July):97-98.
    Account of John Maynard Keynes and Lytton Strachey: "They aimed rather at a life of retirement among fine shades and nice feelings, and conceived of the good as consisting in the passionate mutual admiration of a clique of the *elite*." G.E. Moore, unfairly, has been identified as the source of these aims. Keynes finally escaped this atmosphere "into the great world." Keynes's intellect was the "sharpest and clearest that I have ever known." Reprinted in *Harpers* 206 (January 1953):70-72.

1953

1   ALPERS, ANTONY. *Katherine Mansfield: A Biography*. New York: Alfred A. Knopf, 356 pp.
    Early study with commentary on Mansfield's relationship with Dorothy Brett, Lady Ottoline Morrell, Virginia Woolf, and other Bloomsbury figures. Superceded by 1984 study. (See 1980.2).

2   GARNETT, DAVID. *The Golden Echo*. London: Chatto & Windus, pp. 250-58.
    Autobiographical account of Garnett's activities. Describes his various evenings with "Adrian Stephen and his sister Virginia," who had "recently moved to a lovely house in the middle of the north side of Brunswick Square." Mentions Keynes, Grant, Frederick Etchells. At poker games he also met Gerald Shove, Saxon Sydney-Turner, Karen and Ray Costello, among others: "During my visits, I felt a strange mixture of emotions: the excitement of meeting people who were more charming and more intelligent than the people I met elsewhere--and a feeling of peacefulness, of being at home--almost a premonition of *belonging*, as though I were a stray kitten which had firmly made up its mind that it was going to be adopted." He later comments on the fact that he felt many of the members disliked him, but "Adrian continued to invite me."

3   MacCARTHY, DESMOND. *Memories*. Foreword by Raymond Mortimer. London: MacGibbon and Kee; New York: Oxford University Press, 187 pp.
    Includes "Bloomsbury: An Unfinished Memoir," in which MacCarthy describes the hostility Bloomsbury provoked by the early thirties. Bloomsbury is "neither a movement, nor a push, but only a group of old friends; whose affection and respect for each other has stood the test of nearly thirty years and whose intellectual candour makes their company agreeable to each other."

4   RANTAVAARA, IRMA. *Virginia Woolf and Bloomsbury*. Helsinki. Reprint. Folcroft, Pa.: Folcroft Library Editions, 215 pp.
    "Bloomsbury cannot be properly understood without a comprehension of Virginia Woolf." Important first definition of the Bloomsbury Group, its philosophical underpinnings (via J. McTaggart, G.E. Moore, and Bertrand Russell, among others), and its "aesthetic attitude toward life" (via Clive Bell's *Civilization* [1928]), in relation to Woolf's life.

5   RIDLEY, HILDA. "Leslie Stephen's Daughter." *Dalhousie Review* 33, no. 1 (Spring):65-72.
    Good background study that finds Stephen's influence on Virginia Woolf substantial. Gives framework for Bloomsbury.

6   SANDERS, CHARLES RICHARD. "Lytton Strachey's Point of
    View." *PMLA* 68, no. 1 (March):75-94.
        Study of Strachey's biographic technique which focuses on the
    concept of "point of view" in biography. The ideal of "freedom of mind
    and spirit" comes from Strachey's family background and his Cambridge
    education, and it flourishes in Bloomsbury. Describes the teachings of
    G.E. Moore in relation to this idea: "This both as a disciple of Moore
    and as the son of a distinguished and enthusiastic scientist, Strachey
    found the search for truth full of excitement." Incorporated in *Lytton
    Strachey: His Mind and His Art*. (See 1957.16).

7   ____. *The Strachey Family 1558-1932: Their Writings and Literary
    Associations*. Durham: Duke University Press. Reprint. Westport,
    Conn.: Greenwood Press, 1968. 337 pp.
        Gives history of the Strachey family from the time of Locke
    through the activities of Lytton Strachey, to whom the final chapter is
    devoted, "Giles Lytton Strachey and His Heritage" (pp. 261-95). Gives
    detail of his intellectual growth at Cambridge and his association with
    G.E. Moore, Roger Fry, Leonard Woolf, and others. Describes also
    the period after the publication of *Eminent Victorians* during which
    Strachey was most active in Bloomsbury. This was the time he met
    Dora Carrington and Ralph Partridge.

8   SPENDER, STEPHEN. "Movements and Influences in English
    Literature, 1927-1952." *Books Abroad* 27:5-32.
        Includes some commentary on the importance of Bloomsbury.
    Spender was a defender of the Group.

9   WOOLF, VIRGINIA. *A Writer's Diary: Being Extracts from the
    Diary of Virginia Woolf*. Edited by Leonard Woolf. London:
    Hogarth Press. Reprint. New York: Harcourt, Brace, 1954, 196
    pp.
        Covers the years 1918-1941, including references to various
    Bloomsbury figures. In 1935, for example, she writes about the
    "Bloomsbury baiters," including Wyndham Lewis, Mirsky, and
    Swinnerton. Superceded by the completed diaries, which began to
    appear in 1980.

1954

1   "The Air of Bloomsbury." *Times Literary Supplement* (London) (20
     August):521-23.
         Unsigned review of J.K. Johnstone's *The Bloomsbury Group*.
     Deals with group issue: "Mr. Johnstone's book has one main thesis. He
     sets out to show that the members of the Bloomsbury Group had
     common values stemming from an original gospel, the early Cambridge
     philosophy of G.E. Moore, formulated in his *Principia Ethica*, and
     published in 1904." Concludes by affirming with Johnstone that a
     group identity did exist.

2   BALDANZA, FRANK JR. "The Novels of Virginia Woolf." Ph.D.
     dissertation, Cornell University, 377 pp.
         Woolf's essays reveal that her sensibility was shaped by her
     reading and the interests of her friends in the Bloomsbury. She read
     widely in in English and Russian literature. "From G.E. Moore's
     Principia Ethica she drew her system of values, which put the major
     emphasis on good states of mind, and she developed this value system
     within the tradition of Pater and Wilde's aestheticism at it was passed
     on to her by the theories of Roger Fry and Clive Bell." Divides
     Woolf's work into two categories, novels of fact and novels of vision,
     "although her ultimate aim was to blend the two, as she did in *Between
     the Acts*." See *Dissertation Abstracts* 14:2061-62.

3   BELL, CLIVE. "The Bloomsbury Group." *Times Literary
     Supplement* (London) (August 27):543.
         Letter to the editor. Concerns review of Johnstone's *The
     Bloomsbury Group*.

4   _____. "What Was Bloomsbury?" *Twentieth Century* 155
     (February):153-60.
         Would ask two questions of any commentator on Bloomsbury:
     "(a) Who are or were the members of Bloomsbury? (b) For what do
     they, or did they, stand?" Identifies Molly MacCarthy as source of the
     name, "the Bloomsberries." The story, though, begins in 1899 at Trinity
     College, Cambridge, with the reading group, the "Midnight Society,"
     whose original five members were Lytton Strachey, Leonard Woolf,
     Thoby Stephen, Saxon Sydney-Turner, and Clive Bell. After Cambridge
     the group moved to London and became associated with Vanessa and
     Virginia Stephen: "If ever such an entity as 'Bloomsbury' existed, these

sisters, with their houses in Gordon and Fitzroy Squares, were at the heart of it." Identifies members of "Old Bloomsbury" as well as many who became members later. Questions, finally, whether there really was a group spirit. G.E. Moore influenced some but not all. The members "had precious little in common." Reprinted in *Old Friends*. (See 1956.1).

5   BREWSTER, DOROTHY. *East-West Passages: A Study in Literary Relationships*. London: Allen and Unwin, 223 pp.
      Includes some commentary on the literary relationships that made up Bloomsbury.

6   HAFLEY, JAMES. *The Glass Roof: Virginia Woolf as Novelist*. English Studies no. 9. Los Angeles: University of California Press, 187 pp.
      Full length study of Woolf's novels. States that she became the center of the Bloomsbury Group, but she had very little in common with most of the other members. She was a silent participant and hostess: "It will become more evident in the course of this study that Virginia Woolf was not intellectually in accord with 'Bloomsbury'; it will also become apparent that her own dealings with and solutions to the problems discussed there were precisely her own, and not dependent upon this group of which she was socially at the center."

7   HUGHES, RICHARD. "Bloomsbury." *Spectator*. 192 (11 June):716-19.
      Review of J.K. Johnstone's *The Bloomsbury Group: A Study of E.M. Forster, Lytton Strachey, Virginia Woolf and Their Circle*. Discusses the influence of G.E. Moore's *Principia Ethica* on the young Apostles who, along with the Stephen sisters, were to form the core of Bloomsbury: "The concussion of Moore's ideas and these young men was momentous. For this was the period of history in which dogmatic religion was wholly unacceptable by such minds as these young men had."

8   JOHNSTONE, J.K. *The Bloomsbury Group: A Study of E.M. Forster, Lytton Strachey, Virginia Woolf, and Their Circle*. New York: Noonday Press. London: Secker & Warburg, 315 pp.
      Important early study divided into three major sections, "The Background," which deals with Bloomsbury Philosophy and aesthetics, "Values," which deals with the each writer's attitude toward life, and

"Composition," which deals with the individual works of Forster, Lytton Strachey and Virginia Woolf. Sets out to justify Bloomsbury in relation to the various charges of "snobbishness," "arty," and "Bohemian." Focuses on the literary aspect of the group. Deals with G.E. Moore's influence and somewhat with the influence of Lowes Dickinson, John Ellis McTaggart, and Leslie Stephen. Roger Fry's contribution to Bloomsbury was crucial. Believed that there are some common ideals within the group: "There is a common respect for the things of the spirit; a belief that the inner life of the soul is much more important than the outer life of action or the outer world of material things; an admiration for the individual and for the virtues of courage, tolerance and honesty; a desire that man shall be whole and express himself emotionally as well as intellectually; a love of truth and beauty."

9   LAKE, BERYL. "A Study of the Irrefutability of Two Aesthetic Theories." In *Aesthetics and Language*. Edited by William Elton. Oxford: Basil Blackwell, pp. 100-113.
    Examines the linguistic nature of two aesthetic theories, those of Benedetto Croce and Clive Bell, as well as the assumption that "a theory of aesthetics is based upon, and answers to, matter of fact, albeit very special and sacred matters of fact about Art." Relates Bell's theory of significant form to Roger Fry.

10 "The Listener's Book Chronicle." *Listener* 51 (24 June):11-13.
    Short review of Johnston's *The Bloomsbury Group*. Suggests that there is not enough mention of Clive Bell's role in clarifying the group's aesthetic: "His *Art* was published in 1914, which was a good deal earlier than most of Fry's significant work. But as most of the intercommunications of the group were verbal, it would be difficult to establish priorities."

11 MUIR, EDWIN. "A Study in Bloomsbury." *Observer* (30 May):9.
    Review of Johnston's *The Bloomsbury Group* which gives a general impression of the importance of Bloomsbury and the need for further study.

12 PRICHETT, V.S. "Some Talkers in the Sunset." *New York Times Book Review* 26 (September):36-37.
    Review of Johnston's *The Bloomsbury Group*.

13 RUDIKOFF, SONYA. "The Strains of a Private Life." *Partisan Review* 21, no. 3 (May-June):330-34.
    Review of Virginia Woolf's *A Writer's Diary*. States that Woolf "had many friends and was, as some may recall, the pivot of that remarkable Bloomsbury circle, a society of rare distinction like nothing most people have ever known." Woolf thought too much of the opinions of her circle.

14 SANDERS, CHARLES RICHARD. "Lytton Strachey and the Victorians." *Modern Language Quarterly* 15 (December):335-39.
    Commentary on Strachey's critique of the Victorian era: "Strachey's purpose was not to condemn the Victorian Age as a whole but to subject it to a sifting process by which the good and the bad might be separated." Deals with Strachey's attitudes toward specific Victorian writers. Relates to his association with the more progressive Bloomsbury writers. Incorporated in *Lytton Strachey: His Mind and His Art*. (See 1957.16).

15 SCOTT, GEORGE. "Virginia Woolf." *Adelphi* 30, no. 1:196-76.
    Antagonistic review-article of Virginia Woolf's *A Writer's Diary*, edited by Leonard Woolf (Hogarth Press). Regards the diaries as full of arrogance, "an arrogance big-boned and belligerent." Woolf possesses the arrogance of an aesthete who finds only Bloomsbury figures truly interesting. "How difficult it is to like saints--especially this particular saint, who died only thirteen years ago, and epitomized an intellectual coterie called the Bloomsbury Group." States that the antipathy towards Bloomsbury is the result of its exclusiveness as a club, a clique. Scott distrusts "the self-assured theories of the civilized life." Finally he comments on the need to relate art to life. He calls out to writers "whose creative imaginations will start from the point of recognition of life as it is, not as the dreamer would like it to be."

1955

1 ANNAN, NOEL. "The Intellectual Aristocracy." In *Studies in Social History*. Edited by John H. Plumb. London: Longmans, pp. 243-87.
   Traces the labyrinthine familial relationships within the newly emerging intellectual class of the twentieth century, the lineal descendants of the major intellectuals of the nineteenth century.

2   BALDANZA, FRANK. "*Orlando* and the Sackvilles." *PMLA* 70 (March):274-79.

Evaluates some of the connections between *Orlando* and the world of Vita Sackville-West: "We shall attempt to see how this material was presented through the life and family history of Victoria Sackville-West, who provides in her own books the information we need about her."

3   BINNS, HAROLD. "Strachey and Bloomsbury." *New Statesman and Nation* 49 (23 April):578.

Letter to the editor in response to John Raymond's reassessment of Strachey and Bloomsbury (1955.18). Finds Raymond "searchingly accurate."

4   BLOOMFIELD, PAUL. "Bloomsbury." In *Uncommon People: A Study of England's Elite*. London: Hamish Hamilton, pp. 167-81.

Evaluation of Bloomsbury as special society, a "group of well-bred people" who had "the gift of presenting the traditional values of civilized life in a new, contemporary, characteristic and dangerously infectious idiom." They were in revolt, however: "It was a grand spectacle, to have an intellectual aristocracy so dead set against conventional assumptions and polite cliches." Considers what the Group did as artists and writers.

5   BOWRA, C.M. "Beauty in Bloomsbury." *Yale Review* 44 (March):461-64.

Review of *The Bloomsbury Group* by J.K. Johnstone, which he considers a pioneering study. States that there is no doubt that Bloomsbury believed in and tried to live up to the ideals established by G.E. Moore: "The weakness of the Bloomsbury Group was its narrowness, one might almost say its inhumanity. Moore's doctrine, as they applied it, was ill fitted to an age so rich in disasters as our own, and meant that when other, perhaps less gifted, writers were troubled by the problems of the day the Group paid no attention to them."

6   EPSTEIN, JACOB. *Let There Be Sculpture: An Autobiography*. New York: E.P. Dutton, 294 pp.

Originally published in 1940 as *Let There Be Sculpture*. Revised and extended in 1955. Comments on the negative influence of Roger Fry and his group. "These gentry never hesitated to go out of their

way to damage and undermine an artist, even if he is only a beginner."
Quotes from an article by Fry on Epstein's work.

7   GARNETT, DAVID. "Keynes, Strachey and Virginia Woolf in
    1917." *London Magazine* 2, no. 9 (September):48-55.
        Memories of encounters with several Bloomsbury figures, during
    the First War World, and admiring character sketch of Virginia Woolf.
    Describes his experiences at Asheham, a farmhouse in Sussex: "While
    Clive kept us abreast of the doings of the social world in London and
    the news of Garsington, Maynard Keynes, our other most frequent
    visitor at Firle, told us of the War and the political world."

8   HAMNETT, NINA. *Is She a Lady: A Problem in Autobiography?*
    London: Allan Wingate, 161 pp.
        Autobiographical account that includes commentary on her
    association with Roger Fry and other Bloomsbury figures.

9   HARRIS, SEYMOUR E. *John Maynard Keynes: Economist and
    Policy Maker.* New York and London: Charles Scribner's Sons, 178
    pp.
        Part I, "The Man," deals with Keynes in relation to Bloomsbury.
    Feels that Keynes's candor is a trait that "was strengthened as a result
    of his association with the Bloomsbury Group." This quality also
    reduced the effectiveness of his "power of persuasion."

10 HUNGERFORD, EDWARD A. "Mrs. Woolf, Freud, and J.D.
    Beresford." *Literature and Psychology* 5:49-51.
        Deals somewhat with the importance of the Hogarth Press and
    the introduction of the translation of Freud, which helped to spread his
    literary influence.

11 LAMBERT, GAVIN. "Strachey and Bloomsbury." *New Statesman
    and Nation* 49 (23 April):578.
        Letter to the editor in response to Raymond's reassessment of
    Strachey and Bloomsbury (1955.18). "This reassessment is as
    remarkable for its buoyant inaccuracies as for its silly and uninformed
    gibes at what the writer imagines to have been 'Bloomsbury.'" Points
    out mistakes in judgment in relation to Bloomsbury and to Strachey's
    work.

12   LEHMANN, JOHN. *The Whispering Gallery: Autobiography I*.
      London: Longmans, Green; New York: Harcourt Brace &
      Jovanovich, 342 pp.
          Autobiographical account of a second generation Bloomsbury
      figure in which he describes his meeting with Julian Bell and his work
      on the Hogarth Press for Leonard and Virginia Woolf. He met Bell at
      Cambridge: "Julian Bell was the elder son of Clive and Vanessa Bell, a
      nephew of Virginia Woolf, and one of the most gifted of that fortunate
      second generation of the Bloomsbury giants who inherited the well-laid-
      out gardens of ideas their elders had created, and basked in the
      sunshine of their artistic achievements." Describes his interest in many
      Bloomsbury works, including Strachey's *Landmarks in French Literature*.
      The Bloomsbury parties followed one after the other, with Angelica
      "more often than not the leading spirit." (See also 1060.2).

13   ____. "Working with Virginia Woolf." *Listener* 53 (13 January):60-
      62.
          Describes his experiences working with Leonard and Virginia
      Woolf as manager of the Hogarth Press. For Virginia the publisher's
      life had begun to encroach on the writer's life: "She took an extremely
      active part in reading and in deciding on the manuscripts that came in,
      in planning new series and in persuading authors to write for them."
      Gradually, her role in the press diminished.

14   MOORE, GEOFFREY. "The Significance of Bloomsbury." *Kenyon
      Review* 17 (Winter):119-29.
          Review article on J.K. Johnstone's *The Bloomsbury Group*, giving
      overview of the development of the Group from its early days up to
      World War II. Thinks Johnstone simplifies: "Bloomsbury changed as it
      developed, becoming a microcosm of English intellectual life, weaving
      its strands of influence in a dozen places and arousing those diversified
      feelings which made its name such a two-edged epithet between the
      two wars. Mr. Johnstone's Bloomsbury affords no explanation of such a
      state of affairs. We need to go deeper." The Group was not a group
      "in the sense of having a planned programme or a set of theories which
      its members endeavored to put into practice." Bloomsbury "was the
      first manifestation of the University-intellectual intelligence which was
      to set its mark on high-browed Sunday newspapers, on publishing, on
      the Civil Service, on the B.B.C. and on the Arts Council."

15 NASH, PAUL. *Poet and Painter: Being the Correspondence Between Gordon Bottomly and Paul Nash 1910-1946*. London: Oxford University Press, 246 pp.

Mostly social reference in artistic circle of Bottomly and Nash. Includes commentary on Roger Fry, Omega Workshops, and other Bloomsbury figures.

16 O'CONNOR, WILLIAM VAN. "Toward a History of Bloomsbury." *Southwest Review* 40 (Winter):36-52.

Descriptive history of the Bloomsbury Group with commentary on the various other works that have dealt with the members and the common traits, including memoirs by members, such as Keynes, Desmond MacCarthy, Clive Bell. States that "anyone reading Keynes's *The Economic Consequences of Peace* and Strachey's biographies will immediately recognize the similarity in tone," and "the articles in E.M. Forster's *Two Cheers for Democracy* are in a sense Bloomsbury manifestos: the importance of friendship over politics and institutions, love, the great republic, art for its own sake, and so on." Comments on the various critical studies, including Rantavaara's *Virginia Woolf and Bloomsbury* and J.K. Johnstone's *The Bloomsbury Group*. Goes on to discuss Roger Fry, Clive Bell, and the Post-impressionist exhibitions, as well as the painters associated with Bloomsbury. Concludes with an assessment of the various anti-Bloomsbury articles, including Frank Swinnerton's comments in *The Georgian Literary Scene* and the reviews by F.R. and Q.D. Leavis in *Scrutiny*.

17 PIPPETT, AILEEN. *The Moth and the Star: A Biography of Virginia Woolf*. Boston: Little, Brown, 368 pp.

Early biographical study, based somewhat upon personal admiration: "I met her once, in a Bloomsbury attic, by candlelight, unexpectedly, at a small party some time in the middle nineteen-thirties." Suggests that the negative connotations of "Bloomsbury" never made sense: "Who is right? Those who maintain that the Bloomsbury Circle deliberately shut itself off from contact with ordinary life, or those who feel that it is part of the history of our times?" The answer to such questions "might lie in the personality of the woman herself as apart from the literary artist and social thinker." Extensive commentary of Bloomsbury in relation to Woolf: "If the group of friends and relations who were constantly meeting in Bloomsbury in this prewar time had begun to form a world of their own, it was a world in a state of flux."

18   RAYMOND, JOHN. "Strachey's Eminent Victorians." *New Statesman and Nation* 49 (16 April):545-46.

Antagonistic article on Strachey and Bloomsbury, which have done "so much to bedevil" English life and letters. "Bloomsbury certainly did tend to divide the world into sheep and goats--those who lived in Gordon Square and its spiritual environs, and those who dwelt in the outer intellectual darkness." Bloomsbury is "vulgar." Includes Forster and Woolf in this indictment: "In the face of almost all the issues that vex man's social life--power, religion, sex, money, patriotism--these three great artists either preserve a shirking silence or indulge a brilliant triviality." Article prompted various letters to editor, Harold Binns, "Strachey and Bloomsbury." (16 April):578; Gavin Lambert (16 April):578; St. John-Stevas, "Eminent Victorians." (30 April):616.

19   SACKVILLE-WEST, VITA. "Virginia Woolf and *Orlando*." *Listener* (27 January):157-58.

Commentary on *Orlando*, including extracts from Virginia Woolf's letters to Vita Sackville-West and observations by Sackville-West. States that "the idea of her book *Orlando* was inspired by her own strange conception of myself, my family, and Knole my family home. Such things as old families and great houses held a sort of Proustian fascination for her." Concludes with unpublished passage from the original manuscript.

20   SCOTT-JAMES, R.A. *Lytton Strachey*. London: Longmans, Green, 39 pp.

Surveys Strachey's life through Cambridge and Bloomsbury years.

21   WOOLF, LEONARD. "Coming to London--II." *London Magazine* 2, no. 10 (October):49-54.

Asked by the editor to deal with his first impressions of the London literary world. Describes parties at the Sitwells. Briefly describes his arrival at Cambridge and the founding of the Bloomsbury Group.

1956

1   BELL, CLIVE. *Old Friends: Personal Reflections*. London: Chatto and Windus. New York: Harcourt Brace Jovanovich, 200 pp.

Collection of articles previously published in various magazines, including *Cornhill* and *Twentieth Century*. Includes articles on Lytton Strachey, Maynard Keynes, Roger Fry, Virginia Woolf, and on Bloomsbury in general. He describes, in relation to Strachey, the early days at Cambridge and the Midnight Society which established the tone for the Bloomsbury Group. Keynes is portrayed primarily during World War I. He gives an overview of Roger Fry's artistic development and his primary aesthetic concerns, suggesting that his scientific background was central to his ideas. Tends to be critical. About Virginia Woolf he speaks glowingly, giving full consideration to her feminism.

2   FARR, DENNIS. "Wyndham Lewis and the Vorticisits." *Burlington Magazine* 98 (August):279-80.
        Brief article on Lewis with mention of his initial association with Roger Fry and the Omega Workshops: "Lewis, although briefly linked with Fry's little belated Morris movement (as he described the Omega Workshops in 1915), belonged to a younger generation than Fry and was temperamentally incapable of submitting himself to outside leadership."

3   FORSTER, E.M. "Bloomsbury, An Early Note: February 1929." *Pawn* 3 (November):10.
        Bloomsbury "is the only genuine *movement* in English civilization, though that civilization contains far better and more genuine individuals." Forster also comments further: "Academic background, independent income. Continental enthusiasms, sex-talk and all. They are in the English Tradition."

4   GRAHAM, J.W. "A Negative Note on Bergson and Virginia Woolf." *Essays in Criticism* 6, no. 1 (January):70-74.
        Argues against a close connection between Woolf and Bergson. In Bergson's distinction of intellect from intuition, "we see a definite parallel with the Bloomsbury dichotomy of action and contemplation, the world of ends and the world of means." But these ideas were more directly derived from G.E. Moore.

5   GREEN, DAVID BONNELL. "*Orlando* and the Sackvilles: Addendum." *PMLA* 71, no. 1 (March):268-69.
        Comments on Baldanza article (see 1955.2). The explanation for the change in sex of Orlando can be found in the history of the Sackville family. Orlando's "ceasing to be a man is equivalent to the

ending of the male line in the Sackville family, and his becoming a
woman is equivalent to the beginning of the female representation of
the family in the Sackville-West." Also suggests that the members of
the Bloomsbury are portrayed in the book under various disguises.

6   NICHOLSON, HAROLD. "The Practice of Biography." In *The
     English Sense of Humor and Other Essays*. London: Constable, pp.
     145-59.
         Brief history of the biographical form. During periods of "doubt,
speculation and skepticism, the interest in human behavior increases."
Characterizes Strachey: "Lytton Strachey, with his ironical titters,
emerged as the deftest of iconoclasts; yet Strachey, who enjoyed
paradox more than he respected precision, and who had little sense of
history, exaggerated the lights and shadows of his portraits."

7   "Old Friends Revalued." *Times Literary Supplement* (London) (7
     December):721-22.
         Positive review of *Old Friends* by Clive Bell, *Virginia Woolf and
Lytton Strachey: Letters* edited by Leonard Woolf, and *Virginia Woolf
par elle-meme* by Monique Nathan. Includes full discussion of the
Bloomsbury Group and its characteristics: "They were not always
wholly serious, and playfulness must be expected to excite the
disapproval of ernest mediocrity, of the dunce and the drudge."

8   PETERSON, VIRGILIA. "Growing Up in Bloomsbury." *Saturday
     Review* 39 (8 September):43.
         Review of *The Flowers in the Forest* by David Garnett. Garnett,
as a member of Bloomsbury, is isolated from society, but he writes
about a group "without whose impact the literature, art, and even
politics of England would have today a different shape." Garnett
"represents not a type but a species, *sui generis*, quite impossible to
imagine outside that singular British group--socially privileged,
economically careful and often pinched, intellectually radical, easily
bored, easily intolerant, and wholly internecine in its friendships and its
strife."

9   PRICHETT, V.S. "Bloomsbury and the Ant-Eater." *New Statesman
     and Nation* 52 (17 November):641.
         Review of *Virginia Woolf and Lytton Strachey: Letters*, edited by
Leonard Woolf and James Strachey, and *Old Friends* by Clive Bell.
Describes contrast between world of Bloomsbury as "aesthetic

snobbishness" and the rest of the world: "But we are outside it all, ant-eaters condemned to the species. We gaze back at exceptional personalities."

10   RUSSELL, BERTRAND. *Portraits from Memory, and Other Essays.* London: Allen Unwin, 215 pp.
         Mentions figures from the Bloomsbury group who were important to Russell, including Lytton Strachey, Desmond MacCarthy, E.M. Forster, John Maynard Keynes. This collection does not include *Listener* and *Harpers* articles.

11   WEBB, BEATRICE. *Beatrice Webb's Diaries 1924-1932.* Edited by Margaret Cole. London: Longmans, pp. 130-31.
         Includes some commentary on Bloomsbury. Leonard Woolf was a member of the Fabians.

12   WOOLF, VIRGINIA, and LYTTON STRACHEY. *Virginia Woolf and Lytton Strachey: Letters.* Edited by Leonard Woolf and James Strachey. London: Hogarth Press and Chatto and Windus; New York: Harcourt Brace and Jovanovich, 118 pp.
         These letters include commentary on various Bloomsbury figures. The tone is often associated with the snobbish Bloomsbury attitude.

1957

1   ALLEN, WALTER. "Bloomsbury Water-Spiders." *Nation* 184 (26 January):81-82.
         Review of *Virginia Woolf and Lytton Strachey Letters*, edited by Leonard Woolf and James Strachey (see 1956.12). Suggests that Bloomsbury never existed as a movement or a school, but it did manifest a "common attitude of mind," which can be defined according to John Maynard Keynes as "low habits," meaning irreverence and frivolity, and "austerity," meaning high-thinking. Bloomsbury's members were "intellectually brilliant," were "the transmitters of new ideas, new modes of apprehension." This correspondence, however, will reinforce the idea of Bloomsbury as "lacking in feeling." Keynes had described them as water-spiders skimming the surface.

2   ____. "The Privacy of Bloomsbury." *Nation* 184 (9 March):218-19.
         Review of *Old Friends*, by Clive Bell (see 1956.1): "In the essay

on Bloomsbury he asks whether it ever existed and implies it did not.
Nevertheless, the most valuable parts of the book are those devoted to
his Bloomsbury friends." Suggests that whatever Bell's notion of the
validity of Bloomsbury, his "book is a perfect definition of it" on two
levels, in its snobbishness and in its "exhibition of the values that ruled
it."

3   BELL, QUENTIN. "John Sargent and Roger Fry." *Burlington
     Magazine* 99 (November):380-82.
        Commentary on criticism of Fry in Charles Merrill Mount's *John
Singer Sargent: A Biography.* Corrects the accusation that Fry made use
of Sargent's name in behalf of the Post-impressionist cause without
Sargent's permission. Mount states that because Sargent caught Fry at
this game, Fry's "personal hatred was twisted into attack on artistry and
integrity." Bell points out that Fry had written to the *Nation* on 14
January, 1911, explaining that Sargent had expressed admiration for
Cézanne's early work. Bell also quotes passages from Fry that show his
admiration for Sargent's work.

4   BLOOMFIELD, PAUL. "The Bloomsbury Tradition in English
     Literary Criticism." In *The Craft of Letters in England.* Edited by
     John Lehmann. Boston: Houghton Mifflin, pp. 160-82.
        Characterizes the tradition of literary criticism practiced by
various Bloomsbury figures, especially Virginia Woolf and Lytton
Strachey: "Literary criticism was chiefly practiced in Bloomsbury by
Lytton Strachey and Virginia Woolf, who in the special circumstances
were under obligations to George Moore, a Cambridge philosopher
and critic of morals (most of the men had been at Cambridge); to
Roger Fry, a critic of the plastic arts; to Clive Bell, a critic of
painting and of the arts of living--in which he was reputed to be
something of a connoisseur." Focuses on the personal quality, "the
human touch" in an impersonalized world, in their writing as
important to civilization.

5   BRENAN, GERALD. *South from Granada.* London: Hamish
     Hamilton. Reprint. New York: Farrar, Strauss & Giroux, 1959, pp.
     27-37, 139-46.
        Autobiographical account of various Bloomsbury figures,
Leonard and Virginia Woolf, Lytton Strachey, David Garnett, and
Roger Fry. Chapter 13, "Virginia Woolf's Visit," and Chapter 14,
"Lytton Strachey's Visit," deals with Leonard and Virginia, Lytton

Strachey, as well as other Bloomsbury figures. She would listen to his criticism of her novels: "That was the great thing about 'Bloomsbury'-- they refused to stand on the pedestal of their own age and superiority." Describes Bloomsbury gatherings: "Looking back today it is not, I think, difficult to see that the weakness inherent in the splendid flower of English culture thrown up by 'Bloomsbury' lay in its being so closely attached to a class and mode of life that was dying."

6   EDEL, LEON. *Literary Biography: The Alexander Lectures 1955-1956.* Toronto: University of Toronto Press. Reprint. New York: Anchor Edition, 1959, pp. 87-98.
    Discussion of the biographical techniques of Lytton Strachey and Virginia Woolf. Deals extensively with *Orlando*, "a fantasy in the form of a biography," in relation to Woolf's connections with Harold Nicolson and Lytton Strachey. The idea came from Strachey. Her other biography, *Roger Fry*, is not as evocative: "The Fry biography has certain very fine passages in which Mrs. Woolf writes out her own Bloomsbury Group memories."

7   HAMILTON, IAN. "Review of Two Bloomsbury Books." *Spectator* (December):23-24.
    Review of *Virginia Woolf and Lytton Strachey: Letters*, edited by Leonard Woolf and James Strachey (1956.12) and *Old Friends* by Clive Bell (1956.1). Questions the value of Bloomsbury culture.

8   HARROD, ROY. "Clive Bell on Keynes." *Economic Journal* 67 (December):692-99.
    Commentary on Bell's article on Keynes in *Old Friends* (see 1956.1). Professional economists have protested against Bell's observations because on the whole Bell seems to mock Keynes. Suggests that Bloomsbury partially based not upon mutual admiration but "mutual criticism." Bell's criticism of Keynes involves his "habit of cock-sureness about matters on which he was not well informed" and his "lack of aesthetic discrimination." Harrod refers to his *Life of Keynes* in relation to this criticism. Goes on to argue that Bell is wrong on two points of substance. Bell is wrong about the point at which Keynes "took to speculating." Bell states it was around 1914; Harrod states that it was 1919. Bell is also wrong in stating that Keynes was a conscientious objector during World War I. With Strachey dead, who was the real center of Bloomsbury, no one remains who can write an

adequate tribute to Keynes because Bloomsbury "did not understand
many of the real elements of greatness in their friend."

9   LANE, MARGARET. "On Bloomsbury." *London Magazine* 4, no.
     2:62-64.
         Review of *Virginia Woolf and Lytton Strachey: Letters* (1956.12)
     and Clive Bell's *Old Friends* (1956.1): "The trouble with this eminent
     group of people, so often thought of collectively as Bloomsbury, is that
     they are already far enough away from us to be legendary, while being
     still too near in time for the biographer." The letters are full of
     mockery which has become the chief source of annoyance to those
     outside Bloomsbury.

10   MOUNT, CHARLES MERRILL. *John Singer Sargent: A Biography*.
     London: Cresset Press, 371 pp.
         Study of one of Roger Fry's contemporaries, which includes
     negative commentary on Fry and Bloomsbury. Quentin Bell (1957.3)
     comments on criticism of Fry in this text.

11   MUGGERIDGE, MALCOLM. "The Bloomsbury Brain-Trust."
     New Republic 136 (28 January):16-17.
         Review of *Virginia Woolf and Lytton Strachey: Letters* edited by
     Leonard Woolf and James Strachey (1956.12). States that it would be
     easy to laugh at "this sad, foolish, rather commonplace
     correspondence," but we may find "that we are laughing at ourselves."
     The influence of the group can still be felt: "If most of their works lie
     a moldering in the grave, Brain Trusts and other such popular
     manifestations of the cult of intellectualism go marching on."

12   NEHLS, EDWARD. *D.H. Lawrence: A Composite Biography Vol. 1,
     1885-1919*. Madison: University of Wisconsin Press, 614 pp.
         Biographical study that involves gathering material by various
     people who knew Lawrence during this time period. Includes some
     commentary on and by Bloomsbury figures, especially Lady Ottoline
     Morrell, Bertrand Russell, and David Garnett, which relates to
     Lawrence's association with the Group. Uses excepts from John
     Maynard Keynes's memoir about Lawrence's visit to Cambridge.

13   O'CONNOR, WILLIAM VAN. "Another Chapter on Bloomsbury."
     Kenyon Review 19, no. 2 (Spring):229-36.
         Review article on *Men, Books and Mountains*, by Leslie Stephen,

Old Friends by Clive Bell (1956.1), and *Virginia Woolf and Lytton Strachey: Letters*, edited by Leonard Woolf and James Strachey (1956.12). Describes Bloomsbury as experimental: "In painting and in literature they explored the meanings of *modernism*. And they won a great victory. Sentimentality and philistinism beat a great retreat--even off the book pages of newspapers."

14   ROCHE, PAUL. "Bloomsbury Revisited." *Commonweal* 66 (5 April):17-18.
     Letter to the editor in response to Wagner's article (see 1957.20). Defends Bloomsbury against Wagner's attack. These figures are "the choice and master spirits of their age."

15   ROTHENSTEIN, JOHN. Review *Sargent* by Charles Mount. *Observer* (28 April):15.
     Comments on Mount's statement that Fry felt personal animosity towards Sargent: "Having lately been taken to task for animadversions on the conduct of Roger Fry and several of his friends towards painters outside the Bloomsbury sphere of influence, I was interested in Mr. Mount's account of Fry's personal animosity toward Sargent."

16   SANDERS, CHARLES RICHARD. *Lytton Strachey: His Mind and Art*. New Haven: Yale University Press. Reprint. Port Washington, N. Y.: Kennikat Press, 1973, 381 pp.
     Full-length study of Strachey that includes considerable commentary on his work and on his Bloomsbury associations.

17   SANDILANDS, G.S. "Contemporary British Artists." *Artist* 57 (August):105.
     Includes commentary on the paintings of Duncan Grant and his relation to the Omega Workshops and Bloomsbury.

18   SIMON, IRENE. "Bloomsbury and Its Critics." *Revue des Langues Vivantes* 23, no. 5:385-414.
     Discusses the origin and chief determining influences on the Bloomsbury Group, especially G.E. Moore's *Principia Ethica* and Roger Fry's aesthetic, and its members. Bloomsbury members "felt themselves to form an aristocracy of spirit which was threatened by the philistines outside." Evaluates also the chief adversaries of Bloomsbury, D.H. Lawrence and F.R. Leavis: "The main criticisms of Bloomsbury thus bear on its lack of reverence and of moral sensibility, and on its

distortion of critical standards. Skepticism, cynicism, flippancy, exaggerated cult of self, ignorance of moral responsibility and denial of the Spirit, on the one hand. On the other, coterie-power which sets up social-personal criteria about critical standards."

19   WAGNER, GEOFFREY. "Bloomsbury Revisited." *Books and Bookman* 2 (July):12.
        Violently antagonistic on grounds that Bloomsbury Group were not rebels. They were only "a surface disquiet" and were perfectly "integrated with the status quo." Approaches the Group from Wyndham Lewis's point of view.

20   _____. "Bloomsbury Revisited." *Commonweal* 65 (8 March):589-590.
        Negative commentary on the group based upon his reading of several new texts, including the Strachey-Woolf letters and Johnston's *The Bloomsbury Group*. Forster is the only worthwhile figure: "There remains, thankfully, E.M. Forster. Were it not for him the Bloomsbury movement would go down not merely as a distressing moment in British literature, but as one scarcely civilized."

21   _____. *Wyndham Lewis: A Portrait of the Artist as the Enemy.* New Haven: Yale University Press, 363 pp.
        Comments briefly on Lewis's objections to Bloomsbury and to his problems with Roger Fry. *The Apes of God* ridicules "Bloomsburies." Found the Bloomsbury artists in the Omega Workshops "too dilettantist for his tastes."

22   WAIN, JOHN. "Correspondence." *London Magazine* 4, no. 3 (March):55-57.
        Response to letter by D.J. Enright on Wain's article, "Writer's Prospect." Writers need a grip on contemporary literary history. Uses criticism of Bloomsbury as an example. Iain Hamilton says that current writers "dance on the gave of Bloomsbury" without knowing what lies beneath "their big black boots."

23   WOOD, ALAN. *Bertrand Russell: The Passionate Skeptic.* London: Allen and Unwin. Reprint. New York: Simon & Schuster, 1958, 249 pp.
        Biographical study of Bertrand Russell. Describes Garsington during World War I. Also relates Keynes's acknowledgement of G.E. Moore without mention of Russell at Cambridge. For Russell, World

War I made Russell recognize that "men were not so rational as he had believed. But for Keynes and some of his friends in the 'Bloomsbury' group, the war meant no such crisis of thinking or feeling."

1958

1   CLIVE, JOHN. "More or Less Eminent Victorians: Some Trends in Recent Victorian Biography." *Victorian Studies* 2 (September):5-28.

Survey that deals with Lytton Strachey's influence of Victorian biography. Suggests that he misused and occasionally distorted historical evidence: "He may have been a member of the Bloomsbury Group, but he did not carry its passion for absolute truth and honesty in the expression of thought and feeling about personal relations into the pages of *Eminent Victorians*."

2   DATALLER, ROGER. "Mr. Lawrence and Mrs. Woolf." *Essays in Criticism* 8 (January):48-59.

Brief article which deals somewhat with the association of these two writers within the context of Bloomsbury.

3   DONER, DEAN. "Bloomsbury Correspondence." *Western Review* 22, no. 3 (Spring):237-40.

Review of *Virginia Woolf and Lytton Strachey: Letters*, edited by Leonard Woolf and James Strachey (1956.12). This volume should "prove ammunition for those who dislike Mrs. Woolf, Strachey, and the Bloomsbury group." These letters only show shallowness rather than "penetrate their subjects." Objects to the censorship of portions of the letters. Concludes that these letters will "support the counter-charges of the group's members that it was never a clique; its members were too individualistic and talented to share many opinions in earnest."

4   FIEDLER, LESLIE. "Class War in British Literature." *Esquire* 49 (April):79-81.

Angry young men of 50s reacting explicitly against elitism of Bloomsbury: "What 'Bloomsbury' was historically, even the question of whether it existed at all, does not matter; it has become a *myth*, a handy label for a hated world."

5   IRWIN, W.R. "The Metamorphoses of David Garnett." *PMLA* 73, no. 4 (September):386-92.
    Critical study of Garnett focusing primarily on his two major novels, *Lady into Fox* (1922) and *A Man in the Zoo* (1924). Relates somewhat to the influence of his Bloomsbury association.

6   KALLICH, MARTIN. "Psychoanalysis, Sexuality, and Lytton Strachey's Theory of Biography." *American Imago* 25 (Winter):331-70.
    Commentary on Strachey in relation to the advent of psychoanalysis. Includes letter from James Strachey not reprinted in *The Psychological Milieu of Lytton Strachey*. (See 1961.12).

7   NEHLS, EDWARD. *D.H. Lawrence: A Composite Biography Vol. 2, 1919-1925*. Madison: University of Wisconsin Press, 614 pp.
    Biographical study that involves gathering material by various people who knew Lawrence during this time period. Includes commentary on and by various Bloomsbury figures, especially Dorothy Brett, that relates to Lawrence's association with the Group.

8   O'CONNOR, WILLIAM VAN. "Samuel Butler and Bloomsbury." In *From Jane Austen to Joseph Conrad*. Edited by Robert C. Rathburn and Martin Steinmann, Jr. Minneapolis: University of Minnesota Press, pp. 257-73.
    Suggests that there are connections between Butler and the Bloomsbury Group. It is well know that E.M. Forster was an admirer of Butler and was influenced by him: "It is not so well known that Butler meant a good deal to many of Forster's Bloomsbury friends." Family connections establish the first level of influence. Others, such as Desmond MacCarthy, were influenced by Butler's ideas. Virginia Wool admired Butler's "forthrightness, his willingness to think his own thoughts, and his ability to put them down directly." Bloomsbury "had a lot to do with popularizing Butler."

9   "The Perpetual Marriage." *Times Literary Supplement* (London) (4 July):1-2.
    Review of Virginia Woolf's *Granite and Rainbow* (1958.12). Comments on the relationship between Leonard and Virginia Woolf, as well as on the Bloomsbury world.

10   PLOMER, WILLIAM. *At Home*. London: Jonathan Cape, 210 pp.
     Memories of literary evenings in Bloomsbury.

11   WERNER, ALFRED. "Roger Fry's Discovery of Cézanne." In
     Cézanne: A Study of His Development, by Roger Fry. New York:
     Noonday Press, pp. iii-xv.
         Describes Roger Fry's activities that lead to the discovery of the
     art and importance of Cézanne. Includes commentary on other
     Bloomsbury figures involved in the two Post-impressionist exhibitions.

12   WOOLF, VIRGINIA. *Granite and Rainbow*. Edited by Leonard
     Woolf. London: Hogarth Press, 240 pp.
         Includes essays that relate to Bloomsbury, especially "The New
     Biography," which is a study of the work of Lytton Strachey.

1959

1   BREWSTER, DOROTHY. *Virginia Woolf's London*. London:
    Allen & Unwin; New York: New York University Press, 120 pp.
        "To suggest how some such general impression of London grows
    in our minds as we read the novels and essays in their chronological
    order is the main purpose of the following chapters." Deals also with
    Bloomsbury in relation to the reading of her works.

2   CLUTTON-BROCK, ALAN. "Duncan Grant." *Duncan Grant:
    Retrospective Exhibition*. Exhibition Catalog. London: Tate
    Gallery, pp. 1-6.
        Grant belonged to Bloomsbury by birth and upbringing: "It was
    not generally recognized, until the present Provost of King's College,
    Cambridge, published his ingenious research into the genealogy of Sir
    Leslie Stephen and his circle, how much the ties that held these men
    and women together depended on heredity and family connections."
    Also traces influence on Grant to literary discussions in Bloomsbury, to
    the French Post-impressionists, brought to England by Roger Fry in
    1910 and 1912, and to the Omega Workshops. The catalogue also
    includes "Duncan Grant *Chronology*."

3   DIAMOND, PAMELA. Preface to *Roger Fry: Paintings,
    Watercolours and Drawings*. Exhibition Catalog. Colchester,
    England: Minories, pp. 1-3.

Introduction to Roger Fry's work by his daughter. Gives personal account of his activities, including his work with the Omega Workshops. Deals with Bloomsbury associations as well.

4   GILLIAM, FRANKLIN. *The Garnetts: A Literary Family.*
    Exhibition Catalog. Austin: University of Austin Press.
        Includes preface by David Garnett, "The Garnett Family."
Describes items in the exhibition that relate to Bloomsbury, particularly in relation to David Garnett.

5   HASSALL, CHRISTOPHER. *A Biography of Edward Marsh.* New
    York: Harcourt Brace & World; London: Longmans, Green, 732
    pp.
        Includes some references to Bloomsbury activities in relation to
Edward Marsh's work in literary publication.

6   KEYNES, GEOFFREY. "Henry James in Cambridge." *London
    Magazine* 6, no. 3 (March):50-61.
        Account of Henry James visit to Cambridge to meet with
Charles Sayle, Theodore Bartholomew, and Geoffrey Keynes. James
also met with Maynard Keynes and Harry Norton: "He was bewildered
by the clever scintillating conversation that eddied round him (this was
confirmed by Maynard Keynes himself), and told afterwards of the
incomprehensible utterances made by the Laughing Philosopher, as he
called Harry Norton, one of Maynard Keynes's circle who habitually
followed every remark he made with senseless laughter and giggles."
Desmond MacCarthy was also involved in this visit.

7   LEA, F.A. *The Life of John Middleton Murry.* New York and
    Oxford: Oxford University Press, 378 pp.
        Includes commentary on Murry and Katherine Mansfield's
relationship with Lady Ottoline Morrell, Garsington, and Bloomsbury.

8   LEYBURN, ELLEN DOUGLASS. "Virginia Woolf's Judgment of
    Henry James." *Modern Fiction Studies* 5, no. 2 (Summer):166-69.
        Brief commentary on Woolf's concept of the novel in relation to
the work of Henry James. Deals with the strictures of Edwardian and
Georgian England, which were in conflict with the freedom defined by
Bloomsbury.

9   MELVILLE, ROBERT. "Exhibitions." *Architectural Review* 126
      (August-September):131-33.
          Includes review of Duncan Grant Bell exhibition at the Tate
      Gallery: "The Bloomsbury writers became a pack of intolerant culture
      snobs at the mere mention of the art of painting, and Grant, who was
      tied to them by birth and upbringing, was sensitive to the demands they
      made upon him without having the means to fulfil them."

10   NEHLS, EDWARD. *D.H. Lawrence: A Composite Biography Vol. 3,
      1925-1930.* Madison: University of Wisconsin Press, 767 pp.
          Biographical study that involves gathering material by various
      people who knew Lawrence during this time period. Includes some
      commentary by and about various Bloomsbury figures, particularly
      Dorothy Brett, which relates to Lawrence's association with the Group.
      Some pieces are original for this volume. Rolf Gardiner comments on
      the Cambridge world in 1919, which was dominated by Bloomsbury
      intellectualism: "The dons were steeped in scientific humanism and the
      Bloomsbury elect were the intellectual heros of the hour." Philip
      Trotter comments on the Bloomsbury aesthetic, which was drawn from
      contemporary French art.

11   STRONG, L.A.G. "Memories of Garsington." *London Magazine* 6,
      no. 1 (January):11-16.
          Autobiographical account of Lady Ottoline Morrell: "Too many
      writers have concentrated on what seemed grandiose and absurd, and
      have missed the quality of a great and generous lady." Describes his
      visits to Garsington while at Oxford: "I approached the great house as
      a pilgrim approaches Mecca." Met the Woolfs, T.S. Eliot, and others.

12   WOOLF, LEONARD. "Henry James and the Young Men."
      Listener 62 (9 July):53-54.
          Autobiographical account of his days at Cambridge: "I found to
      my astonishment that there were a number of people near and about
      me with whom I could enjoy the exciting and at the same time
      profound happiness of friendship." Describes meeting with Saxon
      Sydney turner who had "an encyclopedic knowledge of literature, but he
      read books rather in the spirit in which some people collect stamps."
      During the Cambridge years Henry James was at the height of his
      creative powers. They all read the major novels. Woolf's enjoyment of
      these books included some reservations: "There is an element of
      ridiculousness, even phoniness, in them which makes it impossible to

rank them with the greatest or even the great novels." Describes James's visits to the Leslie Stephen in Rye, where the family spent the summer. Lytton Strachey and Saxon came to stay with them too. Later describes James's visit to the second Post-impressionist exhibition, "which he did not much like."

1960

1   "Ethos of an Elite." *Times Literary Supplement* (London) (9 September):1-3.
    Review of Leonard Woolf's *Sowing: An Autobiography of the Years 1880-1904*. Comments on Woolf's description of his Cambridge background and on his association with Lytton Strachey, Clive Bell, Maynard Keynes, and others, as well as on the influence of G.E. Moore. Questions Woolf's evaluation of Desmond MacCarthy. Also looks at Woolf and the intellectual establishment of Bloomsbury, who are "despised, distrusted, and rejected."

2   LEHMANN, JOHN. *I Am My Brother: Autobiography II.* London: Longmans; New York: Reynal & Co, 326 pp.
    Second volume of Lehmann's autobiography (*The Whispering Gallery* [1955.12] is volume one). Again, he describes his relationship with Leonard and Virginia Woolf, as well as his association with the Hogarth Press. This deals primarily with the years of World War II, not with the high years of Bloomsbury activity: "More and more, as the war went on, Leonard left the running of the press to me." He visited Leonard not long after Virginia's death: "I was haunted all the time by the feeling of her presence in the house."

3   PRIESTLY, JOHN B. *Literature and Western Man.* New York: Harper, pp. 113, 311-12.
    Stresses the influence of G.E. Moore on Maynard Keynes and Lytton Strachey, and through them on the Bloomsbury Group. Deals with Strachey and others: "The philosophy belonging to and characteristic of this age came first from Cambridge . . . . The two Cambridge men who rebelled against subjective idealism and ended the long reign of Hegel were G.E. Moore and Bertrand Russell." Sees Virginia Woolf as too dominated by upper-middle class to be a great novelist.

4   QUENNELL, PETER. *The Sign of the Fish.* New York: Viking.
    London: Collins, 217 pp.
        Autobiographical account of various Bloomsbury figures. The
    Chapter, "Camp-Followers," deals extensively with Lady Ottoline
    Morrell and Garsington: "As soon as I had gone up to Oxford, I heard
    discussions of Lady Ottoline Morrell and of the Renaissance court she
    held at Garsington Manor four or five miles beyond the city limits."
    She was not a deeply intelligent women, "but she had a genuine respect
    for intelligence and a gift for promoting intelligence in others." Also
    gives observations about Virginia Woolf, Clive Bell, Lytton Strachey,
    and Edith Sitwell.

5   WOOLF, LEONARD. "After Fifty Years." *New Statesman* 59
    (April):577-80.
        Brief commentary on some aspects of Bloosmbury from one of
    the central members.

6   _____. *Sowing: An Autobiography of the Years 1880 to 1904.*
    London: Hogarth Press; New York: Harcourt Brace Jovanovich,
    224 pp.
        First volume of Woolf's autobiography, including a chapter on
    his childhood and a chapter on his years at Cambridge, where he was a
    member of the Apostles. His association with this society, Woolf says
    formed the basis for Bloomsbury. He developed friendships with
    Lytton Strachey, Clive Bell, Maynard Keynes, and Thoby Stephen. This
    group became the focus of the Bloomsbury Group. Describes the
    importance of G.E. Moore and his doctrine of "nothing mattered except
    states of mind." States that "Bloomsbury grew directly out of
    Cambridge; it consisted of a number of intimate friends who had been
    at Trinity and King's and were now working in London, most of them
    living in Bloomsbury."

1961

1   BANTOCK, G.H. "L.H. Myers and Bloomsbury." In *The Pelican
    Guide to English Literature: The Modern Age.* Edited by Boris Ford.
    Harmondsworth and Baltimore: Penguin Books, pp. 270-79.
        Commentary on the novels of L.H. Myers with a discussion of
    his satire of the Bloomsbury Group: "Myers's analysis of the Pleasance
    of the Arts, a meeting place of contemporary aesthetes, has interest

beyond the novel [*The Root of the Flower*], for here he is satirizing a
prominent literary group of his times, Bloomsbury." He objects to
Bloomsbury because it is aesthetic rather than moralistic. He also found
its elitism distasteful: "Dull, conventional people--people who weren't
lit by the divine spark, had no chance of gaining admission here."

2   BEALES, H.L. "Three Octogenarians." *Political Quarterly* 32
     (January-March):68-70.
         Includes commentary on Leonard Woolf, which involves the
connection between Bloomsbury and the political scene.

3   "Bloomsbury Group." *Listener* 65 (May 4):768.
         Editorial written on the occasion of Vanessa Bell's death: "The
Bloomsbury Group, in fact, reacted violently against the moral-toned,
story telling aspects of Victorian literature and art and the material
world of H.G. Wells, Arnold Bennett, and Bernard Shaw." The Group
did not, however, live in an ivory tower. Leonard Woolf and Keynes
"were concerned with political questions." Relates Bloomsbury revolt
against convention to the current reaction against Bloomsbury: "What
matters above all is the integrity of belief and a vision of beauty. That
was what the Bloomsbury Group had to offer."

4   BRADBROOK, FRANK W. "Virginia Woolf: The Theory and
     Practice of Fiction." In the *Pelican Guide to English Literature*: *The
     Modern Age*. Edited by Boris Ford. Harmondsworth: Peguin
     Books, pp. 257-69.
         "Virginia Woolf's values are those of Bloomsbury." Mutual
admiration that was nearly a form of narcissism.

5   CLUTTON-BROCK, ALAN. "Vanessa Bell and Her Circle."
     Listener 65 (4 May):790.
         Overview of Bloomsbury as large Victorian family involved in all
aspects of culture. Focuses on the painters in the Group: "There was a
family kind of painting as well as of thinking." Concludes that "the
painting of Vanessa Bell, like that of Duncan Grant, may be the
product of Bloomsbury's hedonism, an outlook on life backed up by the
far-reaching doctrine derived from G.E. Moore that an action is good if
its consequences are good and pleasure the most obvious of good
consequences."

6   FRIED, M. "Vanessa Bell: Exhibition of Paintings at the Adams
     Gallery." *Arts* 36 (December):40.
     Review of Vanessa Bell exhibition, which discusses her art in
relation to Bloomsbury and other Bloomsbury artists, including Duncan
Grant and Roger Fry.

7   GARNETT, DAVID. "Some Writers I Have Known: Yalesworth,
     Forster, Moore, and Wells." *Texas Quarterly* 4, no. 3:190-202.
     Personalized account of a second-generation Bloomsbury figure
of E.M. Forster and other writers.

8   HEIBRUN, CAROLYN. *The Garnett Family*. London: Ruskin
     House; George Allen & Unwin, 38 pp.
     Includes some commentary on David Garnett and Bloomsbury.

9   HOFFMAN, FREDERICK J. "*Howard's End* and the Bogey of
     Progress." *Modern Fiction Studies* 7, no. 3 (Autumn): 243-57.
     Evaluates the ideal of progress in Forster's work, using H.G.
Wells as foil: Wells's excessive simplicity and Forster's conscientious
irony seem to me to suggest one of the best ways of judging the impact
of progress upon modern society." One line of development, beginning
with Hume, includes Forster and Bloomsbury.

10   IZZO, CARLO. "Testimonianza sul 'Bloomsbury Group'." In *Studi
     In Onore di Vittorio Lugli e Diego Valeri*. Edited by Carlo Cordie.
     Venice: Pozza, pp. 523-49.
     Intellectual and aesthetic influences on the Bloomsbury Group
(e.g. G.E. Moore, Roger Fry, Clive Bell), and the Group's reputation
and relationships with their contemporaries. [In Italian.]

11   JEGER, LENA M. "Bloomsbury." *Guardian* (25 February):4.
     Discussion of the preoccupation with Bloomsbury and
Bloomsbury figures.

12   KALLICH, MARTIN. *The Psychological Milieu of Lytton Strachey*.
     New York: Bookman Associates, 162 pp.
     Strachey used Freud's views about the unconscious in his study
of personalities: "Knowledge of his direct or indirect indebtedness to
Freud contributes to an understanding of Strachey's special
psychological insights into human nature, among the most important
constituents in modern life writing, and permits an evaluation of his

achievement in biography." Discusses Strachey's "campaign for honesty and truth" in relation to Bloomsbury, sexual freedom, and his experiences as a Cambridge Apostle.

13   NATHAN, MONIQUE. *Virginia Woolf*. Translated by Herma Briffault. New York: Grove Press, 321 pp.
General introduction to Virginia Woolf's life and work, in the context of the Bloomsbury Group and against the background of English life and culture.

14   "A Passage to Ceylon." *Times Literary Supplement* London) (24 November):833-34.
Review of Leonard Woolf's *Growing: An Autobiography of the Years 1904-1911*. Comments on Woolf's years in Ceylon, as well as on his friends from Cambridge who wrote to him of the Bloomsbury activities of which he was to become a part.

15   PLOMER, WILLIAM. Review *Sowing* by Leonard Woolf. *London Magazine* 8, no. 1 (January):69-71.
Gives brief commentary on his days at Cambridge, his association there with Lytton Strachey, Thoby Stephen, Clive Bell, Maynard Keynes, and E.M. Forster, and the influence of G.E. Moore: "They felt suffocated by 'bourgeois Victorianism,' against which they were conscious rebels, and it seemed to them right and a duty to hold nothing sacred and to question all authority."

16   SCHAPER, EVA. "Significant Form." *British Journal of Aesthetics* 1, no. 2 (March):33-43.
Discusses the Clive Bell-Roger Fry theory of significant form in order to branch off from their ideas: "The Bell-Fry theory pre-supposes a substance-quality conception of art ('every work of art has significant form'). My own proposals are based upon a functional approach, according to which it belongs to the function of art (but is by no means the only function of art) to articulate significant form."

17   WOOLF, LEONARD. *Growing: An Autobiography of the Years 1904-1911*. London: Hogarth Press; New York: Harcourt Brace Jovanovich, 256 pp.
Second volume of Woolf's autobiography, which describes mostly his years in civil service in Ceylon but also includes references to his continued association with those back in England who were forming

Bloomsbury. States that he "felt a complete loss of the life which I had lived at Cambridge, its friends and friendship."

1962

1 "The Artist as Biographer." *Times Literary Supplement* (London)(12 October):785-86.
    Deals with the literary biographies of Virginia Woolf and Lytton Strachey.

2 BRENAN, GERALD. *A Life of One's Own.* London: Hamish Hamilton, 219 pp.
    Autobiographical account of various Bloomsbury figures.

3 BREWSTER, DOROTHY. *Virginia Woolf.* New York: New York University Press, 184 pp.
    Study of Woolf's work, with a chapter giving biographical background that relates to Bloomsbury. Describes Bloomsbury's origins in Cambridge and in the philosophy of G.E. Moore. Comments on Bloomsbury-baiters: "Yet there was something very irritating about Bloomsbury."

4 COHN, RUBY. "Art in *To the Lighthouse*." *Modern Fiction Studies* 8:127-36.
    Critical study that includes a discussion of the influence of Roger Fry on the work of Virginia Woolf.

5 CREWS, FREDERICK C. *E.M. Forster: The Perils of Humanism.* Princeton: Princeton University Press, 187 pp.
    Evaluates Forster's "position as a humanist--as a man who places his faith in his world and who takes the individual human norm as the measure of everything." Chapter Two, "Forster and Religion: From Clapham to Bloomsbury," states that "the third, or Bloomsbury, generation of Clapham's descendants was raised in ignorance of theology, and affected to look back on the Christian age with Voltairean amusement." Also deals with Forster's Cambridge years and the origins of Bloomsbury in the Apostles of G.E. Moore.

6 DILLE, ROLAND PAUL. "David Garnett and the Bloomsbury Group." Ph.D. dissertation, University of Minnesota, 230 pp.

Examines "the ideas of David Garnett in relation to the ideas of
the Bloomsbury Group." Evaluates the main aspects of Garnett
through essays and reviews, as well as the eleven novels he wrote
between 1922 and 1959. These works show the shared ideas of
Bloomsbury. See *Dissertation Abstracts International* 22:3895.

7   DUNOYER DE SEGONZAC, ANDRE. Introduction to *Venessa
     Bell: Memorial Exhibition*. Exhibition Catalog. London: Adams
     Gallery, pp. 3-7.
        Introduction to the paintings of Vanessa Bell. Deals with the
importance of Roger Fry and Duncan Grant on Bell's work.

8   GARNETT, DAVID. *The Old Familiar Faces*. London: Chatto and
     Windus. New York: Harcourt Brace and Jovanovich, 167 pp.
        Autobiographical account of his various activities in and out of
Bloomsbury.

9   GRANSDEN, PHILIP. *E.M. Forster*. Edinburgh: Oliver & Boyd;
     New York: Grove Press, 169 pp.
        Includes some commentary on Forster's association with
Bloomsbury and the influence of this group on his thought and fiction.

10   IZZO, CARLO. "Testimonianze sul Bloomsbury Group." *Studi
     Lugli-Valeri* (39):523-49.
        Not seen.

11   KALLICH, MARTIN. "Lytton Strachey: An Annotated Bibliography
     of Writings about Him." *English Literature in Transition* 5:1-77.
        Thorough bibliography with a discussion of the focus of each
article. Those articles that relate specifically to Strachey's Bloomsbury
connection are included in this research guide. Those who want to
work more in depth on Strachey should consult this bibliography for
other aspects of Strachey's work and critical reception.

12   KING, MERTON PRUETT. "The Price of Awareness: Virginia
     Woolf as a Practitioner-Critic." Ph.D. dissertation, University of
     Texas, 312 pp.
        Deals with how Woolf's fiction and nonfiction complement and
supplement each other. Her "biographies and predominantly
biographical essays represent her version of the novelistic biographical

methods brought to twentieth-century English biography by Lytton
Strachey." See *Dissertation Abstracts* 23:1704.

13   KREUTZ, IRVING. "Mr. Bennett and Mrs. Woolf." *Modern
      Fiction Studies* 8:103-15.
          Deals with the artistic conflict between Arnold Bennett and
      Virginia Woolf, taking into account Woolf's Bloomsbury background.

14   LANG, BEREL. "Significance or Form: The Dilemma of Roger
      Fry's Aesthetics." *Journal of Aesthetics and Art Criticism* 21, no. 2
      (Winter):167-76.
          Deals with the conflict in Fry between "systematic aesthetics" and
      the experience of a work of art. One of Fry's major concerns was
      'whether or not the creator of the work had sacrificed formal values for
      those of preconceived ideas, or, in Fry's terms, 'plasticity' for
      'psychology.'" Describes the connection with Clive Bell and with the
      Post-impressionist exhibition.

15   LEHMANN, JOHN. "E.M. Forster: A Refusal to Be Great."
      London Magazine 2 (October):74-8.
          Review by later-generation Bloomsbury member of two books on
      Forster: "The two basic reasons for E.M. Forster's power of survival
      are, first, his extreme subtlety of craftsmanship, and, second, the depth
      of his convictions as a poet-philosopher."

16   WALEY, ARTHUR. Introduction to *One Hundred and Seventy
      Chinese Bars*. Translation by Author Waley. London: Constable,
      pp. 5-6.
          Comments on Roger Fry's Omega Workshops and on Fry's
      interest in Waley's first book, which he wanted to print through the
      Omega. Also comments on Bloomsbury's interest in his translations.

1963

1   BENNET, JOAN. "Virginia Woolf: Critics Who Have Influenced
     Taste." *Times* (London) (25 April):15.
         Brief account of Woolf's importance as a critic. Includes some
     commentary on Bloomsbury.

2   COX, C.B. *The Free Spirit: A Study of Liberal Humanism in the Novels of George Eliot, E.M. Forster, Virginia Woolf, and Angus Wilson*. London: Oxford University Press, 345 pp.

Study of the tradition of liberal humanism in English culture, with special attention to Forster and Woolf in relation to the Bloomsbury tradition.

3   DAINTREY, ADRIAN. *I Must Say*. London: Chatto & Windus, 213 pp.

Autobiographical account that includes some commentary on Bloomsbury figures.

4   DELFORD, J. "Virginia Woolf's Critical Essays." *Revue des Langues Vivantes* 29, no. 2:126-31.

Woolf and Bloomsbury "had a very coherent system of aesthetic values. To them, the creation and the enjoyment of works of art was one of the prime objects in life. To them, the artist's main achievement is the discovery of 'significant form,' that is, the creation of a coherent world where everything is subordinated to a personal perspective." Woolf's criticism attempts "to discover which have governed that particular perspective."

5   FISHMAN, SOLOMON. *The Interpretation of Art: Essays on the Art Criticism of John Ruskin, Walter Pater, Clive Bell, Roger Fry, and Herbert Read*. Berkeley: University of California Press. London: Cambridge University Press, 287 pp.

Chapters on Clive Bell (pp. 73-99) and Roger Fry (pp. 101-142) contain relevant information on Bloomsbury. The Post-impressionists provide Bell "with the ultimate revelation concerning the formal basis of art." Gives full evaluation of "significant form": "Bell's aesthetics appears to lie midway between an excessively purist formalism and an incipient expressionism which threatens the notion of pure form." Relates Fry's and Bell's theory: "It should be noted that in Fry's aesthetics vision is inevitably subordinated to design: the all-important element is form."

6   HAFLEY, JAMES. *The Glass Roof: Virginia Woolf as Novelist*. London: Russell and Russell, 176 pp.

Critical study of Woolf's novel. Bloomsbury helped to form her aesthetic and sense of independence.

7   IRONS, EVELYN. "An Evening with Virginia Woolf." *New Yorker*
    39 (30 March):115-21.
        Personalized account of Woolf and Bloomsbury.

8   LEKAEHMAN, RAYMOND. "John Maynard Keynes." *Encounter*
    21 (December):34-43.
        General evaluation of Keynes, including a discussion of his
    association with Bloomsbury after Cambridge.

9   LEWIS, WYNDHAM. *The Letters of Wyndham Lewis*. Edited by
    W.K. Rose. London: Methuen; Norfolk, Conn.: New Directions.
    580 pp.
        Includes various letters about Bloomsbury and Bloomsbury
    figures. Comments on *The Roaring Queen*, which is in part a parody of
    Bloomsbury, include questions of libel and criticism of "the Bloomsbury
    principle." As late as 1948 he comments on Bloomsbury attacks on his
    written work.

10 MOODY, A.D. *Virginia Woolf*. Edinburgh and London: Oliver &
    Boyd, 78 pp.
        Challenges the *Scrutiny* line of attack on Woolf. Highlights the
    human value and contemporary meaning of Woolf's novels in a chaotic
    age of transition. Traces the development of Virginia Woolf's critical
    reputation in England.

11 MORRELL, LADY OTTOLINE. *Ottoline: The Early Memoirs of
    Lady Ottoline Morrell, 1873-1915*. Edited by Robert Gathorne-Hardy.
    London: Faber & Faber; New York: Alfred A. Knopf, 286 pp.
        Includes vivid accounts of the Bloomsbury world and the
    alternate world created by Lady Ottoline. Discusses various
    Bloomsbury figures, as well as Bertrand Russell and the problems
    associated with the early days of World War I.

12 MORTIMER, RAYMOND. "Desmond MacCarthy: Critics Who
    Have Influenced Taste." *Times* (London) (12 September):13.
        Brief account of MacCarthy as drama critic. Minor references
    to his Bloomsbury background.

13 MORWAT, C.L. "From the Edwardian Age to the Thirties: Some
    Literary Memoirs." *Critical Quarterly* 5 (Summer):157-67.
        Includes some passing references to the impact of Bloomsbury

on literary and artistic culture during this period. Describes the range
of Bloomsbury activities.

14   SIMSON, GEORGE KUPPER. "Lytton Strachey's Use of His
      Sources in *Eminent Victorians*." Ph.D. dissertation, University of
      Minnesota, 312 pp.
          Uses Strachey's "all-pervasive interest in the drama as criterion
      for judging his use of sources." Strachey's biographical work "focused
      on intimate personal relations and dramatic conflicts of mind in a
      manner inspired by G.E. Moore and by his Cambridge and Bloomsbury
      friends." See *Dissertation Abstracts International* 25:2520.

15   SUTTON, DENYS. "Omega Revisited." *Financial Times* (26
      November):24.
          Comment on the history of the Omega Workshops and a new
      exhibition of the work associated with Roger Fry and this organization.

16   SWINNERTON, FRANK. *Figures in the Foreground: Literary
      Reminiscences, 1917-1940.* London: Hutchinson; New York:
      Doubleday, 343 pp.
          Includes a section, "Apostles of Culture" (pp 136-51), which
      elaborates his objections to the elitism of Bloomsbury. They originated
      in the Apostles at Cambridge and continued the elitist ideal in
      Bloomsbury.

1964

1   ALLEN, WALTER. "Review of Morrell Memoirs." *New Republic*
     150 (3 June):27-28.
         Review of Lady Ottoline Morrell's memoirs. Evaluates the
     world created by Morrell and Bloomsbury prior to World War I.

2   BEJA, MORRIS. "Matches Struck in the Dark: Virginia Woolf's
     Moments of Vision." *Critical Quarterly* 6 (Summer):137-52.
         Deals with Woolf's aesthetic moment, which is a vision into the
     heart of reality. Connects Bloomsbury's search for truth to Woolf's
     "moment of vision."

3   BELL, QUENTIN. "Bloomsbury and the Arts in the Early
     Twentieth Century." *Leeds Art Calendar* 55:18-28.
     Text of lecture given at City Art Gallery, Leeds, on 11June 1964.
Tries to explain "the nature of what they call the 'Bloomsbury Group'."
Discusses "writers and politicians, about philosophy and about sex."
The great intellectual adventure "of their lives was the struggle between
faith and reason." And "personally I doubt whether any group *had* ever
been quite so radical in its approach to sexual taboos." The revolt
against Victorian morality "is paralleled by the equally individualistic
revolt against Victorian aesthetics." States that Bloomsbury had ended
by the twenties.

4   _____. "The Omega Revisited." *Listener* 71 (30 January):200-201.
     Personal commentary on the Omega Workshops based upon
exhibition, "The Omega Workshops 1913-1920," at the Victorian and
Albert Museum: "Aesthetically, the Omega presented no surprises for
me: nothing except perhaps the astonishment of finding a shop, a
public place, which looked like my own home." Discusses some of the
criticism of the original Workshops shows. Now he would expect "a
kind of post-Bauhaus desdain for anything so unfunctional, so far from
industrial techniques, so completely lacking in respect for the nature of
the materials that were used." Argues against the comparison to
Morris and the crafts movement. Morris's interests were not those of a
painter.

5   _____. *Roger Fry: An Inaugural Lecture*. Leeds: Leeds University
     Press, 20 pp.
     Lecture delivered at the University of Leeds on 2 December
1963. Compares Fry to Ruskin: "Fry was to a far greater extent an
innovator, a pioneer." He was puzzled by the outcry the Post-
impressionist exhibitions provoked: "Despite all calumnies and
misunderstandings I think that the years between 1910 and 1914 were
the happiest in Fry's life."

6   BELL, QUENTIN, and STEPHEN CHAPLIN. "The Ideal Home
     Rumpus." *Apollo* 80 (October):284-91.
     The publication of Lewis's letters has brought to the attention of
the public the rupture between Lewis and Roger Fry. Suggests that
Virginia Woolf's account of the events "comes closer to the facts."
Quotes various letters from Fry, Spencer F. Gore, and others in

support of this view: "The gravest charge that can be made against Fry is that he may have misunderstood a message."

7   BERMAN, RONALD. "L'Univers Woolfien." *Sewanee Review* 72, no. 1 (Winter):157-66.
     Review-essay based upon various books related to or about the Woolfs: "The supreme values of the men and women who made up Bloomsbury were not only aesthetic but social." The connections between the various members were not only a matter of mind: "It was a sympathy based on class, on family, and, in a sense, on the will to transcend these."

8   BRUNIUS, TEDDY. "An Excursion to Bloomsbury." In *G.E. Moore's Analyses of Beauty*. Sweden: Uppsala, pp. 51-58.
     G.E. Moore was very influential on Bloomsbury indirectly as an aestheticist: "In fact, as a stimulus to so-called Bloomsbury-attitudes this influence cannot be exaggerated." Discusses the criticism of Roger Fry and Clive Bell in relation to Moore. Behind their criticism is the philosophy of Moore, "defending the basic personal assumptions by means of a strategy of inspection trying to distinguish between ends and means. The ends are good states of mind and the means are artistic works refining pictorial significant form."

9   BUNKE, HARVEY C. *The Liberal Dilemma*. Englewood Cliffs, N.J.: Prentice-Hall, 267 pp.
     Describes the history of the liberal ideal, including some commentary on John Maynard Keynes (pp. 132-63) and the liberalism of Cambridge/Bloomsbury.

10   EDEL, LEON. "Review of Morrell Memoirs." *Saturday Review* 47 (June):374.
     Morrell was more a facilitator than a creator. She set up a world for the brilliant and creative. Describes the connection between her world and Bloomsbury during the years prior to World War I.

11   GLENAVY, BEATRICE. *Today We Will Only Gossip*. London: Constable, 187 pp.
     Autobiographical account of various Bloomsbury activities.

12 HASSALL, CHRISTOPHER. *Rupert Brooke: A Biography*. New
    York: Harcourt, Brace & World, 315 pp.
        Includes commentary on Brooke's association with Virginia
    Woolf and other Bloomsbury figures.

13 JONES, MINTA. "Duncan Grant and His World." *Connoisseur* 157
    (December):260.
        Commentary on exhibition of Duncan Grant's work at the
    Wildenstein Gallery. The intellectual atmosphere created by Fry, Clive
    Bell, and Virginia Woolf "explain, in retrospect, the painter's approach
    to art." Intellectual freedom was the password of the Bloomsbury
    Group, and "independent activity in close championship was one of its
    characteristics." Gives brief background of Grant, the French influence
    and the Omega Workshops, with commentary on some of his paintings
    of Group members. His paintings "since the late 1930's have evolved
    into a firmly individual style."

14 LANG, BEREL. "Intuition in Bloomsbury." *Journal of the History of
    Ideas* 25 (April):295-302.
        Finds the concept of Intuition as developed by Bloomsbury
    important: "The concept of intuitive knowledge is . . . worth noting
    both because of the consequent influence of the formulations given it
    by Bloomsbury and because of the clear example of its movement in
    the history of ideas." Sees this idea in Moore, Fry and Keynes as
    linked: "The details of this 'isomorphism' provide a revealing insight
    into the personality and intellect of the figures concerned and the
    'group' they form."

15 MAYHEW, ALICE. "Leonard Woolf's Autobiography."
    Commonweal 81 (20 November):299-302.
        Woolf's autobiography gives an across-the-board view of British
    society. Bloomsbury came into being during this period: "Angus Wilson
    called it a late Victorian heresy, a 'mysticism of godless common sense,'
    and Frank Kermode remarked that its ethics had become decadent
    between Cambridge and London--'the corruption of an elite had
    become the generation of a clique.'" Woolf, however, became involved
    in political action and "found more to life than Bloomsbury." Woolf
    does not tell us what made his friends in Bloomsbury so "charming."

16   PICKVANCE, RONALD. Introduction to *Venessa Bell: Memorial
     Retrospective*. Exhibition Catalog. London: Arts Council, 1-3 pp.
          Gives overview of Bell's work and life, including her association
     with Bloomsbury and various Bloomsbury figures.

17   ____. "Duncan Grant and His World." *Apollo* 80 (November):409.
          Review of exhibition of Grant's work, titled "Duncan Grant and
     His World," at Wildenstein's London galleries. Gives overview of works
     included: "But with Roger Fry and Clive Bell at his side, he was never
     forced or beguiled into practicing, as did Sickert, Wyndham Lewis and
     Paul Nash, the dual trade of painter-critic." Grant's talent needs to be
     enjoyed by the new generation.

18   PRICHETT, V.S. "What Exactly Do You Mean?" *New Statesman*
     67 (8 May):726-27.
          Commentary on Leonard Woolf's *Beginning Again*, the third
     volume of his autobiography: "It has a lot to say about the Apostles at
     Cambridge, about inner Bloomsbury, his conversion to socialism, his
     marriage, country life in Sussex, and the early years of the *New
     Statesmen* under Clifford Sharp, with the Webbs, Shaw, Bennett and
     Wells chirruping in the background." Woolf describes Bloomsbury as "a
     group of friends who are privileged, gay, high-minded rebels against
     Victorian values." Also discusses Leonard Woolf's description of
     Virginia Woolf's struggle with insanity.

19   PRYCE-JONES, ALAN. "Forster of 85: The Endurance of a Case
     Well Stated." *Bookweek* 5 (January):3.
          Assesses value of human heart and mind. Like others in the
     Bloomsbury group, he has tried to define "the something essential" in
     the civilization he writes about.

20   ROBERTS, KEITH. "Duncan Grant: Retrospective at
     Wildenstein's." *Burlington Magazine* 106 (December):584.
          Part of section titled "London" which deals with various
     exhibitions: "Far too many of Grant's later paintings have been
     included. Like his friend and contemporary Vanessa Bell, he reverted,
     after a bold flirtation with fauve principles, to a slack, rather cozy form
     of Impressionism." Suggests that his connection with Bloomsbury is
     misleading. He "was not really *avant-garde* at all (unlike Virginia
     Woolf), but got swept along for a time by the experimental current."

21 _____. "Vanessa Bell: Travelling Arts Council Show." *Burlington Magazine* 106 (April):197.

Part of section titled "London" that deals with various exhibitions. Sees Bell as important, as central to Bloomsbury, but has reservations about her art: "She was undoubtedly sensitive and talented but she was never a very original artist and she did not make the styles she adopted her own in anything like a positive sense." Gives overview of her development as artist, with references to Fauves and Impressionism.

22 RUSSELL, JOHN. "Clive Bell." *Encounter* 23 (December) 47-49.

Commentary on Bell on the occasion of his death. He entered English intellectual life from the day he went up to Trinity College Cambridge and found that his fellow student included Lytton Strachey, Leonard Woolf, and Thoby Stephen. Comments on the quality of Bell's presence: "He had an enormous amount of style in everyday life." Compares him to some other members of Bloomsbury. Concludes by describing his importance as defender of French painting of the period 1880-1914: "He was the right man in the right place at the right moment, and there are not many art-critics of whom that can be said."

23 SMITH, J. OATES. "Henry James and Virginia Woolf: The Art of Relationships." *Twentieth Century Literature* 20:119-29.

Virginia Woolf and Henry James deal both deal with human relationships. Woolf's are created out of the ideals of personal relationship evoked by G.E. Moore.

24 SUTTON, DENYS. Introduction to *Duncan Grant and His World*. Exhibition Catalog. London: Wildenstein & Co., pp. 2-6.

Deals with Duncan Grant's life and work as a Bloomsbury artist. Extensive discussion of his relationship with Bloomsbury figures. Catalog includes "Virginia Woolf" by Duncan Grant.

25 _____. "A Shock for the Troops." *Apollo* 80 (October):260-65.

Editorial on Roger Fry motivated by Quentin Bell's inaugural lecture on Fry at the University of Leeds (1964.5). Fry's interest in Cézanne has a psychological dimension: "Throughout his life he sought painters who affirmed his belief in a visual plasticity: Giotto and then Cézanne." Refers to Virginia Woolf and Clive Bell in reference to Fry's strengths and weaknesses as critic.

26   SYMONS, JULIAN. "Miss Edith Sitwell Have and Had and Heard."
     London Magazine 4, no. 8 (November):50-63.
          Comments briefly on Sitwell's defense of Gertrude Stein in
     Vogue and Desmond MacCarthy's attack of her praise of this "rubbish."

27   WALLIS, NEVILE. "The Bloomsbury Air." *Spectator* 213 (13
     November):637.
          Commentary on Duncan Grant and Bloomsbury written in
     relation to exhibition at Wildenstein Gallery: "Duncan Grant has been
     at the center of the Bloomsbury circle of friends, their intellectual
     candour and freedom of thought influencing English taste most strongly
     for a quarter of a century after 1910." The current interest in
     Bloomsbury may be due to the chaotic condition of the art world. We
     need to see "what humane lessons can usefully be learned" from them.
     "Meantime, the spirit of Bloomsbury persists wherever advanced debate
     and integrity are joined. Its philosophy is echoed in the study of liberal
     subjects increasingly integrated in the Art School course."

28   _____. "Obituary: Clive Bell." *Spectator* 213 (25 September):401.
          Includes commentary on Bell's association with Bloomsbury and
     the Bloomsbury aesthetic.

29   _____. "Vanessa Bell and Bloomsbury." *Connoisseur* 156
     (August):247-49.
          Commentary on exhibition devoted to Vanessa Bell held at the
     Brighton Art Gallery. Gives general description of Bloomsbury values,
     which are often associated G.E. Moore's thought. An understanding of
     the Bloomsbury background is necessary to "to any true appreciation of
     Vanessa Bell's work." Her paintings are eclectic in style and influence:
     "This free expression of a talent not unlike that of a lyrical poet gave
     place, around 1920, to a more intellectual and methodical way of
     painting."

30   _____. "Vanessa Bell and the Bloomsbury Group." *Royal Society of
     Arts Journal* 112 (May):453-55.
          Review of the Memorial Exhibition of Vanessa Bell's paintings.
     Suggests that we have to keep her Bloomsbury background in mind to
     appreciate Bell's art. Her later painting became more methodical:
     "High-bred her intimate realism remained inevitably to the end."

31 "Walter Sickert and Vanessa Bell: Two English Post-Impressionists." *Illustrated London News* 244 (14 March):397.
Illustrations of these two artists' works, with brief commentary.

32 WEBB, MICHAEL. "A Last Flourish of Aestheticism: The Omega Workshops, 1913-20." *Country Life* 135 (2 January):16-17.
Discussion of Roger Fry's Omega Workshops in relation to the aesthetic movement. The ideals of art for art's sake seem to flourish in Fry's creation.

33 WILDE, ALAN. *Art and Order: A Study of E.M. Forster.* New York: New York University Press, 179 pp.
Full-length study of the life and art of E.M. Forster. Includes some material on Bloomsbury.

34 WOOLF, LEONARD. *Beginning Again: An Autobiography of Years 1911 to 1918.* London: Hogarth Press; New York: Harcourt Brace, 289 pp.
Third volume of Woolf's autobiography which gives a trustworthy account of the members of the Bloomsbury Group. Deals with his return to London, marriage to Virginia Stephen, and the beginnings of World War One: "Bloomsbury, in this sense, did not exist in 1911 when I returned from Ceylon; it came into existence in the three years 1912 to 1914." The group used the term Bloomsbury before the outside world adopted it. Describes the philosophical origins of Bloomsbury in Cambridge.

35 ____. "How the Hogarth Press Began." *Bookseller* (11 April):1586-90. Part II (18 April):1664-66.
Personal history of the Hogarth Press, which became the center of Bloomsbury publishing. Woolf describes how the press began modestly and how it emerged into a major cultural force.

1965

1 ALTICK, RICHARD. *Lives and Letters: A History of Literary Biography.* New York: Alfred A. Knopf, pp. 281-300.
Chapter 9, "The Stracheyan Revolution," deals with Strachey's iconoclastic style: "Strachey's work would have been sounder, and its immediate effect on biographical practice healthier, had he not viewed

both his characters and their age with the combination of fastidious disdain and supercilious amusement that was the hallmark of the Bloomsbury group."

2   BELL, QUENTIN. "The Mausoleum Book." *Review of English Literature* 6 (January):9-18.
      "The Mausoleum Book is of interest in that it is the *cri de coeur* of an eminent Victorian, a document in the history of Cambridge skepticism, but above all, I think, because it reveals the force with which a remarkable personality encountered Stephen and lived on in the consciousness of the next generation." Suggests that when the Stephen children moved to Bloomsbury, "they brought with them not only a set of intellectual ideas against which they reacted under the influence of G.E. Moore, but also a set of aesthetic ideas against which they reacted under the influence of Cézanne."

3   CAMPOS, CHRISTOPHER. "The Salon." In *The View of France from Arnold to Bloomsbury*. New York: Oxford University Press, pp. 208-37.
      Bloomsbury was a "pre-war phenomenon." The figures tried to forget "what had happened between 1914 and 1918." They emphasized "a state of mind really belonging to an age that had ended in 1918." Bloomsbury was "genuinely interested in what it thought was France," but it never thought of France "separately from literature or art." Bloomsbury tried to establish a golden age: "We are in an eighteenth-century *salon*, with Virginia Woolf reclining on a *bergere*; Lytton Strachey a thin wizened man, strangely reminiscent of a certain portrait of Voltaire, in a invalid chair by the fire; and Forster, Roger Fry, and Duncan Grant grouped around with powdered wigs and snuff-boxes. The scene is in France." Considers Bloomsbury view of civilization and its sense of values, using works such as Bell's *Civilization*. Always it is removed from reality.

4   COLLET, GEORGES-PAUL. "Jacques-Émile and Virginia Woolf." *Comparative Literature* 17:73-81.
      Jacques-Émile was a painter-writer who helped to introduced Woolf to France. Made connections between her work and painting, which relates to the influence of Fry: "He was among the first to point out what the novelist had in common with the impressionist painters."

5   DICKIE, GEORGE T. "Clive Bell and the Method of *Principia Ethica*." *British Journal of Aesthetics* 5, no. 2 (April):139-43.
    Discusses the parallelism in method "with which G.E. Moore approaches ethics in *Principia Ethica* and the method with which Clive Bell approaches aesthetics in his book, *Art*." Bell tries to "set forth an intuitionist aesthetic theory parallel to Moore's intuitionist ethical theory."

6   EDWARDS, OLIVER. "Dear Desmond." *Times* (London) (13 December):13.
    Brief commentary on Desmond MacCarthy, with some mention of Bloomsbury.

7   ELLIOT, R.K. "Clive Bell's Aesthetic Theory and His Critical Practice." *British Journal of Aesthetics* 5, 2 (April):111-22.
    Suggests that there is an "inconsistency between Bell's aesthetic theory and his critical practice." Bell maintains that the aesthetic value of a work of art depends entirely on its formal quality. In practice, "he draws his reader's attention to irrelevant properties which, it would seem, are likely to distract him from the form of the work."

8   GARNETT, DAVID. *The Flowers of the Forest*. London: Chatto & Windus; New York: Harcourt Brace Jovanovich, 267 pp.
    Additional volume in Garnett's autobiography, in which he describes his relationship with the Bells and other Bloomsbury figures. He married Angelica Bell.

9   _____. "Virginia Woolf." *American Scholar* 34, no. 3 (Summer):371-386.
    Personal account of Garnett's relationship with Virginia Woolf. Deals extensively with Bloomsbury.

10 GERTLER, MARK. *Selected Letters*. Edited by Noel Carrington. Introduction by Quentin Bell. London: Rupert Hart-Davis, 389 pp.
    Gertler was a close friend to Dora Carrington and Lytton Strachey. Letters include commentary and reference to various Bloomsbury figures.

11   GOLDMAN, MARK. "Virginia Woolf as the Critic as Reader."
      PMLA 80 (June):275-84.
          Virginia Woolf's criticism reveals a similar ambition to T.S.
      Eliot's criticism, "an attempt to reach a *via media*, a creative balance
      between reason and emotion, sense and sensibility, the individual critic
      and the impersonal method." The critic's emotional response was
      integral to the Bloomsbury aesthetic. Discusses artistic form in Woolf's
      criticism in relation to Roger Fry, Clive Bell, and "significant form":
      "Pater's reaction against the normal criticism of Carlye, Ruskin, and
      Morris led to a Colridgeian concern with form and an endorsement of
      art for art which may be related to the non-utilitarian ethics of the
      Bloomsbury philosopher, G.E. Moore, whose insistence that art is an
      intrinsic or ethical good influenced Bell and Fry and Virginia Woolf in
      their faith in the self-contained values of art."

12   GRUBBS, FREDERICK. "In But not of: E.M. Forster, Julian Bell,
      and the Liberal Critique." In *A Vision of Reality: A Study of
      Liberalism in Twentieth-Century Verses*. New York: Barnes & Noble.
      pp. 68-97.
          Deals with the liberal tradition in Bloomsbury, tracing it through
      Forster and Julian Bell, who was a second-generation Bloomsbury
      figure.

13   GUIGUET, JEAN. *Virginia Woolf and Her Works*. Translated by
      Jean Stewart. London: Hogarth Press; New York: Harcourt,
      Brace, & World, 201 pp.
          Analytical study of Virginia Woolf with various references to the
      importance of Bloomsbury to her work.

14   INGAMELLS, JOHN. "Cézanne in England 1910-1930." *British
      Journal of Aesthetics* 5, no. 4 (October):341-50.
          The critic often makes people look with "his eyes, or thoughts,
      rather than their own." The critic helps to establish the link between
      the artist and the spectator: "One of the clearest examples of such
      'depth-criticism' is given by the case of Cézanne in England between
      1910 and 1930, when a purely aesthetic doctrine, based on Cézanne's
      work, was accepted by a surprisingly large number of people as a
      means of understanding modern art." Deals extensively with the
      Bloomsbury role in bringing Cézanne to London in the Post-
      impressionist exhibition of 1910: "The status of Cézanne changed in

the post-war years; he came to be regarded less as a Bloomsbury shrine and more as a public issue."

15   MEAGER, R. "Clive Bell and Aesthetic Emotion." *British Journal of Aesthetics* 5, no. 2 (April):123-31.
       Bell's failure to make clear the relationship between aesthetic emotion and significant form was an accident of time and place. Under the influence of G.E. Moore's *Principia Ethica*, "the whole theory of *Art* might be regarded as an attempt to fill out by careful examination of experience part of Moore's own answer to the 'first question of ethics' . . . namely, 'What kinds of things ought to exist for their own sake?' Moore himself answered *inter alia* 'consciousness of beauty'."

16   MICHEL, WALTER. "Rumpus Replied To." *Apollo* (August):132-33.
       States that even Fry's "closest friends and defenders have admitted" that Fry had a "bad side." In the Ideal Home Exhibition controversy, Wyndham Lewis was exposed to this side of Fry.

17   OSBORNE, HAROLD. "Alison and Bell on Appreciations." *British Journal of Aesthetics* 5, no. 2 (April):132-38.
       Comparison and contrast of the theories of artistic appreciation of Archibald Alsion and Clive Bell with no direct reference to Bloomsbury. Describes the influence Bell had on his country "in spreading the demand for that rigour which regards attention to the sensory and formal qualities of a work of art as essential if not always sufficient for aesthetic enjoyment."

18   READ, HERBERT. "Clive Bell." *British Journal of Aesthetics* 5, no. 2 (April):107-10.
       "What I am trying to establish is the possibility that it was Bell who first made Fry aware of the significance of the movement that had come into existence with Cézanne." Bell, though, was a hedonist rather than a philosopher. He wanted to enjoy paintings: "Clive Bell's most serious purpose was to enjoy works of art as part of the enjoyment of life. He became identified with the Bloomsbury 'set,' and was in some sense its protagonist."

19   ROTHENSTEIN, JOHN. *Autobiography*. 2 vols. New York: Holt, Rinehart, Winston, 289 pp.

         Includes commentary on Bloomsbury artists and figures.

20   SITWELL, EDITH. *Taken Care of: The Autobiography of Edith Sitwell*. London: Hutchinson. New York: Athenaeum, 387 pp.

         Deals with her relationship with Bloomsbury and various individual members, including Roger Fry, Virginia Woolf, Lytton Strachey: "I suppose I was always rather odd to look at, from a conventional point of view (and nothing was more unconventionally conventional than the company of Bloomsbury). . . . The Company of Bloomsbury were kind-hearted, and from time to time I entered it on sufferance."

21   SPENDER, STEPHEN. *The Struggle to be Modern* Berkeley and Los Angeles, University of California Press, 210 pp.

         Includes a discussion of E.M. Forster's views on Virginia Woolf's work.

22   SUTTON, DENYS. "The Value of Standards." *Apollo* 81 (January):3-7.

         Deals with Clive Bell and the emergence of aesthetic standards during the twentieth century. The influence of G.E. Moore at Cambridge was central to Bell's thought, as was his marriage to Vanessa Stephen and his association with Roger Fry: "The clue to Bell's approach to art as to life lies in his care for civilized values."

23   WOOLF, LEONARD. "Virginia Woolf: Writer and Personality." *Listener* 73 (4 March):327-28.

         Stresses Virginia Woolf's essentially "normal" interests and attitudes, which were punctuated by moments of great imaginative genius: "I have myself met two people whom you have to call geniuses; one was G.E. Moore the philosopher, and the other was my wife."

1966

1   ANDERSON, PATRICK. "Essays After Tea." *Spectator* (11 November):620.

         Review of Virginia Woolf's *Collected Essays*. Woolf was "neither a scholar nor, in the strict sense, an intellectual. She had little interest

in general ideas." Compares her briefly to Desmond MacCarthy and
F.R. Leavis.

2   BELL, QUENTIN. "Roger Fry." In *Vision and Design: The Life,
    Work and Influence of Roger Fry, 1866-1934.* Exhibition Catalog.
    England: Arts Council and the University of Nottingham, pp. 6-10.
        Discusses Fry as critic, his work as organizer of the Post-
    impressionist exhibitions, as well as the Omega Workshops: "Despite
    his close friendship with Duncan Grant and Vanessa Bell, he was much
    less concerned with contemporary art, particularly after the failure of
    the Omega in 1919, than is usually supposed." Focusing on the
    contradictory points of view his criticism presents: "Yet behind these
    variations of opinion there were, not only those principles which made
    the ready acceptance and candid annulment of opinions a rule of
    thought and conduct, but an underlying consistency of attitude within
    which the antithesis of his taste and views could be synthesized."
    Mentions Fry's connection with Bloomsbury, but states that he "never
    accepted *Principia Ethica* with enthusiasm." He was "very much closer
    to McTaggart, Lowes Dickinson and Ashbee." The Post-impressionist
    exhibitions made Fry the leader of the younger artists in England.

3   BELL, QUENTIN, and STEPHEN CHAPLIN. "Reply with
    Rejoinder." *Apollo* 83 (January):75.
        Letter to the editor concerning Walter Michel's article. Opposes
    view that after their argument in 1913 Roger Fry persecuted
    Wyndham Lewis. Gives text of an unpublished letter from Fry to
    Lewis stating that he hoped "this rather rough episode will not have
    entirely alienated you."

4   CAUSEY, ANDREW. "Roger Fry: Painter, Collector, Critic."
    Illustrated London News 248 (26 March):30-31.
        Includes illustrations of Fry's work, along with brief description
    of his various activities.

5   COCBURN, ALEXANDER. "To and From the Frontier." *Review*
    16 (October):10-16.
        Describes Julian Bell's life and death. The second generation of
    Bloomsbury followed the liberal tradition.

6　　COOPER, BURTON L. "The Cultural Environment of Lytton
　　　Strachey." Ph.D. dissertation, University of Michigan, 184 pp.
　　　　　"The present study is an attempt to describe the intellectual and
social environment of Lytton Strachey and the direction it gave to his
thought and writing." Discusses the traditions of Cambridge rationalism
and social relationships: "These two traditions came together in the
Bloomsbury Group whose membership was closely associated with
Cambridge and who adopted the rationalistic ethics of G.E. Moore and
the structuralist aesthetic of Roger Fry." Strachey's work is guided by
this combination. See *Dissertation Abstracts International*. 27:3039A-
3040A.

7　　CRANSTON, MAURICE. "Harold Nicolson's Diaries." *London
　　　Magazine*, n.s. 6 (December):93-103.
　　　　　Review of *Diaries and Letters, 1930-39*, edited by Nigel Nicolson.
Comments on the relationship with Vita Sackville-West. Deals mostly
with the political dimensions of Nicolson's life. Alludes to his
connections with Bloomsbury and a literary affiliation with the *New
Statesman*.

8　　GAUNT, WILLIAM. "How Well Have They Worn? 16, *Vision and
　　　Design*." *Times* (London) (21 April):17.
　　　　　Deals with the importance of Roger Fry's work, with some
commentary on Fry's Bloomsbury association.

9　　GOLDMAN, MARK. "Virginia Woolf and E.M. Forster: A Critical
　　　Dialogue." *Texas Studies in Literature and Language* 7, no. 4
　　　(Winter):387-400.
　　　　　Comparison of Woolf's and Forster's critical writing:
"Bloomsbury friends and fictional rivals, Forster and Mrs. Woolf
represent two basic, opposing views in a recurring critical dialectic on
the novel." Woolf emphasized experiment and broke with the
Edwardian past: "She criticized Forster for trying to capture the
Georgian sensibility without abandoning the Edwardian form." Forster's
The Longest Journey presents a Bloomsbury view of "personal relations,
the private soul, the importance and possibility of communication in
this world." His method for revealing these qualities lacks
experimentation: "Forster does move closer to the views of Virginia
Woolf, Clive Bell, and Roger Fry in some of the essays included in *Two
Cheers for Democracy*, under the heading of "Art in General." He was
not able to "believe in the value of criticism for art;" it "takes us away

from the creative experience or mystery of the work itself." For Woolf
there is a vital connection between criticism and creativity.

10   HARRISON, CHARLES. "Roger Fry in Retrospect." *Studio* 171
      (May):220-21.
            Commentary on the painting and criticism of Roger Fry. He
      had a major influence on his culture and on his various Bloomsbury
      friends.

11   HUTTON, GRAHAM. "How Have They Worn? 3, The
      Consequences of Mr. Keynes." *Sunday Times* (London) (20
      January):15.
            Brief discussion of John Maynard Keynes. Mentions the
      influence of Bloomsbury.

12   HUWS JONES, E. *Margery Fry: The Essential Amateur.* London:
      Oxford University Press, 278 pp.
            Biographical study that describes Margery Fry's early life. She
      grew up in Bloomsbury.

13   ISHERWOOD, CHRISTOPHER. "Virginia Woolf." In
      Exhumations: Stories, Articles, Verses. New York: Simon & Schuster,
      pp. 132-35.
            Isherwood met Virginia Woolf during the 1920s and became
      associated with the Hogarth Press and other aspects of Bloomsbury
      culture. Personalized account.

14   LEKACHMAN, ROBERT. *The Age of Keynes.* New York:
      Random House; London: John Lane, 324 pp.
            Account of Keynes's life and influence, with brief commentary
      on Bloomsbury (pp. 20, 23-24, 41, 51). States that "the name Lytton
      Strachey is a clue to a significant part of Keynes's life." Bloomsbury
      may be characterized "by common qualities, among them exceptional
      cleverness, great articulateness, extraordinary personal sympathy, and a
      doctrine," derived from G.E. Moore's *Principa Ethica.* During the
      1920s Bloomsbury began to feel that Keynes "had been seduced by the
      attractions of the world of affairs from the single-minded pursuit of
      personal relations."

15   MARIANO, NICKY. *Forty Years with Berenson.* New York: Alfred
      A. Knopf, 187 pp.
          Personal account that deals with some Bloomsbury figures.

16   MELVILLE, ROBERT. "Fry." *New Statesman* 71 (25 March):439.
          Commentary on Fry on the occasion of the exhibition of his work at
      the Arts Council Gallery. Sees Fry as failed painter "who wrote and
      organized exhibitions on the side." The Post-impressionist exhibitions
      constitute his major achievement: "The only exhibition which could do
      him the honour he deserves and reveal the profundity of his insights to
      a new generation would be a selection from the two Post-Impressionist
      exhibitions on which he staked his reputation."

17   MERLE, GABRIEL. "Elements pour une étude biographique de
      Lytton Strachey." *Études Anglaises* 19 (July-September):223-33.
          Includes biographical commentary on Strachey in relation to
      Bloomsbury.

18   MICHEL, WALTER. "Author's Reply." *Apollo* 83 (January):75.
          Reply to Bell and Chaplin (1966.3). Sees their argument as "an
      astonishing simplicity." Corrects "errors in fact in Bell and Chaplin's
      letter."

19   NEVE, CHRISTOPHER. "Roger Fry in 20th Century Art."
      Country Life 139 (31 March):734.
          Brief discussion of the impact of the Post-impressionist
      exhibitions and Fry's theories on the artistic climate of his time in
      relation to exhibition at the Arts Council Gallery, "Vision and Design."
      Suggests that Fry's admiration of Cézanne is not slavish as some critics
      have suggested.

20   NICOLSON, BENEDICT. "Roger Fry and the *Burlington Magazine*."
      Burlington Magazine 108 (October):493.
          Comments in Fry's connection with *The Burlington Magazine*:
      "One would not gather from Virginia Woolf's beautiful biography of
      him the *Burlington Magazine* meant anything more to him than just one
      of innumerable toys to play with. It was much closer to his heart than
      this." Refers further to Fry's support of Cézanne through the pages of
      this journal.

21   NICOLSON, HAROLD. *Diaries and Letters of Harold Nicolson: 1930-1939.* Edited by Nigel Nicolson. New York: Athenaeum, 448 pp.

The introduction by Nigel Nicolson suggests that these diaries and letters form a picture of literary, political and social London in the 1930's. Includes various references to Bloomsbury and Bloomsbury figures: "The Hutchinsons and Keynes arrive. Lydia is very full of the ballet season which she wants to arrange next June. She says that Bloomsbury are old-fashioned. 'Why?' we ask. 'Their morals,' she answers."

22   ROBERTS, KEITH. "Vision and Design: The Arts Council Centenary Exhibition Devoted to Roger Fry." *Burlington Magazine* 108 (May):273.

General commentary on the exhibition, claiming it lacks focus. His major achievement is still the Post-impressionist exhibitions. Recommends that the exhibition should focus on "the aesthetic atmosphere in which he was propounding his revolutionary views."

23   S., D. "Bloomsbury Souvenirs." *Apollo* 83 (June):46-69.

Brief mention of exhibition, with dates and locations, devoted to Roger Fry's life, work, and influence, arranged by the Arts Council. Photographs of various paintings, including Fry's *Vanessa Bell, Clive Bell,* and *Triple Alliance* by Vanessa Bell.

24   SMART, ALASTAIR. "Roger Fry and Early Italian Art." *Apollo* 83 (April):262-71.

Suggests that Fry's work on early Italian art prepared him for his appreciation of Cézanne: "Cézanne, whom he first discovered in 1906 (the year of the artist's death), came as a revelation to him precisely because his work represented to him a return to the principles which the 'anarchic licence of Impressionism' had dissipated." Deals with some aspects of Woolf's view of Fry and with the 1910 Post-impressionist exhibition.

25   STANSKY, PETER, and WILLIAM ABRAHAMS. *Journey to the Frontier: Julian Bell and John Cornford: Their Lives and the 1930's.* London: Constable, 430 pp.

Includes various sections that relate to Julian Bell and Bloomsbury: "A Bloomsbury Childhood," "A Young Apostle," "Searching," "Julian in China," as well as a section on Julian's death in

Spain: "Julian was always conscious of Bloomsbury, of its values and standards, from which he knew he was not to be exempted, conscious also of its high expectations for him; that he was to be not less than its son." Describes the development of the Group from Cambridge to Charleston. Although the intellectual origins of Bloomsbury were masculine and Cambridge, "the most important person in Julian's life, from its very beginning to its very end, was his mother, the gifted and beautiful Vanessa Bell."

26   STONE, WILFRID. *The Cave and the Mountain: A Study of E.M. Forster*. London: Oxford University Press, 430 pp.
        Full study of Forster with significant material on Bloomsbury, especially chapter 3, "The Apostolic Ring." Relates Bloomsbury, through the Apostles, to the Clapham Sect: "To understand Forster we don not go primarily to Bloomsbury, or to the Moorean renaissance that helped cement the interests and friendships forming that coterie; we go--as Clive Bell has suggested--to the Apostles. This group made Forster's coming to Cambridge an epiphany: The tradition of the Apostles, from the earliest days, was such as to give Forster a footing independent of Clapham, upon which he could negotiate with those formidable ancestors. Suggests that Bloomsbury's "liberalism was emphatically a liberalism detached from political engagement." Gives background to the pre-Bloomsbury world of Cambridge, including influence of G. Lowes Dickinson, J.M.E. McTaggart, G.E. Moore, Nathaniel Wedd, and Roger Fry.

27   TROUTMAN, PHILIP. "Roger Fry--Painter." In *Vision and Design: The Life, Work and Influence of Roger Fry 1866-1934*. London: Arts Council; University of Nottingham, pp. 11-15.
        Describes Fry's development as painter: "Painting continued to be the activity which meant most to him, which alone gave him a sense of fulfillment." The Post-impressionist aesthetic merged with his own to produce a flurry of artistic activity. Also comments on trip to Turkey with Clive and Vanessa Bell. The Omega Workshops did not inhibit his artistic output, although "a large proportion of the time spent on painting was dedicated to design for the Omega." During his last years he was a solitary figure.

28   WARNER, M. "The Webbs, Keynes, and the Economic Problem in the Inter-War Years." *Political Studies* 14 (February):81-86.
        Gives overview of social problems during the inter-war years.

Includes some commentary on Keynes in relation to the Bloomsbury background.

29   WOOLF, VIRGINIA. *Letters of Virginia Woolf: Volume I 1888-1912.* Edited by Nigel Nicholson and Joanne Trautmann. New York: Harcourt Brace Jovanovich, 589 pp.
        Includes references to Woolf's early association with Bloomsbury figures at Cambridge and later in Bloomsbury. The development of the group is fully drawn in these letters.

1967

1   ANDERSON, PATRICK. "The Apostle of Bloomsbury." *Spectator* 219 (13 October):429-30.
        Review of the first volume of Michael Holroyd's *Lytton Strachey.* Questions the excessive length. Gives brief overview of associations with Bloomsbury at Cambridge and with G.E. Moore.

2   BELL, QUENTIN. *Victorian Artists.* London: Routledge & Kegan Paul; Cambridge: Harvard University Press, 123 pp.
        Includes an essay that deals with Roger Fry and the new aesthetic associated with Bloomsbury art criticism: "Sickert and the Post-Impressionists" (pp. 85-94).

3   BOULTON, DAVID. *Objection Overruled.* McGibbon & Kee. 174 pp.
        Memoir that includes commentary on various Bloomsbury figures.

4   BULLOCK, ALAN, and MAURICE SHOCK. *The Liberal Tradition from Fox to Keynes.* Oxford: Clarendon Press, 289 pp.
        Bloomsbury evolved out of the Liberal tradition. John Maynard Keynes drew on Cambridge and the thought of G.E. Moore.

5   "Candid Friends." *Times Literary Supplement* (London) (9 November):1049-50.
        Review of Michael Holroyd's *Lytton Strachey: A Critical Biography.* The commentary centers on the Bloomsbury ideal of candor. Truth and candor were central to the Group. The idea was promoted by the writings of G.E. Moore.

6   EDELSTEIN, J.M. "Twilight in Bloomsbury." *New Republic* 157 (25 November):264.
      Review of Michael Holyrod's *Lytton Strachey: A Critical Biography*. Deals with the elitism of the Group.

7   EGBERT, D.D. "English Art Critics and Modern Social Radicalism." *Journal of Aesthetics and Art Criticism* 26, no. 1 (Fall):31-4.
      Evaluates the connection between English art criticism and social radicalism. The current trend seems to be away from social radicalism. Includes a discussion of Roger Fry and his friends, including Leonard Woolf, who was sympathetic to Fabian socialism: "Fry, unlike his friend and fellow member of the Bloomsbury Group, the art critic Clive Bell, always rejected non-representational art both in his own painting and in his criticism, even though he was essentially interested in the *form* of objects depicted." Looks at the connection between Fry and the Fabian Society. Also deals with Fry and Wyndham Lewis, who broke from Fry's Omega Workshops.

8   GRIGSON, GEOFFREY. "Apostolic." *Listener* 78 (12 October):473.
      Review of the first volume of *Lytton Strachey* by Michael Holroyd which comments on the anti-homosexualism in the text: "He analyzes the milieu of 'Bloomsbury,' which expands from the refinements of Apostolic homosexuality."

9   HARRISON, CHARLES. "Abstract Painting in Britain in the Early 1930's." *Studio International* 173 (April):180.
      Deals with the influence of the aesthetic theories of Clive Bell and Roger Fry in relation to the advent of abstract painting.

10 HOLROYD, MICHAEL. *Lytton Strachey: A Critical Biography*. London: William Heinemann. New York: Holt, Rinehart and Winston. Vol. 1: *The Unknown Years, 1880-1910*, 475 pp. Vol. 2: *The Years of Achievement, 1910-1932*, 754 pp.
      Exhaustive biographical study with extensive information on Strachey's Bloomsbury connections. Chapter 10 in volume one, for example, is titled "Bloomsbury: The Legend and the Myth" and suggests that "it was on a superfine mixture of arrogance and diffidence, of ambitious talent and crippling shyness, that the Bloomsbury Group was largely founded." Aims to correct the view of

Bloomsbury that has resulted from "public imagination," especially that it was a "strategically planned and predetermined literary movement." Volume 2 deals in part with Garsington, Strachey's relationship with Dora Carrington and other Bloomsbury related matters. Garsington was an "Arcadian colony where she [Lady Ottoline] resolutely acted out the part of evangelical patroness to writers and artists of her" liking.

11 HUDSON, DEREK. "Harold Nicolson." *Quarterly Review* 305 (April):163-71.
  "The influence of Harold Nicolson on twentieth-century English literature has been deeper than is generally realized outside the world of letters." He "accepted the revolution in biographical writing associated with the name of Lytton Strachey." Deals briefly with his marriage to Vita Sackville-West.

12 KELVIN, NORMAN. *E.M. Forster.* Preface by Harry T. Moore. Carbondale: Southern Illinois University Press, 196 pp.
  Study relating Forster's life to his work. Alludes to his background at Cambridge and his connections to Bloomsbury: "Excluding Forster's writing, the two main biographical facts of the years succeeding Cambridge are his travels and his association with the Bloomsbury group."

13 KIELY, JAMES JOSEPH. "Harold Nicolson: A Critical Study of a Modern Biographer's Method." Ph.D. dissertation, Boston University, 418 pp.
  A "critical study of the aims and tendencies of modern biography in its evolution as an art form." Nicolson's achievements span the period from Strachey to the present. Deals with Strachey's and Bloomsbury's influence on early work. Evaluates his indebtedness to these influences. See *Dissertation Abstracts International* 28:1821A.

14 MAY, KEITH M. "The Symbol of Painting in Virginia Woolf's *To The Lighthouse*." *Review of English Studies* 9:91-98.
  Deals in part with the influence of Roger Fry on Virginia Woolf.

15 MORPHET, RICHARD. Preface to *Vanessa Bell: Drawings and Design*. Exhibition Catalog. London: Folio Fine Art, pp. 1-4.
  Introduction to the work of Vanessa Bell. Her design theory was drawn from both Roger Fry and Clive Bell.

16   _____. "The Significance of Charleston." *Apollo* 86 (November):342-
        45.
        Charles "expresses both a pattern of life and a visual style; it
makes especially evident, in a way that a museum or a book cannot,
the fusion of these two characteristics into a single sensibility."
Describes house and its decorative contents. "The many decorations
make apparent the inter-relation" of literary, artistic, and philosophical
concerns.

17   NICOLSON, HAROLD. *Diaries and Letters.* Vol. 2, *The War Years,
        1939-1945.* Edited by Nigel Nicolson. New York: Athenaeum, 511
        pp.
        The introduction by Nigel Nicolson describes some of the
Bloomsbury context for the diary entries and letters that follow.
Includes letters from Nicolson to Vita Sackville-West. Some reference
to Bloomsbury and Bloomsbury figures: "Vita says our mistake was
that we remained Edwardian for too long, and that if in 1916 we had
got in touch with Bloomsbury, we should have profited more than we
did by carrying on with Mrs. George Keppel, Mrs. Ronald Greville and
the Edwardian relics."

18   POSS, S. "To the Woolf House." *Nation* 204 (6 February):187-88.
        Deals with Monks House, the country home of Leonard and
Virginia Woolf.

19   PROUDFIT, SHARON WOOD. "The Fact of the Vision of
        Virginia Woolf and Roger Fry's Post Impressionist Aesthetic." Ph.D.
        dissertation, University of Michigan, 286 pp.
        The similarity between "Fry's Post-Impressionist aesthetic and
Mrs. Woolf's aesthetic philosophy is striking, and even more notable is
a similarity in formulation and articulation of their critical ideas."
Explores the "nature and significance of the intellectual relationship in
order to determine what impact that relationship had upon the
formulation of Mrs. Woolf's theory of fiction and her practice as a
writer."

20   ROTHENSTEIN, JOHN. *Brave Day Hideous Night.* Vol. 2 of his
        autobiography. New York: Holt, Rinehart, Winston, 286 pp.
        Includes some commentary on his association with Bloomsbury
artists.

21   RUSSELL, BERTRAND. *The Autobiography of Bertrand Russell 1872-1914.* London: Allen and Unwin, 210 pp.
      All three volumes of Russell's autobiography published in 1975. (See 1975.23).

22   SUTTON, DENIS. "Jacques Copeau and Duncan Grant." *Apollo* 86 (August):138-41.
      Analysis of the collaboration between Jacques Copeau and Duncan Grant. Copeau met Grant during his visit in 1912 to lecture on French literature on the occasion of the Second Post-Impressionist exhibition. Describes the work Grant did as set and costume designer for various Copeau productions. The costume designs for the production of *Pelleas et Melisande*, staged in 1918, was done at Charleston, with the help of other Bloomsbury figures.

23   THOMSON, GEORGE H. *The Fiction of E.M. Forster.* Detroit: Wayne State University Press, 304 pp.
      Study of Forster's fiction as romance in which his "symbols achieve archetypal significance and mythic wholeness." Suggests that Forster's Bloomsbury association deserves a place in any consideration of Forster's background. Uses Leonard Woolf as authority on the Group: "Cambridge, London, Bloomsbury, and a tradition of close association among the intelligentsia, all these centripetal forces are at work in shaping the society of Bloomsbury." States that "if Bloomsbury existed at all, Forster belonged."

24   WOOLF, LEONARD. *Downhill All the Way: An Autobiography of the Years 1919-1939.* London: Hogarth Press; New York: Harcourt, Brace & World, 259 pp.
      Fourth volume of Woolf's autobiography, which begins in the year Leonard and Virginia purchased Monks House. States that he has "reached the period in my autobiography in which our lives and the lives of everyone have become penetrated, dominated by politics." Virginia, however, was the "least political animal that has lived since Aristotle invented the definition." But she is not like the "invalidish lady living in an ivory tower in Bloomsbury." Describes the parties at Garsington and Bedford Square held by Lady Ottoline Morrell: "Ottoline's Bedford Square was even more a salon than her Garsington." Vita Sackville-West enters their lives. Comments significantly on the founding of Bloomsbury and the Memoir Club: "The original thirteen members of the Memoir Club, identical with the

original thirteen members of Bloomsbury, were all intimate friends, and it was agreed that we should be absolutely frank in what we wrote and read."

25   ____. "Strachey." *New Statesman* (6 October):267.
    Commentary on Lytton Strachey by one of his closest Bloomsbury friends.

26   ____. "Virginia Woolf: Literary Reputations and Earnings." *Bookseller* (8 April):1842-44.
    Gives details of Virginia Woolf's literary activities. Explains world of Hogarth Press.

1968

1   AMORUSO, VITO. *Virginia Woolf*. Bari: Adriatica Editrice, 127 pp.
    The opening section of this study discusses Woolf in relation to Bloomsbury.

2   ANDERSON, PATRICK. "Just Good Friends." *Spectator* 220 (31 May):742-43.
    Commentary on Bloomsbury based on Quentin Bell's *Bloomsbury*: "In my opinion Bloomsbury does represent an attitude which, for all the individual differences, is as distinctive as a tone of voice or the interior of one of those houses Mr. Bell describes so deliciously."

3   BEDIENT, CHARLES. "Review of *Lytton Strachey*." *Nation* 206 (20 May):670-71.
    Review of Michael Holyrod's biography. Sees Bloomsbury as overrated.

4   BELL, QUENTIN. *Bloomsbury*. London: Weidenfeld and Nicolson; New York: Basic Books, 189 pp.
    Study of Bloomsbury by a second-generation member of the Group, with chapters titled "Bloomsbury Before 1914," "The War," "Bloomsbury After 1918," and "The Character of Bloomsbury." Suggests that the world was in need of "Bloomsbury liberation": "The need was for a new honesty and a new clarity in personal relations, and

I think that everyone in what was to become Bloomsbury felt this." Bloomsbury was feminist and libertarian. Defines the Group as consisting of twenty members. Emphasizes the Group's belief in rationalism. Something that can be called Bloomsbury continued to exist after World War I.

5   BRIDGEMAN, ELIZABETH. *"Bloomsbury." Apollo* 88 (July):72-73.
     Review of Quentin Bell's *Bloomsbury*, summarizing some aspects of Bell's book. Comments finally that "the most perplexing feature of Bloomsbury is that, apart from isolated incidents--Roger Fry's first Post-Impressionist exhibition or the publication of Lytton Strachey's *Eminent Victorians*, in 1918--there was no culmination of their ideas and way of life." Complains that Bell "makes little attempt to analyze the relationship between the characters of Bloomsbury and the work produced by them." Feels that writings and paintings were English, provincial, and unsophisticated by European standards.

6   BROPHEY, JAMES D. *Edith Sitwell: The Symbolist Order.* Carbondale: Southern Illinois University Press, 170 pp.
     Study of Sitwell that deals somewhat with her criticism of Bloomsbury.

7   "County Cork and W.C.1." *Times Literary Supplement* (London) (4 July):704.
     Deals with Somerville, Ross, and the Bloomsbury Group.

8   DEVAS, NICOLETTE. *Two Flamboyant Fathers.* London: Collins, 276 pp.
     Discusses Leslie Stephen's relationship to his children. Also describes the emergence of Bloomsbury in relation to the Stephen family background.

9   GARNETT, DAVID, ed. *The White/Garnett Letters.* London: Jonathan Cape, 178 pp.
     Includes commentary by Garnett on his Bloomsbury activities.

10   GODFREY, DENIS. *E.M. Forster's Other Kingdom.* Edinburgh: Oliver & Boyd. New York: Barnes and Noble.
     Forster was influence by Bloomsbury.

11   GRIGSON, GEOFFREY. "Lytton's Effigy." *Listener* 79 (22
      February):246-47.
          Negative review of volume two of *Lytton Strachey*, by Michael
      Holroyd, based upon Strachey's hatred of lower classes: "Given his
      pretensions, this is a monster speaking, however intelligent, however
      coruscating--or flashy." Uses references to Lady Ottoline Morrell and
      T.S. Eliot.

12   GROSSKRUTH, PHYLLIS. *Leslie Stephen*. London: Longmans,
      36 pp.
          Gives information on the family background of Stephen
      Children: pp. 14-15.

13   HEILBRUN, CAROLYN G. "The Bloomsbury Group." *Midway:
      A Magazine of Discovery in the Arts and Sciences* 9, no. 2
      (Autumn):71-85.
          Evaluative article defending Bloomsbury against various sneers:
      "The men and women of Bloomsbury were extraordinarily accomplished
      both in their individual lives and works and in the life of love and
      friendship they shared." Discusses "the ascendancy of reason which
      excludes violence but not passion," androgyny, homosexuality: "They
      were civilized even if, as Virginia Woolf remarked of Clive Bell's book
      on that subject, civilization turns out to be a lunch party at 50 Gordon
      Square. Civilization is capable of worse things, and usually achieves
      them."

14   HIMMELFARB, GERTRUDE. "Review of *Lytton Strachey*." *New
      Republic* 158 (18 May):33-35.
          Includes extensive commentary on the Bloomsbury milieu and its
      intellectual background.

15   HOFFMANN, CHARLES G. "Fact and Fantasy in *Orlando*:
      Virginia Woolf's Manuscripts Reviews." *Texas Studies in Literature
      and Language* 10 (Fall):435-44.
          Critical study, which deals somewhat with the relationship
      between Vita Sackville-West and Virginia Woolf.

16   HOLROYD, MICHAEL. "Biographer: Interview." *New Yorker* 44
      (25 May):27-28.
          Interview with Michael Holroyd. He discusses his biography and
      the world of Bloomsbury of which Lytton Strachey was a part.

17 HYNES, SAMUEL. *The Edwardian Turn of Mind*. Princeton: Princeton University Press, 278 pp.
   Deals with the influence of Bloomsbury and Bloomsbury figures during this period.

18 JACOBSON, DAN. "The Bloomsbury Idea." *Commentary* 45 (March):79-80.
   Review of Leonard Woolf's *Downhill All the Way*. Expresses low opinion of Bloomsbury work, but he finds Leonard Woolf's autobiography appealing. Suggests that the contradictions in his character come through, "reflected in the sometimes startling juxtapositions of the social groups among which he has lived."

19 JOHNSTONE, J.K. "World War I and the Novels of Virginia Woolf." In *Promise of Greatness: The War of 1914-1918*. Edited by George A. Panichas. London: Cassell, pp. 528-40.
   The ultimate effect "of the war on the individuals who survived it was on the inner life, and Virginia Woolf, to a much greater extent than has been generally recognized, is a chronicler, if not of the contemporary events themselves, of what is at least as significant, the effect of contemporary events on individuals." Deals with general reactions among the Bloomsbury Group to the war, and traces allusions to combat through Woolf's work: "The war heightened her awareness of flux, impermanence, and death, causing her to value personal experience the more and to examine the more closely the experience of the present moment."

20 JULIEN, HERSHEY. "Virginia Woolf: Post-Impressionist Novelist." Ph.D. dissertation, University of New Mexico, 212 pp.
   Virginia Woolf's experiments in the novel involve "to a significant degree an attempt to apply to the art of fiction the aesthetic theories of Post-Impressionism, especially as they are articulated by Roger Fry in the early years of the twentieth century." See *Dissertation Abstracts* 29:4490A.

21 KEYNES, CHARLES. *The Letters of Rupert Brooke*. London: Macmillan, 348 pp.
   Includes some letters that relate to Brooke's association with Virginia Woolf and other Bloomsbury figures.

22   LEAVIS, F.R., ed. *A Selection From Scrutiny.* 2 vols. Cambridge: Cambridge University Press, 1: 312 pp.; 2: 320 pp.
      Includes various essays that relate to Bloomsbury and to the Leavises quarrel with the Group.

23   LEHMANN, JOHN. *A Nest of Tigers: The Sitwells in Their Times.* London: Macmillan. Boston: Little, Brown, 294 pp.
      Biographical study in which the Sitwell family is related to Bloomsbury: "The picture would suggest a certain rather more than formal diplomatic inter-relationship between the foreground Sitwell group and the Bloomsbury group in the nearer middle distance, such as a relationship between two states who respect and yet at the same time suspect one another." Characterizes the ambivalent relationship the Sitwells had with Bloomsbury. States that the closest friend among all the Bloomsbury figures to the Sitwells was Aldous Huxley.

24   MORPHET, RICHARD. "Bloomsbury Review." *Studio* 176 (July):49.
      Brief commentary on Bloomsbury artists.

25   MORTIMER, RAYMOND. "E.M. Forster: The Art of Being Individual." *Sunday Times* (London) (29 December):51.
      Commentary on Forster by one of his Bloomsbury friends. Forster was part of the individualistic tradition.

26   NICOLSON, HAROLD. *Diaries and Letters.* Vol. 3, *The Later Years, 1945-1962.* Edited by Nigel Nicolson. New York: Athenaeum, 448 pp.
      Introduction by Nigel Nicolson. Includes various letters from Harold Nicolson to Vita Sackville-West and commentary on other Bloomsbury figures: "I read the Lytton-Virginia letters and am appalled by their silliness, dirtiness and cattishness."

27   PANICHAS, GEORGE A. "The Bloomsbury Cult." *Modern Age* 12, no. 2 (Spring):210-16.
      Review of Leonard Woolf's *Downhill All the Way: An Autobiography of the Years 1919-1939.* Gives overview of reaction to Bloomsbury, including Wyndham Lewis's and F. R. Leavis's negative commentary: "Undoubtedly, the Bloomsbury-Cambridge world was guilty of little tattle and of the more insidious element of self-congratulation that made so much fuss over the writings of Lytton

Strachey, and perhaps Virginia Woolf herself." Also describes the impact of World War I on the Bloomsbury world.

28   PRYCE-JAMES, ALAN. "World of Lytton Strachey." *Commonweal* 88 (10 May):231-34.
    Personal account of a Bloomsbury "recruit": "Very few echoes of Bloomsbury talk still survive. And in all this Lytton Strachey was a commanding figure, at any rate during the last ten years of his life. It is presumably their Bloomsbury passion for truth-telling which has led to some of those still alive to permit such a huge disinterment of ancient scandal and flimflam."

29   RAMLOV, PREBEN. "Bloomsbury og Virginia Woolf." In *Fremmede digtere i det 20 arhundrede*. Copenhagen.
    Not seen.

30   REES, GORONWY. "A Case for Treatment: The World of Lytton Strachey." *Encounter* 30 (March):71-83.
    Review-essay of Michael Holroyd's *Lytton Strachey*. Questions whether Strachey deserves such a massive study. Describes the source of his direction in life in relation to his Cambridge experience, especially in the Apostles and later in London under Fry's influence. Also evaluates the issue of homosexuality as part of the Bloomsbury world.

31   ROSEN, S.M. "Keynes Without Gadflies." In *The Dissenting Academy*. Edited by T. Roszak. New York: Pantheon Books, pp. 62-91.
    Discussion of John Maynard Keynes. Includes some commentary on his association with Bloomsbury and the importance it had to his economic thought.

32   SALTER, ELIZABETH. *The Last Years of a Rebel: A Memoir of Edith Sitwell*. London: Bodley Head, 116 pp.
    Personal commentary on Sitwell, which includes some minor references to her association with Virginia Woolf and Bloomsbury.

1969

1   BELL, QUENTIN. "Last Words from Bloomsbury." *Spectator* (18

October):512.
    Review of Leonard Woolf's *The Journey, Not the Arrival, Matters*.
Suggests that Leonard's virtues and limitations as a political thinker
relate to his Bloomsbury association. He ended by seeing his political
work as useless: "He had a genius for friendship (an essential
qualification for entry into Bloomsbury)."

2   BROGAN, DENIS. "The Last of Bloomsbury." *Spectator* (23
    August):236.
    Obituary of Leonard Woolf: "The death of Leonard Woolf
removes the last and, for me, the most attractive of the
'Bloomsberries.'" Discusses the view that Leonard Woolf was an
intelligent, political writer who did not quite come off: "I am inclined
to believe that some of his limitations were due to his being embedded
in the Bloomsbury Group by his marriage to Virginia Woolf." Suggests
that there is a thinness in the achievement of most of the Bloomsbury
Group, despite the impressive minds and real genius of Maynard
Keynes and E.M. Forster.

3   FAIRFIELD, J. "Out of Her Time: Lady Ottoline." *Vogue* 154
    (September):442-47.
    Discusses the world created by Lady Ottoline Morrell at
Garsington and in London. Also describes her literary associations with
Virginia Woolf and other Bloomsbury figures.

4   FLEISHMAN, AVROM. "Woolf and McTaggart." *ELH* 36, no. 4
    (December):719-38.
    The fundamental language of McTaggart's metaphysics "connects
it with the world of Woolf's fiction, in which selves, perceptions and
emotions make up the metaphysical substance of the universe." This
connection explains a tendency in Woolf's novels to "envision a unity
that persists in the here-and-now, a unity independent of the synthetic
power of the mind and, apparently, even of the heart or any other
human faculty." Woolf ultimately breaks with McTaggart in her
attitude toward death, "for despite his awareness of man's tragic
limitations, his philosophy remains at heart an attempt to offer the
atheist some consolation in expectations of an after-life."

5   FRANKS, GABRIEL. "Virginia Woolf and the Philosophy of G.E.
    Moore." *Personalist* 50 (Spring):222-40.
    Evaluates the importance of the writing of G.E. Moore for

Virginia Woolf. She became aware of Moore through her brother,
Thoby, who attended Cambridge and along with other Bloomsbury
figures fell under Moore's spell.

6   GARNETT, DAVID. "Forster and Bloomsbury." In *Aspects of E.M.
    Forster*. Edited by Oliver Stallybrass. New York: Harcourt, Brace
    & World. pp. 29-35.
        Gives general sense of Bloomsbury. Suggests that Forster was
    "on the periphery rather than at the heart of the circle." His friendship
    with Leonard Woolf brought him into the group.

7   GROSS, JOHN. *The Rise and Fall of the Man of Letters: English
    Literary Life Since 1800*. London: Weidenfeld & Nicolson, 270 pp.
        Deals with Bloomsbury in relation to the tradition of letters in
    England.

8   HARROD, ROY. "The Arrested Revolution." *New Statesman* 79 (5
    December):808-10.
        Reassessment of Keynes. Identifies two sources of power in
    Keynes's life, the intellectual tradition of his family and his Cambridge
    friends who formed the Bloomsbury Group: "These young men
    constituted a circle of higher culture, broader vision and finer sensitivity
    than was to be found at Cambridge High Tables or in College at Eton."

9   HENIG, SUZANNE. "D.H. Lawrence and Virginia Woolf." *D.H.
    Lawrence Review* 2:665-71.
        Describes the literary relationship between these two figures,
    which relates to the Bloomsbury context. Lawrence hated Bloomsbury.

10 LEHMANN, JOHN. *In My Own Time: Memoirs of Literary Life*.
    Boston: Little, Brown, 167 pp.
        Describes Virginia Woolf's relationship with Lehmann and his
    literary periodicals, *New Signatures* and *New Writing*, in the late thirties
    and early years of the war.

11 _____. "Leonard Woolf." *Times Literary Supplement* (London) (30
    October):1258-259.
        Review of Leonard Woolf's autobiography. He is the last of the
    major Bloomsbury figures.

12   McDOWELL, FREDERICK P. "Recent Books on Forster and on Bloomsbury." *English Literature in Transition* 12:135-40.
      Review of various texts on Forster, some of which relate directly to Bloomsbury, including Quentin Bell's *Bloomsbury*, Leonard Woolf's *Sowing, Growing, Beginning Again, Down Hill All the Way*, Michael Holroyd's *Lytton Strachey*. All of these works have "the value of original documents," for they are by members of the group.

14   PLOMER, WILLIAM. "Leonard Woolf and His Autobiography." *Listener* 82 (17 August):789-91.
      Review of Leonard Woolf's *The Journey, Not the Arrival, Matters*. Deals briefly with the relation of Virginia and Leonard Woolf, as well as the atmosphere in Western Europe around the time of World War I.

15   ROBSON, WILLIAM. "Leonard Woolf." *New Statesman* 78 (22 August):251.
      Obituary notice on Leonard Woolf, which discusses his contributions to British culture: "A notable part of Leonard Woolf's contribution to English Literature was the way in which he made it possible for Virginia Woolf to express her genius as a writer."

16   RUSSELL, JOHN. "Julia Strachey." *Times Literary Supplement* (London) (19 June):665-66.
      Review of Julia Strachey's memoir. Deals with her Bloomsbury background.

17   SHONE, RICHARD. Introduction to *Duncan Grant: The Murals, Berwick Church*. Exhibition Catalog. Published by the Tower Art Gallery, Eastbourne, for the exhibition of Berwick Church Paintings, pp. 1-4.
      Gives history of the murals and their importance to the Bloomsbury artists involved. Describes Roger Fry's involvement.

18   _____. Introduction to *Duncan Grant: Portraits*. Exhibition Catalog. Cambridge: Arts Council, Cambridge Gallery, pp. 2-5.
      Introduction to the work of Duncan Grant. Describes the influence of Roger Fry on Grant's painting.

19   TAYLOR, DAVID GEORGE. "Roger Fry: A Study of His
      Theories of Art." Ph.D. dissertation, University of Toronto, 219 pp.
           Deals with Fry's aesthetic theories. "The aesthetic content of a
      work of art is thus seen as an expressed, 'formal,' 'autotelic' unity,
      though *not* as a *theoretical* one, and its analysis is regarded as
      incomplete and distortive if divorced from such a dichotomy of critical
      approach as these 'two' unities suggest. Does not relate much of Fry
      to his Bloomsbury associates. See *Dissertation Abstracts International*
      32:403A.

20   THOMSON, GEORGE H. "E.M. Forster, Gerald Head, and
      Bloomsbury." *English Literature in Transition* 12:87-91.
           Forster's 1929 note on Bloomsbury invokes Gerald Heard's
      theory of evolving civilization and advancing consciousness: "Our
      understanding of the complexity of Forster's relationship to Bloomsbury
      is enriched by an awareness of Heard's theory."

21   WATT, DONALD J. "G.E. Moore and the Bloomsbury Group."
      English Literature in Transition 12:119-34.
           Moore's work offers "a significant clue to the beliefs of some of
      Bloomsbury's most seminal convictions." Evaluates the view of Leonard
      Woolf, Virginia Woolf, E.M. Forster, Lytton Strachey, Keynes, Clive
      Bell, and Roger Fry. Concludes that Moore's overall moral and
      aesthetic effect on Bloomsbury extended beyond *Principia Ethica*: "In
      fine, Moore was at once an inspiration and a challenge to several
      members of Bloomsbury--an inspiration in his bold analysis of values in
      support of their highest ideals, a challenge in his steady personal
      example."

22   WILKINSON, PATRICK. "Forster at King's." In *Aspects of E.M.
      Forster: Essays and Reflections Written for His Ninetieth Birthday*.
      Edited by Oliver Stallybrass. New York: Harcourt, Brace & World.
      pp. 13-28.
           Relates to Forster's experience at Kings College, Cambridge.
      Like other Bloomsbury figures, the Cambridge experience was a high
      mark in his intellectual life.

23   WOLLHEIM, RICHARD. "Saving Civilization." *Listener* 81 (15
      May):684-85.
           Deals with the artistic ideals of Bloomsbury in relation to the
      concept of civilization.

24　WOOLF, LEONARD. *The Journey Not the Arrival, Matters: An Autobiography of the Years 1939-1969.* London: Hogarth Press. Reprint. New York: Harcourt Brace Jovanovich, 1970, 217 pp.

Fifth volume of Woolf's autobiography, which begins with a chapter on "The Death of Virginia" and is followed by a chapter on "The Hogarth Press." Gives a sense of the last phase of Bloomsbury and the impact of World War Two on the psychology of his generation: "It was as if one had been violently hit on the head." States that "it was this feeling of hopelessness and helplessness, the foreknowledge of catastrophe with the forces of history completely out of control, which made the road downhill to war and the outbreak of war so different in 1939 from what they had been twenty-five years before." In 1938 he entered into partnership with John Lehmann in the Hogarth Press.

1970

1　ACKERLEY, J.R. *E.M. Forster: A Portrait.* London: Ian McKelvie, 153 pp.

Includes some commentary on Forster's relation with Bloomsbury, from its origin in Cambridge with the Apostles, to London and to Garsington with Lady Ottoline Morrell.

2　ANDERSON, PATRICK. "E.M. Forster." *Spectator* (13 June):793-94.

Refers to Forster's association with Bloomsbury and to his interaction with Virginia Woolf.

3　ANNAN, LORD. "Leonard Woolf's Autobiography." *Political Quarterly* 41 (January-March):35-41.

Review of Leonard Woolf's *The Journey Not the Arrival Matters.* Comments on how Woolf's political work and public service related to the Bloomsbury world of which he was a part: In this last volume Leonard Woolf, therefore, is still debating a dilemma which the Apostles had debated in his day as an undergraduate. Should those who care for truth, for the distinction between right and wrong, and for the private virtues exemplified by the communion between friends, despise the world of politics and the compromises of political action?"

4　_____. "Morgan Forster Remembered." *Listener* 83 (18 June):826.

Refers to Bloomsbury briefly in relation to Forster.

5   CARRINGTON, DORA. *Carrington: Letters and Extracts from Her
     Diaries*. Edited by David Garnett. London: Jonathan Cape.
     Reprint. New York: Holt, Rinehart & Winston, 1971, 514 pp.
          Includes preface by David Garnett and "Carrington's Early Life"
     by Noel Carrington, Dora Carrington's brother. These letters and
     extracts from Carrington's diary give her perspective on the Bloomsbury
     world with which she became involved. The letters are often written to
     Various Bloomsbury figures, such as Lytton Strachey, to whom
     Carrington was devoted, Gerald Brenan, and Virginia Woolf. Garnett
     suggests in his preface that Carrington did not quite fit into the
     Bloomsbury Group; she "entered it more as an appendage of Lytton
     Strachey's than in her own right." Lady Ottoline Morrell, however,
     knew Carrington before she met Strachey. Noel Carrington describes
     Carrington's early home life and her opposition to conventionality.

6   EDEL, LEON. "Personal History." *Saturday Review* 53 (11
     April):34-35.
          Biographical commentary on Leonard Woolf which includes a
     discussion of Woolf and Bloomsbury.

7   EDELSTEIN, J.M. "Fitting Farewell." *New Republic* 162 (4
     April):26-28.
          Commentary on Leonard Woolf. Describes his Bloomsbury
     connection as well as his independence in relation to his political
     thought.

8   EKMAN, ROSALIND. "The Paradoxes of Formalism." *British
     Journal of Aesthetics* 10, no. 4 (October):350-58.
          Suggests that in order to make sense of Clive Bell's theory of
     significant form and to understand the real point of formalism, it is
     necessary to make a closer analysis of the form-content distinction: "I
     take my clue for the analysis I will offer from Bell's own many
     acknowledgements to the philosophy of G.E. Moore." When Bell's
     ideas are evaluated in light of Moore's theory of value, "the apparent
     paradoxes in Bell's theory, especially those generated by the form-
     content distinction, will be resolved."

9   FURBANK, P.N. "The Personality of E.M. Forster." *Encounter* 35
     (November):61.
          Commentary on E.M. Forster by his biographer. Makes some
     connections between Forster and the Bloomsbury milieu.

10   GERVAIS, DAVID. "Leonard Woolf's Autobiography." *Cambridge
      Quarterly* 5 (Spring-Summer):82-98.
          Commentary on the various volumes of Leonard Woolf's
      autobiography, which have proven to be reliable sources for a
      discussion of Bloomsbury and Woolf's Bloomsbury activities.

11   HOLROYD, MICHAEL. "Rediscovery: The Bloomsbury Painters."
      Art in America 58 (July):116-23.
          A revival in interest in Bloomsbury has taken place in literature,
      "while the Bloomsbury painters have by comparison been curiously and
      unjustly ignored." Explains the lack of sophistication in British art and
      gives a history of the Bloomsbury artists after the Post-impressionist
      exhibition of 1910. Discusses Duncan Grant, Vanessa Bell, Henry
      Lamb, Dora Carrington, Mark Gertler, and Simon Bussy: "Bloomsbury
      was essentially the product of an age of transition, and, perhaps, for
      this reason, much of their work was very erratic."

12   LIKPE, WILLIAM. "The Omega Workshops and Vorticism."
      Apollo 91 (March):224-31.
          Describes the connections between Roger Fry's Omega
      Workshops, which included work by Vanessa Bell and Duncan Grant,
      and Vorticism: "The figurative work produced at the Omega
      Workshops, while in some ways suggesting the influence of the English
      Post-Impressionists, also drew on the elements of the contribution of
      the Vorticists, notably their primitive and 'stick-like' style."

13   McCLURE, J. DERRICK. "Diversions of Bloomsbury." *American
      Speech* 45, nos. 3-4 (Fall-Winter):278-83.
          Review of *Diversions of Bloomsbury: Selected Writings on
      Linguistics* by R.H. Robins, which has nothing to do with the
      Bloomsbury Group: "Readers for whom the name *Bloomsbury* suggests
      the languid life of English fin-de-siecle high society should not be put
      off by the title of this anthology. R.H. Robins is about as far from
      languid or affected as a writer can be."

14   MORPHET, RICHARD. Introduction to *Vanessa Bell: Paintings
      and Drawings*. Exhibition Catalog. London: Anthony d'Offay
      Gallery, pp. 1-3.
          Evaluates Vanessa Bell's work in relation to her affiliation with
      Bloomsbury and other Bloomsbury artists.

15   RICHTER, HARVENA. *Virginia Woolf: The Inward Voyage.*
     Princeton: Princeton University Press, 273 pp.
          Study of Woolf's "subjective methods--not only the ways by which
     her reader is led 'inland' to the consciousness of her characters, but
     also the means by which he senses its very geography and climate."
     Chapter 2 deals with the influence of Bloomsbury and G.E. Moore on
     Woolf: "Governed by G.E. Moore's 'scientific method,' the Bloomsbury
     attitude was outwardly rational and questioning but also inward-turning,
     examining philosophical and aesthetic questions from an intuitive or
     neo-mystical standpoint."

16   ROBSON, W.W. "Liberal Humanism: The 'Bloomsbury' Group."
     In *Modern English Literature.* London: Oxford University Press, pp.
     93-102.
          Important study of the tradition of liberal humanism in relation
     to Bloomsbury. Deals with the origins in Cambridge and the
     expression of these ideals in the works of various Bloomsbury writers,
     including John Maynard Keynes, E.M. Forster, and Leonard Woolf.

17   RUNYAN, ELIZABETH. "Escape from the Self: An
     Interpretation of E.M.Forster, D.H. Lawrence, Virginia Woolf."
     Ph.D. dissertation, Kent State University, 226 pp.
          "Concentration on the self, which is characteristic of much
     modern literature, is often accompanied by an effort to escape from
     the confines of this self." This dissertation evaluates the major novels
     of Forster, Lawrence, and Woolf in light of this tendency. Briefly
     mentions Bloomsbury in relation to Woolf. See *Dissertation Abstracts
     International* 31:5423A.

18   SAKAMOTO, KIMINOBU. *Tozasareta Taiwa--V. Woolf No Bungaku
     to Sono Shuhen* [*Solitary dialogue--V. Woolf's literature and circle*].
     Tokyo: Ofusha.
          Not seen. In Japanese.

19   SEYMOUR, WILLIAM KEAN. "E.M. Forster: Some Observations
     and a Memory." *Contemporary Review* 217 (August):84-86.
          Includes some commentary on Forster's Bloomsbury connections.

20   SITWELL, EDITH. *Selected Letters 1919-1964.* Edited by John
     Lehmann and Derek Parker. New York: Vanguard Press, 376 pp.
          Letters to V. Woolf, John Lehn, and others. Comments on

Bloomsbury figures: "I've been having a lot of trouble with silly little Bloomsburys lately. They think that it matters to me if they, and people like Desmond MacCarthy, like my poetry. It doesn't. I don't expect them to. They've civilized all their instincts away."

1971

1   BEJA, MORRIS. *Epiphany in the Novel*. Seattle: University of Washington Press, 287 pp.
  Chapter V: Virginia Woolf; "Matches Struck in the Dark" (pp. 112-47), relates the development of the novel to the work of G.E. Moore, Roger Fry, and Clive Bell.

2   BELL, QUENTIN. "The Biographer, the Critic, and the Lighthouse." *Ariel* 2, no. 1 (January):94-101.
  Commentary on Mitchell A. Leaska's *Virginia Woolf's Lighthouse*. Uses Woolf's letters to Roger Fry as a vehicle for evaluating her method. Deals with the intellectual interaction of Fry, Vanessa Bell, and Virginia Woolf. States that Leaska is not a biographer. Bell uses a more biographical point of view.

3   BLYTHE, RONALD. "Bloomsbury Group." In *Penguin Companion to English Literature*. Edited by David Daiches. New York: McGraw Hill; Harmondsworth: Penguin Books, p. 54.
  Gives brief, general introduction to various aspects of the Bloomsbury Group and to the major figures involved. Lists some appropriate works.

4   CHALFANT, THOMAS HAIGHT. "The Marriage of Granite and Rainbow: Virginia Woolf as Biographer." Ph.D. dissertation, University of Wisconsin, 326 pp.
  This dissertation examines Virginia Woolf's biographical criticism and theory as well as her biographical essays; her partial mock biographies, *Flush* and *Orlando*; and her one full-scale biography, *Roger Fry*. She writes as "Fry's champion. This partisanship weakens her prose and renders the portrait somewhat unrealistic." Looks at "granite fact" and the "rainbow of personality" in her biographical technique. See *Dissertation Abstracts* 32:3298A.

5 DOLLE, ERIKA. *Experiment und Tradition in der Prosa Virginia Woolfs*. Munich: Wilhelm Fink.

Her estimate of the novelistic theories of Forster are of special interest in studying his principles of Development. [In German.]

6 FISHER, HERMANN. "Virginia Woolf, 1882-1941." In *Englishe Dichter der Moderne: Ihr Leben Undwerr*. Edited by Rudolf Suhuel and Dieter Riesner. Berlin: Schmidt, pp. 299-316.

Discusses Virginia Woolf in relation to the Bloomsbury milieu. Deals with her inheritance of intellectual skepticism. [In German.]

7 FRY, PHILLIP, and JAMES W. LEE. "An Interview in Austin with John Lehmann." *Studies in the Novel* 3, no. 1 (Spring):80-96.

Interview with Lehmann during the time he was a visiting professor at the University of Texas. Discusses his relationship with Virginia and Leonard Woolf, as well as his work on the Hogarth Press. Discusses the depiction of the dissolution of his partnership with Leonard Woolf, which Woolf described in *The Journey Not the Arrival Matters*.

8 HARTWELL, R.M. "The Young Keynes." *Spectator* (11 September):373-74.

Deals with Keynes during his years at Cambridge when he first met many of the figures who were to form Bloomsbury.

9 HOLROYD, MICHAEL. *Lytton Strachey and the Bloomsbury Group: His Work, Their Influence*. Harmondsworth: Penguin, 400 pp.

Major study of Bloomsbury in relation to Lytton Strachey. Chapters cover the origin of the Group at Cambridge, the Bloomsbury artists, and other aspects of the relationships that made up Bloomsbury.

10 ____. "Lytton Strachey by Himself." *Encounter* 36 (January):21-6.

Amended version of Holroyd's introduction to *Lytton Strachey by Himself*. (See 1971.22).

11 HULCOOP, JOHN F. "Virginia Woolf's Diaries: Some Reflections After Reading Them and a Censure of Mr. Holroyd." *Bulletin of the New York Public Library* 75:301-10.

Comment on Woolf's relationship with Lytton Strachey and other Bloomsbury figures as depicted in her diaries.

12   KIRK, RUSSELL. *Eliot and His Age*. New York: Random House.
      Rev. and enl. ed. La Salle, Illinois: Sherwood Sugden & Co., 1984,
      476 pp.
          Describes Eliot's relation to Bloomsbury: "Any other such
      seeker might have been found vexatious or ridiculous by Bloomsbury;
      but that circle could not dismiss Eliot with a sneer or a chuckle. He
      knew his poets, his metaphysics, and even his theologians."

13   LAKSHMI, VIJAY. "Virginia Woolf and E.M. Forster: A Study in
      Inter Criticism." *Banasthali Patrika* 16:8-18.
          Discusses the critical relationship between Virginia Woolf and
      E.M. Forster. Includes commentary on the commonality of their
      Bloomsbury association as it relates to their criticism of each other's
      work.

14   McLAURIN, ALLEN. "Aesthetics and Bloomsbury, With Special
      Reference to the Works of Virginia Woolf." Ph.D. dissertation.
      University of Wales, Cardiff, 287 pp.
          Published as *Virginia Woolf: The Echoes Enslaved*. (See 1973.33).

15   PHILLIPS, ANN H. "The Anonymous Self: A Study of Virginia
      Woolf's Novels." Ph.D. dissertation, Stanford University, 256 pp.
          Relates Woolf's work to the visual arts. "Unlike the
      Impressionist in art and literature, she did not wish to subordinate
      impersonal nature to the individual's experience of it. Chapters one
      and two differences between Monet and Cézanne and connect Woolf to
      the artistic perspective of Cézanne. "The third chapter talks about the
      extent of Virginia Woolf's exposure to Post-impressionist art through
      her close friend Roger Fry." See *Dissertation Abstracts International*
      32:5801A.

16   ROSE, MARTIAL. *E.M. Forster*. New York: Arco Press, 137 pp.
          Includes some commentary on Forster and his work in relation
      to Bloomsbury.

17   ROSENBAUM, S.P. "The Philosophical Realism of Virginia Woolf."
      In *English Literature and British Philosophy*. Edited by S.P.
      Rosenbaum. Chicago and London, pp. 316-56.
          Woolf "had her own ideas about the nature of philosophy as well
      as the novel." Explores influences, especially G. E. Moore's

epistemology and ethics. Uses Woolf's novels as focus, including *Mrs. Dalloway*, *To the Lighthouse*, and *Orlando*: "In her last two novels Virginia Woolf is less preoccupied with consciousness and perception than in her four preceding novels."

18 ROSS, MICHAEL L. "The Mythology of Friendship: D.H. Lawrence, Bertrand Russell, and 'The Blind Man.'" In *English Literature and British Philosophy*, edited by S.P. Rosenbaum. Chicago and London: University of Chicago Press, pp. 285-315.
　　The friendship of Russell and Lawrence started off promisingly. They had been introduced by Lady Ottoline Morrell. Describes the problems that emerged as a result of Lawrence's visit to Cambridge and the Bloomsbury crowd with Russell. Uses the story and Lawrence's non-fiction to show that "like the liberal humanitarians whom Lawrence attacks in "The Crown," Russell and Lady Ottoline 'have corruption within themselves as sensationalism"; they, too--on the level of personal relations--"destroy life for the preserving of a static, rigid form, a shell.'"

19 SENCOURT, ROBERT. *T.S. Eliot: A Memoir.* Edited by Donald Adamson. New York: Dodd, Mead; London: Garnstone Press, 266 pp.
　　Autobiographical account of Eliot's activities, which includes commentary on his relationship with Bertrand Russell, Lady Ottoline Morrell, and Bloomsbury: "Bertrand Russell continued his guardianship of Tom by introducing him to Lady Ottoline Morrell and also to Bloomsbury. Russell himself belonged to the circle which was to make Bloomsbury famous." Also describes the meeting between Virginia Woolf and Eliot.

20 SPATER, GEORGE A.. "The Monks House Library." *American Book Collector* 21, no. 4 (January):18-20.
　　Description of the books in the Woolfs' library, many of which relate to the Bloomsbury friends, such as Clive Bell and Roger Fry.

21 _____. "The Paradise Road Publications of the Hogarth Press." *American Book Collector* 21, no. 7:18.
　　Description of the publishing activities of the Hogarth Press that became central to the Bloomsbury Group.

22   STRACHEY, LYTTON. *Lytton Strachey by Himself: A Self Portrait*.
      Edited with Introduction by Michael Holroyd. London: Macmillan;
      New York: Holt, Rinehart & Winston, 184 pp.
           Portrait of Strachey given through his diaries and other personal
      texts, including "Trinity Diary of 1902," "August 6, 1905," "Diary--1910,"
      "Conscientious Objector," and other entries. Holroyd's introduction (pp.
      1-12) and commentary on each section discusses his Bloomsbury
      association, such as his activities as an Apostle, a friend of Lady
      Ottoline Morrell, and a member of the Memoir Club. His evocation of
      Bloomsbury will probably convert no one: "Those who detest the
      group will be confirmed in their antipathy by this picture of a life of
      crowded leisure and of easy privilege in the midst of war. But others
      will undoubtedly be fascinated by what is a unique view of this gifted
      circle."

23   WEBB, IGOR MICHAEL. "Sense and Sensibility: A Study of the
      Influence of English Aesthetics From Ruskin to Roger Fry on Ford
      Madox Ford and Virginia Woolf." Ph.D. dissertation, Stanford
      University, 292 pp.
           "The premise of this study is that the writing of Ford Madox
      Ford and Virginia Woolf can best be understood in the light of English
      aesthetics from Ruskin to Roger Fry. Ford's novels depend on the
      experience of the Pre-Raphaelites; Virginia Woolf's more generally on
      the ideas of "The Last Romantics," and especially on the work of Roger
      Fry." Focuses in relation to Woolf on her interest in "the concept of
      formal relationships as a means of illuminating the unconscious." Roger
      Fry's "influence is especially apparent here." See *Dissertation Abstracts
      International* 32:4638A.

24   WOODESON, JOHN. "Survey." In *Mark Gertler: Retrospective*.
      Exhibition Catalog. Colchester, England: The Minories, pp. 1-4.
           Includes some commentary on Gertler's association with Dora
      Carrington and Lytton Strachey.

                                    1972

1   ARCHER, W.G. "A Tribute to Roger Fry." *Apollo* 96
      (October):360-62.
           Article written in relation to the publication of *The Letters of
      Roger Fry*, edited by Denys Sutton. Fry "dominated English art-criticism

for almost thirty years." He stressed "the supreme importance of structural unity and formal organization." Describes some aspects of his correspondence with Bloomsbury figures.

2   BAGNOLD, ENID. "Virginia Woolf." *Adam International Review* 37:15.
       Memoir of a brief meeting with Virginia Woolf in Sussex in the early forties: "When I came to London at nineteen Bloomsbury was a kind of glittering village with no doors. It hovered ungeographically and had, to my mind, only one inhabitant--a woman with a magnet."

3   BELL, CAROLYN W. "A Study of Virginia Woolf's 'Moment of Vision.'" Ph.D. dissertation, University of Texas at Austin, 208 pp.
       "Examines the implications of the experience Woolf called the 'moment of vision'--that fleeting apprehension of a stable reality which transcends the flux of ordinary clock and calendar time." A portion of this study deals with the biographical context of the 'moment' by focusing on G.E. Moore's influence on Bloomsbury and "on Woolf's quasi mystical experiences as they were recorded in *A Writer's Diary*." See *Dissertation Abstracts International* 34:761A.

4   BELL, QUENTIN. Introduction to *Clive Bell at Charleston*. Exhibition Catalog. London: Gallery Edward Harvane, pp. 2-9.
       Includes commentary on Bell's relationship to Bloomsbury and the influence of his aesthetic on Bloomsbury figures. Deals primarily with his years with Vanessa and Duncan Grant at Charleston farmhouse.

5   _____. *Virginia Woolf: A Biography*. Vol. 1, *Virginia Stephen 1882-1912*. Vol. 2, *Mrs Woolf 1912-1941*. London: Hogarth Press; New York: Harcourt Brace and Jovanovich, 1:228 pp.; 2:300 pp.
       Biographical study: "the purpose of the present volume is purely historical; and although I hope that I may assist those who attempt to explain and to asses the writing of Virginia Woolf, I can do so only by presenting facts which hitherto have not been generally known and by providing what will, I hope, be a clear and truthful account of the character and personal development of my subject." Volume One gives details about the establishment of the Stephen's Bloomsbury home and Bloomsbury's Cambridge origins. G.E. Moore's *Principia Ethica* was "regarded practically as the gospel of their time." Volume Two describes Bloomsbury activities through Woolf's death in 1941: "After

Christmas there was one last Bloomsbury celebration, Angelica's twenty-first birthday party which, since wartime shortages had not yet made themselves felt, could be celebrated with some *éclat*."

6   CHAPMAN, ROBERT T. "The 'Enemy' vs Bloomsbury." *Adam International Review* 37:81-84.

Surveys Wyndham Lewis's published attacks on Virginia Woolf and Bloomsbury, which started with his ordeal with Fry over the Ideal Home exhibition: "This *imbroglio* marked the beginning of Lewis's lifelong feud with the 'aesthetic-politicians' of Bloomsbury whose world, he wrote in *Blasting and Bombarding* [1937] resembled the 'afternoon tea-party of a perverse spinster.'"

7   DIAMAND, PAMELA FRY. "An Appreciation of Jeanne Coppel." *Virginia Woolf Quarterly* 1, no. 1 (Fall):28-32.

Reflections on Jeanne Coppel and on the elegance of her collages. Briefly describes her arrival at the Omega Workshops.

8   DUNLOP, IAN. "The Post-Impressionists." In *The Shock of the New: Seven Historic Exhibitions of Modern Art*. London: Weidenfeld & Nicolson, pp. 120-61.

Commentary on the reaction to and the significance of the two Post-impressionist exhibitions Roger Fry organized. Describes Fry's background and his "conversion to Post-Impressionism." The real "impact of the exhibition was felt not so much by Walter Sickert and his circle but by a younger group, in particular the Bloomsbury painters Duncan Grant and Vanessa Bell." Bloomsbury was eager to join the fight.

9   FALKENHEIM, JACQUELINE V. "Roger Fry and the Beginnings of Formalist Art Criticism." Ph.D. dissertation, Yale University, 256 pp.

Deals with the development in Fry's mind of the requirements for formal design and with the artistic events in England that provided the context for Fry's ideas. The two Post-impressionist exhibitions helped the British public understand "the aesthetic assumptions of the new art." See *Dissertation Abstracts International* 33:6814A. This dissertation has been revised and published as part of Studies in the Fine Arts: Criticism (No. 8), Ann Arbor, Mich.: UMI Research Press. See Falkenheim, *Roger Fry and the Beginnings of Formalism*. 1980.21.

10 FIRCHOW, PETER. *Aldous Huxley: Satirist and Novelist.* Oxford: Oxford University Press; Minneapolis: University of Minnesota Press, 203 pp.

Critical study that relates aspects of Huxley's work to Bloomsbury, which reacted negatively to *Crome Yellow*. Suggests that he questioned the intellectual mood: "He saw that the intellectual emperor had no clothes (even if the emperor happened to come from Bloomsbury)."

11 FRY, ROGER. *The Letters of Roger Fry.* 2 vols. Edited with introduction by Denys Sutton. London: Chatto & Windus, 1:367 pp; 2:345 pp.

Letters include extensive commentary on Bloomsbury figures and activities. Sutton's introduction (pp. 1-95) gives complete evaluation of Fry's life and work, including commentary on Bloomsbury's involvement in the 1910 and 1912 Post-impressionist exhibitions and the Omega Workshops. Deals also with his relationships with Lady Ottoline Morrell and Vanessa Bell.

12 GOONERATNE, YASMINE. "Leonard Woolf's 'Waste Land': *The Village in the Jungle.*" *Journal of Commonwealth Literature* 7, no. 1 (June):22-34.

Analysis of Woolf's novel that also briefly compares it to Eliot's *The Waste Land* suggesting that Eliot may owe something to the "drought' section of the opening chapter in the novel. Woolf was Eliot's publisher for some time, and his Ceylon experience was known to Eliot, "as it was to the others of Woolf's Bloomsbury circle, and it is hardly probable that the poet had not read Woolf's 1913 novel, reprinted as often as it was before 1923."

13 GOTTLIEB, FREEMA. "L.W.: The Creative Writer." *Adam International Review* 37:66-70.

Leonard Woolf's main intention was to be a creative writer, although his "reputation appears to rest, not on any single achievement, but on the unique network of relationships, both public and private, in which he played a part." His interest in creative writing was probably "inculcated by the whole Apostolic Cambridge ethos which prized the life of contemplation above that of action." Evaluates *The Wise Virgins* in relation to Bloomsbury: "Leonard's search for truth led him ultimately to the abnegation of fiction, to the only story he could write with any gleaming of veracity, the story of himself."

14   GRINDEA, MIRON. "The Stuff of Which Legends are Made."
      Adam International Review 37:2-14.
            Overview of Virginia Woolf and Woolf scholarship by the editor
      of *Adam* as an introduction to this issue of the journal. Refers to
      Bell's biography, Fry's letters, edited by Dyns Sutton, and *Reflections of
      Virginia Woolf*, edited by Joan Russell Noble: "Most of the new
      materials cover, of course, Bloomsbury, that unique set whose gifted
      minds have for more than half a century stimulated each other. The
      information one receives illuminates one's often distorted picture of the
      group; but it is a light which also serves to deepen and define the
      shade." Describes Leonard Woolf and Virginia in relation to the
      Hogarth Press.

15   HAYMAN, RONALD. *Literature and Living: A Consideration of
      Katherine Mansfield & Virginia Woolf*. London: Covent Garden
      Press, 22 pp.
            Brief comparative study of these two writers in relation to the
      period, including the Bloomsbury context. Also compares the husband-
      wife relationship of both writers. Concludes that "for both writers,
      stories and characters are a substitute for living and having children.
      The difference is that Katherine Mansfield's characters are strong
      enough to get away from her while Virginia Woolf's never manage to
      break the umbilical cord."

16   HEINE, ELIZABETH. "Rickie Elliot and the Cow: The Cambridge
      Apostles and *The Longest Journey*." *English Literature in Transition*
      15, no. 2:116-34.
            Discussion of the symbolic significance of images and phrases in
      Forster's novel, including a full discussion of his Cambridge experience
      with the Apostles. The shift in Forster from McTaggart's Hegelian
      idealism to G.E. Moore's *Principia Ethica* and to Lytton Strachey's
      psychological probings represent a shift for Forster from Victorianism
      to modernism. Deals with influence of other figures, including Roger
      Fry and Leonard Woolf.

17   KENNEDY, RICHARD. *A Boy at the Hogarth Press*. London:
      Heinemann; New York: Aeolian Press, 87 pp.
            Kennedy's account of some of his experiences working for the
      Hogarth Press. Presents a rather critical portrait of Leonard as a
      demanding, authoritarian employer.

18 LAING, D.A. "An Addendum to the Virginia Woolf Bibliography." *Notes and Queries* 19:338.

Comments on unlisted item in B.J. Kirkpatrick's *A Bibliography of Virginia Woolf*, the essay Woolf wrote as a forward to the exhibition catalog of Vanessa Bell's paintings held in March, 1934, in the Lefevre Galleries: "The essay, which is only a page in length, is mainly interesting for the way in which it touches upon so many of Virginia Woolf's basic thoughts about art in so short a space." Equates Woolf's commentary to Clive Bell and Roger Fry's view of artistic form.

19 LUCAS, ROBERT. *Frieda Lawrence: The Story of Frieda von Richthofen and D.H. Lawrence.* Munich: Kindler Verlag. Translated by Geoffrey Skelton. New York: Viking Press, 1973, 308 pp.

Evaluation of the relationship of D.H. Lawrence and Frieda, including commentary on their association with Dorothy Brett and Lady Ottoline Morrell: "Lady Ottoline collected celebrities in the same way that a schoolboy collects stamps." Characterizes Garsington's unconventionality.

20 LUEDEKING, LEILA M.J. "Bibliography of Works by Leonard Sidney Woolf (1880-1969)." *Virginia Woolf Quarterly* 1, no. 1 (Fall):120-40.

Introduction to bibliography gives overview of Woolf's publishing and political activities, including discussion of his work with Virginia on the Hogarth Press: "Being both literary editor of the *Nation and Athenaeum* and publisher at The Hogarth Press greatly facilitated Leonard Woolf's and Virginia Woolf's efforts to get the works of promising writers published."

21 MacKNIGHT, NANCY MARGARET. "Vita: A Portrait of V. Sackville-West." Ph.D. dissertation, Columbia University, 242 pp.

Biographical study which deals with Sackville-West's family background, marriage to Harold Nicolson, relationship with Virginia Woolf: "The two women were friends for nearly twenty years." Separate chapter deals with Vita in Bloomsbury, which includes some private letters to the author from David Garnett. Includes commentary on Roy Campbell's attack on Bloomsbury in "The Georgiad." See *Dissertation Abstracts International* 35:7914A.

22   MEDCALF, STEPHEN. "The Village in the Jungle." *Adam International Review* 37:75-80.
        Commentary on Leonard Woolf's novels. Relates this work somewhat to his Cambridge background and to the Bloomsbury friends he met there.

23   MICHEL-MICHOT, P. "Bloomsbury Revisited: Carrington's Letters." *Revue des Langues Vivantes* 38, no. 4:421-37.
        Review article of *Carrington: Letters and Extracts from Her Diaries* edited by David Garnett. This work provides "some fresh material for an appraisal of Bloomsbury values." The actual attitudes of Bloomsbury in terms of "human intercourse" and "personal affections" only show up "in the life they led, to which we have access only through the autobiographies, diaries and letters of the members of the group and of those connected with it." Gives overview of Carrington's life and various relationships. Her relationship with Lytton Strachey "involved her much too much in people, and not the kind of people who were likely to help her since, as we have seen, she felt isolated among them and hardly got any response from them." Some of the material here "reveals Bloomsbury's limitations on the human level, their superior attitude and their lack of human sympathy for outsiders."

24   NOBLE, JOAN R. *Recollections of Virginia Woolf by Her Contemporaries*. New York: William Morrow; London: Peter Owen, pp. 207.
        Includes essay by various Bloomsbury figures relating to Woolf's association with the Bloomsbury Group.

25   OLSON, STANLEY. "North from Richmond, South from Bloomsbury." *Adam International Review* 37:70-74.
        Brief note on the early days of the Woolfs' Hogarth Press: "The Hogarth Press was always seen by both husband and wife as a mere diversion, and both were anxious that it should remain so, even if in three years they could no longer deny its emergence into an independent entity." Deals also with the early publishing relationship with Katherine Mansfield.

26   PAINTER, GEORGE. "Proust and Virginia Woolf." *Adam International Review* 37:17- 23.
        Deals with the importance of Proust to Woolf and other

Bloomsbury figures. A letter appeared in a special issue of *Nouvelle Revue Francaise* on the occasion of Proust's death declaring that "he restored to use life as we had known and experienced it, but enriched, made beautiful and magnificent by the alchemy of art." This letter was signed by "the majority of the Bloomsbury Group."

27 ROBINSON, AUSTIN. "John Maynard Keynes: Economist, Author, Statesman." *Economic Journal* 82 (June):531-46.
    General article on Keynes. Deals with his Cambridge background and his connection with Bloomsbury.

28 RUBENSTEIN, ROBERTA. "Virginia Woolf and the Russian Point of View." *Comparative Literature Studies* 9, no. 2 (June):196-206.
    An evaluation of Woolf's interest in Russian literature which includes some consideration of her work on the Hogarth Press and the publication of works by Russian authors.

29 SAYERS, R.S. "The Young Keynes." *Economic Journal* 82 (June): 591-99.
    Deals with Keynes at Cambridge, where he met Leonard Woolf, Lytton Strachey, and other Bloomsbury figures. Also deals with his membership in the Apostles, which formed the basis of the Bloomsbury ideal.

30 SPATER, GEORGE A. "Monks House, 1970." *Virginia Woolf Quarterly* 1, 1 (Fall):106-9.
    Verbal tour of Monk's house, describing objects there that related to the Woolfs and their world. "There are many reminiscences of Bloomsbury."

31 SPENDER, STEPHEN. "Duncan Grant." In *Duncan Grant: Watercolours and Drawings*. Exhibition Catalog. London: Anthony d'Offay Gallery, n.p.
    "Duncan Grant paints a world which is to some extent identifiable with that of Virginia Woolf and Vanessa Bell, Roger Fry and Clive Bell. Visually speaking the idea behind this is what is called environmental." When one connects "him with Bloomsbury one thinks of rooms in houses which are 'Duncan and Vanessa' and Omega."

32   TRAUTMANN, JOANNE. "A Talk with Nigel Nicholson." *Virginia Woolf Quarterly* 1, no. 1 (Fall):38-44.

Interview. Deals with Bloomsbury and Virginia Woolf's love affair with Vita Sackville-West: "On May 21, 1971, in the process of writing a long essay on the friendship of Virginia Woolf and Vita Sackville-West, I spoke to Nigel Nicolson at Sissinghurst. He talked about his parents, Bloomsbury, *Orlando*, and, of course, about Virginia Woolf." States that Vita felt they should have profited more from Bloomsbury: "The central core of Bloomsbury, of course, was really pre-war." And in the twenties Bloomsbury had "a sort of second wind." Describes the first meeting of Vita and Virginia Woolf.

33   VAIZEY, MARINA. "Bloomsbury." *Connoisseur* 179 (February):147.

Review of series of exhibitions at the Gallery Edward Harvane on the theme of Bloomsbury. The first exhibition, in the winter of 1971, was called "The World of Lytton Strachey." The second exhibition, "Ottoline," was held in the autumn of 1972: "Bloomsbury in the visual arts is refined, elegant and sensitive in tone, a delicate dilution in many cases of the Post-impressionists which indeed the Bloomsberries had sponsored in England."

34   WATSON, SARA R. *V. Sackville-West*. New York: Twayne, 164 pp.

Tries to establish Vita Sackville-West's position "in the mainstream of English literature, particularly in the history of the novel." Her Bloomsbury connections, especially her association with Virginia Woolf, "lend a particular interest to her work and to her biography." Chapter Two is "*Orlando*: Friendship with Virginia Woolf and the Bloomsbury Group," which describes the association of Harold Nicolson and Vita Sackville-West with Bloomsbury from approximately 1919 onward and gives the background of the Group.

35   WATTS, JANET. "Dear Quentin: Janet Watts Interviews Mr. Bell of Bloomsbury." *Virginia Woolf Quarterly* 1, no. 1 (Fall):111-16.

Commentary on Quentin Bell based upon personal interview. When he was a child all Bloomsbury "meant to him was 'that one's parents were odd and different, because they didn't believe in the war, or in God.'" Bloomsbury life in the Sussex house was "a spartan affair." He became conscious of Bloomsbury as a group in the 1920s: "Then, Duncan Grant was at the center of the London Group of Artists;

Roger Fry was drawing enormous crowds to his lectures; Lytton
Strachey's and Virginia Woolf's books were gaining acclaim." In the
1930s attitudes changed: "Obviously, I was in Bloomsbury--of
Bloomsbury--as a child: but with a very definite feeling, as I grew up,
that I was critical of it--and that my friends were even more critical."
Reprinted from *Arts Guardian* (London) (14 June 1972).

36   WEES, WILLIAM C. *Vorticism and the English Avant-Garde.*
      Toronto and Buffalo: University of Toronto Press, 273 pp.
      Deals with the impact of the Post-impressionist exhibitions, the
Omega Workshops, and the Bloomsbury Group in modern British
culture: "The shock created by Post-Impressionism would not have
been so great had England not been so oblivious to the currents of
change in continental art from the 1860s on." "Coteries," Chapter 4
(pp. 53-72), deals with the various intellectual and artistic groups that
emerged after the 1910 exhibition, including the Omega Workshops and
some commentary on the Friday Night, which Vanessa Bell established,
and the Bloomsbury Group in general.

37   WOODESON, JOHN. *Mark Gertler: Biography of a Painter, 1891-*
      1939. London: Sidgwick & Jackson, 413 pp.
      Biographical account to the painter who was involved with Dora
Carrington, Lytton Strachey and Lady Ottoline Morrell, among other
Bloomsbury figures: "Mark had met Lytton Strachey in 1914 at
Ottoline's, where the thirty-five-year-old writer was a frequent guest,
often dominating the conversation with his brilliance. His urbanity and
learning were impressive and Mark willingly agreed to further
meetings." Describes fully the relationship between Carrington and
Gertler, including many long extracts from letters from each, as well as
Carrington's relationship with Strachey. Later, Roger Fry became
interested in Gertler's work: "Roger Fry, who had been watching his
work with increasing interest, now made friendly approaches, inviting
Mark to take part in an exhibition of 'copies' at his Omega Workshops
in April 1917, and in shows of modern art which he organized at
Birmingham in July and at Heal's, London, in October." Ottoline's
Garsington became a second home for Gertler.

38   WOOLLEY, KATHI. "Film Review: Duncan Grant at Charleston."
      Virginia Woolf Quarterly 1, no. 1 (Fall):118.
      Brief review of "Duncan Grant at Charles," which presents an

informal interview between Quentin Bell and Grant. Feels that the film assumes too much knowledge of Bloomsbury.

39 ZINK, DAVID D. *Leslie Stephen*. New York: Twayne Publishers, 237 pp.
 Includes some commentary on the Stephen children who were to form the core of the Bloomsbury Group. Gives sense of the intellectual background they inherited from their father.

1973

1 BAZIN, NANCY TOPPING. *Virginia Woolf and the Androgynous Vision*. New Brunswick: Rutgers University Press, 251 pp.
 Woolf discovered that her life with her brothers and sister in Bloomsbury only partially liberated her; she was unsure of herself and shy. Here begins her quest for the androgynous vision. Connects this concept to the artistic theories of Roger Fry and Clive Bell.

2 BEDFORD, SYBILLE. *Aldous Huxley: A Biography*. London: Chatto and Windus/William Collins. Reprint. New York: Alfred A. Knopf; Harper & Row, 1974, 769 pp.
 Biographical study which includes references to Huxley's relationship with various Bloomsbury figures, especially Lady Ottoline Morrell at Garsington during World War I. Relates *Crome Yellow* to Garsington.

3 BELL, MILLICENT. "Virginia Woolf Now." *Massachusetts Review* 14, no. 4 (Autumn):655-87.
 Exploratory essay on the character of Virginia Woolf in relation to our own time which involves her Bloomsbury association: "She was a Bloomsbury rationalist and atheist, after all." Discusses Bloomsbury and androgyny, the Hogarth Press, and other aspects of Woolf's life: "The young founders of Bloomsbury had, of course, no consciousness that they were a 'movement.' Cultural history may very well be a consequence of accidents of prominence gained by certain groups and persons--not all of them of individual importance--whose behavior and ideas are probably shared by many persons in society in their time."

4 BELL, QUENTIN. "Roger Fry's Letters." *Burlington Magazine* 115 (January):50-51.
Review of *The Letters of Roger Fry* edited by Denys Sutton (see 1972.11). This volume gives a good sense of Fry's life. Sutton's introduction, which is a short life and appreciation of Fry, is a welcome addition. Woolf's biography is flawed because she deferred to the feelings of the Group members involved. Describes the stages of Fry's life, including the middle period, which consisted of his work in behalf of the Post-impressionist and the Omega Workshops.

5 BLUNT, ANTHONY. "From Bloomsbury to Marxism." *Studio International* 186 (November):164-68.
Autobiographical account of Blount's life during 1920s and 1930s, including his association with Bloomsbury: "But the most important thing for us was the discovery of what was then modern art. And Modern Art in 1923 meant Cézanne first and the other Post-Impressionists, who were still regarded in this country as dangerous revolutionaries." His days at Cambridge were dominated by Bloomsbury ideals. With very few exceptions, "Bloomsbury was not interested in politics. The exceptions were Leonard Woolf and Goldie Lowes-Dickinson, but they were interested in politics in quite different ways." Marxism hit Cambridge in 1933.

6 BOBBITT, JOAN. "Lawrence and Bloomsbury: The Myth of a Relationship." *Essays in Literature* 1, no. 3:31-43.
Suggests that the "Lawrence-Bloomsbury relationship did not fail; it simply failed to materialize." Gives evidence showing the lack of actual contact between Lawrence and the various Bloomsbury personaliries. Analyzes the assorted accounts of Lawrence's antagonism toward the Group: "Did Lawrence in fact feel the intense dislike that the Bloomsbury group attributes to him? If so, was it personal or theoretical or perhaps a combination of both." Identifies aspects of the Group's aesthetics which would have been objectionable to Lawrence: "The Bloomsburies were certainly not his kind of people, and after a brief acquaintance, Lawrence was the first to admit that fact. However, if any real antipathy did exist between them, it was primarily disinterest."

7 BREE, GERMAINE. "Two Vintage Years: France 1913; England 1922." *Virginia Woolf Quarterly* 1, no. 4 (Summer):19-30.
Identifies the changing intellectual landscape in France and

England in relation to the dates 1913 and 1922. In 1913 "in the English cluster the names Virginia Woolf, Roger Fry, Clive Bell, Lytton Strachey point to the so-called Bloomsbury group." There are parallels between the milieu of Andre Gide in France and Bloomsbury in England, with Virginia Woolf as its center, including a similar sexual preoccupation, belief in literature as a form of high art, blend of individualism and aesthetic fastidiousness.

8   BRETT, DOROTHY, and JOHN MANCHESTER. "Reminiscences of Katherine." *Adam International Review* 38:84-92.
        Brett's account of her meeting with Katherine Mansfield at Lady Ottoline Morrell's country home, Garsington, and subsequent meetings up to Mansfield's death.

9   CHAPMAN, ROBERT. "The Malefic Cabal." In *Wyndham Lewis: Fictions and Satires.* New York: Barnes & Noble, pp. 83-98.
        Expanded version of "The 'Enemy' vs 'Bloomsbury.'" (See 1972.6.)

10   CONNOLLY, CYRIL. *Enemies of Promise.* Rev. ed. London: Andre Deutsch, 187 pp.
        Includes personalized commentary on Bloomsbury based upon his connection with some of the members of the Group.

11   DIAMOND, PAMELA FRY. "Recollections of Roger Fry and the Omega Workshops." *Virginia Woolf Quarterly* 1, no. 4 (Summer):47-55.
        The establishment of the Workshops was a "courageous thing." Mentions Fry's Letter to Wyndham Lewis as containing the germ of the idea for Omega. The project was "a financial failure but a portent that left its mark on all applied art of the future."

12   DUFFY, MAUREEN. *A Nightingale in Bloomsbury Square.*
        Play produced in Hampstead Theatre Club.

13   EDMISTON, SUSAN. "Bloomsbury: A Good Address in the Geography of the Mind." *New York Times* (18 March):X 1, 9.
        Literary guide to the Bloomsbury area, giving history of the Bloomsbury Group with Virginia Woolf as the center of focus: "In an England just out of the shadow of Queen Victoria, it was horrifying. Virginia and Vanessa, such well-bred girls, were talking late into the

night--and unchaperoned, too--with these strange young men from Cambridge."

14 EDWARDS, RALPH. "The Wizard's Wand." *Connoisseur* 182 (February):112-13.
    Review of *The Letters of Roger Fry* edited by Denys Sutton (1972.11): "Roger Fry is among the few members of the Bloomsbury circle who a later generation have successfully defied 'the iniquity of oblivion.'" Sees him as a peripheral figure: "From the first Fry lacked some of the more distinctive Bloomsbury traits--the arrogant self-esteem, consciousness of innate superiority and lofty destain of the unenlightened beyond the pale."

15 FETZER, LELAND. "The Bunin-Koteliansky-Lawrence-Woolf Version of 'The Gentleman from San Francisco.'" *Virginia Woolf Quarterly* 1, no. 4 (Summer):31.
    Deals with Leonard Woolf's work with the Hogarth Press. There were in reality two translations of Bunin's story, one which appeared in *The Dial* and "a second done by Koteliansky, Lawrence, and Leonard Woolf and published by the Hogarth Press."

16 FLOOD, DAVID H. "Leonard Woolf's *The Village in the Jungle*: A Modern Version of Pastoral." *Virginia Woolf Quarterly* 1, no. 4 (Summer):78-86.
    Commentary on Woolf's novel in relation to the pastoral tradition: "Man has become an alien in his world instead of achieving harmony and identity with it; nature itself has become a cruelly indifferent jungle instead of a nurturing garden; and man seeks to exploit his fellow man for personal gain instead of working together with him."

17 FORRESTER, VIVIANE. *Virginia Woolf*. Paris: Editions de La Quinzaine Litteraire, 79 pp.
    Transcriptions of seven ORTF broadcasts (January 1973). Describes the Bloomsbury Group, the operations of the Hogarth Press, etc.

18 GARBER, LAWRENCE A. "Bloomsbury Biography." Ph.D. dissertation, University of Toronto, 217 pp.
    A study of the "art of biography as conceived and practiced by various members of the Bloomsbury Group." By focusing on their

efforts in biography, "this thesis attempts to construct some general notion of their characteristics of the Group, as well as to examine their contributions to the development of modern biography." Involves close and extensive reading of "three experimental biographies: *Orlando, Elizabeth and Essex* and *Marianne Thorton.*" See *Dissertation Abstracts International.* 35:1098A-99A

19   GARDNER, PHILIP, ed. *E.M. Forster: The Critical Heritage.* London and Boston: Routledge & Kegan Paul, 498 pp.
    The extensive introduction deals in part with Virginia Woolf's reaction to Forster's work, as well as the mixed reaction of F.R. Leavis because of Forster's Bloomsbury association. Includes articles by various Bloomsbury figures, including Virginia Woolf, Desmond MacCarthy, and Edith Sitwell.

20   GERSH, GABRIEL. "The Letters of Roger Fry." *Art Journal* 32, no. 3 (Spring):350-52.
    Review of *The Letters of Roger Fry*, edited by Denys Sutton (1972.11). Gives overview of Fry's life, including some commentary on the Post-impressionist exhibitions and the Omega Workshops.

21   GRINDEA, MIRON. "Only on K.M.?--notes and footnotes to a biography." *Adam International Review* 38:2-18.
    Introduction by the editor to a special issue of *Adam* on Katherine Mansfield, which describes the relationship between Virginia Woolf and Mansfield, as well as the Garsington world of Lady Ottoline Morrell.

22   GUIGET, JEAN. "La biographie de Virginia Woolf par Quentin Bell." *Études Anglaises* 26:331-37.
    Commentary on Quentin Bell's biographical study of Virginia Woolf. Feels that more could be done.

23   HAIGHT, GORDON S. "Virginia Woolf." *Yale Review* 62 (Spring):426-31.
    Review of *Virginia Woolf: A Biography,* by Quentin Bell and *Reflections on Virginia Woolf*, edited by Joan Russell Noble. Gives overview of the Bloomsbury Group, using Virginia Woolf as center of focus: "Thoby's sisters fitted easily into their pattern of conversation, in which complete candor was the rule."

24 HANQUART, EVELYNE. "Humanisme féministe ou humanisme au féminin: Une lecture de l'oeuvre romanesque de Virginia Woolf et E.M. Forster." *Études Anglaises* 26:278-89.

Comparative study of the humanistic qualities of Virginia Woolf's and E.M. Forster's fiction. Deals with the common ground of their Bloomsbury experience and association.

25 HARDWICK, ELIZABETH. "Bloomsbury and Virginia Woolf." *New York Review of Books* (8 February):15-18.

Review of Quentin Bell's *Virginia Woolf: A Biography* and *Lytton Strachey: The Really Interesting Question and Other Papers*, edited by Paul Levy. Slightly revised and reprinted in *Seduction and Betrayal: Women and Literature*. (See 1974.13.)

26 HEILBRUN, CAROLYN G. "The Bloomsbury Group." In *Toward a Recognition of Androgyny*. New York: Alfred Knopf, pp. 115-67.

"I write of Bloomsbury not as the apotheosis of the androgynous spirit, but as the first actual example of such a way of life in practice." Two things made Bloomsbury unique: "It produced more works of importance than did any similar group of friends" and "it was androgynous." "Masculinity and femininity were marvelously mixed in its members." Comments on the Group's opposition to jealousy: "The fusion within the Bloomsbury group, perhaps for the first time, of 'masculinity' and femininity' made possible the ascendancy of reason which excludes violence but not passion." Evaluates some Bloomsbury work, especially Lytton Strachey's and Virginia Woolf's, in relation to androgyny.

27 HEINE, ELIZABETH. "The Significance of Structure in the Novels of E.M. Forster and Virginia Woolf." *English Literature in Transition* 16, 4:289-306.

Deals with Woolf's and Forster's practice of "implementing the Bloomsbury idea of 'significant form' in their novels" in relation to current structuralist theory, particularly that of Levi-Strauss: "The basic question about why form is significant seems to be answered similarly by both Bloomsbury and modern science. That is, the answer depends on the person who is questioning and his own preference in the matter."

28   HENIG, SUZANNE. Review of *Portrait of a Marriage*, by Nigel
      Nicolson. *Virginia Woolf Quarterly* 1, no. 4 (Summer):90-91.
          "This is the most amazing book to be written about members of
      Bloomsbury or their friends which has come out in recent years--and
      the most truthful and honest one."

29   _____. Review of *Virginia Woolf: A Biography*, by Quentin Bell.
      Virginia Woolf Quarterly 1, no. 2 (Winter):55-69.
          Negative review, listing eighteen specific weaknesses or
      omissions. Bell lacked "the most obvious qualifications for such an
      important undertaking: a thorough knowledge, familiarity with and love
      of literature; objective distance; knowledge of research and scholarly
      principles and techniques, or even any formal academic training."
      Leonard Woolf emerges as the true hero of the book. "The scholarly
      biography is yet to be written."

30   _____. "Ulysses in Bloomsbury." *James Joyce Quarterly* 10:203-8.
          Gives history of the Woolf's consideration of *Ulysses* for
      publication by the Hogarth Press. Evaluates Virginia Woolf's hostility
      to Joyce's work, focusing, in part, on her aversion to the sexual content:
      "Virginia Woolf's reluctance to accept *Ulysses* as a masterpiece was
      founded on a triad of emotional responses: subject matter, class
      snobbery, and personal and professional jealousy."

31   HUXLEY, JULIETTE. "Ottoline." *Adam International Review*
      38:92-93.
          Personal account of Morrell and Garsington: "While at
      Garsington, I was privileged to meet many people of note, for the
      house was always full at weekends, and several friends stayed for weeks
      at a time, such as Bertrand Russell, Lytton Strachey, Mark Gertler,
      Dorothy Brett, and many others." States that "the Bloomsbury set
      thrived on being funny at everyone's expense."

32   McDOWELL, FREDERICK P.W. "E.M. Forster and Goldsworthy
      Lowes Dickinson." *Studies in the Novel* 5, no. 4 (Winter):441-56.
          Discusses the influence on Forster of Dickinson based upon
      Forster's *Goldsworthy Lowes Dickinson* and *The Autobiography of G.
      Lowes Dickinson*: "*Goldsworthy Lowes Dickinson* is, ultimately, more
      significant for what it reveals about Forster than for what it tells us
      about Dickinson. Yet the latter aspects of the book is important, since
      Dickinson was formative upon those who were to make up

Bloomsbury." Involves some discussion of other Bloomsbury figures, including Keynes and Virginia Woolf.

33   McLAURIN, ALLEN. *Virginia Woolf: The Echoes Enslaved*. New York: Cambridge University Press, 232 pp.
        Part I, "Roger Fry and Virginia Woolf" (pp. 17-94), does not deal as much with similarity between Fry's theories and Woolf's technique. Deals rather with "common problems," particularly the idea of representation or the connection between art and life, which will allow comparison to other writers and aestheticism. Discusses Woolf's work in relation to such issues as "verisimilitude and illusion," "sensation in language and art," "autonomy," "craftsmanship," "colour," and "space."

34   MANTZ, RUTH. "In Consequence: Katherine and Kot." *Adam International Review* 38:95-107.
        Biographical account of the association of Katherine Mansfield and Koteliansky, including connections with some Bloomsbury figures, particularly Dorothy Brett, in whose flat Mansfield resided.

35   MAY, DERWENT. "'Christ or a Saucepan': The Baleful Indifference of Roger Fry." *Encounter* 40 (February):55-59.
        Review of *The Letters of Roger Fry*, edited by Denys Sutton (1972.11). The period during which Fry organized the two Post-impressionist exhibitions "represent the high point of his work as a critic." From 1913 on his criticism becomes reckless, "reckless in the sense, at any rate, that his criticism henceforth does not pay the same close attention to paintings as it had done previously."

36   MEYERS, JEFFREY. "D.H. Lawrence and Homosexuality." *London Magazine* 13, no. 4 (October-November):68-98.
        Discussion of Lawrence's attitude toward homosexuality, which includes some of his associations with Bloomsbury figures, including Maynard Keynes, Duncan Grant, and Francis Birrell.

37   ____. Review of *Mark Gertler* by John Woodeson. *Virginia Woolf Quarterly* 1, no. 3 (Spring):80-84.
        Comments on the Carrington-Strachey relationship: "Both Carrington and Strachey wished she were a boy." Finds little new in this biography.

38   MORPHET, RICHARD. "The Art of Vanessa Bell." In *Vanessa
      Bell: Paintings and Drawings*. Exhibition Catalog. London: Anthony
      d'Offay Gallery, pp. 2-7.
          Describes Bell's association with Duncan Grant and Roger Fry.

39   _____. "Bloomsbury Portraits." *Studio International* 193 (January-
      February):68-70.
          Review of Richard Shone's *Bloomsbury Portraits*: "Bloomsbury
      artists were pioneers in a 20th-century willingness to look at what was
      actually there in a picture, and--rather than conforming to society's
      prejudiced, restricted mode of vision--to be open to the emotions it
      expressed. This attitude was apparent in their determination as artists
      to express directly in their paintings the truth of their own perceptions
      and emotions, whatever these might be."

40   NAREMORE, JAMES. *The World Without Self: Virginia Woolf and
      the Novel*. New Haven and London: Yale University Press, 259 pp.
          Includes some commentary on the influence of the Bloomsbury
      world on Virginia Woolf and her sense of self.

41   NICHOLSON, NIGEL. *Portrait of a Marriage*. London:
      Weidenfeld & Nicolson; New York: Athenaeum, 235 pp.
          Vita Sackville-West's autobiography with commentary by Nigel
      Nicolson. Parts I and III are Vita's autobiography; parts II and IV are
      commentaries on the autobiography. Part V contains a justification for
      the book and an evaluation of Vita's love affairs with Geoffry Scott and
      Virginia Woolf, who she first met in 1922. At one point Vita wrote to
      Harold about Virginia: "I think she is one of the most mentally
      exciting people I know. She hates the wishywashiness of Bloomsbury
      young men."

42   OZICK, CYNTHIA. "Mrs. Virginia Woolf." *Commentary* 56, no.
      2:33-34.
          Comments and questions about Virginia Woolf's life, occasioned
      by Bell's biography.

43   PARSONS, TREKKIE. "Virginia Woolf's Last Letters." *Times
      Literary Supplement* (London) (13 July):808.
          States that she has deposited in the British Library Woolf's last
      three letters, two to Leonard Woolf and one to Vanessa Bell, written

before her death. The opposite page shows one of the last letters with comments written by Leonard.

44   RICHARDS, CHRIS. "The Aesthetic Theories of Roger Fry, Clive Bell, and Susanne Langer: Some Comparisons." *Virginia Woolf Quarterly* 1, no. 3 (Spring):22-31.
       Each figure endeavors "to account for the response the work of art provokes in the person disposed to contemplate it." Discusses Fry's critical method in *Last Lectures* and Bell's concept of "significant form."

45   SPATER, GEORGE A. "The Monks House Library." *Virginia Woolf Quarterly* 1, no. 3 (Spring):60-65.
       Deals with books in Monks house, some of which have been sold. Identifies books that relate to Bloomsbury. Reprinted from *American Book Collector* 21, no. 4 (1971):18-20.

46   SPENCE, KEITH. "Country Refuge from Bloomsbury: Lord's Wood, Marlow." *Country Life* 154 (15 November):1579-84.
       Bloomsbury figures, in spite of their urbane image, had links with the countryside: "Another retreat, Bloomsbury mire by association than direct contact, was Lord's Wood, high on the beech-covered hills north of Marlow, in Buckinghamshire," built by Mary Sargant-Florence. Her studio provided "the most tangible links between Lord's Wood and the Bloomsbury Group, or to be more precise between Lord's Wood and Lytton Strachey." Her daughter, Alix, married James Strachey, Lytton's younger brother. Describes these relationships and the contents of the home.

47   SPENDER, STEPHEN. "A Certificate of Sanity." *London Magazine* 12, no. 6 (February-March):137-40.
       Review of Quentin Bell's *Virginia Woolf: A Biography*. Quentin handles the complex and personal relationship with Virginia Woolf well, "a triumph of detachment." The biography is "remarkably civilized" and "coming so much out of the heart of things, that it should be so is high testimony to the group, from which he himself derives, which Quentin unhesitatingly calls Bloomsbury (a name his aunt did not at all like, by the way. Once reading something of mine in which I used it she threatened to call William Plomer and me, then close neighbors in that part of London, 'Maida Vale')." Bloomsbury figures "had a genuine passion for civilization even if they had a rather narrow view of it." Bloomsbury "was in part the soil which Virginia Woolf required in

order that she might flower, above all because it centered on a cult of friendship and 'personal relations.'" Woolf also shared some of the faults of Bloomsbury, "snobbishness and gentility, and what Wyndham Lewis unkindly described as a way of 'peeping at life.'"

48   STEVENS, MICHAEL. *V. Sackville-West: A Critical Biography*.
      London: Uppsala; New York: Scribners, 192 pp.
          Evaluates the life and work of Vita Sackville-West, with
      references to her association with Virginia Woolf and other Bloomsbury
      figures. Primary focus is the work.

49   STRACHEY, LYTTON. *The Really Interesting Question and Other
      Papers*. Edited with introduction by Paul Levy. London:
      Weidenfeld & Nicolson; New York: Coward, McCann &
      Geoghegan, 177 pp.
          Includes correspondence, articles, and commentaries not
      published during Strachey's lifetime, which include references to
      Bloomsbury figures. Levy's introduction describes Strachey's years in
      the Cambridge Apostles and G.E. Moore's influence: "To the
      Apostolic mind anything, even behavior condemned by most of the
      world, was a fit subject for serious consideration, dignified discussion,
      and the exercise of humor."

50   TRAUTMANN, JOANNE. *The Jessamy Brides: The Friendship of
      Virginia Woolf and V. Sackville-West*. University Park: Pennsylvania
      State University Press, 57 pp.
          A detailed study of the evolution of the friendship between Vita
      Sackville-West and Virginia Woolf which tells "us a great deal about
      Virginia Woolf, about attraction--particularly between women--about the
      relationship of literary friendships to creativity, and about the
      culmination of this particular friendship in *Orlando*." Looks at Virginia
      Woolf and the Bloomsbury world, as well as its background, in 1922,
      when she and Vita first met.

1974

1   ALEXANDER, JEAN. *The Venture of Form in the Novels of
     Virginia Woolf*. Port Washington, N. Y.: Kennikat Press, 237 pp.
         The introduction questions studies that deal with Bloomsbury
     and particular intellectual influences, such as her Cambridge friends

and G.E. Moore's philosophy. We need to refocus studies of Woolf's
work: "Biography, personality, and milieu have been studiously avoided
in the following chapters because I believe these factors have proved
misleading as a guide to Virginia Woolf's fiction."

2   BELL, QUENTIN. "Art and the Elite." *Critical Inquiry* 1, no. 1
     (September):33-46.
     Historical account of the relationship between art and the social
or intellectual elite which includes a section on Roger Fry and the first
Post-impressionist exhibition: "Roger Fry is surely right when he
suggests that the elitist game is played rather with the cultural
framework around the picture than with the picture itself."

3   _____. "Letter to the Editor." *Twentieth Century Literature* 20, no. 4
     (October):241.
     Offers corrections to Ellen Hawkes Rogat's review of his
biography of Virginia Woolf, especially the comments about Clive Bell's
intellectual development.

4   BELL, VANESSA. *Notes on Virginia's Childhood.* Edited by
     Richard J. Schaubeck, Jr. New York: Frank Hallman, 10 pp.
     Memoir by Vanessa about their childhood. "I cannot remember
a time when Virginia did not want to be a writer and I a painter."
Limited edition, 300 copies.

5   BERGONZI, BERNARD. "Who Are You?" *New Review*
     (November):50-54.
     Negative evaluation of the Bloomsbury Group, with an overview
of recent scholarship. Deals with the mystique that surrounded this
group and with the various figures who were members, such as Lady
Ottoline Morrell. "Bloomsbury was not in fact a powerful creative
source, whatever the talents of its individual members." Ford Madox
Ford and Ezra Pound were the significant figures of this period.
"Virginia Woolf is the one Bloomsbury figure who now looks like a
major modern writer." Reprinted as "The Bloomsbury Pastoral" in *The
Myth of Modernism and Twentieth Century Literature.* (See 1986.3.)

6   CONKLIN, ANNA M. "Historical and Sociocultural Elements in the
     Novels of Virginia Woolf." Ph.D. dissertation, University of North
     Carolina at Chapel Hill, 150 pp.
     "Factual substrata" on which Woolf's works are based need to be

explored. Have already dealt extensively with "life at its source." "The hidden life of personality, after all, interacts with an external world of fact which has been conditioned by history and is therefore modified by powerful social forces which Virginia Woolf, living in the atmosphere of Bloomsbury, could not fail to take into account." See *Dissertation Abstracts International* 35:3730A.

7   CORK, RICHARD. Introduction to *Vorticism and Its Allies*.
      Exhibition Catalog. London: Arts Council; Hayward Gallery, pp. 5-
      26
          Deals with Bloomsbury in relation to Wyndham Lewis and
Vorticism. In the early days of the twentieth century, Lewis and others
"looked as if they would be happy to identify themselves with the
Bloomsbury contingent." Also describes Lewis in relation to Omega
Workshops. "The Fitzroy Square honeymoon did not last long,
however. A personal antipathy between Fry and Lewis, which had
already shown itself on previous occasions, erupted into outright conflict
when Spencer Gore discovered that Fry had stolen a *Daily Mail*
commission to design a 'Post-Impressionist Room' at the October 1913
Ideal Home Exhibition."

8   CRICHTON, FENELLA. "London Letter." *Art International* 18
      (January):14-17, 25.
          Includes commentary on Vanessa Bell, whose paintings are on
display at the Anthony d'Offay Gallery, as one of the central members
of Bloomsbury. Describes her association with Bell, Fry, and others.
Her paintings show more spontaneity than the concentration on formal
elements advocated by Fry.

9   _____. "London Letter." *Art International* 18 (November):37- 46.
          Describes Vanessa Bell "as one of the first artists in this country
to produce abstract art." Her association with Fry's Omega Workshops
was part of this trend.

10   GADD, DAVID. *The Loving Friends: A Portrait of Bloomsbury*.
      New York: Harcourt Brace, 210 pp.
          Admiring study of the lives rather than the works of various
Bloomsbury members: "Human beings are less available than their
works and always more complex and exciting. There is infinitely more
in Lytton Strachey than in *Eminent Victorians*, and Roger Fry's
aesthetics are dull compared with Roger Fry. This book then is

concerned with people who happen to be writers and artists rather than with the work by which they are well known." Includes separate chapters on Bloomsbury's beginnings and Cambridge, on Lady Ottoline Morrell and Dora Carrington, On Wartime Bloomsbury. Concludes with Virginia Woolf's death in 1941.

11   GARNETT, DAVID. "Friends and Friendship." *Spectator* (12
       October):467-68.
       Personalized account of the ideals of human relationships that
were central to Bloomsbury.

12   HAIGHT, GORDON S. "The Permissive Edwardians." *Yale Review*
       63, no. 3 (Spring):416-21.
       Review of Nigel Nicolson's *Portrait of a Marriage*. Vita Sackville-
West "believed that she was rebelling against such hypocrisy by
flaunting the convention that 'women should love only men, and men
only women'." Discusses mostly her relationship with Violet Trefusis,
but also comments of Virginia Woolf's involvement.

13   HARDWICK, ELIZABETH. "Bloomsbury and Virginia Woolf." In
       Seduction and Betrayal: Women and Literature. New York: Random
       House, pp. 125-39.
       Meditative evaluation of the nature of the Bloomsbury world
and of Virginia Woolf's relationship to it, including asides on Gertler,
Ottoline Morrell, Lytton Strachey, and others: "Then the force of
Bloomsbury and 'brightest things that are theirs' claimed the mind.
The wood smoke, a life still courteous and unconventional, people
handsome and malicious and serious and never boring--and as all of
this swells and inflates there is reason for gratitude and pride." Deals
briefly the sexual practices of the Group.

14   HENIG, SUZANNE. "The Bloomsbury Group and Non-Western
       Literature." *Journal of South Asian Literature* 10, no. 1:73-82.
       Deals with Bloomsbury's reaction to Oriental literature: "The
actual contribution of Bloomsbury to non-Western literature was four-
fold in origin: 1. translation of non-Western works; 2. elements of non-
Western literature found in their work; 3. publication and support of
unknown non-Western writers; and 4. the impact of Bloomsbury's
oriental interest on younger writers." Deals with Arthur Waley's
translations, and with Oriental elements in Virginia and Leonard
Woolf's, E.M. Forster's, and T.S. Eliot's work.

15   HUNGERFORD, EDWARD A. "Visiting Monks House Papers at the University of Sussex." *Virginia Woolf Miscellany* 2:5-6.
        Papers donated to the University of Sussex, some of which related to the Woolfs and Bloomsbury.

16   JONES, ENID HUWS. "Roger Fry: A Quaker Interpreter of Art." *Friends Quarterly* 18 (July):320-26.
        Deals with Fry's Quaker background, which relates to the ideals of Bloomsbury.

17   MARTIN, RICHARD. *The Love That Failed: Ideal and Reality in the Writings of E.M. Forster*. The Hague: Mouton, 231 pp.
        Chapter Two (pp. 36-45) is titled "Moore, Bloomsbury, and Personal Relations." Describes Forster's Cambridge background and the influence of G.E. Moore's ideal that "by far the most valuable things, which we know or can imagine, are certain states of consciousness, which may be roughly described as the pleasures of human intercourse and the enjoyment of beautiful objects." Considers some aspects of Forster's relation to the Bloomsbury Group: "Essentially Bloomsbury was a group of intelligent, privileged, and creative people, doing their utmost to live out Moore's ethical and aesthetic ideals in an atmosphere which was in the world without being of it. In this last respect they differ from Forster, who, while choosing to live very much in and with the world, finally finds his ideals becoming more and more unreal, more and more unrelated to the reality of experience."

18   MEYERS, JEFFREY. "The Paintings in Forster's Italian Novels." *London Magazine* 13, no. 6 (February-March):46-62.
        Discussion of Forster's use of painting in his Italian novels as a way of revealing character. Deals with the influence of Roger Fry on Forster in this context, especially in relation to *The Ascension of St. John* by Giotto: "Forster's interest in and attitude toward this painting was undoubtedly influenced by the essay on Giotto by his close friend Roger Fry, which first appeared in the *Monthly Review* of 1901."

19   MOORE, HARRY T. *The Priest of Love: A Life of D.H. Lawrence*. London: William Heinemann, 397 pp.
        Revised edition of Moore's biographical study, *The Intelligent Heart*, originally published in 1954. Includes extensive commentary on the relationship between Bertrand Russell, Lady Ottoline Morrell, and

Lawrence. Also comments on Lawrence's association with and hatred for Bloomsbury. Ottoline was living in two worlds.

20 MORRELL, LADY OTTOLINE. *Ottoline at Garsington: Memoirs 1915-1918.* Edited with introduction by Robert Garthorne-Hardy. London: Faber & Faber, 304 pp.
     Lady Ottoline Morrell's personal commentary on the parallel Bloomsbury world she created at Garsington Manor and on various Bloomsbury figures. Includes separate chapters on many figures, "Lytton Strachey," "Katherine Mansfield and Virginia Woolf in London, 1917," and "Garsington--A Beautiful Theatre. Lytton and Carrington Start Their Friendship." Garthorne-Hardy suggests in the introduction that tales about Ottoline "taken from Bloomsbury must be looked on with the doubt which a serious historian applies to old, unlikely and uncorroborated tradition."

21 MYERS, JOHN BERNARD. "Roger Fry's Letters." *Art in America* 62, no. 1 (January-February):120-21.
     Review of *Letters of Roger Fry* edited by Denys Sutton (1972.11). Faults Woolf's biography because of her lack of candor: "Candid as the Bloomsberries were about each other, not even Virginia Woolf could have plumbed further without causing embarrassment to some one or another." Feels that the results of the Omega Workshops are dreadful.

22 NICOLSON, BENDICT. "No Klimts for Newcastle." *Burlington Magazine* 116 (March):123.
     Editorial dealing with the disappointing "display of twentieth-century art in our public collections." Identifies Fry's exhibitions in 1910-1912 as "the decisive turning of the tide" of conservatism."

23 RATCLIFF, CARTER. "Art Criticism: Other Minds, Other Eyes." *Art International* 18 (September):49-54.
     Gives evaluation of art criticism from 1913-1925, using the Armory Show of 1913 as starting point: "The occasion set off a debate between two energetic teams of critics, those who could and those who could not accept the most radical new art." The two sides maintained similar assumptions about art. Includes a brief discussion of Clive Bell's concept of significant form in relation to the changing view of art: "Having broken the 'conservatives' link between significance and beauty, he goes on to finish the job: reference or description, as Bell calls it, cannot have esthetics value, and 'art is above morals.'"

24   REES, JENNY. "What's New in the Bloomsbury Industry?" *Sunday Times Magazine* (London) (3 February):58-61.
       Discusses the "Neo-Bloomsbury gossip": "The boundaries of Bloomsbury have spread, too, and the cast list expands considerably as a result." What Bloomsbury actually produced seems to have been forgotten.

25   RICHARDSON, BETTY. "Beleaguered Bloomsbury: Virginia Woolf, Her Friends, and Their Critics." *Papers on Language and Literature* 10, no. 2 (Spring):207-21.
       Review essay on many recent studies of Bloomsbury and Bloomsbury figures, all of which suggest a shift of interest in the Group: "It is not surprising that Bloomsbury, with its hatred of Bloodshed and dullness, of violence and corruption, of commercialism and machine-tooled humans, should find a new audience today; it is rather more surprising that present-day studies of Bloomsbury so often lack proportion and that so much basic scholarly work remains to be done." Sees the need for more work on Bertrand Russell and Maynard Keynes.

26   ROGAT, ELLEN HAWKES. "Letter to the Editor." *Twentieth Century Literature* 20, no. 4 (October):242.
       Response to Quentin Bell's letter above. Still questions Virginia Woolf's "complex feelings about her brother-in-law."

27   _____. "The Virgin in the Bell Biography." *Twentieth Century Literature* 20, no. 2 (April):96-113.
       Extended commentary on Quentin Bell's biography of Virginia Woolf. Woolf as woman not as writer is the central problem in the work. Involves some discussion of Woolf's Bloomsbury association and the influence of Bloomsbury ideals on her artistic development. Questions how Bell deals with the issue of Bloomsbury's sexual frankness, for example, and virginity.

28   ZYTARUK, GEORGE J. "Dorothy Brett's Letters to S.S. Koteliansky." *D.H. Lawrence Review* 7:240-74.
       Letters edited with brief introduction. Brett was the only one of Lawrence's friends who was willing to leave England to "found a little colony where there shall be no money but a sort of communism as far as necessaries of life go." Brett, who was associated with Bloomsbury and Lady Ottoline Morrell's circle, became involved with Lawrence's

circle as well, which included other Bloomsbury figures too, Mark Gertler and Dora Carrington. The letters describe various Bloomsbury figures.

1975

1 ANNAN, NOEL. "Keynes Remembered: Cambridge and Coterie." *Times Literary Supplement* (London) (2 May):469-71.
   Review of *Essays on John Maynard Keynes*, edited by Milo Keynes. Discusses the importance of Cambridge and Bloomsbury. The War placed a strain on Keynes and his friendships. Compares Bloomsbury's hatred of war and the current generation's hatred of Vietnam.

2 BELL, ALAN. "Miss Virginia and Her Friends." *Times Literary Supplement* (London) (19 September):1038-39.
   Review of *The Letters of Virginia Woolf: Volume One.* Comments on the forming of the Bloomsbury Group: "Thoby's death widened the circle of friends. Clive Bell married her sister soon afterwards, and Lytton Strachey and others of the Stephen boys' friends came more into her life."

3 BRAITHWAITE, R.B. "Keynes as Philosopher." In *Essays on John Maynard Keynes.* Edited by Milo Keynes. Cambridge: Cambridge University Press, pp. 237-46.
   Overview of Keynes's philosophic thought, including a discussion of G.E. Moore's influence: "G.E. Moore's *Principia Ethica* (1903) appeared at the end of Keynes's first undergraduate year at Cambridge, and was received as the new gospel by him and his circle of friends." Evaluates this influence in relation to Keynes's "My Early Beliefs."

4 BRENAN, GERALD. *Personal Record, 1920-1972.* New York: Alfred A. Knopf; London: Jonathan Cape, 381 pp.
   Memoir that includes commentary on Bloomsbury friends.

5 BROWN, DAVID. Introduction to *Duncan Grant: A 90th Birthday Exhibition of Paintings.* Exhibition Catalog. Edinburgh: Scottish National Gallery of Modern Art, pp v-vii.
   Brief introduction to the life and work of Grant. Stayed with his uncle and aunt in London, one of whose children was Lytton Strachey:

"Strachey later shared with Grant a circle of friends including Vanessa Bell, Virginia and Leonard Woolf, Clive Bell, Maynard Keynes, Roger Fry and others." Style change during the years 1910-1914 under the influence of Russian Ballet and the two Post-impressionist exhibitions. Describes progress toward abstract art.

6   BUCKLE, RICHARD. "On Loving Lydia." In *Essays on John Maynard Keynes*. Edited by Milo Keynes. Cambridge: Cambridge University Press, pp. 49-59.
        Bloomsbury missed the point over Lydia Lopokova. Describes adverse responses to Lydia by Vanessa Bell, Virginia Woolf, and others. Includes letters from Lydia to Buckle.

7   BYWATER, WILLIAM G., JR. *Clive Bell's Eye*. Detroit: Wayne State University Press, 249 pp.
        Critical study that includes some comparison of Clive Bell and Roger Fry. Includes "A Checklist of the Published Writings of Clive Bell," by Donald A. Laing.

8   CARRINGTON, NOEL. "Decorative Artists of the Twenties: Dora Carrington." *Country Life* 158 (17 July):157-58.
        Commentary on Carrington, with references to her relationship with Lytton Strachey and the Bloomsbury Group in general.

9   CLARK, RONALD W. *The Life of Bertrand Russell*. London: Jonathan Cape. Reprint. New York: Alfred A. Knopf, 1976, 766 pp.
        Biographical study of Bertrand Russell, with two chapters that relate to Bloomsbury associations, Chapter 6, "Ottoline" (pp. 129-65), and Chapter 8 "Ottoline: Ebbing Tide" (pp. 199-224). Discusses early meetings with Keynes and Lytton Strachey at Cambridge and the developing relationship between Lady Ottoline Morrell and Russell: What had started as primarily an emotional relationship rapidly developed into a complementary intellectual partnership in which Russell poured out his hopes and plans and philosophical ambitions without inhibition." Also describes Russell's agnosticism in relation to Ottoline's influence: "But she was nevertheless beginning to sap the high wall of agnosticism with which he had surrounded himself." Various incidents at Garsington Manor are recounted in Chapter 8: "Russell, like many others, almost made Garsington his second home."

10   COLMER, JOHN. *E.M. Forster: The Personal Voice.* London and
      Boston: Routledge & Kegan Paul, 243 pp.
      Forster saw himself in relation to tradition. Looks at the
synthesis between Forster's life and his work. Stresses the limited
connection between Forster and Bloomsbury; he moved "on the
periphery" only, and after 1916 "the gulf between his Bloomsbury
friends and himself widened and he felt that he couldn't go there for
any sort of comfort and sympathy."

11   DARROCH, SANDRA JOBSON. *Ottoline: The Life of Lady
      Ottoline Morrell.* New York: Coward, McCann & Geoghegan, 317
      pp.
      Describes her life in Bedford Square and Garsington, which
relate directly to her Bloomsbury association. Virginia Woolf met
Ottoline in 1909: "Though Ottoline has been described as 'the
patroness of Bloomsbury' and the 'high priestess of Bloomsbury,' she
was never remotely near to being a member of the group. Her
relationship with its members fluctuated, and was deeper with some
(particularly Lytton, Virginia, and, for a time, Clive Bell) than others."

12   DELANY, PAUL. "Lawrence and E.M. Forster: Two Rainbows."
      D.H. Lawrence Review 8, no. 1 (Spring):54-62.
      Discussion of visual works that relate to D.H. Lawrence's novel,
The Rainbow, including Post-impressionist designs by Roger Fry that
appeared on E.M. Forster's work *The Celestial Omnibus*: "The front
and rear endpapers . . . are decorated with a design by Roger Fry that
is obviously similar in composition to Lawrence's rainbow drawing."

13   DONNELL, CAROL A. "The Problem of Representation and
      Expressionism in Post-Impressionist Art." *British Journal of Aesthetics*
      16, no. 3 (Summer):226-38.
      Includes a discussion of Roger Fry and Clive Bell in relations to
Post-impressionism in England.

14   EDER, DORIS. "Bloomsbury Revisited." *Book Forum* 1
      November):528-38.
      Review of *The Bloomsbury Group: A Collection of Memoirs,
Commentary, and Criticism* edited by S.P. Rosenbaum: "We have what
may be the definitive sourcebook for the study of Bloomsbury."
Concludes that "after threading his way through a labyrinth of differing
opinions, the reader . . . emerges with the conviction that Bloomsbury

existed all right, that indeed it dominated English literary life from the
teens through the thirties, and that it is eminently worth study."
Wonders "just how rational was Bloomsbury?"

15   EHRENPREIS, IRVIN. "Bloomsbury Variations." *New York Review
      of Books* (17 April):9-12.
         Review of S.P. Rosenbaum's anthology, *The Bloomsbury Group*,
      David Gadd's *The Loving Friends*, and Gerald Brenan's *Personal Record,
      1920-72*. Offers some basic definitions of Bloomsbury's character,
      including rationalism, honesty, and the pursuit of truth, much of which
      is related to G.E. Moore's thought: "Large doses of reality can only be
      compounded in an air of extreme tolerance; and this of course is
      quintessentially the atmosphere of Bloomsbury."

16   FRACKMAN, NOEL. "Duncan Grant." *Arts Magazine* 49 (June):5.
         Review of Grant exhibition at the Davis and Long Galleries:
      "An original member of the Bloomsbury Group, that witty, sometimes
      outrageous cluster of intellectuals who enriched the London scene for
      several decades before, during, and after the First World War, Duncan
      Grant conveys through his art the liveliness that must have animated
      the group as a whole."

17   GARNETT, DAVID. "Maynard Keynes as Biographer." In *Essays
      on John Maynard Keynes*. Edited by Milo Keynes. Cambridge:
      Cambridge University Press, pp. 254-59.
         Commentary by second generation Bloomsbury figure.

18   "Grantsmanship." *Apollo* 102 (July):71.
         Brief mention of Duncan Grant exhibition at the Davis and
      Long Gallery in New York City: "Keynes is a household word over
      here, while you'd never know there was a painter in Bloomsbury."

19   HOLROYD, MICHAEL. "Virginia Woolf and Her World." *Horizon*
      17, no. 3 (Summer):48-57.
         Looks at the world of which Woolf was a part, including
      Bloomsbury.

20   KEYNES, MILO. "Maynard and Lydia Keynes." In *Essays on John
      Maynard Keynes*. Edited by Milo Keynes. Cambridge: Cambridge
      University Press, pp. 1-8.
         Personal account by Keynes's nephew describing family meetings

with Lydia and Maynard Keynes. Briefly discusses Lydia's background. Relies on quotations from Bloomsbury figures who knew Keynes, including Clive Bell, E.M. Forster. Lydia had some difficulty fitting in with the Bloomsbury Group: "Bloomsbury, however, early discovered her gaiety and infectious laughter."

21 LEHMANN, JOHN. *Virginia Woolf and Her World*. New York: Harcourt Brace Jovanovich; London: Thames & Hudson, 128 pp.
       Deals with Bloomsbury figures in relation to Woolf and her world. Brief account, but by one who was involved in the group and managed the Hogarth Press for a number of years. Gives history of Hogarth Press and its various managers. Includes various photographs and illustrations.

22 LEVY, PAUL. "The Bloomsbury Group." In *Essays on John Maynard Keynes*. Edited by Milo Keynes. Cambridge: Cambridge University Press, pp. 60-72.
       Overview of the Bloomsbury Group, using Keynes as the focus. Begins with one of the meetings of the Memoir Club at Keynes's house in Sussex in 1938. Looks back at the development of the Group from its Cambridge origins in the Apostles. Discusses the "higher sodomy" issue of this period and Keynes's various relationships, including his association with the "neo-pagans." During the war Bloomsbury "thought more often of Goethe and Bach than of Kizer Bill." Deals also with those who were conscientious objectors during the war. Concludes with Keynes's marriage to Lydia Lopokova: "His Bloomsbury friends adored her as a party guest but had doubts about whether a prima ballerina could possibly also have a suitable mind."

23 LUKE, PETER. *Bloomsbury*. New York: Alfred A. Knopf, 176 pp.
       Play, mostly about Strachey and Dora Carrington. Other figures from Bloomsbury come in throughout. Inaccurate representation.

24 MAJUMDAR, ROBIN, and ALLEN McLAURIN, eds. *Virginia Woolf: The Critical Heritage*. London and Boston: Routledge & Kegan Paul, 467 pp.
       Includes extracts from articles and reviews about Virginia Woolf's work, many of which relate her both positively and negatively to Bloomsbury aesthetics. Most of the relevant articles are also listed in this research guide. The editors give an extensive review of Woolf's critical reception for each work, as well as a general review of her

reception in France. Their introduction (pp. 1-46) includes a discussion of her association with Bloomsbury: "She gave much to, and gained a great deal from members of this group, especially Lytton Strachey and Roger Fry, whose researches, respectively into biography and the visual arts, were paralleled by her experiments in fiction." Her association with the group has to be taken into account in assessing the critical reception of her work.

25   MARGETTS, MARTINA. "Duncan Grant." *Connoisseur* 188 (April):321.
    Review of two Duncan Grant exhibitions, "Duncan Grant: Recent Paintings" at Anthony d'Offay Gallery and "Duncan Grant" at the Tate Gallery: "By relationship and inclination, Duncan Grant belongs to the socially and intellectually elitist Bloomsbury group, whose spirit of independent inquiry and self-criticism nurtured Grant's style and subject matter." Relates him to Fry and the Post-impressionist painters.

26   MORPHET, RICHARD. "Notes." In *Duncan Grant: Ninetieth Birthday Display*. Exhibition Catalog. London: Tate Gallery, pp 12-26.
    Includes some commentary on Grant's art in relation to Bloomsbury, Roger Fry, and Vanessa Bell.

27   MORRELL, LADY OTTOLINE. "K.M." In *Katherine Mansfield: An Exhibition*. Austin: Humanities Research Center, University of Texas at Austin, pp. 8-15.
    Memoir that describes Mansfield in relation to the Bloomsbury world of which Morrell and others were a part. Exhibition catalog includes descriptions of items, letters in particular, that related to the relationship between Mansfield and Ottoline.

28   PROCTOR, DENNIS. "Keynes Remembered: The Essential Values." *Times Literary Supplement* (London) (2 May):472.
    Mentions the importance to Keynes of Bloomsbury and his Bloomsbury friends.

29   ROBINSON, AUSTIN. "A Personal View." In *Essays on John Maynard Keynes*. Edited by Milo Keynes. Cambridge: Cambridge University Press, pp. 9-23.
    Robinson is pleased that this collection is considering Keynes as

more than an economist: "What sort of a person was he, this versatile polymath, this academic who was through his adult life a man of action, this intimate both of 'Bloomsbury' and of those that inhabited the corridors of power." Bloomsbury "clearly changed all his thinking." Also suggests that Keynes moved away from Bllomsbury in later years in part because of the lack of acceptance of Lydia and partly because he had moved into other worlds.

30   ROSENBAUM, S.P., ed. *The Bloomsbury Group: A Collection of Memoirs, Commentary and Criticism*. Toronto: University of Toronto Press, pp. 444.

Anthology of material about the Bloomsbury Group divided into four sections: "Bloomsbury on Bloomsbury," which "contains the basic memoirs and discussions of the Group itself by twelve of its original members," "Bloomsberries," a term coined by Molly MacCarthy, which includes "a series of essays on ten members of Bloomsbury and their importance in the Group," "Bloomsbury Observed," which "contains reminiscences of the Group by their contemporaries," and "Bloomsbury Criticism and Controversies," which contains "selections from the most influential, articulate, or representative critics of Bloomsbury, along with some rejoinders from the Group." The "Foreword" states that the volume is based upon two assumptions: the Bloomsbury Group existed and the Bloomsbury Group is worth serious study. Each section and essay is preceded by introductory material. Also includes "A Bloomsbury Chronology," "Bibliographies," and "Identifications," which gives important people and places mentioned in the text. Several items are published here for the first time. "Saxon Sydney-Turner: Towards a Descriptive Definition of Bloomsbury," an extract from a letter to Virginia Woolf in 1919, questions whether Oliver Strachey and Barbara Hiles Bagenal should be considered members and suggests how Bloomsbury came about. "Vanessa Bell: Notes on Bloomsbury" states that Bloomsbury ceased to exist with the First World War. Rosenbaum also includes an exchange between George Bernard Shaw, Clive Bell, and Desmond MacCarthy which relates to the Bloomsbury aesthetic but does not directly refer to Bloomsbury. All other items reprinted in this anthology are listed in this research guide.

31   RUOTOLO, LUCIO P. "Living in Monks House." *Virginia Woolf Miscellany* 4:1-2.

Personal account of the world of Monks house, which became one of the country homes of Bloomsbury.

32   RUSSELL, BERTRAND. *The Autobiography of Bertrand Russell*.
      London: Unwin Books, 751 pp.
          Single volume edition of Russell's autobiography. Includes
      extensive commentary of his relationship with Lady Ottoline Morrell
      and other Bloomsbury figures, especially during the years of World War
      I: "I underwent a process of rejuvenation, inaugurated by Ottoline
      Morrell and continued by the War."

33   RYLAND, GEORGE. "The Kingsman." In *Essays on John Maynard
      Keynes*. Edited by Milo Keynes. Cambridge: Cambridge University
      Press, pp. 39-48.
          Deals with the importance of the Cambridge experience to
      Keynes, including his association with the Apostles, which was part of
      the origin of Bloomsbury.

34   SHONE, RICHARD. "Duncan Grant." *Burlington Magazine* 117
      (March):186.
          Review of Duncan Grant exhibition at the Tate Gallery: "His
      association with Bloomsbury has been more hindrance than help."
      Describes paintings that show his early "determination to master a
      traditional manner of painting." Most of the paintings shown date from
      the 1910-1920 period.

35   _____. "Friday Club." *Burlington Magazine* 117 (May):279-84.
          Gives history of "The Friday Club," which was founded by
      Vanessa Bell, including the dates of the various exhibitions: "It has
      usually been seen as a Bloomsbury-oriented club but with such
      members as John Nash, Derwent Lees, and Wadsworth on its hanging
      committee, its scope was wider than has generally been admitted." The
      1910 "Friday Club" exhibition "showed work that was cognizant of
      recent French painting." In 1913 the Bloomsbury painters left the
      "Friday Club" to form "The Grafton Group."

36   _____. Introduction to *Duncan Grant and Bloomsbury*. Exhibition
      Catalog. Edinburgh: Fine Art Society, pp. 1-3.
          Includes commentary on Duncan Grant's relationship with
      Bloomsbury, especially with Vanessa Bell and Roger Fry.

37   SHONE, RICHARD, and DUNCAN GRANT. "The Picture
     Collector." In *Essays on John Maynard Keynes*. Edited by Milo
     Keynes, pp. 280-89.
        Deals with the friendship of Keynes and Duncan Grant, which
     contributed to Keynes's interest in modern French and English
     paintings: "Until Keynes's marriage to Lydia Lopokova in 1925, Duncan
     and Vanessa Bell were his closest friends in London, his chief
     confidants and the 'keepers of his conscience.'" Describes the start of
     his collecting during World War I, in conjunction with acquiring
     paintings for the National Gallery, and several items in his collection.
     Concludes with a list of the more important paintings in the Keynes
     collection.

38   TAIT, KATHARINE. *My Father Bertrand Russell.* New York and
     London: Harcourt Brace Jovanovich, 211 pp.
        Deals briefly with Russell's relationship with Lady Ottoline
     Morrell (pp. 42-46, 154): "She was glamourous, exotic, aristocratic,
     artistic, everything that Quaker Alys was not, and he had known her
     slightly, disapprovingly, for many years." States that he was in awe of
     Ottoline.

39   TRAUTMANN, JOANNE. "The Story of the Woolf Letters."
     Virginia Woolf Miscellany 3:1-2.
        Alludes to aspects of Woolf's life that relate to Bloomsbury.

40   VAIZEY, MARINA. "London." *Artnews* 74 (March):82-88.
        General review of London galleries, including commentary on
     Duncan Grant exhibition at the Tate, an exhibition of drawings at the
     Southover Gallery in Lewes, near Charleston, and two exhibitions
     following one another at Anthony d'Offay's.

41   WOOLF, VIRGINIA. *The Flight of The Mind: The Letters of
     Virginia Woolf,* Vol 1, *1882-1912.* Edited by Nigel Nicolson and
     Joanne Trautmann. London: Hogarth Press. New York: Harcourt
     Brace Jovanovich, 531 pp.
        Introduction by Nigel Nicolson. These early letters include many
     to Vanessa after she married Clive Bell, others to Clive Bell and to
     Lytton Strachey. Some have direct references to Bloomsbury. At this
     point she finds some of the group a great trial: "Oh, women are my
     line and not these inanimate creatures." There are various references
     to "Thursday Evenings" and Vanessa's "Friday Club." Nicolson states in

his introduction that many readers will be surprised "to find how slowly she discovered her lifelong friends among Thoby's, how indifferent she remained for several years to the Bloomsbury style of living and talking."

42 WORKMAN, GILLIAN. "Leonard Woolf and Imperialism." *Ariel* 6, no. 2: 5-21.
   Discussion of Leonard Woolf's views on imperialism based upon his experiences in the foriegn service and his writings. Relates somewhat to his Bloomsbury associations and to his Cambridge background.

43 ZWENDLING, ALEX. "Virginia Woolf in and out of Bloomsbury." *Sawanee Review* 83 (Summer):510-23.
   Commentary on the current interest in Bloomsbury and Bloomsbury figures, discussing many recent studies: "There is, I think, one additional reason for the current interest in Bloomsbury--the feeling of nostalgia for a world in which culture still seemed coherent rather than hopelessly fragmented, in which the present was fed by the past, and in which a group of intimate friends could discuss books, paintings, and ideas without posing as authorities or parading their expertise."

1976

1 BELL, ALAN. "Bare-Foot into the Past." *Times Literary Supplement* (London) (4 June):677.
   Review of *Virginia Woolf: Moments of Being,* edited by Jeanne Schulkind. Suggests that this work adds to the Virginia Woolf canon, rather than to the bulk of recent Bloomsbury literature, which concentrates on biographical detail in a way that prevents adequate attention to the literary works.

2 BELL, MILLICENT. "Portrait of the Artist as Young Woman." *Virginia Quarterly Review* 52:670-86.
   Includes commentary on Woolf's artistic development in realtion to Bloomsbury.

3   BELL, QUENTIN. Introduction to *Word and Image VII: The Bloomsbury Group*. Exhibition Catalog. London: National Book League and The Hogarth Press, pp. 5-7.

What is being offered is not the familiar territory of Bloomsbury. It was in "1910 that Bloomsbury really opened its eyes." Cézanne had replaced G.E. Moore as major intellectual force in the group. Comments on selection criteria in exhibition: "On the one hand I have tried to show by means of images the sudden and dramatic aesthetic redirection of which Bloomsbury was one of the chief agents, the change from the world of Watts to that of Post-impressionism. . . . Secondly I have tried to draw attention to what may perhaps be considered the type of Bloomsbury, the point at which the visual aesthetic of the group meets that literary from through which it is most commonly approached." Catalog is divided into ten sections: "Victorian Origins," "Cambridge," "Duncan Grant and Vanessa Bell," "Adrian Stephen," "Clive Bell," "Lytton Strachey," "John Maynard Keynes and Lydia Keynes," "Leonard and Virginia Woolf, the Hogarth Press," "Saxon Sydney-Turner, E.M. Forster and Others," "Roger Fry."

4   BRINK, ANDREW. "Russell to Lady Ottoline Morrell: The Letters of Transformation." *Russell* 21-22 (Spring-Summer):3-15.

Article dealing with the influence of relationship with Lady Ottoline Morrell on Russell's development: "As documentation the letters make credible Russell's change from brilliant but limited mathematical logician into the fuller human being he became." The letters between these two figures are used "mainly as accomplishments in a literary form of which Russell became a master, a form for long a an important branch of literature." Shows Ottoline's interest in visual arts and Russell's response: "Though no aesthete (never responding to Roger Fry's call to a new visual aestheticism), Russell was surprisingly amenable to Ottoline's prescription for his soul's growth through the arts."

5   CALLOW, STEVEN D. "A Biographical Sketch of Lady Anne Thackeray Ritchie." *Virginia Woolf Quarterly* 2, nos. 3-4 (Summer-Fall):258-93.

Traces the significant events in the life of Anne Thackeray Ritchie, daughter of William Thackeray, from her birth in 1837 to her death in 1919. Of interest to Bloomsbury is the description of Anne's friendship with Leslie Stephen after the death of his first wife, Anne's sister Harriet Thackeray Stephen.

6   CORK, RICHARD. *Vorticism and Abstract Art in the First Machine Age.* Vol. 1, *Origins and Development.* Vol. 2, *Synthesis and Decline.* Berkeley and Los Angeles: University of California Press, 592 pp.

Exhaustive evaluation of Vorticism in a broad social and cultural context, including its relationship to Bloomsbury and Bloomsbury artists. Volume One includes chapters on "The First Stirrings of Revolt: Lewis, Pound, and the Post-Impressionist Exhibition," "The Impact of the Futurist and Cubist Invasion of the English Rebels," "Student Unrest at the Slade, and "Dissension at the Omega," all of which involve a consideration of the aesthetics of Roger Fry, Clive Bell, and Bloomsbury. Volume two deals less directly with Bloomsbury, but the artists evaluated are often described in relation to the Bloomsbury milieu. Deals especially with the relationship between Wyndham Lewis and Bloomsbury, which is characterized as "dissension in the ranks of the English avant-garde."

7   CRUIKSHANK, MARGARET. "Buggery in Bloomsbury." *Gay Literature* 5:22-24.

Commentary on the negative criticism of homosexuality, especially in relation to Michael Holroyd's biography of Lytton Strachey: "Seeing Strachey as a representative homosexual and seeing him through a fog of prejudice, the biographer is unable to account for Strachey's uniqueness." Sees the path of Carolyn Heilbrun's *Toward a Recognition of Androgyny* as more promising. (See 1973.26.)

8   DAVIS, RUSSELL. "The Bloomsbury Industry." *Observer Magazine* (25 April):16-19.

Commentary on the growth of interest in Bloomsbury and Bloomsbury figures.

9   DINNAGE, ROSEMARY. "Garsington Manners." *Times Literary Supplement* (London) (4 June):677.

Review of Sandra Darroch's *Ottoline.* Asks, "What was the Ottoline phenomenon really about?" She is something of "a work of art, reflecting the fantasies of those who knew her." Finds little new in the biography "that has not appeared in other Bloomsbury biographies or in Ronald Clark's life of Russell."

10   ____. "The World and the Whirlpool." *Times Literary Supplement* (London) (24 September):1206-07.

Review of *The Letters of Virginia Woolf,* Vol. 2, *1912-1922.*

Vanessa Bell is chief of the corespondents: "Queen of the circle to whom the letters were sent is Vanessa; by far the largest number out of the total are written to her. It is something in Virginia's own attitude perhaps that brings the word 'queen' to mind; we feel her always ready to make something of a myth out of her 'dear dolphin,' her earth-goddess and substitute mother."

11   EDER, DORIS. "Louis Unmasked: T.S. Eliot in *The Waves*." *Virginia Woolf Quarterly* 2, nos. 1-2 (Winter-Spring):13-27.
        Sees T.S. Eliot as the prototype for Lewis in Virginia Woolf's *The Waves*. Gives background of the association between Eliot and Leonard and Virginia Woolf, including the publication by the Hogarth Press of Eliot's *Poems* (1919) and *The Waste Land*: "Bloomsbury's attitude to Eliot was curiously compounded of condescension on the one hand and awe on the other--an attitude similar to that his companions felt toward Louis in *The Waves*."

12   ____. Review of *The Bloomsbury Group: A Collection of Memoirs, Commentary and Criticism*, edited by S.P. Rosenbaum. *Virginia Woolf Quarterly* 2, nos. 1-2 (Winter-Spring):159-69.
        Discusses common questions associated with Bloomsbury, including whether it existed and the membership: "What I had not realized before which Rosenbaum's collection brings home strikingly is how self-critical Bloomsbury was. Its reputation not withstanding, it was a mutual criticism not a mutual admiration society." Book raises some questions, including "just how rational was Bloomsbury?"

13   EDWARDS, MARY IRENE. "Inheritance in the Fiction of Victoria Sackville-West." Ph.D. dissertation, University of Nebraska, pp. 210.
        Deals primarily with the fiction of Vita Sackville-West. Includes some commentary on the relationship with Virginia Woolf and Bloomsbury. See *Dissertation Abstracts International* 37:982A-83A.

14   FARR, DENNIS. "Clive Bell's Eye." *Apollo* 103 (May):451.
        Review of William G. Bywater's *Clive Bell's Eye*. Finds the work to be a "somewhat arid, hermetic dissertation" too devoted to philosophy rather than the wider context of Bell's idea of "significant form": "Yet it was Fry, not Bell, who developed the thesis into a more or less viable critical system by concentrating on 'plastic' rather than 'significant' form."

15   FASSLER, BARBARA CAROL. "The 'Bond of Love' in the Novels
      of Victoria Sackville West." Ph.D. dissertation, University of Iowa,
      340 pp.
            Deals primarily with the novels of Vita Sackville-West. Includes
      some commentary on her relationship with Virginia Woolf and
      Bloomsbury in general. See *Dissertation Abstracts International* 37:982A.

16   FRENCH, ELIZABETH BOYD. *Bloomsbury Heritage: Their
      Mothers and Their Aunts.* New York: Tapinger; London: Hamish
      Hamilton, 161 pp.
            Study of the backgrounds of various Bloomsbury figures: "My
      disposition as a student of literature has always been to know the
      authors themselves who are responsible for the works that I enjoy, and
      to understand the soil from which they sprang. With the Bloomsbury
      writers I was thus led to trace the connection between their families
      and some of the families in the Clapham Sect." Decided to focus on
      the extraordinary women in these families. "The Pattle Sisters" chapter
      deals with "a fabulous bevy of women known in Victorian society" who
      were the maternal grandmother and grand aunts of Virginia Stephen
      and Vanessa Stephen: "Lady Somers and Lady Dalrymple survived into
      the twentieth century, the only ones of the Prattle great aunts whom
      Vanessa and Virginia Stephen, in the early days of the Bloomsbury
      Group, could have known besides their grandmother, Mrs. Jackson."
      The next chapter, "Julia Prinsep Duckworth Stephen, nee Jackson
      (1846-1895)," deals with the background of Vanessa and Virginia
      Stephen's mother. "Jane Maria Strachey, nee Grant" deals with the
      mother of Lytton Strachey: In 1919, Lady Strachey and her daughters
      Pippa and Marjorie moved to No. 51 Gordon Square, a tall row house
      on the east side of the square, right in the heart of the emerging
      Bloomsbury Group's homes. Here Lady Strachey settled down to write
      her memoirs, just as the inner circle of the group was forming its own
      Memoir Club." "Anne Issebella Ritchie, nee Thackery (1837-1919),"
      deals with the older sister of Leslie Stephen's first wife. She represents
      "a more conservative and religiously orthodox, though still liberally
      feministic influence on the Group." The final chapter, "Mary Josefa
      MacCarthy, nee Warre-Cornish," deals with the founder of the Memoir
      Club and a direct member of the Bloomsbury Group.

17   GAITHER, MARY E., and J. HOWARD WOOLMER. *Checklist of
      the Hogarth Press.* Andes, N.Y.: Woolmer & Brotherson, 216 pp.
            Includes essay by Gaither, "The Hogarth Press: 1917-1938,"

which describes the growth and editorial policies of the press during the years of Leonard and Virginia Woolf's partnership.

18   GARNETT, DAVID. "Lady into Woolf." *New Statesman* 91 (11 June):777-78.
       Review of Virginia Woolf's *Moments of Being* (see 1976.50). Describes the harm that George Duckworth did to Virginia's psyche. Vanessa "was never in any real danger: she was a far stronger character than Virginia." Also discusses Virginia's snobbery.

19   GISH, ROBERT. "Mr. Forster and Mrs. Woolf: Aspects of the Novelist as Critic." *Virginia Woolf Quarterly* 2, nos. 3-4 (Summer-Fall):255-69.
       "The purpose here is to explain what Forster and Woolf said about each other's novels and to submit that what they said was determined as much by their respective critical statements as by their novels." Deals with the dynamic of their literary relationship.

20   HENIG, SUZANNE. "Bibliography of the Hogarth Press." *Virginia Woolf Quarterly* 2, nos. 1-2 (Winter-Spring):106-52.
       Bibliography of books published by the press Leonard and Virginia Woolf established and which published many of the books of Bloomsbury figures.

21   _____. "Review of *Virginia's Childhood*, by Vanessa Bell." *Virginia Woolf Quarterly* 2, nos. 1-2:175.
       "A charming memoir by Virginia's beloved sister Vanessa about their childhood. . . . One only wishes that there were more to this scant volume of only ten unnumbered leaves of text."

22   ISHERWOOD, CHRISTOPHER. *Christopher and His Kind: 1929-1939*. New York: Farrar, Strauss & Giroux, 339 pp.
       Third personal autobiographical account that includes commentary on the literary life of London during this period and briefly on Isherwood's relationship with John Lehmann and other Bloomsbury figures, especially Leonard and Virginia Woolf.

23   KUSH, KATHERINE DAVIDSON. "Virginia Woolf and F.H. Bradley: Metaphysical Idealism in Fiction and Philosophy." Ph.D. dissertation, University of Michigan, 150 pp.
       The first chapter deals with Woolf as a philosophical novelist,

"noting that she has most often been linked to realist and psychological philosophers, especially G.E. Moore and Henri Bergson." See *Dissertation Abstracts International* 37:6500A-01A.

24   LAING, DONALD ALEXANDER. "The Published Writings of Roger Fry and Clive Bell: Checklists and Commentary." Ph.D. dissertation, University of Toronto, 226 pp.
     "If we are to appreciate fully Fry's and Bell's significance in the cultural life of their time, and if we are to examine their influence thoroughly, we must base our judgement on a more complete knowledge of their writings." The Fry entries number 816, with almost 400 essays by Fry published anonymously. The Bell list includes 462 entries, more than fifty of which appeared anonymously. The commentary focuses on three major themes: the power of society to corrupt genuine art, a belief in a knowledge of the art of Cézanne as an antidote to the corruption, and the effort to foster a critical spirit in the British public. See *Dissertation Abstracts International* 39:2256A-57A.

25   LEHMANN, JOHN. "Early Virginia." *London Magazine* 15 (February-March):121-24.
     Commentary on Lehmann's early association with Virginia Woolf.

26   LUMSDEN, IAN G. Introduction to *Bloomsbury Painters and Their Circle*. Exhibition Catalog. New Brunswick, Canada: Beaverbrook Art Gallery, pp.7-16.
     Introduction to the Bloomsbury Group in relation to the work of artists in the circle. Bonding among the Bloomsbury Group based upon friendship and an attitude toward life expounded in G.E. Moore's *Principia Ethica*. Prior to 1910 most of the group was literary in orientation: "With the induction of Roger Fry, the most senior member, into Bloomsbury, came a more worldly appreciation of the plastic arts along with a retinue of English and French painters whom he had become friendly with through his myriad activity in the arts as a painter, art historian, and curator." Briefly describes the artistic development of Vanessa Bell and Duncan Grant, including Simon Bussy's influence on Grant, as well as the evolution of the Omega Workshops.

27 MacDOWELL, FREDERICK. *E.M. Forster: An Annotated Bibliography of Writings bout Him.* Dekalb: Northern Illinois University Press, 878 pp.

Extensive annotated bibliography which includes many references to Forster's Bloomsbury association. All important commentaries in relation to Bloomsbury are included in this research guide. Useful for finding further commentary on Forster not related directly to his Bloomsbury association.

28 McLAUGHLIN, THOMAS MICHAEL. "Approaches to Order in Bloomsbury Criticism." Ph.D. dissertation, Temple University, 220 pp.

Bloomsbury shares common intellectual traits, particularly the obsession with artistic order. "This study attempts to show that the techniques and language" of Bloomsbury's critical writing "imply an unstated set of aesthetic assumptions which guide their specific judgments and interpretations." See *Dissertation Abstracts International* 37:2175A.

29 MEYEROWITZ, SELMA S. "Class Perspectives and the Works of VirginiaWoolf." Ph.D. dissertation, Wayne State University, 450 pp.

Includes some commentary that relates to Woolf's position within the elite structure of Bloomsbury. See *Dissertation Abstracts International* 36:74442A.

30 MOERS, ELLEN. *Literary Women.* New York: Doubleday. Reprint. London: W.H. Allen, 1977, 336 pp.

General commentary on the literature of women which includes a discussion of Virginia Woolf and her relationship to the intellectual milieu of Bloomsbury.

31 MOGGRIDGE, D.E. *John Maynard Keynes.* London: Fontana/Collins; Baltimore: Penguin Books, 190 pp.

Chapter One, "Prologue," deals with Keynes in relation to the Bloomsbury Group. "Keynes was a product of Victorian and Edwardian England." His interests and activities broadened as he became involved with friends at Cambridge and other groups. "Of these, perhaps the most important to his development was membership in the group eventually known as Bloomsbury." Deals with his years at Cambridge in the Apostles and the influence of G.E. Moore. As a result of these associations he re-examined personal relations and morality. Developed a sense of liberation. Carries this influence into his politics and economic thought.

32   MOORE, HENRY T. "Virginia Woolf and Three Recent London Plays." *Virginia Woolf Quarterly* 2, nos. 3-4:382-82a.
Critical review of plays recently produced in London, including Peter Luke's *Bloomsbury*. The play does not occur in Bloomsbury "and only a few of the accredited 'Bloomsberries' appear."

33   MORRELL, LADY OTTOLINE. *Lady Ottoline's Album: Snaps and Portraits of Her Famous Contemporaries (and Herself), Photographed for the Most Part by Lady Ottoline Morrell. From the Collection of Her Daughter, Julian Vinogradoff.* Introduction by Lord David Cecil. Edited by Carolyn G. Heilbrun. New York: Alfred A. Knopf, 117 pp.
Large number of photographs of Bloomsbury figures and others who visited the Morrell's at Garsington. Includes brief foreword by Julian Morrell Vinogradoff describing Ottoline's habits as a photographer. Introduction by David Cecil focuses on Ottoline's life and her desire to live life "on the same plane as poetry and music." Also gives a personal reminiscence of his association with her in 1921: "I was captivated alike by the house and by its chatelaine."

34   NEWBERRY, JO. "Russell and the Pacifists of World War I." In *Russell in Review: The Bertrand Russell Centenary Celebrations at Manchester University.* Edited by J.E. Thomas and Kenneth Blackwell. Toronto: Samuel Stevens, Hakkert, pp. 33-55.
"The subject of this paper is of course the never-ending wickedness of Russell during the First World War, and his compulsion to say things displeasing to tyrants and kings." Also deals briefly with Russell's relations with D.H. Lawrence and Lady Ottoline Morrell. Dose not relate him directly to the Bloomsbury pacifists.

35   NICOLSON, BENEDICT. "The Burlington Magazine." *Connoisseur* 191 (March):177-83.
History of the *Burlington Magazine*, which Roger Fry helped to salvage in 1903 and edited for many years starting in 1909. In this journal he promoted the work of Cézanne.

36 RANTAVAARS, IRMA. "Bloomsbury Today." *Virginia Woolf Quarterly* 2, nos. 3-4 (Summer-Fall):281-83.
Overview of recent Bloomsbury criticism. Deals mostly with David Gadd's *Loving Friends* (See 1974.10). In Gadd's book "Practically everything concerning their work is left out." Finally, though, this work "sheds light on some aspects of Bloomsbury with reliability and sympathy."

37 ROSENBAUM, S.P. "Bertrand Russell: The Logic of a Literary Symbol." In *Russell in Review: The Bertrand Russell Centenary Celebrations at Manchester University*. Edited by J.E. Thomas and Kenneth Blackwell. Toronto: Samuel Stevens; Hakkert, pp. 57-87.
Looks at Russell as a symbolic significance in a number of literary works. Moore's influence probably resulted in Russell's work having no literary impact. Describes Russell's introduction to T.S. Eliot, Lady Ottoline Morrell and the Bloomsbury Group. Comments on Lawrence's depiction of Russell in *Women in Love*, Huxley's depiction in *Chrome Yellow*, and Campbell's depiction in *The Georgiad* in relation to Garsington and Bloomsbury.

38 ____. "Gilbert Cannan and Bertrand Russell: An Addition to the Logic of a Literary Symbol." *Russell* 21-22 (Spring-Summer):16-25.
Article dealing with three novels by Gilbert Cannan, *Pugs and Peacocks*, *Sembal*, and *The House of Prophecy*, in relation to their depiction of the life and times of Bertrand Russell. Includes discussion of Ottoline Morrell and Garsington, as well as other Bloomsbury figures: "The final scenes of *Pug and Peacocks* take place at Birch-End, a Garsington-like country home complete with a Lytton Stracheyesque character named Sopley." Concludes that the literary value of these novels "is not very high, and therefore these novels do not contribute much to the logic of Russell as a literary symbol." But they remain interesting when compared with Russell as literary symbol in Eliot, Lawrence, and Huxley.

39 ROSENTHAL, MICHAEL. "Virginia Woolf." *Partisan Review* 43, no. 4:557-69.
Describes the emergence of Woolf as a major literary figure: "To begin with, it is clear that the rediscovery of Woolf is part of the larger phenomenon of the canonization of Bloomsbury which has been in the process for the past seven or eight years." The interest is not scholarly: "People await the newest revelations about the personal

intrigues with much the same interest as Dickens's readers anticipated each new installment by the master." States that "if Woolf is to survive as other than a precious oddity of the modernist movement, it will be neither as a member of a coterie, a radical feminist, nor a prophetic androgynist."

40   RUOTOLO, LUCIO P. Preface to *Freshwater: A Comedy by Virginia Woolf*. New York: Harcourt Brace Jovanovich, pp. vii-xi.
      Brief commentary on the play which Virginia Woolf wrote for "one of a number of theatrical evenings that had characterized 'Bloomsbury' parties since the early 1920s." Discusses preparations for the play during the summer of 1934.

41   SAKAMOTO, KIMINOBU. "V. Woolf no Zahyo" [The coordinates of V. Woolf]. *Eigo Seinen* 122:119-21.
      Review article on numerous recent studies of Virginia Woolf and Bloomsbury. [In Japanese.]

42   SCHAEFER, JOSEPHINE O'BRIEN. "Moments of Vision in Virginia Woolf's Biographies." *Virginia Woolf Quarterly* 2, nos. 3-4 (Summer-Fall):294-303.
      In her biographies Woolf "concentrates upon a moment in time when the self is brought into clear focus," and "she tries to recreate the sudden illumination so that the reader may share it." Describes these aims in relation to work on Roger Fry and Vita Sackville-West.

43   SCHLACK, BEVERLY ANN. "Portrait of the Artist as Young Woman: The Letters of Virginia Woolf." *Literature and Psychology* 26, nos. 3:118-23.
      Review-article based on *The Letters of Virginia Woolf*, Vol. 1, *1882-1912*, edited by Nigel Nicolson, giving overview of Woolf's attitudes as represented in her letters: "We learn that the birth of what came to be known as the Bloomsbury Group did not inspire Virginia with unqualified awe or submissive respect." In letters to figures like Lytton Strachey and Saxon Sydney-Turner, "she continues to fight off her conglomerate fears of marriage, motherhood and spinsterhood with defensive humor."

44   SHIELDS, E.F. "Bloomsbury Revisited." *Queens Quarterly* 83, 1 (Spring):103-5.
      Review of Rosenbaum's *The Bloomsbury Group: A Collection of*

Memoirs, Commentary and Criticism: "Although Bloomsbury reached its peak of influence in the twenties and thirties, only in the past fifteen years has the full story of its members begun to be told." Mentions sexual freedom and suggests that the works "conformed, on the surface at least, to conventional sexual mores."

45 SHONE, RICHARD. *Bloomsbury Portraits: Vanessa Bell, Duncan Grant, and Their Circle*. Oxford: Phaidon Press; New York: E.P. Dutton, 272 pp.
       Study of the work of Duncan Grant and Vanessa Bell in relation to the Bloomsbury milieu. The major section of the book deals with the period of 1910-20, the most active time in the lives of these artists, including the Post-impressionist exhibitions, World War I, Omega Workshops, and the move to Charleston: "From all these changes and new experiences and experiments, certain themes emerge and roots are put down which I have tried to develop in the less detailed later sections of the book." Sees Vanessa Bell as pivotal figure in Bloomsbury, not Lytton Strachey or Virginia Woolf.

46 SKIDELSKY, ROBERT. "Keynes and the Revolt Against the Victorians." *Spectator* (1 May):14-16.
       Traces Keynesian economics back to a changed attitude to life dating from his days in Cambridge and London in the 1900s," a period which involves the Bloomsbury Group: "At its center was an overwhelming sense that life was to be lived for the present, not for the past or the future." In this development two names stand out: G.E. Moore in philosophy and Lytton Strachey in love. Reprinted in *The End of the Keynesian Era: Essays on the Disintegration of the Keynesian Political Economy*, ed. Robert Skidelsky (New York: Holmes & Meier, 1977), pp. 1-9.

47 VAIZEY, JOHN. "Keynes and the Cambridge Tradition." *Spectator* (29 May):20-22.
       Minor reference, in relation to Keynes and Cambridge economics, especially Alfred Marshall, to the "Bloomsbury urge *epater le bourgeois*; if there were two ways of saying something, he chose the more shocking." Reprinted in *The End of the Keynesian Era: Essays on the Disintegration of the Keynesian Political Economy*, ed. Robert Skidelsky (New York: Holmes & Meier, 1977), pp. 10-17.

48   WEBB, EUGENE. "Pozzo in Bloomsbury: A Possible Allusion in
      Beckett's *Waiting for Godot.*" *Journal of Modern Literature* 5, no. 2
      (April):326-31.
           Argues that the name "Pozzo" in *Waiting for Godot* is an allusion
      to Keynes, whose nickname was "Pozzo," and Bloomsbury: "The Pozzo
      of Beckett's play is not much of a philosopher, or at least not a very
      articulate one, but to the extent that he does express a vision of the
      good life, it has strong similarities to that of Pozzo of Bloomsbury."

49   WOOLF, VIRGINIA. *The Diary of Virginia Woolf*, Vol. 1, *1915-
      1919.* Edited by Anne Olivier Bell. London: Hogarth Press, 486
      pp.
           Includes various references to and about Bloomsbury figures,
      especially about the development of the Group prior to World War I.

50   _____. *Moments of Being: Unpublished Autobiographical Writings.*
      Edited with introduction by Jeanne Schulkind. New York: Harcourt
      Brace Jovanovich. Sussex: University Press, 207 pp.
           Includes memoirs that relate to Woolf's background an to
      Bloomsbury. "Reminiscences," written for Julian Bell, deals with Julia
      Stephen, Stella Duckworth, and Vanessa Bell. "A Sketch of the Past"
      deals with Virginia's childhood from the perspective of 1939-1940 and
      takes her, through the figure of her mother, to St. Ives, Cornwall, and
      Talland House where the Stephens spent their summer holidays from
      1882 to 1894. The last three selections were written for the Memoir
      Club, the regrouping of many of the original members of Bloomsbury:
      "22 Hyde Park Gate," "Old Bloomsbury," and "Am I a Snob?"
      Schhulkind states that Woolf "charts the development of 'Bloomsbury'
      from its serious, truth-seeking, Cambridge-oriented origins, through its
      period of notoriety, to what, in some respects at least, was its antithesis,
      the society of London hostesses such as Margot Asquith and Sibyl
      Colefax."

51   _____. *The Question of Things Happening: The Letters of Virginia
      Woolf*, Vol. 2, *1912-1922.* Edited by Nigel Nicolson and Joanne
      Trautmann. London: Hogarth Press; New York: Harcourt Brace
      Jovanovich, 627 pp.
           Woolf's letters include various references to Bloomsbury and are
      often written to Bloomsbury figures. She alludes to Bloomsbury
      parties, to the 1917 Club, the founding of the Memoir Club, and to the
      character of Gordon Square: "Gordon Square is like nothing so much

as the lions house at the Zoo. One goes from cage to cage. All the animals are dangerous, rather suspicious of each other, and full of fascination and mystery." Nigel Nicolson's "Introduction" also describes the character of Bloomsbury, along with the nature of Leonard and Virginia's marriage: "One quality they shared with all Bloomsbury was dedication. This may seem difficult to reconcile with the wild parties in Gordon Square and Virginia's coruscating letters, but a serious intent always qualified their fun."

1977

1 ANNAN, NOEL. "Forster's Self-Discovery." *Listener* 98 (4 August):155-56.

Transcript of talk about P.N. Furbank's *E.M. Forster.* Involves some personal observations about Forster at King's College, Cambridge. Deals with lack of interest in Forster. Mentions Hugh Trevor-Roper's denouncement of the whole Bloomsbury Group in the *Times Literary Supplement.*

2 BARRON, T.J. "Before the Deluge: Leonard Woolf in Ceylon." *Journal of Imperial and Commonwealth History* 6 (October):47-63.

Deals with Leonard Woolf's work, somewhat in relation to his Bloomsbury background.

3 BELL, ALAN. "Artists' Workshops." *Times Literary Supplement* (London) (13 May):597.

Review of *Bloomsbury Portraits* by Richard Shone. This is not just another Bloomsbury book: "The Group will come bobbing up from time to time, but Mr. Shone's rather inadequate summaries of their general attitude to Society or the First World War show that he has done best to stick to the artistic side."

4 ____. "Rodmell and Its Routine." *Times Literary Supplement* (London) (28 October):1256.

Review of Spater and Parsons's *A Marriage of True Minds: An Intimate Portrait of Leonard and Virginia Woolf:* "George Spater and Ian Parsons have set out to give us not just another Bloomsbury book, but a short study of the joint lives of two of its most important members." Leonard Woolf dominates the study.

5   BROWN, CAROLE O. "The Art of the Novel: Virginia Woolf's
     The Voyage Out." Virginia Woolf Quarterly 3, nos. 1-2 (Winter-
     Spring):67-84.
        "No one asserts strongly enough the fundamental importance of
     painting in Virginia Woolf's novels, from the very beginning, and I
     should like to examine her first novel, *The Voyage Out*, which has been
     substantially ignored by critics." Deals with the connections between
     Vanessa Bell, Clive Bell, Roger Fry, and Virginia Woolf's work as
     novelist. In her first novel we find "the painterly qualities of her later
     fiction present in two ways, as ideas put into the mouths of characters
     and as techniques that are realized in the structure of the novel."
     Deals with Fry's five emotional elements of design as technique in the
     novel.

6   CECIL, LORD DAVID. "Lady Ottoline Morrell and Her Circle."
     Illustrated London News 265 (February):57-60.
        Commentary, including illustrations, on Lady Ottoline Morrell's
     associations, which included Bertrand Russell, Lytton Strachey, and
     several other Bloomsbury figures.

7   DINNAGE, ROSEMARY. "A Medium for Mischief." *Times
     Literary Supplement* (London) (7 October):1130.
        Review of *A Change of Perspective: The Letters of Virginia Woolf,
     1923-1928*, edited by Nigel Nicolson. Comments on the "glorious
     profusion" in this volume. Letters to Vita Sackville-West make up a
     third of the collection, including vivid comments about their
     relationship.

8   EDEL, LEON. "The Group and the Salon." *American Scholar* 46
     (Winter 76-77):116-24.
        Review-article on *The Letters of Virginia Woolf*, edited by Nigel
     Nicolson and Joanne Trautmann, *The Loving Friends*, by David Gadd,
     The Bloomsbury Group, edited by S.P. Rosenbaum, *Ottoline at
     Garsington: The Memoirs of Lady Ottoline Morrell, 1915-1918*, edited by
     Robert Gathorne-Hardy, and *Ottoline: The Life of Lady Ottoline Morrell*,
     by Sandra Darroch. To understand the flow of current books on
     Bloomsbury we must go back to another book, Michael Holroyd's life
     of Lytton Strachey. Its errors "fixed for too long the picture of
     Bloomsbury's men as gamboling satyrs spending a lifetime on weekends,
     and its women, notably Virginia Woolf, as wraiths." Morrell was not a
     member of Bloomsbury. She "created a distinct world of her own that

bore no resemblance to Bloomsbury." Also identifies Carrington and Vita Sackville-West as not really Bloomsbury.

9   EDER, DORIS L. "Portrait of the Artist as a Young Woman: Virginia Woolf." *Book Forum* 3:336-44.
     Review-article dealing with Virginia Woolf's *Letters*. Comments on her developing association with Bloomsbury and various Bloomsbury figures.

10   "The Fine Arts Society." *Burlington Magazine* 119 (January):57.
     Review of "Bloomsbury Portraits," an exhibition organized to coincide with the publication of Richard Shone's *Bloomsbury Portraits*. The show does "nothing to alter the view that Bloomsbury is of far more interest in a literary as opposed to a pictorial context."

11   FURBANK, P.N. *E.M. Forster: A Life*. Vol. 1. New York: Harcourt Brace Jovanovich, 260 pp.
     Volume one of Furbank's two volume biography, published together in 1978. (See 1978.18.)

12   GANDILLAC, MAURICE and JEAN GUIGUET, eds. *Virginia Woolf: Colloque de Cerisy: Virginia Woolf et le Groupe de Bloomsbury*. Paris: Union Generale d'Éditions, 263 pp.
     Gathering of seven papers, and transcriptions of subsequent discussions, presented during the Cerisy-la-Sable colloquium on "Virginia Woolf and Bloomsbury" in August 1974, together with Guiguet's introductory comments. Guiguet's introduction suggests that the point of the conference is to debate the existence of Bloomsbury and to determine whether it can be placed on any kind of map--critical, intellectual, geographical, political, psychological, or sociological. Guiguet's article "Les Vacances et l'Engagement" analyzes the process of "being away" as a necessary step toward later engagement. "Bloomsbury and France" by Peter Fawcett looks at the connections between the group and France. David Daiches' article "The London of Virginia Woolf" considers the distinct qualities the Bloomsbury district had for Virginia Woolf. It was intellectual and bohemian, definitely not bourgeois or chic. David Garnett's "John Maynard Keynes, Biographer" gives a detailed comparison of Strachey, Fry and Keynes in relation to biographical writing. "Virginia Woolf and Lytton Strachey," by Gabriel Merle, suggests that aside from some surface similarities, the work of these two figures is very different. "Reflections of a Theme: Virginia

Woolf and Water," by Marie-Paule Vigne, looks at references to water in Woolf's novels. "Virginia Woolf and Criticism," by Anthony Inglis, suggests that changes in critical methods mean that Woolf must be re-evaluated. The conclusion of the volume, also by Guiguet, questions whether any connections between Woolf and Bloomsbury have been usefully established: "I believe we have modified the extreme position I took by saying that Bloomsbury is only a myth."

13 GILLESPIE, DIANE FILBY. "Virginia Woolf's Miss Latrobe: The Artist's Last Struggle Against Masculine Values." *Woman and Literature* 5, no. 1:38-46.
   Deals with the world of masculine values, most often defined by the Cambridge world of her brother, Thoby, and other Bloomsbury figures, such as Leonard Woolf, Clive Bell, and Lytton Strachey.

14 GLENDINNING, VICTORIA. "The Gods of Garsington." *Times Literary Supplement* (London) (18 February):178.
   Review of *Lady Ottoline's Album*, edited by Carolyn G. Heilbrun. Comments on the photographs of Bloomsbury figures, and those of Lady Ottoline herself: "We have a better view of the gods at play."

15 GORDON, LYNDALL. *Eliot's Early Years*. Oxford and New York: Oxford University Press, 174 pp.
   Through Bertrand Russell, Eliot met Clive Bell and other figures in Bloomsbury, including Lady Ottoline Morrell, "but he remained an outsider," nor was he ever completely accepted by them. In 1917 the Egoist Press published his first volume, copies of which Clive Bell distributed at Garsington. "Lytton Strachey applauded Eliot's talent."

16 HEINE, ELIZABETH. "E.M. Forster and the Bloomsbury Group." *Cahiers Victoriens et Edouardiens* 4-5:43-52.
   Forster was never central to Bloomsbury: "The ways in which he did or did not belong provide further definitions of the qualities and limits of both the group as a whole and of Forster himself." Finds that Forster's activities in and attitudes toward the group were ambivalent. His attitudes are reflected in *The Longest Journey*, *Howard's End*, and *Maurice*. He gained from contact with members of the group, even if he did not find himself completely one of them.

17 HEINEMANN, JAN. "The Revolt Against Language: A Critical Note on Twentieth-Century Irrationalism with Special Reference to the Aesthetico-Philosophical Views of Virginia Woolf and Clive Bell." *Orbis Litterarum* 32, no. 2:212-28.

This article attempts "to shed light on the linguistic aspects of modern irrationalist philosophy as they appear in the writings of Virginia Woolf and Clive Bell." Concentrates on "problems relating to aesthetics and philosophy, omitting biographical detail." Asserts that "the basic attitude behind the aesthetico-philosophical theories of Woolf and Bell coincides with a profoundly skeptical view of Western civilization prevalent among European intellectuals of the early 20th century."

18 HEWISON, ROBERT. *Under Siege: Literary Life in London 1939-1945.* New York: Oxford University Press, 219 pp.

Study of literary life in London during this period which involves brief evaluation of the end of Bloomsbury: "Shortly afterwards a bomb on Tavistock Square destroyed the Woolfs' former home. Bloomsbury was literally coming to an end."

19 HOLZMAN, MICHAEL. "Silences in the Text: *Virginia Woolf and Lytton Strachey: Letters*." *Virginia Woolf Quarterly* 3, no. 1-2 (Winter-Spring):33-37.

Brief article about the missing passages in *Virginia Woolf and Lytton Strachey: Letters* edited by Leonard Woolf, whose editing "leaned heavily toward omission." Deals with three types of omissions: names, invitations to dinner and tea, and unflattering remarks about personalities. Includes the missing passages.

20 HULCOOP, JOHN. "'The only way to keep afloat': Work as Virginia Woolf's *raison d'etre*." *Women's Studies* 4, no. 2-3:223-45.

Virginia Woolf's work was not merely her pleasure: "More than that, it was her major means of survival, her *raison d'etre*." Deals somewhat with her relationship with Leonard and other Bloomsbury figures, especially during the final years of her life.

21 KENNEY, EDWIN J., JR. "The Moment, 1910: Virginia Woolf, Arnold Bennet, and the Turn of Century Consciousness." *Colby Library Quarterly* 13, no. 1 (March):42-66.

Commentary on Woolf's famous statement, "on or about December, 1910, human character changed," in relation to her personal life, as well as in relation to social and political change. Includes full discussion of her relationship with Thoby, Vanessa, Clive Bell, and Roger Fry: "Therefore I think Woolf is deadly accurate about her choice of the date 1910, for the change in her bit of the world (and here I think Bell is showing the Bloomsbury fault of limiting his vision to Bloomsbury occurrences) corresponded to changes going on within the national public life of Britain, and she knew it. During the year of the first Post-impressionist exhibition, women, workers, Irishmen, and members of Parliament were changing their ways of regarding themselves and one another; older conventions of thought, feeling, and politics were breaking down without the immediate creation of new structures to take their place."

22   LEE, HERMIONE. *The Novels of Virginia Woolf.* London: Methuen, 237 pp.
     Critical study with assorted references to Bloomsbury and Bloomsbury figures: "Virginia Woolf's novels seem to have become more interesting, and are more widely read, because of the vogue for Bloomsbury. But what makes Bloomsbury intriguing has not, perhaps, really very much to do with what makes Virginia Woolf an important novelist."

23   LEHMANN, JOHN. "Return to the Hogarth Press: 1937." *Virginia Woolf Quarterly* 3, no. 1-2 (Winter-Spring):65-66.
     Commentary on the events surrounding Lehmann's return to the Hogarth Press in 1937 motivated by the discovery of letters and unknown facts about the incident. Includes excerpts from letters of Leonard and Virginia Woolf and Lehmann. The result was that Lehmann purchased half a share in the Hogarth Press.

24   L'ENFANT, JULIE. "'A Lady Writing': Virginia Woolf Chronicle." *Southern Review* 13, no. 3 (July):456-67.
     Commentary on Virginia Woolf's life in relation to recent publications by her, including *Moments of Being, The Letters of Virginia Woolf,* and *Freshwater: A Comedy.* Discusses her autobiographical works and the incidents in her life which led to the establishment of Bloomsbury.

25 McLAUGHLIN, THOMAS M. "Clive Bell's Aesthetic: Tradition
and Significant Form." *Journal of Aesthetics and Art Criticism* 35, no.
4 (Summer):433-43.
Bell has been unfairly criticized: "When Bell's entire career is
considered, a more fully developed aesthetic system than his detractors
have been willing to recognize is apparent." The system depends on
Bell's formulation of a theory of tradition which provides a coherent
explanation of the process by which form is imposed on the world, and
which anticipates at least in part many of the objections raised against
him. Briefly mentions Fry and G.E. Moore in relation to Bell.

26 MARCUS, JANE. "'No More Horses': Virginia Woolf on Art and
Propaganda." *Women Studies* 4, nos. 2-3:265-90.
Questions whether the coupling of art and propaganda is a
"mutilation" to Woolf. Deals with the relationship of Woolf's politics to
other Bloomsbury figures and associates, such as E.M. Forster and
Leonard Woolf, as well as Wyndham Lewis and Q.D. Leavis.

27 MARQETTS, MARTINA. "Bloomsbury Portraits." *Connoisseur* 194
(January):139-40.
Review of Richard Shone's *Bloomsbury Portraits* commenting on
the absence of significant discussion of the Bloomsbury Group: "Mr.
Shone does not see the group as being important in either the personal
or artistic development of Grant or Vanessa Bell."

28 MECKIER, JEROME. "Philip Quarles's *Passage to India*: Jesting
Pilate, Point Counter Point, and Bloomsbury." *Studies in the Novel* 9
(Winter):445-67.
Involves a discussion of Huxely's satire of various Bloomsbury
novels in *Point Counter Point*, including *A Passage to India* and *To the
Lighthouse*: "Where Forster tests Bloomsbury values in India to
discover their universal validity, Huxley sets a chapter in India to reveal
that discontinuity between men and between mind and matter is
worldwide." Bloomsbury ideals come under fire through Huxley's novel:
"By dismissing the Bloomsbury Group, particularly Forster, Huxley
contends that Bloomsbury is an inadequate idea; its idealist philosophy
cannot speak to the modern period."

29   MEYERS, JEFFREY. "Virginia and Leonard Woolf: Madness and
      Art." In *Married to Genius*. New York: Barnes & Noble, pp. 92-
      112.
            Competent, brief account of Virginia Woolf's marriage.

30   MIROIU, MIHAI. *Virginia Woolf*. Bucharest: Editura Univers, 384
      pp.
            Two opening chapters are devoted to surveying the social and
      cultural influences of Virginia Woolf's late Victorian childhood and the
      Bloomsbury Group.

31   MOORE, MADELINE. "Virginia Woolf's *The Years* and Years of
      Adverse Male Reviewers." *Women's Studies* 4, nos. 2-3:247-63.
            Deals in part with W.H. Mellers's negative review in *Scrutiny*,
      which was primarily based upon objections to Bloomsbury aesthetics.
      Suggests that the objections are not merely based upon hatred of
      "curiously tepid Bloomsbury prose" into which Woolf sometimes slips:
      "The novel is diminished then by the limitations of her sex."

32   MORPHET, RICHARD. "Bloomsbury Portraits." *Studio
      International* 193 (January-February):68-70.
            Review of Richard Shone's *Bloomsbury Portraits*: "The
      Bloomsbury artists were pioneers in a 20th century willingness to look
      at what was actually there in a picture, and--rather than conform to
      society's prejudiced, restricted mode of vision--to be open to the
      emotions, whatever these might be."

33   OZICK, CYNTHIA. "The Loose Drifting Material of Life." *New
      York Times Book Review* (2 October):7, 40, 41.
            Review of *The Diary of Virginia Woolf*, Vol.1, *1915-1919*. Woolf's
      diary gives us few psychological surprises. All the names are here,
      Strachey, Clive Bell and Roger Fry, Duncan Grant and Mark Gertler.

34   ROCHE, PAUL. Introduction to *Duncan Grant*. Exhibition
      Catalog. Rye: Rye Art Gallery, pp. 2-6.
            Commentary on Grant as artist by one of Grant's most intimate
      friends.

35   SCHAEFER, J. O'BRIEN. "*Three Guineas* and *Quack Quack!* Read
      Together." *Virginia Woolf Miscellany* 7:2-3.
            These two works, one by Virginia and one by Leonard Woolf,

should be read as companion pieces. Shows some of the artistic
influence that developed between these two figures.

36   SHONE, RICHARD. *The Century of Change: British Painting Since
      1900*. Oxford and New York: Phaidon Press; E. P. Dutton, 324 pp.
      Includes some commentary on the Bloomsbury Artists.

37   SILVER, B.R. "Virginia Woolf and the Concept of Community."
      Women's Studies 4, nos. 2-3:291-98.
         Relates Woolf's concept of community to the Elizabethans and
      the Elizabethan playhouse. Connects the community of Oxbridge to
      Bloomsbury prior to World War I.

38   SPATER, GEORGE, and IAN PARSONS. *A Marriage of True
      Minds: An Intimate Portrait of Leonard and Virginia Woolf*. London
      and New York: Harcourt Brace Jovanovich, 210 pp.
         Introduction by Quentin Bell describes value of this study and of
      Bloomsbury. Biographical study, beginning with the early years of both
      Virginia Stephen and Leonard Woolf. Extensive use of primary
      materials. Full description of early Bloomsbury but critical of any real
      association which could be called "late Bloomsbury."

39   SPEAR, R.E. "Acquisitions: 1975-76." *Oberlin College Bulletin* 34,
      no. 1 (76-77):11.
         Comments on paintings by Roger Fry ("Vanessa Bell Sewing")
      and Duncan Grant ("Design for a Window Seat") acquired by Oberlin
      College.

40   SQUIER, SUSAN MERRILL. "The Politics of Street Haunting:
      Virginia Woolf and the City." Ph.D. dissertation, Stanford
      University, 291 pp.
         Deals with Woolf's residence in Bloomsbury. See *Dissertation
      Abstracts International* 38:5468A-69A. Published as *Virginia Woolf and
      London*. (See 1985.34.)

41   STEELE, ELIZABETH, KAREN REYNDERS, and JUDITH
      LANGE. "Glossary-Index to Virginia Woolf's *Orlando*." *Virginia
      Woolf Quarterly* 3, nos. 1-2 (Winter-Spring):38-64.
         Glossary-Index to help those teaching this novel. Includes
      reference to Vita Sackville-West, the Sackvilles, and their country
      home, Knole.

42   STEWART, J.I.M. "The Victim of Bloomsbury." *Times Literary Supplement* (London) (27 May):642.
      Review of *The Diary of Virginia Woolf*, Vol. 1, *1915-1919*, edited by Anne Olivier Bell: "It cannot be maintained that, as a person, the Virginia Woolf now so largely revealed is likely to make a favourable initial impression on a reader not already acquainted with the quality of her courage and the pitch of her spirit."

43   SUTTON, DENYS. "And is There Honey Still . . . ?" *Apollo* 105 (January):77-78.
      Review of Richard Shone's *Bloomsbury Portraits*. States that "modern enthusiasts are keener about the lives of the Bloomsberries than about their works. This is perhaps understandable, for their achievement is on the meager side." Very critical of Shone's book, identifying errors in fact: "Mr. Shone's ignorance about the cultural background of the period is surprising."

44   TAYLOR, DAVID G. "The Aesthetic Theories of Roger Fry Reconsidered." *Journal of Aesthetics and Art Criticism* 36, no. 1 (Fall):63-72.
      Asserts that Fry's later work did not perpetuate the severities of his earlier criticism but rather was a vigorously liberalized, interpretative theory of the plastic arts. Argues against Morris Weitz's view that "Fry's theory of the appreciation of art is on the whole a reiteration of Bell's."

45   THAYER, JACQUELINE GAILLET. "Virginia Woolf: From Impressionism to Abstract Art." Ph.D. dissertation, University of Tulsa, 125 pp.
      "The affinities of Virginia Woolf's work with Impressionism and Post-Impressionism have been repeatedly noted by her critics. This study in addition examines the relationship of Woolf's art to the contemporary development in the visual arts from Impressionism to abstract art." States that "the metaphysical dimension of Virginia Woolf's art can be significantly examined in the light of G.E. Moore's concept of the material and the spiritual and Roger Fry and Clive Bell's concern with spirituality in art." Places Woolf's art within and without the Bloomsbury circle. See *Dissertation Abstracts International* 38:1419A.

46 TOMALIN, CLAIR. "Millionaire." *New Statesman* 93 (17 June):816-18.
Review of *The Diary of Virginia Woolf*, Vol. 1, *1915-1919*, edited by Anne Olivier Bell, commenting on the happiness apparent in this first volume. Comments on some of the relationships with various Bloomsbury figures, including Philip Morrell and Desmond MacCarthy.

47 WELLEK, RENE. "Virginia Woolf as Critic." *Southern Review* 13, no. 3 (July):419-37.
Overall evaluation of Woolf's critical writing which also comments on the influence of G.E. Moore: "Philosophical Woolf was no idealist, no Bersonian, not even a British empiricist but a fervent adherent of G.E. Moore, whom she studied with real effort in 1908 and even quoted in her novels."

48 WOOLF, VIRGINIA. A Change of Perspective: *The Letters of Virginia Woolf*, Vol. 3, *1923-1928*. Edited by Nigel Nicolson and Joanne Trautmann. London: Hogarth Press; New York: Harcourt Brace Jovanovich, 600 pp.
Introduction by Nigel Nicolson. Includes various letters about and to Bloomsbury figures: "I wish to God that Tomlin, Penroses, and Andersons had never left Bloomsbury. The rooms ring with their bright Bugger-Bloomsbury up to date bragging." Near the end of this period she suggests that "very little of old Bloomsbury is left." Nicolson states in his introduction that "these years, 1923 to 1928, were happy and successful for the Woolfs. Everything, in the end, turned out right." The relationship with Vita Sackville-West occurs during this period: "Ours was a friendship which might have disintegrated before it became an intimacy. There was much in Vita--Vanessa felt this--that was alien to Bloomsbury."

1978

1 ADAMS, ROBERT M. "Help with Virginia." *Times Literary Supplement* (London) (4 August):895.
Review of Heromine Lee's *Novels of Virginia Woolf* and Mitchell A. Leaska's *The Novels of Virginia Woolf From Beginning to End*. Suggests that Lee's account is sensible, without a detour through "the well-publicized sexual byways of the Bloomsbury Group."

2   ALLEN, PETER. *The Cambridge Apostles: The Early Years*.
    Cambridge: Cambridge University Press, 266 pp.
        History of the early years of the secret society which was to help
form Bloomsbury as it evolved out of associations developed at
Cambridge. Deals briefly with Bloomsbury figures who were members
of the Apostles, including Leonard Woolf, E.M. Forster, Lytton
Strachey, Jon Maynard Keynes. States that "the freedom and intensity
of relations among the Apostles could breed contempt for the relations
usually found among non-Apostles, and the Society sometimes
developed what looked to outsiders like a fixation on the enormous
importance of the difference between inside and outside," which is
related to Bloomsbury attitudes.

3   ALSOP, SUSAN MARY. *Lady Sackville: A Biography*. London:
    Weidenfeld & Nicolson; New York: Doubleday, 273 pp.
        Biographical study of Vita Sackville-West's mother, with
references to Virginia Woolf and Bloomsbury during the 1920s. Lady
Sackville states: "Vita dined at Virginia Woolf's, and told me how
brilliant the conversation was. I really understand how and why the
child likes the Bloomsbury people, who seem to appreciate her as she
deserves."

4   ANNAN, LORD. "The Art of Friendship." *Times Literary
    Supplement* (London) (24 March):334-36.
        Review of *E.M. Forster: A Life*, P.N. Furbank. Unlike other
Bloomsbury figures, Forster made his name before the war. Love "for
Forster meant friendship." But the feelings were too literary, as with
other figures in Bloomsbury. Compares him to the relationship
between Virginia Woolf and Vita Sackville-West, which needs no
literary allusions.

5   BEHM, CARL III. "E.M. Forster and the Modern World: A Study
    of the Cultural Themes in His Fiction, Essays, and Other Writings."
    Ph.D. dissertation, University of Maryland, 349 pp.
        "This dissertation examines the cultural themes of E.M. Forster
(1879-1970), whose liberal humanism was made to stand the tests of
war, cultural decline, and mass society which distinguish the modern
world." See *Dissertation Abstracts International* 39:4933A.

6   BLUNT, KATHERINE. Review of *The Letters of Virginia Woolf,*
     vols. 1 -3, edited by Nigel Nicolson. *Virginia Woolf Quarterly* 3, nos.
     3-4 (Summer-Fall):330-40.
         Gives overview of letters and events. Finds third volume most
appealing. Comments on Bloomsbury during World War I:
"Bloomsberries, many of them conscientious objectors, were scattered,
working as farm laborers in return for exemption." Discusses her
attitudes toward various figures as revealed in her letters.

7   BRINK, ANDREW. "Lady Ottoline Morrell's Life." *Russell* 29-
     32:75-83.
         Review of Sandra Jobson Darroch's *Ottoline: The Life of Lady
Ottoline Morrell* and *Lady Ottoline's Album,* edited by Carolyn G.
Helbrun: "Garsington is legendary as a World War I Mecca for
pacifists. It is natural that Sandra Darroch should draw attention to
Garsington as a cultural generating point, a sort of extension of
'Bloomsbury' with which the Morrells were closely associated."
Wonders whether this biography will reduce Ottoline's status to "a
precursor of sexual 'liberation,' a false ideal of our time."

8   BROWN, CAROLE O. "The Art of the Novel: Virginia Woolf's
     The Voyage Out." *Virginia Woolf Quarterly* 3, nos. 3-4 (Summer-
     Fall):68-84.
         Deals with the relationship between Fry and Woolf.

9   CAMPBELL, MARY J. Review of *The Diary of Virginia Woolf,* Vol.
     1, *1915-1919,* edited by Anne Olivier Bell. *Virginia Woolf Quarterly*
     3, nos. 3-4 (Summer-Fall):341-42.
         Suggests that for the Bloomsbury coterie scholar a new
dimension has been added with these diaries. Includes long extracts
from the diaries.

10   CARRINGTON, NOEL. *Carrington: Paintings, Drawings and
     Decorations.* Foreword by Sir John Rothenstein. Oxford: Oxford
     Polytechnic Press, 95 pp.
         Rothenstein suggests that Carrington as artist has been almost
forgotten. Comments on her writing also. Noel Carrington gives an
overview of Carrington's life, which includes commentary on her years
at the Slade, where she met Mark Gertler, Dorothy Brett, and others.
Carrington met Lytton Strachey in 1915 at Asheham, the Woolf's home
in Sussex: "Strachey was one of the central figures in the Cambridge-

Bloomsbury elite." Describes the developing and complex relationship with Strachey. Devotes separate section to her marriage to Ralph Partridge. Includes prints, some in color, of her various paintings.

11   CARROLL, BERENICE A. "'To Crush Him in Our Own Country': The Political Thought of Virginia Woolf." *Feminist Studies* 4, no. 1 (February):99-131.
        Woolf is seldom seen as a political writer; "the political content of her writings goes completely unnoticed." Suggests that "in interpreting Woolf's novels, it is necessary to recognize that, particularly in the more mature works, there is hardly a word without significance, and that the significance is often a well-concealed political message." Deals somewhat with Bloomsbury thought and ideals and with the political thought of Leonard Woolf in relation to Woolf's novels.

12   CLARKE, LORD. "Duncan Grant." *Adam* 41 (1978):7-8.
        Brief commentary on Grant's art, which includes his Bloomsbury association and his relationship with Vanessa Bell.

13   CLARKE, PETER. "A Peculiar Kind of Socialist." *Times Literary Supplement* (LOndon) (29 September):1072.
        Review of Duncan Wilson's *Leonard Woolf: A Political Biography*: "The association of Leonard Woolf with Bloomsbury seems inescapable." But this biography resists its scope. The author "dispels any suspicion that this is the mere epiphenomenon of Bloomsbury, and it hardly impinges upon the territory magisterially annexed by Quentin Bell in his biography of Virginia Woolf."

14   DELANY, PAUL. *D.H. Lawrence's Nightmare: The Writer and His Circle in the Years of the Great War.* New York: Basic Books, 420 pp.
        Various chapters deal with world of Lady Ottoline Morrell and Bloomsbury figures. "Interlude at Bedford Square" (pp. 45-50) gives background of Morrell and her parties at Bedford Square, which included E.M. Forster, Dora Carrington, Duncan Grant, and D.H. Lawrence. "Lawrence and Forster: First Skirmish with Bloomsbury" (pp. 50-57) evaluates Lawrence's plan for the utopian colony Rananim and his early dealings with Forster, particularly in relation to the latter's homosexuality. "Ottoline, Russell, and Revolution" (pp. 64-74) describes the association of Lawrence and Russell through Ottoline Morrell: "Before his disillusionment with Ottoline, however, Lawrence

saw his move to Garsington as an opportunity to create a sacred precinct of the 'new life,' with herself as its oracle." "Lawrence at Trinity" (pp. 77-81) gives the background to the "Apostles" and describes Lawrence's negative reactions to his visit to Trinity College, Cambridge, where he met G.E. Moore, Maynard Keynes, and others. "A Visit from David and Frankie" describes Lawrence's relationship with David Garnett and Francis Birrell, with commentary on their Bloomsbury association: "The prevalence of homosexuality in the Bloomsbury circle caused Lawrence to deliberately slam the door on relationships that might have been both intrinsically rewarding and a support in his later troubles with the authorities." "Ottoline: The Tyranny of Will" (pp. 91-93) describes Ottoline as depicted in *Women in Love*. "Garsington: The Nucleus of a New Belief" (pp. 109-18) deals further with Russell and Lawrence at Ottoline's estate.

15 ____. "Lawrence and Forster: First Skirmish with Bloomsbury." *D.H. Lawrence Review* 11, no. 1 (Spring):63-72.
Reprinted in *D.H. Lawrence's Nightmare*, by Paul Delany. (See 1978.14.)

16 DINNAGE, ROSEMARY. "Angel in the House." *Times Literary Supplement* (London) (6 January):7.
Review of Virginia Woolf's *The Pargiters*, edited by Mitchell A. Leaska, which is an early manuscript version of *The Years*. Deals briefly with the relationship between Leonard and Virginia during the composition of the text.

17 DRABBLE, MARGARET. "A Woman's Life." *New Statesman* 96 (3 November):585-86.
Review of *A Reflection of the Other Person: The Letters of Virginia Woolf, 1929-1931*, edited by Nigel Nicolson; *Woman of Letters: A Life of Virginia Woolf*, by Phyllis Rose; and *Leonard Woolf: A Political Biography*, by Duncan Wilson. Minor references to Virginia Woolf's relationship to her husband and her sister Vanessa.

18 FURBANK, P.N. *E.M. Forster: A Life.* 2 vols. New York: Harcourt Brace Jovanovich, 359 pp.
Biographical study with many references to Forster's Bloomsbury associations. Volume One deals extensively with Cambridge and the Apostles, which "had recently entered a particularly brilliant era,

through the influence of G.E. Moore." The relationship and clash with Virginia Woolf and Forster is described in terms of "Bloomsbury style."

19 GORSKY, SUSAN RUBINOW. *Virginia Woolf.* Boston: Twayne, 173 pp.

Study that aims to be a "unified introduction to Virginia Woolf as literary and social theoretician, fiction writer, human being, and representative of the modernists." Includes extensive commentary on Woolf's Bloomsbury association in "Bloomsbury: The Growth of an Artist" and in "Mrs. Woolf" (pp. 19-27): "The spirit of free thought encouraged Virginia to develop her own independence, and their sense of faith in the possibilities of art encouraged her to seek in her own fiction ways to express her vision of the new world, one which Bloomsbury was helping to define and to shape."

20 GOTTLIEB, FREEMA. "Reality and Romance: Leonard Woolf's Portraiture of Virginia Woolf in Various Early Writings." *Virginia Woolf Quarterly* 3, no. 3-4 (Summer-Fall):199-205.

Discusses *The Wise Virgins* as an autobiographical novel that is the literary expression of Leonard's love for Virginia: "The quality of Leonard's feeling for Virginia during their courtship and the early days of their marriage is reflected in the autobiographical novel, *The Wise Virgins* (1914), which he had in hand at the time, and which can be read simply as a poem in praise of his wife, and a literary expression of his love for her." Describes the emerging relationship between Leonard and Virginia. Compares *The Wise Virgins* to "Aspasia," a character sketch of Virginia.

21 HAMPSHIRE, STUART. "The Heavy Victorian Father." *Times Literary Supplement* (London) (10 February):159.

Review of *Sir Leslie Stephen's Mausoleum Book* edited by Alan Bell. This book supports Lytton Strachey, who emphasized the romantic remoteness of eminent Victorians, "who usually did not talk and write, and therefore apparently did not feel, in ways that seem to us natural and unforced."

22 HENIG, SUZANNE. "If Virginia Woolf Were Alive Today." *Virginia Woolf Quarterly* 3, nos. 3-4 (Summer-Fall):217-21.

Considers what Virginia Woolf's art would be like had she not committed suicide. Reviews her interaction with various Bloomsbury figures, including Lady Ottoline Morrell, Lytton Strachey, and others to show her contradictory character: "She accepted the hospitality of Lady Ottoline Morrell, a rich noblewoman whom history will remember as the patroness of Bloomsbury and the mistress of Bertrand Russell, yet was capable of mocking her cruelly in letters to Lytton Strachey and in her own diary."

23 _____. "Interview with Christopher Isherwood." *Virginia Woolf Quarterly* 3, nos. 3-4 (Summer-Fall):157-65.

Asks him about the stir Bloomsbury has created in our own time: "I don't think Woolf needs any partisan." States that he did not know Bloomsbury figures all that well: "I just knew Forster, but he wasn't as Bloomsbury as all that. I didn't know Vanessa Bell, Clive Bell, or Duncan Grant." He knew Keynes through the theatre and his wife, Lydia Lopoknova.

24 KENDZORA, KATHRYN. "'Life stand still here': The Frame Metaphor in *To the Lighthouse*." *Virginia Woolf Quarterly* 3, nos. 3-4 (Summer-Fall):252-67.

To fully understand the formal experiment in *To the Lighthouse*, it is important to see it as part of "the general experimentation with new forms which was characteristic of all the arts in the late nineteenth and early twentieth centuries." Uses Cézanne and Roger Fry as basis of Woolf's desire to "realize the underlying structures, the significant formal pattern." Suggests that the philosophical influence of Fry is more clearly "documented than Bergson's since Fry was a member of the Bloomsbury Group and Virginia Woolf was his biographer."

25 KING, FRANCIS. *E.M. Forster and His World*. Charles Scribner's Sons, 128 pp.

Includes brief description of his association with the Cambridge Apostles and his later connections with Bloomsbury: "What Forster also derived from the Apostles, as later from the Bloomsbury Group, was a sense of belonging to an elite, a Blessed Band of Brothers."

26 LEHMANN, JOHN. *Thrown to the Woolfs*. Introduction by Phyllis Rose. London: Weidenfeld & Nicolson; New York: Holt, Rinehart & Winston, 164 pp.

Bittersweet memories of Lehmann's association with the Hogarth Press, which was central to Bllomsbury, with the Woolfs together, and with Leonard Woolf in the forties, expanded and modified from earlier publication in light of more recent memoirs by others and newly

published documents, such as Virginia Woolf's *Diaries* and *Letters*.
Phyllis Rose states in the introduction that "the history of the Hogarth
Press is exciting because it suggests the triumph of imagination over
capital, the creative mind over the managerial." Lehmann states that
he has not confined himself to his relations and work with the Woolfs
themselves; he has "tried to give a picture of . . . [his] relations with
the writers who were already, or came to be, published by the press."

27   LESSER, SIMON. "Creativity versus Death: Virginia Woolf (1882-
      1941)." *Hartford Studies in Literature* 10:49-69.
          General overview of Virginia Woolf's despondency and
breakdowns, with speculations on her psychology. Deals with her
relationship with Leonard and other Bloomsbury figures.

28   LEVY, PAUL. "The Colours of Carrington." *Times Literary
      Supplement* (London) (17 February):200.
          Commentary on the artistic reputation and life of Dora
Carrington: "Dora Carrington's personality must have been magnetic.
She was obviously the sort of woman whose attraction for most men--
and for a few other women--was utterly irresistible." Describes her
relationship with Strachey, the problems with her lack of education by
Bloomsbury Standards, and the influence on her art by Mark Gertler.

29   LYON, GEORGE ELLA HOSKINS. "The Dilemma of the Body in
      Virginia Woolf and E.M. Forster." Ph.D. dissertation, Indiana
      University, 141 pp.
          Explores "the paradoxical treatment of the bodily experience in
Virginia Woolf's and E.M. Forster's fiction, the circumspection and
reserve they show despite their pleas for the unity of body and spirit
and for honesty in dealing with all facets of human life." Compares
fours sets of novels: *The Voyage Out* and *The Longest Journey*, *Mrs.
Dalloway* and *Howard's End*, *Orlando* and *Maurice*, and *Between the
Acts* and *A Passage to India*. See *Dissertation Abstracts International*
39:873A-74A.

30   MEYERS, JEFFREY. *Katherine Mansfield: A Biography*. London:
      Hamish Hamilton. Reprint. New York: New Directions, 1980, 386
      pp.
          Includes Chapter Ten, "Garsington and Bloomsbury, 1916-1917"
(pp. 130-48), which deals with Mansfield's relationship with Lady
Ottoline Morrell, Bertrand Russell, and Virginia Woolf. Compares and

distinguishes Mansfield's and Virginia Woolf's temperaments and attitudes, and summarizes their acquaintance.

31   PARTRIDGE, FRANCES. *A Pacifist's War*. London: Hogarth Press, 176 pp.
         Memoir which deals with various Bloomsbury figures during World War One, including Lytton Strachey, Duncan Grant and others.

32   PEARSON, JOHN. "'In Full United Swing'--The Sitwells Remembered." *Listener* 100 (30 November):731-33.
         Discussion of the Sitwells based primarily upon personal association by John Pearson, Frank Margo, Harold Acton, Peter Quennell, William Walton, John Piper, and John Lehmann.

33   _____. *The Sitwells: A Family Biography*. New York and London: Harcourt Brace Jovanovich, 534 pp.
         Full biographical study of the Sitwells, Edith, Osbert, and Sacheverell, which includes many references to Bloomsbury activities and figures. During the 1918-1919 period, the Diaghilev Ballet became "the rage with London's intellectuals, particularly with Bloomsbury." When the Sitwells threw "a full-scale party for the Russian Ballet at Swan Walk on 12 October, Bloomsbury arrived in force. Indeed, it was here that Maynard Keynes first met Lopokova, and started the most unlikely union of all between Bloomsbury and the Ballet Russes." Describes the cultural struggle during the 1920s, the experimentalists against the traditionalists, including the middle class and the popular press, which involved Bloomsbury and which centered on the French Art Exhibition.

34   PERL, JED. "Bloomsbury Painters and Their Circle." *Arts Magazine* 52 (May):18.
         Review of "Bloomsbury Painters and Their Circle," a traveling exhibition organized by the Beaverbrook Art Gallery in New Brunswick, Canada. This show "tells the story of a group who loved the French tradition too much." These artists were unable "to assimilate the essential lessons of Cubism: the canvas as center of a universe of extended possibilities, the prism of cubist space."

35   PIMLOTT, BEN. "De haut en bas." *New Society* 46 (5 October):30-31.
         Review of Duncan Wilson's *Leonard Woolf: A Political*

Biography. Few now think of Leonard Woolf as a politician. He is known as a "man of letters--critic, essayist, editor, journalist, publisher, husband of Virginia Woolf, friend of Lytton and Maynard: one of the mythic figures at the center of the Bloomsbury firmament." Describes G.E. Moore's influence in relation to Woolf's political ideals.

36   POOLE, ROGER. *The Unknown Virginia Woolf.* Cambridge: Cambridge University Press, 285 pp.
       Deals somewhat with the psychology of Woolf in relation to Bloomsbury.

37   ROBBINS, RAE GALLANT. *The Bloomsbury Group: A Selected Bibliography.* Kenmore, Wash.: Price Guide Publishers, 223 pp.
       Lists works by and about major figures in the Bloomsbury Group, Clive Bell, Vanessa Bell, E.M. Forster, Roger Fry, Duncan Grant, Maynard Keynes, Desmond MacCarthy, Molly MacCarthy, Andian Stephen, Karin Costelloe Stephen, Lytton Strachey, Saxon Sydney-Turner, Leonard Woolf, Virginia Woolf, as well as some later additions to the group, Angelica Bell, Julian Bell, Quentin Bell, David Garnett.. Secondary works includes only books or portions of books about the group. Limited selection.

38   ROSE, PHYLLIS. "Portrait of a Woman of Letters." *Partisan Review* 45, no. 3:446-57.
       Portrait of Woolf's temperament: "People who knew her frequently described her like a fairy-tale princess, so unusual as to be otherworldly, so elegant of build, with such deep-set eyes, so wraithlike, so distinguished, and so fragile." Her relationship with figures like Lady Ottoline Morrell "flattered her self-esteem." Describes also early years with Vanessa and Gerald Duckworth. Briefly suggests some connections with E.M. Forster.

39   _____. *Woman of Letters: A Life of Virginia Woolf.* New York: Oxford University Press, 298 pp.
       Biographical study "which aims to place Virginia Woolf's work in a biographical context." Includes separate chapters on "Bloomsbury," "Lytton Strachey and Leonard Woolf," and "V. Sackville-West and Androgyny." Describes the masculine element in Bloomsbury's origin: "Virginia Woolf's vision of Cambridge is inseparable from the experience of exclusion." The early period of Bloomsbury form the basis for her novels: "The mythic period of Woolf's life was over by

World War I." Virginia's love for Vita "seems to have fueled" her imagination.

40   RUDIKOFF, SONYA. "Afraid of Virginia Woolf?" *American Scholar* 47 (Spring):245-54, 270-71.
     "Who would have imagined that in 1962 Virginia Woolf as a literary figure would be made to stand for that old culture?" Question what Virginia Woolf stands for in Albee's play, and discusses the emergence of Woolf studies in various English departments. Includes many references to Bloomsbury: "Perhaps earlier readers were too beguiled by her graceful tours around the library, her essays, Bloomsbury, the cozy world of lunches and teas, of universities, squares, and servants, where there were always links to the great world and always some niece of an earl to be seen." Also evaluates the feminist criticism generated by Woolf studies.

41   SHAW, VALERIE. "The Secret Companion." *Critical Quarterly* 20, no. 1 (Spring):70-77.
     Commentary on Woolf related to the publication of *The Diary of Virginia Woolf*, Vol. 1, *1915-1919*, edited by Anne Olivier Bell and *Books and Portraits: Some Further Selections from the Literary and Biographical Writings of Virginia Woolf*, edited by Mary Lyon: "Virginia Woolf herself was thankful to be on the inside and thus immune from the hypnotic fascination 'Bloomsbury' exerted even then over 'the sane and the insane alike.'"

42   TEAVER, WILLIAM. "Just Carrington." *Observer Magazine* (12 March):28-29.
     Commentary, with various illustrations, on Dora Carrington's artistic development. Includes commentary on Carrington's association with Bloomsbury, especially through her relationship with Lytton Strachey.

43   VANDERWERFF, WHITNEY GROVE. "Virginia Woolf as Equilibrist: The Moment of Vision and the Androgynous Mind." Ph.D. dissertation, University of North Carolina at Greensboro, 398 pp.
     This study asserts that "Virginia Woolf's novels reflect her fictive search for a balance between what she called the masculine and feminine sides of the brain." Minds that have achieved an balance of these opposing forces are called "androgynous," and "through characters

whose minds reflect such balance and wholeness, Virginia Woolf conveys the experience of the moment of vision." Chapter Two concerns Woolf's social and cultural milieu. "It finds the Stephen household representative of the Victorian patriarchy and explains that in Bloomsbury, Virginia Stephen found the androgynous ideal realized socially as well as aesthetically." See *Dissertation Abstracts International* 39:3606A-7A.

44 WATNEY, SIMON. "Duncan Grant, 1885-1970." *Virginia Woolf Miscellany*:1-2.
Brief commentary on Duncan Grant and his connection with Vanessa Bell and Virginia Woolf.

45 WILSON, DUNCAN. *Leonard Woolf: A Political Biography.* Assisted by J. Eisenberg. New York: St. Martin's Press; London: Hogarth Press, 282 pp.
A biographical study limited to Leonard Woolf's political activities. Includes commentary on his years at Cambridge, his involvement with the Labor Movement and the Fabians, and his political theories. The commentary is limited but relates well to the Bloomsbury world which Leonard inhabited. Gives sense of the politics of Bloomsbury as shown through Leonard's activities.

46 WONG, SAU-LING CYNTHIA. "A Study of Roger Fry and Virginia Woolf from a Chinese Perspective." Ph. D. dissertation, Stanford University, 475 pp.
"This dissertation is not a comparative study of historical influences, for Bloomsbury's contacts with Chinese culture were very meager. Instead, it uses certain Taoist-Zen terms as foci for interpretation, as short-hand labels for a configuration of ideas peripheral to the Judaeo-Christian tradition but felt to be central to Fry's, Woolf's, and the Taoist-Zen world-view." See *Dissertation Abstracts International* 38:7353A.

47 WOOLF, VIRGINIA. *The Diary of Virginia Woolf*, Vol. 2, *1920-1924.* Edited by Anne Olivier Bell and Andrew McNeillie. London: Hogarth Press; New York: Harcourt Brace Jovanovich, 371 pp.
Entries include commentary on Bloomsbury and Bloomsbury figures. E.M. Forster, for example, is "critical of the East as of Bloomsbury." Raymond Mortimer squirms "in Cambridge company." She quotes him as saying, "you can't imagine what it has been to me

getting to know Bloomsbury. They're different human beings from any I thought possible."

48 _____. A Reflection of the Other Person: *The Letters of Virginia Woolf*, Vol. 4, *1929-1931*. Edited by Nigel Nicolson and Joanne Trautmann. London: Hogarth Press; New York: Harcourt Brace Jovanovich, 442 pp.

Introduction by Nigel Nicolson. Includes letters to and about various Bloomsbury figures, including some commentary on the famous Alice-In-Wonderland party for Angelica's eleventh birthday. Nicolson states that she wrote less to her Bloomsbury friends during this period, "but when one of her oldest friends, Lytton Strachey, fell seriously ill in December 1931, there was no doubt where Virginia's deepest affections lay."

1979

1 ANNAN, NOEL. "Georgian Squares and Charmed Circles." *Times Literary Supplement* (London) (23 November):19-29.

Review of *Bloomsbury: A House of Lines*, by Leon Edel. The sexual interests of the group are less interesting than "the changes in the interests and the development of the personalities." Suggests that we still recoil from such work: "Some hypertrophy of the heart seems to strike the defenders of Bloomsbury." Bloomsbury saw life as a comedy.

2 "Appeal for Charleston." *Antique Collector* 50 (October):71.

Brief commentary on Charleston, identifying its importance as the country seat of Bloomsbury. Includes an appeal for help in saving this house.

3 BEER, JOHN. "'The Last Englishman': Lawrence's Appreciation of Forster." In *E.M. Forster: A Human Exploration*. Edited by G.K. Das and John Beer. New York: New York University Press, pp. 245-68.

Deals with connections between Lawrence and Forster: "The point which one notices again and again is that the two writers are handling similar themes, with Lawrence in each case one stage further along the road." Suggests that the "respective differences of the men

define themselves well in their respective relationships with the
Bloomsbury Group." Forster's relationship was more equivocal.

4   BELL, QUENTIN. "Bloomsbury and the 'Vulgar Passions.'" *Critical
     Inquiry* 6, no. 2 (Winter):239-56.
         Evaluates Bloomsbury politics in relation to the view that the
group was more aesthete than political. The list of names reminds us
"that Bloomsbury produced authors who were not primarily or not
wholly concerned with aesthetics but with social problems and indeed
that there were some whom we should hardly think of as 'literary
artists' but rather as social theoretists who made use of language."
Deals with World War I, Virginia Woolf's feminism, Keynes, Leonard
Woolf, Bell and others.

5   ____. "Charleston." *Architectural Review* 166 (December):394-96.
         Article written in relation to the appeal to save Charleston, the
home of Vanessa Bell and Duncan Grant: "It is not so much a house
as a phenomenon. A place, that is, where the effects of time have
been so much arrested that we can observe a way of life and a work
which belongs, properly speaking, to a long vanished society."
Describes, with photographs, the interior of the house, including the
designs, based upon Post-impressionist aesthetic, by Grant, Bell, Fry
and others.

6   CAVALIERO, GLEN. *A Reading of E.M. Forster.* Totowa, NJ:
     Rowman & Littlefield, 187 pp.
         Suggests that "of necessity the biographical factor has to be
taken into account" in any reading of Forster. Gives details of
background at Cambridge and his association with Bloomsbury: G.E.
Moore's "ideas were the intellectual air he breathed, and were what put
him in sympathy with his Bloomsbury friends, with whom his name has
otherwise been too readily associated."

7   CURRIER, SUSAN. "Virginia Woolf: A Whole Vision and a
     Whole Aesthetic." Ph.D. dissertation, University of Massachusetts,
     260 pp.
         Describes the development of Woolf's fiction: "Her goal was to
unite the multiple dimensions of our lives in a whole vision and a
whole art." The third chapter deals with Woolf's use of "Impressionistic
stylistic methods to defamiliarize the false perspectives to which we are
most accustomed and Post-Impressionistic structural methods to achieve

a 'true reality' in their stead." See *Dissertation Abstracts International* 40:1480A.

8   EDEL, LEON. *Bloomsbury: A House of Lines.* New York: J.B. Lippincott, 288 pp.

Biographical study. Deals with the early lives and associations of Bloomsbury up to the beginnings of the Memoir Club. Deals with nine members: Clive Bell, Vanessa Bell, Roger Fry, Duncan Grant, Maynard Keynes, Desmond MacCarthy, Lytton Strachey, Leonard Woolf, Virginia Woolf. Excludes E.M. Forster, Ottoline Morrell and other associated figures. "Having abandoned the idea of writing nine essays . . . I resolved to seek my truths in both an episodic structure and a psychological interpretation of Bloomsbury's past."

9   FASSLER, BARBARA. "Theories of Homosexuality as a Source of Bloomsbury's Androgyny." *Signs* 5, no. 2 (Winter):237-51.

Asserts that there is a connection between theories of androgyny and Bloomsbury homosexuality: "Theories familiar to Bloomsbury hold homosexuality to be caused by a unique fusion of masculine and feminine elements. Notions about androgyny were closely intertwined with ideas about homosexuality." Deals with "trapped soul theory, " which is "linked to another image cluster pervasive and important both within the discussions of homosexuality and within the work of Bloomsbury: the body as clothing for the soul; actual clothing as a disguise, as a symbol of one's true sex, or as a prop to one's role; and masculine or feminine behavior as either a cover for, or a revelation of, the soul's true sex."

10   FENTON, TERRY. "Roger Fry (1866-1934): Painter as Critic, Critic as Painter." *Latern* 3, no. 3:137-40.

Commentary on Fry as painter focusing on the influence of the Post-impressionists on his work. His art changed from late-Victorian naturalism around 1909 "as a result of his growing appreciation of French Post-Impressionist painting." Comments on the difference between his conservative later art and his advanced critical writing.

11   FROMM, HAROLD. "Virginia Woolf: Art and Sexuality." *Virginia Quarterly Review* 55, no. 3 (Summer):441-59.

Discusses Woolf's emergence as a central literary figure and her separation from Bloomsbury. Focuses on feminist identification with Woolf and evaluations of Woolf's sexuality. Uses biographical material that relates her to her Bloomsbury background, particularly in relation to homosexuality. Concludes that "however 'aetherial' her daily life and however restrained her sexual activities, Virginia Woolf was a extraordinarily sentient person who was fully aware through firsthand feelings of her own of the nature and the complexity of the sensual life."

12   FURBANK, P.N. "Forster and 'Bloomsbury Prose.'" In *E.M. Forster: A Human Exploration: Centenary Essays*. Edited by G.K. Das and John Beer. New York: New York University Press, pp. 161-66.
      Deals with two aspects of Forster's prose, the "Bloomsbury" quality and the use of metaphor. In his study of Keats, as in Virginia Woolf's study of the Brownings, the "obliqueness and teasing refusal of the high road is a distinctively Bloomsbury trait." Cites Strachey as basis in the dismantling of Victorianism. Compares Forster's prose to the work of Virginia Woolf as well.

13   GALLAGHER, SARAH VAN SICKLE. "The Fiction of the Self: Virginia Woolf and the Problem of Biography." Ph.D. dissertation, State University of New York at Buffalo, 173 pp.
      Examines Woolf's biographical works and their influence on her fiction. Also discusses the autobiographical writings in *Moments of Being*. Includes discussion of *Orlando* and *Roger Fry*. See *Dissertation Abstracts International* 39:7339A.

14   GILLESPIE, DIANE FILBY. "Vanessa Bell, Virginia Woolf, and Duncan Grant: Conversation With Angelica Garnett." *Modernist Studies: Literature and Culture, 1920-1940* 3, no. 3:151-58.
      Interview with Angelica Garnett in which she considers the differences between Virginia Woolf and Vanessa Bell. Also deals with Vanessa's relationship with Duncan Grant. She describes some of her reservations about the traditional way in which the two sisters are viewed. States that "the sort of arrogance that most people complain of in connection with Bloomsbury, particularly in connection with her, was really a defense mechanism and I don't think she realized it."

15   GINDIN, JAMES. "A Precipice Marked V." *Studies in the Novel* 11, no. 1 (Spring):82-98.
      Comments on the relationship between Virginia Woolf and Vita Sackville-West in relation to Woolf's "fear of her own identity dissolving

in the chaos of total commitment to someone or something else and her consequent emphasis on the need for careful and conscious control." Uses evidence primarily from Woolf's letters and diaries.

16   HALPERIN, JOHN. "Bloomsbury and Virginia Woolf: Another View." *Dalhousie Review* 59 (Autumn):426-42
Reviews the multiplicity of attitudes and varying popular reputation of the Bloomsbury Group: "Virginia Woolf represents what is both good and bad about Bloomsbury, and a lot of what is most interesting and contradictory about it." She demonstrates in her life and work "what seems to me one of the things most typical of Bloomsbury: its brilliant creative energy on the one hand and its paucity of warmth, of human feeling, on the other."

17   HAWKES, ELLEN. "Introduction to 'Friendships Gallery.'" *Twentieth Century Literature* 25, 3-4 (Fall-Winter):270-73.
Introduction to this "early example of Virginia Woolf's way of expressing her affection and admiration for a woman friend," Violet Dickinson, and compares this to Vita Sackville-West as described in *Orlando*. Dickinson's relationship with Woolf was important "during the difficult years when her father died, when her brother Thoby died, when Vanessa's marriage to Clive Bell put her at a distance, when in short all seemed to conspire against her, that is all except her friend Violet Dickinson."

18   HEINE, ELIZABETH. "The Earlier *Voyage Out*: Virginia Woolf's First Novel." *Bulletin of Research in the Humanities* 82 (Autumn):294-316.
Commentary on the various manuscripts related to *Voyage Out* in the Berg Collection of the New York Public Library. Mentions her interaction with various Bloomsbury figures when she submitted the manuscript to Gerald Duckworth in 1913 and when it was published in 1915. Also traces the revisions and associations with Bloomsbury figures.

19   ____. "E.M. Forster's *Commonplace Book*." *Contemporary Review* 234 (May):251-55.
Review of *Commonplace Book*, by E.M. Forster, with brief commentary on some Bloomsbury connections: "Bloomsbury *aficionados* will be rewarded with Forster's note on the group as a

literary movement, in which he regrets, along lines suggested by Gerald Heard, what he takes to be the intellectual's fear of emotion."

20   HINTIKKA, JAAKKO. "Virginia Woolf and Our Knowledge of the External World." *Journal of Aesthetics and Art Criticism* 38 (Fall):5-14.
     "In the history of recent ideas, there are few gaps as glaring as the failure of almost all scholars to study in any real depth the interplay of philosophical and literary methods, values, and doctrines in the Bloomsbury group." Claims that there is a close connection "between Bloomsbury fiction and the epistemology and ontology of Russell, Moore, and Whitehead" but deals mostly with the connections between Russell's philosophy and Woolf's fiction. Doubts there was direct influence: "However, there is indirect influence which is very real indeed. . . . All that Virginia Woolf needed to reach an intuitive grasp of several of Russell's themes was to give certain familiar Platonic questions a slightly new twist, a twist which Virginia Woolf could easily have acquired through the almost subconscious osmotic processes of conversation and listening."

21   HOY, PAT C., II. "E.M. Forster: Pagan Humanist." Ph.D. dissertation, University of Pennsylvania, 476 pp.
     "This study examines the relationship between Forster's interest in the body and his literary vision and highlights the changes in that vision from the earliest stories and sketches in the *Independent Review* through the six novels." Includes full evaluation of Forster's debate with Virginia Woolf over poetic and symbolic technique.

22   HUTCHEON, LINDA. "Revolt and Ideal in Bloomsbury." *English Studies in Canada* 5, no. 1 (Spring):78-93.
     Discussion of revolt and ideal in sex and art in Bloomsbury: "What ever the individual or social reasons for this revolt, it seems evident that Bloomsbury did want to lead the way to change in educated public opinion on sexual mores." Deals with the connection between sexual revolt and artistic creation, especially in relation to the homosexuality of Forster, Lytton Strachey, and Virginia Woolf. The major concern of Bloomsbury was love and human relations in general: "In the last Bloomsbury novels, the land that says 'No--not yet' and those 'hidden faces' suggest a very intimate connection of sex and art."

23 ____. "'Sublime Noise' for Three Friends: E.M. Forster, Roger
Fry, and Charles Mauron." *Modern Studies: Literature and Culture
1920-1940* 3:141-58.
   Reprinted in *E.M. Forster: Centenary Revaluations*, ed. Judith
Scherer Herz and Robert K. Martin, pp. 84-98. (See 1982.17.)

24 HYNES, SAMUEL. "Mr. and Mrs. Leonard Woolf." *New York
Times Book Review* (25 February):11, 31.
   Review of Roger Poole's *The Unknown Virginia Woolf* and
Duncan Wilson's *Leonard Woolf: A Political Biography*. Deals with the
dynamic of the relationship between Leonard and Virginia Woolf in
which he states that Leonard's problem with politics is mirrored in his
relationship with Virginia: "He offered to men and nations the advice
of a rational man (as he had offered it to Virginia), and men and
nations went on with their political insanities."

25 LEHMANN, JOHN. "Ringside View." *London Magazine* 18
(February):99-102.
   Review of *Facades* by John Pearson, which was published in
America under the title *The Sitwells: A Family's Biography*. States that
he "was a close friend of both Edith and Osbert during the last quarter
of a century of their lives, and I sometimes wondered whether I was
reading about the same people." The Sitwells "attracted lightning as
Bloomsbury never did, partly because they deliberately picked quarrels
with the established literary world."

26 L'ENFANT, JULIE. "A Mind Running Loose: New Views of the
Private Virginia Woolf." *Southern Review* 15 (Summer):688-95.
   Review-essay on the first two volumes of *The Diary of Virginia
Woolf*, edited by Anne Olivier Bell; *Virginia Woolf: Sources of Madness
and Art*, by Jean O. Love; and *The Unknown Virginia Woolf*, by Roger
Poole. Deals with various aspects of Woolf's relationships with
Bloomsbury figures: "Poole presents Leonard Woolf, moreover, as the
quintessence of a reductive Bloomsbury rationalism."

27 LEVY, PAUL. *Moore: G.E. Moore and the Cambridge Apostles.*
London: Weidenfeld & Nicolson; New York: Holt, Rinehart &
Winston, 335 pp.
   Evaluates the impact of G.E. Moore on British culture, with
some focus on Bloomsbury: "A less documentable claim I have heard
made about the breadth of Moore's influence--on the world outside

that of Bloomsbury and of philosophy--is that of the effect of the propagation of the 'Ideal Utilitarian' position of *Principia Ethica*." Throughout this study, Levy alludes to Bloomsbury and Bloomsbury figures in relation to Moore's thought and character.

28   McDOWELL, FREDERICK P.W. "Forster Scholarship and Criticism for the Desert Islander." In *E.M. Forster: A Human Exploration*. Edited by G.K. Das and John Beer. New York: New York University Press. pp. 269-82.
        Overview of significant criticism of Forster, with commentary on various works that relate Forster to Bloomsbury.

29   MAXWELL-MAHON, W.D. "E.M. Forster: The Last of the Apostles." *Latern* 29, no. 1 (December):20-25.
        General account of Forster's life and work. Cambridge remained his spiritual and intellectual home. Identifies the Apostles as the nucleus of the Bloomsbury Group: "This assembly of intellectual and artistic talent, an extension of Cambridge University, stood in the same relationship to early twentieth-century cultural society as Dr. Johnson did to the eighteenth century. *The Longest Journey* came out of the influence of this group. Comments on various Bloomsbury reactions to this novel.

30   MEYEROWITZ, SELMA. "*The Hogarth Letters*: Bloomsbury Writers on Art and Politics." *San Jose Studies* 5, no. 1:76-85.
        Evaluation of the Bloomsbury Group during the 1930s based upon a reading of *The Hogarth Letters* (1933): "Bloomsbury writers expressed their concern with the social, artistic, economic, and political issues affecting individual consciousness and international life." This volume embodies "the philosophy toward art, literature, and politics of both the Hogarth Press and the Bloomsbury Group." Concludes that the "social upheaval of the 1930s made Europe, including Bloomsbury, aware that social values and conventions and political ideology could threaten individual and social survival. *The Hogarth Letter* reveal that Bloomsbury writers used literature, and especially the Hogarth Press, to express their political consciousness and their views on the role of art and literature in society."

31   MOORE, MADELINE. "*Orlando*: An Edition of the Manuscript." *Twentieth Century Literature* 35, nos. 3-4(Fall/Winter):303-7.
        Introduction and commentary, published along with the edition.

Deals with the relationship of Woolf and Sackville-West, as well as Woolf's developing theory of biography: "Like Stern, Woolf sought to explode the fact-bound nature of fiction by externalizing the self-consciousness of the author or 'biographer' herself. In Vita Sackville-West, she discovered a modern prototype whose complexity called for the self-conscious fantasies which permeate *Orlando*."

32   NEVE, CHRISTOPHER. "A Last Outpost of Bloomsbury: Why Save Charleston?" *Country Life* 166 (29 November):1994-97.
        Article written in behalf of the appeal to save Charleston, the Home of Vanessa Bell and Duncan Grant. Gives brief history of Charlestoon, including various photographs: "The irresistible attraction of Charleston is that it is the last surviving example of a house decorated and re-decorated over a long period by Vanessa Bell and Duncan Grant, and lived in or visited constantly by countless other artists and writers connected with Bloomsbury who affected its appearance and contributed to its extraordinary atmosphere."

33   ROSENBAUM, S.P. "Conversation with Julian Fry." *Modernist Studies: Literature and Culture, 1920-40* 3:127-40.
        Interview with Julian Fry dealing with his recollections of his father and of Bloomsbury. Comments on John Rothenstein's criticism of Bloomsbury and on the pacifism during World War I in relation to Fry's Quaker background: "Yes, but Bloomsbury was an intellectual concern not a religious concern. The Garsington people of Lady Ottoline Morrell were intellectually convinced conscientious objectors."

34   _____. "*The Longest Journey*: E.M. Forster's Refutation of Idealism." In *E.M. Forster: A Human Exploration*. Edited by G.K. Das and John Beer. New York: New York University Press, pp. 32-54.
        Evaluates G.E. Moore's influence on Forster, especially as displayed in *The Longest Journey*. Related to Bloomsbury adoption of his philosophy: "Perhaps the simplest way to show how Moore's rejection of Idealism for Realism is changed into something rich and even strange in *The Longest Journey* is to go through, one by one, the ideas that followed the original inspiration."

35   ROSENTHAL, MICHAEL. *Virginia Woolf*. New York: Columbia University Press, 270 pp.
        Stresses the primacy of form for Woolf in order to "provide a

focus which is not only central to her development as a writer but also
honors the complexity and merits of each individual work." Chapter
Two (pp. 19-34) deals extensively with Bloomsbury. Discusses the
various positive and negative definitions of Bloomsbury and cautions
against the "unqualified acceptance of any of the Bloomsbury myths."
It is "important to remember the most significant feature of
Bloomsbury is not the style it affected but the work it produced."

36   RUAS, CHARLES. "An Interview with Nigel Nicolson." *Book
      Forum* 4:618-35.
          Nicolson's memories of Virginia Woolf (1922-39), impressions of
her character (as contributing editor for her *Letters* and *Diaries*), and
portrait of her relationship with his mother, Vita Sackville-West.

37   RUDIKOFF, SONYA. "How Many Loves Had Virginia Woolf"
      Hudson Review 32, no. 4 (Winter 1979-1980):540-66.
          Commentary on Woolf's various relationships and attachments,
with remarks on some of the recent research on Woolf's life and time:
"Thus, when the series of attachments and losses in Woolf's life is
considered, the fact that such losses were exceedingly familiar to any
late Victorian family makes Woolf's own intensity about specific
attachments the more significant; she distanced herself from what has
been called the late Victorian 'pornography of death'" but was not
without the capacity for intense emotional display herself, as her
childhood history amply demonstrates." Includes discussions of her
relationship with her sister, Vanessa, and her reaction to her marriage
to Clive Bell, her relationship with her early suitors, Saxon Sydney-
Turner and Sidney Waterlow, and her relationship with Vita Sackville-
West: "Marriage was really just a more private version of Bloomsbury
life, however, and when Woolf became ill, the marriage modified the
Bloomsbury form but without essential change."

38   SHONE, RICHARD. "Portsmouth." *Burlington Magazine* 121
      (October):79-84.
          Review of Vanessa Bell Centenary Exhibition at Portsmouth
Museum and Art Gallery. Her later work is distinctly less interesting.
The work produced between 1910 and 1920 shows "serene audacity."
She is important also "as the sister of Virginia Woolf, a 'liberated'
woman and central figure in Bloomsbury."

39   SILVER, BRENDA R. "'Anon' and 'The Reader': Virginia Woolf's
     Last Essays." *Twentieth Century Literature* 25, no. 3-4
     (Fall/Winter):356-65.
          Introduction and commentary on these essays which are
     published in this issue. Deals briefly with the influence of Vita
     Sackville-West during this period, the late 1930s into 1941.

40   SKIDELSKY, ROBERT. "Keynes and the Restructuring of
     Liberalism." *Encounter* 52 (April):29-32, 34-39.
          General article on Keynes and political theory: "Keynes's
     political achievement can be fully appreciated only against the
     background of his times." Of crucial importance to Keynes's theory of
     unemployment and to the psychology of expectation is his "complex
     reaction to the Victorian moral legacy." He opposed the view that the
     duty of saving, or abstinence, should be seen as supreme virtue at the
     "expense of the 'arts of production as well as those of enjoyment'."
     This view "might have been expected from a member of Bloomsbury
     and an intimate friend of Lytton Strachey."

41   SPALDING, FRANCES. "Carrington." *Burlington Magazine* 121
     (January):47-48.
          Review of *Carrington: Paintings, Drawings and Decorations*, by
     Noel Carrington. Describes the revival of interest in Carrington's life
     and work, due to the publication of related studies, such as *Mark
     Gertler: Selected Letters*, edited by Noel Carrington, and Michael
     Holroyd's *Lytton Strachey*. Briefly describes her relationship with
     Lytton Strachey.

42   _____. Introduction to *Vanessa Bell 1879-1961*. Exhibition Catalog.
     Sheffield, England: Mappin Art Gallery, pp. 3-7.
          Gives background to Vanessa Bell, including her association with
     Roger Fry, Duncan Grant, and other Bloomsbury figures.

43   _____. "Vanessa Bell and Charleston." *Connoisseur* 202
     (October):143.
          Review of Vanessa Bell Centenary Exhibition held at the
     Mappin Art Gallery, Sheffield, and at the Portsmouth Museum and Art
     Gallery. Mentions the controversy over the possible destruction of her
     home Sussex farmhouse, Charleston, "which reflects a sensibility and a
     life-style that influenced the lives of these talented individuals and
     affected their work." Describes some aspects of the exhibition: "Even

when she returns in the 1920s to a more naturalistic style, her compositions remain bold and architectonic." States that the Post-impressionists released in her "a sudden burst of confidence in her own expression."

44   SPILKA, MARK. "New Life in the Works: Some Recent Woolf Studies." *Novel* 12, no. 2 (Winter):169-84.
       Review article giving overview of recent criticism of Virginia Woolf, some of which relates to Bloomsbury. Focuses on the connections between Woolf's life and her art made possible by the publication of memoirs and autobiographical writings. Studies discussed include Jean O. Love's *Virginia Woolf: Sources of Madness and Art*, Phyllis Rose's *Woman of Letters: A Life of Virginia Woolf*, and Roger Poole's *The Unknown Virginia Woolf*.

45   _____. "The Robber in the Bedroom; or, The Thief of Love: A Woolfian Grieving in Six Novels and Two Memoirs." *Critical Inquiry* 5:663-82.
       Chapter from his book, *Virginia Woolf's Quarrel with Grieving*. (See 1980.54.)

46   STANLEY, THOMAS F. "Bloomsbury: History, Myth, and Metaphor." *Southern Review* (Summer)15:696-701.
       Review-essay on various books related to Bloomsbury, including *Bloomsbury Heritage* by Elizabeth French Boyd and *Bloomsbury Portraits* by Richard Shone. Suggests that only recently are those associated with Bloomsbury, other than Virginia Woolf, Maynard Keynes, and E.M. Forster, being studies on the basis of their individual achievement.

47   STRACHEY, RICHARD. *A Strachey Child*. Exeter, England: A. Wheaton, 151 pp.
       First part of an autobiography by Lytton Strachey's nephew, also a Bloomsbury figure, with reference to Lytton and other Bloomsbury figures, including Duncan Grant, Vanessa Bell, and Virginia Woolf.

48   TRIVEDI, H.K. "Forster and Virginia Woolf: The Critical Friendship." In *E.M. Forster: A Human Exploration*. Edited by G.K. Das and John Beer. New York: New York University Press, pp. 216-30.
       Summarizes Virginia Woolf's and E.M. Forster's personal relationship and their responses to each other's works. The

relationship existed within the wider context of Bloomsbury: "In fact, Forster came to Virginia Woolf through his induction into Bloomsbury, and to Bloomsbury through 'the Apostles.'" Relationship with Leonard was at least as close as with Virginia.

49   WEBB, EUGENE. "The Spiritual Crisis: Keynes, Beckett, Baudelaire." *Soundings* 62:130-43.
     Includes some commentary on Keynes's Bloomsbury association.

50   WILSON, D.G. "Charles Lamb and Bloomsbury." *Charles Lamb Bulletin*, n.s. 26 (April):21-24.
     Deals with some resemblances between Charles Lamb and Virginia Woolf as well as with "the wider field of Bloomsbury." Discusses both figures in relation to madness and brings in Bloomsbury in relation to its Cambridge origin: "So it appears that the affinities which I see, and which I have discussed here between two such outwardly different authors as Virginia Woolf and Charles Lamb, and which are based essentially on the fact that both represent a Romantic reaction to a rigid classical form of writing, were apparent even in the very early years of our century, and those who formed and influenced the Bloomsbury 'group' (undefined as it is, we all recognize a Bloomsbury person when we see one) also formed a large proportion of those who did honour to the 'immortal memory' of Charles Lamb at Cambridge from 1909 to the First World War."

51   WOOLF, VIRGINIA. *The Sickle Side of the Moon: The Letters of Virginia Woolf*, Vol. 5, *1932-1935*. Edited by Nigel Nicolson and Joanne Trautmann. London: Hogarth Press. New York: Harcourt Brace Jovanovich, pp. 476.
     Introduction by Nigel Nicolson. Includes letters about and to various Bloomsbury figures. Mentions in one letter that the "Bloomsbury Group" is "merely a journalistic phrase which has no meaning that I am aware of," and in another that "to dwell upon Bloomsbury as an influence is liable to lead to judgments that, as far as I know have no basis in fact." Later comments that Lady Ottoline Morrell's memoirs, which she sent to Virginia to read, reveals "old Bloomsbury at its height." Nicolson comments that these were not happy years for Virginia; Roger Fry and Lytton Strachey had died. Vita Sackville-West remained one of her closest friends.

1980

1   ALLENTUCK, MARCIA. "Greville Texidor's *These Dark Glasses*:
    Bloomsbury in New Zealand." *World Literature Written in English* 19,
    no. 2 (Autumn):227-32.
        Establishes a connection between Texidor's novel *These Dark
    Glasses* (1949) and the Bloomsbury Group: "This is, in fact, a novel
    with characters easily identifiable with members of Bloomsbury and
    their hangers-on." The artist who is the focus of the novel is Mark
    Gertler. Suggests that Texidor, "neither stridently feminist nor
    revolutionary," has managed to "convey many of the issues which would
    be engaging us more than three decades later."

2   ALPERS, ANTONY. *The Life of Katherine Mansfield*. New York:
    Viking Press, 466 pp.
        Biographical study meant to replace *Katherine Mansfield: A
    Biography* (1953). Describes Mansfield's relationship with Lady
    Ottoline Morrell in Chapter 12, "Gower Street and Garsington" (pp.
    215-35) and with Virginia Woolf in Chapter 14, "Katherine and
    Virginia, 1917-1923 (pp. 247-61), as well as her association with
    Bloomsbury through the final break in 1921. Sydney Waterlow was
    Murry's lodger in his house in Hampstead. Earlier, Lady Ottoline
    Morrell had initiated an affair with John Middleton Murry, which
    became a part of Bloomsbury gossip: "The espionage element in
    Bloomsbury is one of its neglected moral aspects." Also includes
    information on Dorothy Brett.

3   ATLAS, JAMES. "The Letters of Virginia Woolf." *New York Times
    Book Review* (5 October):1, 34-35.
        Review of *The Letters of Virginia Woolf*, Vol. 4, *1936-1941*, along
    with Hilton Kramer's review of Frances Spalding's *Roger Fry*, under the
    general title, "Bloomsbury: Last Letters and a Life." Comments on her
    defense of Bllomsbury against the charge that it was effete.

4   "Atticusnote." *Sunday Times* (London) 16 (March), 32b.
        Brief story, "Bloomsbury Leanings," about Richard, who was
    asked whether, being surrounded by so many homosexuals in
    Bloomsbury, he had any homosexual leanings: "More leant upon than
    leanings, I'd have thought," Garnett replied.

5   BEER, JOHN. "Forster, Lawrence, Virginia Woolf and
     Bloomsbury." *Aligarth Journal of English Studies* 5, no. 1:6-37.
        Questions the prevailing attitude that Lawrence was an isolated
"fighter for the voice of the ordinary people" against the literary
establishment "dominated by Bloomsbury and far removed from
ordinary realities." Evaluates the Cambridge world, including work by
Russell and Moore, and the connection between Forster and Virginia
Woolf. Suggests that Lawrence was not an uncompromising opponent
of Bloomsbury. *The Longest Journey* points to a "subterranean link
between Lawrence and Bloomsbury."

6   BELL, ALAN. "Disenchantment of a Diplomatist." *Times Literary
     Supplement* (London) (14 November):1279.
        Review of James Lees-Milne's *Harold Nicolson: A Biography
1886-1929* and *Harold Nicolson: Diaries and Letters, 1930-1964*, edited
by Stanley Olson. Comments on the connection between Harold
Nicolson's resignation and his wife's developing association with
Bloomsbury: "The finer nuances of personalities observed at the
conference table are replaced by the equally delicate problem of his
and his wife's relations with Bloomsbury, where her connection with
Virginia Woolf and his own correspondence with Clive Bell by no
means betoken general acceptance."

7   BELL, QUENTIN. "Haphazard Gift of Sensibility." *Times Literary
     Supplement* (London) (21 March):307-8.
        Review of Francis Spalding's *Roger Fry: Art and Life*: "He was a
major figure, perhaps *the* major figure, in that group of friends which
people call Bloomsbury." States that Woolf's biography of Fry is "an
uneasy book in which one feels the authoress has ventured into an
unfamiliar territory." Fry's "social stance is reflected in his aesthetic
doctrines." Questions whether Fry's insistence upon the democratic
experience has received the attention it deserves.

8   ____. "Vanessa Bell and Duncan Grant." *Crafts* 42 (January):26-
     33.
        Fully illustrated assessment of the decorative works of Vanessa
Bell, Duncan Grant and other Bloomsbury figures: "Neither Vanessa
Bell nor Duncan Grant were in any true sense of the word craftsmen.
They were painters who, about the year 1910, turned to decoration."

9   BERGONZI, BERNARD. "An Artist and His Armour." *Times Literary Supplement* (London) (31 October):1215-17.
    Review of various books on Wyndham Lewis: Jeffery Meyers's *The Enemy: A Biography of Wyndham Lewis* and *Wyndham Lewis: A Revaluation*, Timothy Materer's *Vortex: Pound, Eliot, and Lewis*, and Fredric Jameson's *Fables of Agression: Wyndham Lewis, the Modernist as Fascist*. Agrees with Meyers that Lewis was in the right in his quarrel with Roger Fry and the Omega Workshop: "But as a result of it, Lewis earned the intense and undying opposition of the Bloomsbury Group--who previously had been well disposed towards the young artist and writer--which certainly harmed his later reputation."

10 BERNIKOW, LOUISE. *Among Women*. New York: Harmony, 289 pp.
    Essentially biographical survey of Virginia Woolf's relationship with women focusing on her roles as a sister to Vanessa Bell, as a friend to Katherine Mansfield, and as a lover to Vita Sackville-West.

11 BLUME, MARY. "Bucolic Bloomsbury." *Artnews* 79 (September):229-30.
    Article in relation to the fund-raising appeal, launched by Quentin Bell and Angelica Garnett, to save Charleston, Sussex, the home of Vanessa Bell and other Bloomsbury figures: "Keynes wrote *The Economic Consequences of Peace* there, Bell his major book, *Civilization*, and Strachey corrected the proofs of *Eminent Victorians* within its walls." The farmhouse should be saved for both its literary associations and for its example of Bloomsbury's visual side.

12 BOSHOFF, PHILIP PETER. "Virginia Woolf's Verbal Alchemy." Ph.D. dissertation, Purdue University, 337 pp.
    Woolf faced the problem throughout her life of how to "represent her characters' and narrators' shifting perceptions without making her writing too idiosyncratic to be understood." Deals with various aspects of culture during Woolf's life, including "the significance of the so-called Bloomsbury group, particularly of Roger Fry and his 'Essay in Aesthetics,' on Woolf's own artistic theories." See *Dissertation Abstracts International* 41:3571A-72A.

13 CAWS, MARY ANN. "Bloomsbury in Cassis." *American Society Legion of Honor Magazine* 50, no. 3 (Winter 1979-80):153-60.
    Describes the role of the small, French village Cassis in the life

of some of the Bloomsbury figures: "Once I visited the outlying (and uplying) domain where I was told several Bloomsburyians had stayed, I was convinced that this landscape could indeed enter the imagination of those artists and writers, as Cassis itself did." Deals primarily with Leonard and Virginia Woolf, Clive and Vanessa Bell, and Duncan Grant.

14 CHAPMAN, ROBERT. "Letters and Autobiographies." In *Wyndham Lewis: A Revaluation.* Edited by Jeffrey Meyers. Montreal: McGill-Queen's University Press, pp. 15-28.
      Commentary on Lewis's work with references to the Ideal Home Rumpus: "If the Ideal Home Rumpus had not occurred, Lewis would have had to invent it. His relationship with the Omega--that 'arty-crafty conception, with a "post-impressionist" veneer'--was never very good, and the very public row which blew up because of a misplaced commission was finely staged managed by Lewis."

15 COLLINS, L. Review of Duncan Grant Exhibition. *Art and Artists* 14 (April):10-13.
      Commentary on Grant's work and his connection with Bloomsbury.

16 COOMBES, JOHN. "British Intellectuals and the Popular Front." In *Class, Culture, and Social Change.* Edited by Frank Gloversmith. Sussex: Harvester Press; N. J.: Humanities Press, pp. 70-100.
      This discussion of the Popular Front in British political history involves some Bloomsbury figures, including Clive Bell and Leonard Woolf: "Woolf's monolithic liberal humanism reveals itself, politically, in unquestioning acceptance of the similarly monolithic notion that human history is not that of conflict, but of an eternalized ruling class." Stephen Spender's ideas in *Forward from Liberalism* need to be understood in relation to Virginia Woolf's "The Artist and Politics" and the Bloomsbury Group.

17 CRABTREE, DEREK, and ANTHONY P. THIRLWALL, eds. *Keynes and the Bloomsbury Group.* London: Macmillan; New York: Holmes & Meier, 100 pp.
      Collection of essays from the Fourth Keynes Seminar held at the University of Kent in 1978. Major articles include "Cambridge Intellectual Currents of 1900," by Derek Crabtree; "A General Account of the Bloomsbury Group," by Richard Shone; "The Significance of

'Bloomsbury' as a Social and Cultural Group," by Raymond Williams; and "Recollections and Reflections on Maynard Keynes," by Quentin Bell. Crabtree looks at the Cambridge antecedents of Bloomsbury, with commentary on the idealism of McTaggart and refutation of idealism by G.E. Moore. Shone describes the character of the Bloomsbury milieu: "In the climate of their youth, at the time Bloomsbury came into being, it seemed a pressing necessity to reduce, compress, to prick the balloons of bombast and rhetoric, to flush from art and thought and daily life the impurities of another age." He sees them as an important part of the revolution in manners and personal relations. Williams discusses the idea of Bloomsbury as a group: "For this is the real point of social and cultural analysis of any developed kind: to attend not only to the manifest ideas and activities, but also to the positions and ideas which are implicit or even taken for granted." The members have achieved "eminence by association." "Social conscience," especially in the work of Leonard Woolf and Maynard Keynes, was a factor in the group's development. Bell gives a personal view of Keynes from his perspective as a child growing up in Bloomsbury: "I do not remember the time when I did not know Maynard and from the first I found him extraordinarily attractive and wonderfully kind."

18   CUNNINGHAM, JOHN. "Bloomsbury's Home Still Blooms--And May Yet Survive." *Manchester Guardian* (12 January):17.
     Describes a visit to Charleston, Vanessa Bell's farmhouse home, to see Duncan Grant. The national Trust has accepted the house on principle, but large sums need to be raised still to save the house. Also interviews Angelic Garnett and Quentin Bell: "They sit on either side of the stove, an elderly brother and sister whose childhoods are separated by a decade or so, recalling a child's eye view of Bloomsbury."

19   DeSALVO, LOUISE A. *Virginia Woolf's First Voyage: A Novel in the Making.* Totowa, N.J.: Rowman & Littlefield, 202 pp.
     Describes the evolution of the novel in terms of Woolf's activities during this period, including her association with Bloomsbury beginning in the autumn of 1904. She began to associate with Lytton Strachey and Clive Bell, as well as Leonard Woolf when he returned from Ceylon. As her life changed the novel changed.

20   DINNAGE, ROSEMARY. "Away from the Agonies." *Times*
       Literary Supplement (London) (18 April):435.
           Review of *The Diary of Virginia Woolf*, vol. 3, *1925-1930*, edited
       by Anne Oliver Bell: "Perhaps we have had enough of this Woolfiana,
       volume on volume? The Bloomsbury Goldrush, which has unearthed so
       much trivia, may well make readers feel so; but the answer must still
       be no. Are there many (any?) other writings that come close to
       transposing the feel of day-to-day life--imaginative life and practical life-
       -as these diaries do?"

21   FALKENHEIM, JACQUELINE V. *Roger Fry and the Beginnings of*
       Formalism. Ann Arbor, Mich.: UMI Research Press, 234 pp.
           Revision of Ph.D. dissertation. (See 1972.9)

22   FFRENCH-FRAZIER, NINA. "A New York Letter." *Art*
       International 24, nos. 1-2 (September-October):75-77.
           Commentary on exhibition *Vanessa Bell (1879-1961)*: "What a
       delight then to meet Vanessa Bell, face to face at last--center stage--on
       her own turf." Suggests that "it is never quite possible to disentangle
       Vanessa Bell from the ubiquitous Bloomsbury Group."

23   FREEDMAN, RALPH. "The Form of Fact and Fiction: *Jacob's*
       Room as Paradigm." In *Virginia Woolf: Revaluation and Continuity*.
       Edited by Ralph Freedman. Berkeley: University of California Press,
       pp. 123-40.
           Woolf's novels manifest the "tension between fiction and life."
       In her postwar novels "beginning with *Jacob's Room*, these two aspects
       of art are brought together in most striking forms." Evaluates the
       novel in part in relation to Bloomsbury and G.E. Moore, "which
       represent such a vital aspect of her ideology and art" in relation to
       "idealist" and "realistic" explanation of the process of awareness.

24   GALASSI, SUSAN GAIL. "Vanessa Bell." *Arts Magazine* 54, no. 10
       (June):7.
           Less is known about the Bloomsbury artists than about literary
       Bloomsbury. Gives overview of Bell's career, including her association
       with Roger Fry and the Omega Workshops: "On balance, Bell can be
       appreciated not only for the iconoclasm of her early years but for her
       commitment to traditions in English art as seen in her lifelong interest
       in portraiture and landscape, her love of the applied arts, and her

ability to satirize which she carried forward in a quiet way into the
twentieth century."

25   GARNETT, DAVID. *Great Friends*. New York: Athenaeum, 215
      pp.
           Autobiographical account that includes some commentary on his
      Bloomsbury friends.

26   GLOVERSMITH, F. "Defining Culture: J.C. Powys, Clive Bell,
      R.H. Tawney & T.S. Eliot." In *Class, Culture, and Social Change*.
      Edited by Frank Gloversmith. Sussex: Harvester Press; New Jersey:
      Humanities Press, pp 26-43.
           Evaluates the ideas of culture developed by Powys, Bell, Tawney,
      and Eliot. Bell evolves a sort of "aestheticized sociology." Establishes
      some connections to Bloomsbury thought in *Civilization*, especially to
      G.E. Moore's work. Also suggests some connections to Virginia Woolf.

27   GROSSKURTH, PHYLLIS. "Between Eros and Thanatos." *Times
      Literary Supplement* (London) (31 October):1225-26.
           Review of *Leave the Letters Till We're Dead: The Letters of
      Virginia Woolf*, Vol. 4, *1936-1941*, edited by Nigel Nicolson and Joanne
      Trautman dealing mostly with Virginia's suicide. Deals with the
      relationship between Leonard and Virginia during her final years, with
      material drawn from other sources, such as Quentin Bell's biography.

28   GUNAWARDANA, A.J. "Village in the Jungle." *Sight and Sound*
      49 (Winter 79-80):26-27.
           Relates to movie production and Woolf's work. Has some
      commentary on Woolf's Bloomsbury background as introduction to him
      as figure.

29   HAMPSHIRE, STUART. "The Good Habit of Indecision." *Times
      Literary Supplement* (London) (18 January):53.
           Review of Paul Levy's *Moore: G.E. Moore and the Cambridge
      Apostles*: "In a pettish reaction against too much Bloomsbury
      biography, some writers have tried to belittle this Cambridge and
      Bloomsbury circle. In a reasonable historical perspective this cannot be
      done." This group of "thinking men" deserves serious study.

30   HERZ, JUDITH SCHERER. "Forster's Three Experiments in
     Autobiographical Biography." *Studies In Literary Imagination* 13, no.
     1:51-67.
          Forster dealt somewhat with his background at Cambridge and
     its continuation as Bloomsbury.

31   HOLROYD, MICHAEL. "Looking Back at Bloomsbury." *Times*
     (London) (1 March):8.
          Commentary on Lytton Strachey's reputation on the centenary of
     his birth in relation to the group of studies that relate to Bloomsbury.
     Gives some brief history of the various generations of Bloomsbury. In
     the 1930s sexual politics was replaced by economic politics: "The
     process had been caused by an infiltration of the second generation
     Bloomsbury by the Fabian ethic."

32   HOLROYD, MICHAEL, and PAUL LEVEY. Introduction to *The
     Shorter Strachey*. New York: Oxford University Press, pp. vii-xii.
          During Strachey's years in the Apostles at Cambridge he
     replaced G.E. Moore as its chief member. When *Queen Victoria* was
     published he was regarded as "the greatest lion of the Bloomsbury
     pride."

33   HUSAIN, S. WIGAR. "Lytton Strachey: Major Bibliographies."
     Aligarth Journal of English Studies 5, no. 2:211-28.
          Questions the appeal of Strachey's work on the grounds that it is
     entertaining and the denunciation of his work for its lack of historical
     accuracy: "The dazzling surfaces and the impeccable form of the
     biographies combined with the popular notion of the author's
     Bloomsbury background, might have distracted, at least part of the
     reader's attention, from that keenly felt and highly organized experience
     of history that had gone into the creation of the underlying wholes of
     solid and vibrant meaning."

34   HYMAN, VIRGINIA R. "Late Victorian and Early Modern:
     Continuities in the Criticism of Leslie Stephen and Virginia Woolf."
     English Literature in Transition 23:144-54.
          Deals with the connection between the literary criticism of father
     and daughter in relation to the movement from Victorian to modern.
     Bloomsbury was part of the modernized aesthetic.

35   KRAMER, HILTON. "Roger Fry." *New York Times Book Review*
     (5 October):1, 34-35.
          Review of *Roger Fry: Art and Life*, by Frances Spalding, along
     with James Atlas's review of *The Letters of Virginia Woolf*, Vol. 6, under
     the general title, "Bloomsbury: Last Letters and a Life." Woolf's
     esteem for Fry "was greater, certainly, than for any other member of
     the Bloomsbury Group that she and Vanessa had done so much to
     create in the years before World War I and that by 1928 was firmly
     established as a potent force in the London cultural scene." His work
     undertaken before he joined Bloomsbury seems undervalued.

36   LEES-MILNE, JAMES. *Harold Nicolson: A Biography 1886-1929*.
     London: Chatto & Windus. Reprint. Hamden, Conn.: Archon
     Books, 1982, 429 pp.
          First volume of a biographical study, which deals with Nicolson's
     marriage to Vita Sackville-West, his diplomatic career, and his
     association with Bloomsbury: "Lytton Strachey represented in Harold
     Nicolson's eyes the kernel of Bloomsbury. But he was personally and
     physical distasteful to him." Nicolson was devoted to Clive Bell and "he
     acknowledged and admired the genius of Virginia Woolf and Maynard
     Keynes."

37   LOVE, J.O. "*Orlando* and Its Genesis: Venturing and
     Experimenting in Art, Love and Sex." In *Virginia Woolf: Revaluation
     and Continuity*. Edited by Ralph Freeman. Berkley: University of
     California Press, pp. 188-218.
          Orlando emerged during the period Woolf was most
     experimental and venturesome: "Her personal venturing was
     epitomized by her relationship with Vita Sackville-West, in some
     respects another anomaly. It was the only one of her several intense
     friendships with women known to have included a physical relationship
     and thus to have been a testing ground for what she had supposed to
     be her peculiarity in love--Sapphism." Describes the dynamic of this
     relationship. The ultimate comment on the affair was *Orlando*: "In a
     decisive way, then, the venture into eroticism had ended with *Orlando*
     and in a sense the book became a requiem mass for that part of
     Virginia's life."

38   McLAUGHLIN, THOMAS M. "Virginia Woolf and Bloomsbury."
     Contemporary Literature 21, no. 4 (Autumn):639-45.
          Review of Leon Edel's *Bloomsbury: The House of Lions* and

Roger Poole's *The Unknown Virginia Woolf*: "Fueled by concern with
sex roles and experimental life styles, interest in Bloomsbury has
generated two interdependent lines of biographical research. One has
resulted in the publication of journals, diaries, letters, and scholarly
biographies dealing with almost every figure associated with
Bloomsbury, while the other, directed toward the nonspecialist, has
produced informal, belle-lettristic narratives emphasizing Bloomsbury's
involvement in continuing cultural and sexual controversies." These two
studies "clearly fit into the second category."

39   MARCUS, JANE. "Enchanted Organs, Magic Bells" *Night and Day*
      as Comic Opera." In *Virginia Woolf: Revaluation and Continuity*.
      Edited by Ralph Freedman. Berkeley: University of California
      Press, 97-122.
           Day and Night depends "structurally on Mozart, stylistically on
      Jane Austen, and thematically on Ibsen." Identifies these influences in
      relation to some Bloomsbury activities: "*Day and Night* is an anti-war
      novel: it is against the 'sex war,' the most important political issue in
      Edwardian England, and it is against the misogyny of Cambridge-
      Bloomsbury culture, which appropriated the classics and music as male
      property." Reprinted in *Virginia Woolf and the Languages of Patriarchy*,
      pp. 18-35. (See 1987.19.)

40   MARKER, SHERRY. "The Luminous Ghosts of Bloomsbury."
      Horizon 27 (December):64-69.
           Discusses Bloomsbury in relation to their houses, from 46
      Gordon Square to Monk's House and Charleston Farm. Leonard
      Woolf said: "What cuts the deepest channels in our lives are the
      different houses in which we live." States that there is a Bloomsbury of
      the mind. The Bloomsbury figures were literary revolutionaries. The
      move to Bloomsbury horrified friends of the Stephen family, including
      Henry James and Thomas Hardy.

41   MEISEL, PERRY. *The Absent Father: Virginia Woolf and Walter
      Pater*. New Haven and London: Yale University Press, 249 pp.
           Woolf "succeeds Pater among principal English critics, and it is
      with Pater that her principal literary relationship is to be found."
      Includes commentary on Woolf's Bloomsbury associations that relate to
      the influence of Pater, including a discussion of Bloomsbury
      homosexuality and aestheticism. Suggests that Pater and G.E. Moore
      matched each other in the "equally insistent emphasis on the authority

of one's personal judgment and the rejection of the authority of mere tradition and inherited taste."

42   MEYERS, JEFFREY. *The Enemy: A Biography of Wyndham Lewis.* Boston and London: Routledge & Kegan Paul, 391 pp.
      Includes a chapter, "Omega Workshops and Rebel Art Center, 1913-1914" (pp. 39-54), which deals with Lewis's quarrel with Roger Fry which "began his lifelong conflict with Bloomsbury and permanently damaged his ability to earn his living as an artist." Evaluates the clash with Lewis over the Ideal Home Exhibition and over whether Fry used his influence to hurt Lewis's artistic career. Sides with Lewis in both cases.

43   MOORSOM, SASHA. "Last Outpost of Bloomsbury." *Illustrated London News* 268 (June):87, 89-90.
      Deals with Charleston, the farmhouse home of Vanessa Bell and Duncan Grant. Includes illustrations.

44   MORPHET, RICHARD. "Roger Fry: The Nature of His Painting." *Burlington Magazine* 122 (July):478-88.
      Fry has been much discussed due to interest in Bloomsbury, but Fry's "work as a painter has been overshadowed by his fame as a critic." Two new studies, Francis Spalding's *Roger Fry: Art and Life* and Donald A. Laing's *Roger Fry, An Annotated Bibliography of the Published Writings,* and the re-issue of Virginia Woolf's biography, give cause to look at Fry from a more balanced perspective: "Virginia Woolf and Francis Spalding both make clear that Fry's work as painter was not secondary to his activity as a critic." Gives evaluation of Fry's work using reference to these studies: "With that near-signature of a Bloomsbury painting, the insistent vertical line which ties the design as a whole to the recilinearity of the canvas, these devices assisted a close interweaving of the pictorial scheme."

45   NICOLSON, HAROLD. *Diaries and Letters, 1930-1964.* Edited and ondensed by Stanley Olson. Introduction by Nigel Nicolson. London: Collins, 436 pp.
      Condensed versions of the letters and diaries edited by Nigel Nicolson. (See 1966.20, 1967.17, and 1968.21.)

46 PETERS, PAULINE. "Lunching with Bloomsbury Industry." *Sunday Times* (London) (21 September):37g.

Description of lunch at Sissinghurst Castle with Nigel Nicolson, son of Vita Sackville-West and Harold Nicolson. The scene is a throwback to the Bloomsbury days, which are evoked by various volumes of Virginia Woolf's letters Nicolson has edited.

47 PRITCHARD, WILLIAM. "Literary Criticism as Satire." In *Wyndham Lewis: A Revaluation.* Edited by Jeffrey Meyers. Montreal: McGill-Queen's University Press, pp. 196-210.

Virginia Woolf and Bloomsbury were among those satirized: "She is reduced to a sort of 'party-lighthouse'; by looking at her apology in 'Mr. Bennett and Mrs. Brown' we can find out the going Bloomsbury line on modern literature."

48 PRITCHETT, V.S. "David Garnett." *New Yorker* 56 (18 August):89-92.

Commentary on Garnett and Bloomsbury based upon Garnett's *Great Friends*: "The Garnett family were outside the Apostolic traditions of Bloomsbury. They were not souls." Garnett's portraits of Forster, Lytton Strachey, J. M. Keynes, and Virginia Woolf "have an air of dé jà vu." They have been pushed elsewhere and remind us of other Bloomsbury portraits.

49 RETTIG, CYNTHIA BESTOSO. "The Continuing Battle Against the Philistines: Virginia Woolf's Cultural Criticism." Ph.D. dissertation, University of Michigan, 402 pp.

States that Woolf "drew heavily upon the Victorian idea of culture in criticizing her own society. Her early rebellion against the Victorians was more limited than is generally assumed, for in denouncing Victorian qualities like narrow-mindedness and hypocrisy, she reiterated in substance what the major Victorian critics had already said." Aspects of her life illustrate her broad knowledge of the world and the varied pattern of her life, including the Hogarth Press and her husband's political work. See *Dissertation Abstracts International* 41:682A-83A.

50 ROBBINS, ROBIN. "Matters of Seriousness." *Times Literary Supplement* (London) (21 November):1319.

Review of William Walsh's *F.R. Leavis*. Leavis's criticism is more active and intelligent than that produced by Bloomsbury: "Even

Virginia Woolf could allow herself to intrude as the star of a critical essay, playing not even to the gallery but to a private box."

51 ROSE, JONATHAN. "Moore and His Apostles." In *The Edwardian Temperament*. London and Athens: Ohio University Press, pp. 40-49.
Deals with the origin of Bloomsbury at Cambridge and the influence of the teaching of G.E. Moore. Describes also the advancement of Moore's ideals in Bloomsbury and the significance of Bloomsbury to Edwardian culture.

52 SHONE, RICHARD. Introduction to *Vanessa Bell 1879-1961: A Retrospective Exhibition*. New York: Davis & Long Co., pp. 3-7.
Gives overview of Vanessa Bell's life and artistic development, including her association with Bloomsbury, the Omega Workshops, and Duncan Grant. It was after her marriage to Clive Bell that her career as an artist "took wing." She was not merely engaged in formal values in art: "By 1919 audacious experiment was over" for her art. The catalog includes a chronology and commentary by Shone on the individual paintings.

53 SPALDING, FRANCES. "'Duncan Grant Designer' at the Brighton Museum and Art Gallery." *Burlington Magazine* 122 (March):214-15.
Exhibition review that states that Bloomsbury decorative art is unorthodox: "It follows no theory, is grossly individualistic, and its anarchic style wanders at will from pure abstraction to representational motifs." This exhibition traces Grant's decorative achievement up to his death in 1978: The "hedonistic element in Bloomsbury decorations irritates purists and seriously troubles accepted canons of taste."

54 _____. *Roger Fry: Art and Life*. London: Paul Elek; Granada. Berkeley: University of California Press, 304 pp.
Full-length biographical study including various references to Fry's Bloomsbury activities and associations. In Roger Fry there is "no separation between" his life and work: "His multi-faceted life grew directly out of the variety of his interests and activities." States that "when Fry entered Bloomsbury the group had already formed a closed corporation, held together not by a set of rules or a mutually-shared doctrine, but by a less easily defined, subtle chemistry." Fry shared "Bloomsbury's primary belief--that civilization, in order to develop, must depend on intellectual honesty; likewise, he shared their distrust of

society, with its love of display, fame, power and easy success, and he
confirmed their contempt for Philistinism, vulgarity and over-emphasis."

55   SPILKA, MARK. *Virginia Woolf's Quarrel with Grieving.* Lincoln:
     University of Nebraska Press, 142 pp.
          Chapter three, "Funeral Gloom," deals with relationship to
     Thoby and the household setup after the death of Leslie Stephen.
     "Free of the trifling and effusive Duckworths, free of their father's
     glooms and rages, they seemed to be living at last in the Edwardian
     present."

56   STONE, WILFRED. "The Future of Forster Biography." *Biography*
     3, no. 3:253-61.
          Suggests that there is still need for additional information in
     Forster biography. Furbank could have dealt more with the
     social/historical background. Comments on Strachey biography and
     homosexuality.

57   STRACHEY, BARBARA. *Remarkable Relations.* London:
     Hogarth Press, 128 pp.
          Memoir that deals with Strachey family and some aspects of the
     Bloomsbury activities.

58   SUTTON, DENYS. "Discoveries." *Apollo* 112 (July):2-5.
          Editorial on the interest in art of other countries around the
     turn of the century, including Fry's work in this area: "Fry's interest in
     the decorative arts, which led to the foundation of the Omega
     Workshops, was partly fuelled by his experience of Oriental ceramics."

59   SYMONS, JULIAN. "Viewpoint." *Times Literary Supplement*
     (London) (18 April):437.
          General commentary on the word *clique* in relation to the
     various literary movements of this century with several references to
     Bloomsbury. Sees some positive characteristics of such associations:
     "Yet even those, like me, who are able to restrain their admiration for
     the literary products of Bloomsbury, there seems no denying that the
     social, sexual, and intellectual interchange of the Woolfs, Stracheys, and
     others produced work of interest that would never have been written if
     'Bloomsbury' had not existed."

60   TOULMIN, STEPHEN. "Moore: G.E. Moore and the Cambridge
     Apostles, by Paul Levy." *New Republic* (30 August):29-32.
          Review with commentary on Moore's philosophical approach and
     Bloomsbury's idealization of him: "Moore's Bloomsbury followers,
     however, understood him to be enthroning Art and Friendship--
     particularly friendship between men--as the supreme occasions for
     'good' states of mind."

61   VELLACOTT, JO. *Bertrand Russell and the Pacifists in the First
     World War*. Brighton: Harvester Press; New York: St. Martin's
     Press, 234 pp.
          Deals in part with Russell's association with Lady Ottoline
     Morrell and other figures connected with Bloomsbury who were active
     in the pacifists movement during World War I.

62   WALSH, WILLIAM. *F.R. Leavis*. London: Chatto & Windus. 189
     pp.
          Biographical study that deals with Leavis's quarrel with
     Bloomsbury as expressed in the pages of *Scrutiny*.

63   WATNEY, SIMON. *English Post-Impressionism*. New York:
     Eastview; London: Studio Vista, 218 pp.
          Deals with Roger Fry, Bloomsbury and the Post-impressionist
     exhibitions. The English Post-impressionists included Fry, Vanessa Bell,
     and Duncan Grant, as well as other painters associated with
     Bloomsbury and the Omega Workshops.

64   WILLIAMS, RAYMOND. "The Bloomsbury Faction." In *Problems
     in Materialism and Culture*. London: Macmillan, pp. 155-56.
          Bloomsbury appeared as an elite faction within Edwardian
     society. Rather than being a part of modernism, the Group was
     emblematic of class distinction and Victorian society.

65   WOOLF, VIRGINIA. *The Diary of Virginia Woolf*, Vol. 3, *1925-
     1930*. Edited by Anne Olivier Bell and Andrew McNeillie. London:
     Hogarth Press; New York: Harcourt Brace Jovanovich, 384 pp.
          Entries deal with various Bloomsbury figures and issues. In
     relation to Harold Nicolson, for example, she states that "as a family
     we distrust anyone outside our set, I think. We too definitely decide
     that so & so has not the necessary virtues. I dare say Harold has not

got them." She also talks about her "Bloomsbury evenings" with Roger Fry, Clive Bell and others.

66 _____. *Leave the letters till we're dead: The Letters of Virginia Woolf,* Vol. 6, *1936-1941.* Edited bu Nigel Nicolson and Joanne Trautmann. London: Hogarth Press; New York: Harcourt Brace Jovanovich, 556 pp.

Introduction by Nigel Nicolson. Last volume of Woolf's letters, in which she often refers to Bloomsbury: "A young man the other day sent me a book in which he perpetually used 'Bloomsbury' as a convenient hold for everything silly, cheap, indecent, conceited, and so on. These letters, Nicolson observes, "add immeasurably to our knowledge of Bloomsbury. They record its growth and gusto, illuminate it. defend it, and consciously claim for it, as in her remarkable letter to Nicolson Benedict, for which we also happily posses her very different draft, a significant role in social and intellectual history."

1981

1 ANNAN, NOEL. "A Spontaneous Liberality." *Times Literary Supplement* (London) (31 July):859-62.

Review of L.P. Wilkinson's *A Century of King's 1873-1973* and *Kingsmen of the Century, 1873-1973.* Includes some commentary on Maynard Keynes, the Apostles, and the Bloomsbury Group.

2 ANSCOMBE, ISABELLE. *Omega and After: Bloomsbury and the Decorative Arts.* London: Thames & Hudson, 176 pp.

Gives full history of the development of the Omega Workshops out of the Post-impressionist aesthetic and the involvement of various Bloomsbury figures, especially Vanessa Bell and Duncan Grant. Includes a considerable amount of biographical detail, as well as illustrations.

3 BARKER, NICOLAS. "A Humanist in His Time." *Time Literary Supplement* (London) (6 November):1290.

Review of Geoffrey Keynes's *The Gates of Memory.* Suggests that his "craftsman's" approach to life kept him "out--had he wished to be in it, which he did not--the Bloomsbury Group." His brother, John Maynard Keynes, was a natural link. Also describes association with the Woolfs and Lydia Lopokova.

4   BAYLEY, JOHN. "The Muse à la mode." *Times Literary
     Supplement* (London) (31 July):863-64.
         Review of Victoria Glendinning's *Edith Sitwell*: "Edith Sitwell
     must be admitted to have been both style and fashion." Nothing on
     Bloomsbury, mostly comments on her poetry.

5   BELL, QUENTIN. "Historic Houses: Charleston, Memories of the
     Bloomsbury Group." *Architectural Digest* 38 (March):172-76.
         Photo-essay describing the unique qualities of Charleston, the
     home of Vanessa Bell, Clive Bell, and Duncan Grant: "But Charleston
     is, in a different way, valuable. It represents, in visible terms, a way of
     life that resulted in a particular kind of domestic decoration." This
     decoration is "un-English, for English decoration tends nearly always to
     be tremendously tasteful and proper."

6   BELL, VANESSA. *Vanessa Bell's Family Album*. Edited by
     Quentin Bell and Angelica Garnett. London: Jill Norman &
     Hobhouse, 87 pp.
         Brief account of the Stephen children by Vanessa.

7   BRINK, ANDREW. "The Education of Roger Fry." *Russell* 2, no. 1
     (June):69-77.
         Review of Frances Spalding's *Roger Fry: Art and Life*. Gives
     overview of Fry's life, with commentary on his association with
     Bloomsbury, and focuses on the problem of Fry's reputation. Describes
     the relationship between Bertrand Russell and Fry, who knew each
     other from Cambridge. Relates, too, to Lady Ottoline Morrell.
     Concludes that "if there are the beginnings of a different book on the
     'real Roger Fry,'" it is not a book that Bloomsbury admirers seem to
     want at the moment."

8   BROYARD, ANATOLE. "Perennial Bloom." *New York Times
     Book Review* (18 October):51.
         General reaction to Bloomsbury based upon Frances Partridge's
     Love in Bloomsbury. Relates the "Bloomsbury" spirit to the American
     literary scene in the 1980s.

9   BUFKIN, E.C. "The Woolfs and Other Lions." *Georgia Review* 35
     (Spring):190-94.
         Review of Leon Edel's *Bloomsbury: The House of Lions*, Phyllis
     Rose's *Woman of Letters: A Life of Virginia Woolf*, Michael Rosenthal's

Virginia Woolf, and the reprint of Leonard Woolf's *The Wise Virgins*.
The recent publication of critical studies, biographies, autobiographies,
memoirs, letters and diaries related to the Bloomsbury Group has
"made apparent the need for a synthesis of the relationships of these
particular individuals." *The Wise Virgins* "is engaging solely for its
personal view of Bloomsbury and the portrayal, especially, of Virginia
Stephen." Edel makes a mistake by ending his study with the Memoir
Club in 1920 and by leaving out figures like Lady Ottoline Morrell and
E.M. Forster. Rosenthal offers good introduction to Bloomsbury and
Rose gives an excellent account of Woolf in the 1930s, a supplement to
Edel.

10   CAREY, JOHN. "The English Flamingo." *Sunday Times* (London)
      (2 August):35.
          Review of Victoria Glendinning's *Edith Sitwell*. Comments of
      Sitwell's association with various literary figures, including Virginia
      Woolf and E.M. Forster.

11   EDMONDS, MICHAEL. *Lytton Strachey: A Bibliography*. New
      York: Garland Press, 157 pp.
          Comprehensive bibliography with brief introduction which
      describes his Bloomsbury connections. The entries give publishing
      history.

12   ELBORN, GEOFFREY. *Edith Sitwell: A Biography*. New York:
      Doubleday, 322 pp.
          Full-length biographical study with various references to
      Bloomsbury and to Virginia Woolf: "Edith was not a constant visitor to
      the Bloomsbury teas, for although she liked Virginia personally, and
      was fascinated by her appearance, she cared very little about her work."
      Edith found the "pretentiousness in the Bloomsbury Group's behavior"
      unacceptable.

13   FLEISHMANN, AVROM. "To Return to St. Ives: Woolf's
      Autobiographical Writings." *ELH* 48 (Fall):606-18.
          Includes some comentary on Woolf's life relevant to Bloomsbury.

14   GARNETT, ANGELICA. "Duncan Grant." In *Duncan Grant*.
      Exhibition Catalog. London: Anthony d'Offay Gallery, pp. 3-7.
          Commentary by his natural daughter, which describes his work
      and gives an impression of their life at Charleston.

15 GINDIN, JAMES. "Method in the Biographical Study of Virginia Woolf." *Biography* 4, no. 2 (Spring):95-107.

Some ethnobiographic studies of Virginia Woolf are almost inevitable, "given her father's articulate and public prominence (and a number of diaries and collections of letters by and about him survive, going back two generations), her mother's legendary status and earthly death, and Bloomsbury's close connections and capacities for defining and re-defining itself." Evaluates the method in some current biographical studies.

16 GLENDINNING, VICTORIA. *Edith Sitwell: The Unicorn Among Lions*. London: Weidenfeld & Nicholson; New York: Alfred A. Knopf, 393 pp.

Sitwell had "a personal fame and a public persona and appearance that she enjoyed and exploited, but which drove the private woman further and further into the shadows." Deals with Bllomsbury and the Sitwells from 1918, at the end of World War One, in relation to Diaghilev's Ballets Russes. Describes Edith's chilled reaction to Bloomsbury and her personal relationship with many Bloomsbury figures, including the conflict between Edith, Virginia Woolf, and Vita Sackville-West.

17 GRIFFIN, GAIL B. "Braving the Mirror: Virginia Woolf as Autobiographer." *Biography* 4, no. 2 (Spring):108-18.

Discusses Woolf's autobiographical method in relation to many pieces that deal with Woolf and Bloomsbury.

18 GRIFFIN, NICHOLAS. "The Acts of the Apostles." *Russell* 1, no. 1 (Summer):71-82.

Review-essay of Paul Levy's *Moore: G.E. Moore and the Cambridge Apostles*: "Since much of this information is important for understanding the intellectual concerns of Moore, Russell, the Bloomsbury Group and the Cambridge Apostles, it is impossible to ignore the book." Finds problems with the book, though. Agrees with Levy's assertion that Moore's influence on Bloomsbury was at least partly personal: "His almost palpable integrity, the seriousness with which he pursued the truth, his high-mindedness, his lack of reverence for metaphysical obscurity and his childlike innocence were all qualities which endeared him to Bloomsberries."

19 GUPTARA, PRABHU S. "A Strachey Child." *Biography* 4, no. 2:175-78.

Review of two autobiographical texts by Rochard Strachey, nephew of Lytton Strachey and an author of children's books, *A Strachey Child* and *A Strachey Boy*: "But what could be better suited to a children's author than his own childhood, first in India, and then among the young Bloomsburys in pre-World War I England?" Strachey does not disown snobbery. Discusses his faith in relation to Bloomsbury's rationalism.

20 HARRIS, CHARLES. *English Art and Modernism, 1900-1939*. London: Allan Lane; Bloomington: University of Indiana Press, pp. 45-113.

Two chapters deal with Bloomsbury subjects, Chapter 3 "'Post-Impressionism' and the 'New Movement'" (pp. 45-74) and Chapter 4 "Cubism, Futurism, Vorticism" (pp. 75-113). "'Post-Impressionism' and the 'New Movement'" gives overview of the period, with full discussion of the exchange of ideas among the Bloomsbury figures involved in the art world during the early years of the twentieth century. Gives special attention to the aesthetics of Roger Fry and Clive Bell as Bloomsbury critics. Brings in Duncan Grant and Vanessa Bell: "None of the 'inner circle' of Bloomsbury were really very competent painters, though Vanessa Bell and Duncan Grant produced much of their most technically progressive work during the few years on either side of 1912, buoyed on the high tide of Post-Impressionism." Omega, like the Post-impressionist exhibitions, was "very much a Bloomsbury enterprise." "Cubism, Futurism, Vorticism" evaluates the conflicts between Roger Fry and Wyndham Lewis, as well as the many differences between Bloomsbury attitudes and those of the Futurists and Vorticists: "Where Bloomsbury took pride in its considerable homosexual membership, the Futurists and the English rebels struck attitudes of aggressive heterosexuality."

21 HARROD, DOMINICK. "John Maynard Keynes: 'Keynes Never Averted His Gaze from the Real World.'" *Listener* 105 (8 January):34-36.

Commentary on Keynes during the years between the First and Second World Wars. He was still involved with Bloomsbury: "But Bloomsbury was important to Keynes, the economist, in more ways than the affection and friendship of his friends, the artistic dimension it added to his dry Cambridge upbringing." Living among these impractical, but worthwhile, people, emphasized for him the purpose of thr economic realities, that is, to try to make life better.

22 HEACOX, THOMAS. "Proust and Bloomsbury." *Virginia Woolf Miscellany* 17 (Fall):2.
    Proust was important to the literary ideals of Bloomsbury.

23 HEILBRUN, CAROLYN G. "Virginia Woolf in Her Fifties." *Twentieth Century Literature* 27, 1 (Spring):16-33.
    Reprinted in *Virginia Woolf: A Feminist Slant*, pp. 236-253. (See 1983.25.)

24 HILL, KATHERINE C. "Virginia Woolf and Leslie Stephen: History and Literary Revolution." *PMLA* 96, no. 3 (May):351-62.
    Establishes the relationship between Virginia Woolf and Leslie Stephen more positively: "Leslie Stephen made it difficult for Virginia to write, but he also gave her the tools she needed to write." Shows how Stephen's ideas carry over into Virginia Woolf's adult life and her sense of literary tradition, with some connections to Bloomsbury.

25 HORWELL, VERONICA. "Edith--A Golden Giraffe in Profile." *Sunday Times* (London) (2 August):28.
    Interview with Victoria Glendinning about her biographical study of Edith Sitwell. Comments on the relationship of figures during this period, especially Vita Sackville-West.

26 KENNEDY, THOMAS C. "Russell and the Pacifists." *Russell* 1, no. 1 (Summer):83-88.
    Review of Jo Vellacott's *Bertrand Russell and the Pacifists in the First World War*. Includes minor references to relation with D.H. Lawrence and Bloomsbury.

27 KEYNES, SIR GEOFFREY. *The Gates of Memory*. Oxford: Oxford University Press, 428 pp.
    Autobiographical account which includes some commentary on John Maynard Keynes and his association the Cambridge Apostles and Bloomsbury.

28 KLEIN, DAN. "Fired With Enthusiasm." *Connoisseur* 207 (September):116-17.
    Interview with Quentin Bell on the occasion of an exhibition of

his recent work in conjunction with the Fulham Pottery. Bell comments on Bloomsbury and on his mother Vanessa Bell and Duncan Grant. He suggests that Bloomsbury is very visible in his work. The Bloomsbury aesthetic is difficult to explain: "It is easier to talk about my own aesthetic in rather negative terms."

29 LEES-MILNE, JAMES. *Harold Nicolson: A Biography 1930-1968*. London: Chatto & Windus; Hamden, Conn.: Archon Book, 403 pp.
Second volume of the biographical study, which deals in part with his relationship with Vita Sackville-West and various Bloomsbury figures. Includes less information than volume one.

30 LEONARD, DIANE R. "Proust and Virginia Woolf, Ruskin and Roger Fry: Modernist Visual Dynamics." *Comparative Literary Studies* 18, no. 3 (September):333-43.
Evaluates the visual dimension in the work of Proust and Virginia Woolf, with the aesthetic origins traced to Ruskin and Roger Fry respectively. Woolf discovered techniques akin to Cézanne's in Proust's work. Proust was able to draw on Ruskin, whereas the Bloomsbury Group was not: "Proust had the necessary distance, in space if not in time, whereas Woolf, Fry and the other 'Bloomsberries' were huddled at the base of this eminent Victorian, and saw him only through the distortions of their proximity."

31 MARCUS, JANE. "Liberty, Sorority, Misogyny." In *The Representation of Women in Fiction*. Edited by Margaret Higgonnet and Carolyn Heilbrun. Baltimore: Johns Hopkins University Press, pp. 35-51.
In order to "catapult women into history Woolf analyzed the notions of liberty, equality, and fraternity of her forefathers and her friends. Female liberty, equality, and sorority were her goals." Deals with background of Apostles and its influence on the male society of the Bloomsbury milieu. Reprinted in *Virginia Woolf and the Languages of Patriarchy*, pp. 75-95. (See 1987.19.)

32 O'BRIEN, EDNA. *Virginia: A Play*. London: Hogarth Press. Rev. ed. New York: Harcourt Brace Jovanovich, 1985, 73 pp.
Drama based on Virginia Woolf's life and work, focusing on her relationship with Leonard Woolf and Vita Sackville-West. Draws on Woolf's diaries and letters, as well as on Leonard Woolf's

autobiography. First performed in 1980 in Canada at the Stratford
Shakespeare Festival.

33   PARTRIDGE, FRANCES. *Love in Bloomsbury: Memories*. Boston:
      Little, Brown, 244 pp.
         Autobiographical account by Frances Marshall, who was to
      marry Ralph Partridge, which describes Bloomsbury from the inside.
      Certain chapters deal more specially with Bloomsbury: "London and
      Bloomsbury," "The Definitive Years," and "Gordon Square." Suggests
      that the Bloomsbury voice came from the Strachey family and the
      Cambridge intellectuals combined. Bloomsbury was "quite uninterested
      in conventions, but passionately in ideas: "Comfort didn't rank high in
      Bloomsbury houses (though beauty did), but there would be good
      French cooking, and wine at most meals." Deals extensively with Dora
      Carrington, Lytton Strachey, Duncan Grant and other Bloomsbury
      figures.

34   PETERS, MARGOT. "Group Biography: Challenges and Methods."
      In *New Directions in Biography*. Edited by Anthony M. Friedson.
      Honolulu: University Press of Hawaii, pp. 41-51.
         "Group biography may be defined as the interweaving of a
      number of lives by one writer to show how they interact with each
      other." Bloomsbury is a subject ready-made for group biography.
      Discusses place motif in relation to Bloomsbury. Refers to Edel's
      Bloomsbury: The House of Lions.

35   PILE, STEPHEN. "Bloomsbury's Debt to Mrs. Higgens." *Sunday
      Times* (London) (1 February):32.
         Mrs. Higgens cared for the various members of the Bloomsbury
      Group who lived at Charleston. A portrait of her by Vanessa Bell is
      on display in the house: "Working from 8 am until 10 pm, Mrs
      Higgens made the Bloomsbury Group possible." She has no intention
      of writing her memoirs.

36   ROSEN, AMY. "The Pulse of Colour: A Study of Virginia Woolf."
      Ph.D. dissertation, State University of New York at Buffalo, 236 pp.
         Examines the relationship of "colour to thought, feeling, and
      sensation in the work of Virginia Woolf." Involves some discussion of
      the influence of Bloomsbury: "Chapter Two examines theories of
      colour from Aristotle to the Bloomsbury Group." Treats the influence

of Vanessa Bell's theories of painting on Woolf. See *Dissertation Abstracts International* 42:1650A.

37   ROSENBAUM, S.P. "Bloomsbury Letters." *Centrum* 1, no. 2 (Fall):113-19.
        Discusses the place of Bloomsbury letters in the literary history of the group: "The place of Bloomsbury letters in this idea of literary history has to do, first, with the fictive and non-fictive, public and private genres of letters they wrote, then with the transitive nature of letters that must be taken into account in their interpretation, and finally with the textual interconnections that letters display in Bloomsbury's literary history."

38   _____. "Preface to a Literary History of the Bloomsbury Group." *New Literary History* 12, no. 2 (Winter):329-44.
        Gives the beginnings of a literary history of the two generations of the Bloomsbury Group. The need for a literary history of Bloomsbury is based upon the "incongruity of the kinds of books that have been written about the Group and its members. Books about the lives of the Group and their interrelations have had little to say about their writings, whereas studies of the individuals' writings say almost nothing about how these are related to the writings of the other members." The literary history of Bloomsbury must deal with "a series of texts written by a group of friends." Deals with the interconnectedness of Bloomsbury texts.

39   SCAMMELL, MICHAEL. "A Chinaman in Bloomsbury." *Times Literary Supplement* (London) (10 July):789.
        Discusses Chen Chun Yeh, who turned up at the PEN Club conference in Copenhagen. Yeh, during the late 1940s, became "a familiar figure in Bloomsbury and Cambridge, at which time he wrote short stories and novels in English and contributed to several reviews." He had obtained a scholarship to King's College, Cambridge, "where he was taken up by members of the Bloomsbury elite--Maynard Keynes, Duncan Grant, Leonard Woolf, the Garnetts."

40   SHONE, RICHARD. "Duncan Grant on a Sickert Lecture." *Burlington Magazine* 123 (November):671-72.
        Includes the text of Grant's comments on Sickert and on Sickert's lecture to the School of Painting and Drawing. Shoe offers a brief biographical introduction to the event. Sickert had lunched with

Vanessa Bell prior to the lecture. Grant's notes on the lecture include references to various Bloomsbury figures.

41   STRACHEY, RICHARD. *A Strachey Boy*. London: Peter Owen, 160 pp.
      Autobiographical account by Richard Strachey. Describes Lytton Strachey, Bloomsbury, and other Bloomsbury figures.

42   ____. *A Strachey Childhood*. Oxford: Simonette Strachey, 151 pp.
      Autobiographical account of Lytton Strachey's nephew, describing his life as a child in India, where he spent his first three years, and then in Bloomsbury.

43   STRAWSON, GALEN. "The Interests of the Patient." *Times Literary Supplement* (London) (1 January):15-16.
      Negative review of Stephen Trombley's "*All that Summer She was Mad*": *Virginia Woolf and Her Doctors*. Argues with the view that Leonard and Virginia were unhappy: "It is suggested, or implied, more or less directly, that Leonard Woolf was (always) unsympathetic to his wife, and insensitive in her regard; that they were not happy together-- that they were never happy together; and that Quentin Bell and almost all those who knew the couple were wrong about this."

44   STROUSE, LOUISE F. "Virginia Woolf: Her Voyage Back." *American Imago* 38, no. 2 (Summer):185-203.
      Describes Woolf's struggles with insanity. Often deals with her relationship with other figures who made up Bloomsbury.

45   TROMBLEY, STEPHEN. "*All That Summer She Was Mad*": *Virginia Woolf and Her Doctors*. London: Junction Books. Also published as *All Summer Long She Was Mad: Virginia Woolf, Female Victim of Male Medicine*. New York: Continuum, 338 pp.
      Describing Woolf's dealings with various doctors and her struggle with insanity. Also involves considerable discussion of her relationship with various Bloomsbury figures.

46   WILKINSON, L.P. *A Century of Kings, 1873-1972*. Cambridge: Cambridge University Press, 183 pp.
      Includes commentary on some of the figures who were to be central to Bloomsbury, including E.M. Forster, Leonard Woolf, and others. Also comments on the Apostles.

47 _____. *Kingsmen of a Century, 1873-1972*. Cambridge: Kings
Gallery, 394 pp.
   Deals with various figures associated with the origin of
Bloomsbury.

1982

1 ALEXANDER, PETER. *Roy Campbell: A Critical Biography*. New
   York and Oxford: Oxford University Press, 277 pp.
      Describes Campbell's brief encounter with Bloomsbury figures
   and life. His dislike of Bloomsbury was based upon his hatred of
   wealth and his wife's affair with Vita Sackville-West.

2 ALLEY, HENRY M. "A Rediscovered Eulogy: Virginia Woolf's
   'Miss Janet Case: Classical Scholar and Teacher.'" *Twentieth
   Century Literature* 28, no. 3 (Fall):290-301.
      The influence of Janet Case on Virginia Woolf has not been
   adequately evaluated. The association of the two ended sometime after
   April 1907, "with Case feeling somewhat intimidated by 'the new
   Bloomsbury life' and fearing rejection."

3 BACK, KURT W. "Clapham to Bloomsbury: Life Course Analysis
   of an Intellectual Aristocracy." *Biography* 5, no. 1 (Winter):38-52.
      Considers the possibility of combining the methods of the
   individual biographer and the sociological study of the group for the
   analyzing the evolution of the nineteenth-century Clapham Set into the
   Bloomsbury Group: "The pre-eminence of the intellectual aristocracy
   did not outlast the pre-eminence of the nobility in politics. Both had to
   contend with recruits from new sources." Describes Bertrand Russell,
   Lady Ottoline Morrell, and Vita Sackville-West in relation to this trend.

4 BAKER, DENYS VAL. "From Bloomsbury to Cornwall."
   Geographical Magazine 54 (March):169-70.
      Woolf's holidays spent in Cornwall had a profound influence on
   her work. Gives local description of places which can be seen today.
   Alludes to other Bloomsbury figures in this connection.

5 BLUME, MARY. "That Amazing Bloomsbury Group." *Vogue* 172
   (October):188, 197.
      Discussion of Charleston, the Sussex farmhouse of Vanessa Bell,

and the art and literature created there. Also comments on the
attempts to restore and preserve Charleston. Suggests that "it is a
popular fallacy to think of the 'Bloomsberries' as rich and leisured."

6   BULL, DAVID. "Two Women Intellectuals in a Changing World:
     V. Woolf and B. Webb." *Annali della Facolta di Lettere e Filosofia*
     35, nos. 2-3 (May-December):225-249.
         Deals somewhat with the social-cultural world during the early
years of the twentieth century. Includes Woolf's association with
Bloomsbury.

7   BUMPUS, JUDITH. "Contemporary Art Society." *Art and Artists*
     193 (October):3-9.
         Looks at the past and present "of the society that occupies a
very special place in the vanguard of art appreciation. It has taken
new art to out of the way places, broadened the horizons of the young
and opened the eyes of the old." Includes some commentary on Roger
Fry's role in the society and the controversy over Post-impressionism.

8   COHEN, EDWARD H. "An Uncollected Poem by Vita Sackville-
     West." *English Language Notes* 19, no. 2 (Winter 1981-1982):129-31.
         Discusses two great losses Vita Sackville-West suffered: her
ancestral home, Knole, and her right to an independent existence.
Brief mention of Virginia Woolf's observations about Vita.

9   CURTIN, DEANE W. "Varieties of Aesthetic Formalism." *Journal
     of Aesthetics and Art Criticism* 40, no. 3 (Spring):315-26.
         Formalism no longer dominates the discussion of painting as it
did in years past. It is still the most important critical position of the
century. Discusses Roger Fry's role in establishing formalism in
relation to the Post-impressionists.

10   DeSALVO, LOUISE A. Introduction to *Melymbrosia*, by Virginia
     Woolf. New York: New York Public Library, pp. xiii-xliv.
         Introduction to the earliest draft of Woolf's novel, *The Voyage
Out*, which includes commentary on the making of the novel. She
discussed her anxiety over the novel among her Bloomsbury friends.

11   ____. "Lighting the Cave: The Relationship Between Vita
        Sackville-West and Virginia Woolf." *Signs* 8, no. 2 (Winter):195-214.
            Summarizes Virginia Woolf's love relationship with Sackville-
        West, which coincided with "the most productive period of each of their
        lives" (1923-33) and speculates on their influences on each other's
        creativity: "The love that they developed provided a solid, central base
        from which they could each look anew at their childhoods, at their
        family histories, at how each had become the woman that she now was.
        This re-examination resulted in profound changes for both."

12   DONNELLY, FRANCES. "The Bloomsberries: Snobbish, Sniping
        and Self-Absorbed." *Listener* 108 (5 August):6-7.
            Relates to program on the group, "A Boom in Bloomsbury": "I
        suspect my own attitude towards the Bloomsberries, compounded
        equally of dislike, envy and fascination, is a fairly typical one."
        Comments on what the Group was and seemed to represent, with
        reference to various studies that have poured forth recently: "But
        perhaps the greatest nostalgia that the Bloomsbury memory evokes is
        the amount of time and leisure they had for cultivating friendships.
        They were freed from the most menial tasks and enjoyed the kind of
        freedom that nowadays only students can briefly experience."

13   EDEL, LEON. "Biographer and Subject: Lytton Strachey and Van
        Wyck Brooks." *Prose Studies* 5, no. 3 (December):281-293.
        Deals somewhat with Stracehy and Bloomsbury.

14   ____. "The Madness of Virginia Woolf." In *Stuff of Sleep and
        Dreams: Experiments in Literary Psychology*. New York: Harper &
        Row, pp. 192-203.
            The sources of Virginia Woolf's tragic and heroic struggle with
        madness can be found in her confusion of infantile sexual feeling.
        Survey's Virginia Woolf's relationships with her father and step-
        brothers, her phobias, and her attitudes toward death. Gives some
        background to the early relationship between sisters.

15   FURBANK, E.M. "The Philosophy of E.M. Forster." In *E.M.
        Forster: Centenary Revaluations*. Edited by Judith Scherer Herz and
        Robert K. Martin. London: Macmillan; Toronto and Buffalo:
        University of Toronto Press, pp. 37-51.
            Forster had a "set of theories (not just beliefs) about existence
        which had multiple application and formed a worked out system."

Connects Forster's philosophy to Bloomsbury and, in particular, to
Cambridge, although he questions the influence of G.E. Moore's "mode
of argument about Idealism."

16   HERZINGER, KIM A. *D.H. Lawrence in His Time: 1908-1915*.
      Lewisbury: Bucknell University Press; London: Associated
      University Presses, 237 pp.
           Comments on Lawrence's life in relation to the literary and
      cultural scene in pre-war England. Includes a chapter on Bloomsbury,
      "Extensions: Cambridge and Bloomsbury" (pp. 172-79): "Many of the
      elements in the Georgian sensibility that Lawrence had found
      dangerous and had violently rejected in 'England, My England,'--the
      sense of extended adolescence, the underlying lust for war, the failure
      to confront the reality of a decaying England with the necessary
      toughness--were crystallized in a more influential form in the
      Cambridge-Bloomsbury milieu."

17   HUTCHEON, LINDA. "'Sublime Noise' for Three Friends: Music
      in the Critical Writings of E.M. Forster, Roger Fry, and Charles
      Mauron." In *E.M. Forster: Centenary Revaluations*. Edited by Judith
      Scherer Herz and Robert K. Martin. London: Macmillan; Toronto:
      University of Toronto Press, pp. 84-98.
           Images of music "significantly inform the writings, both critical
      and creative, not just of Forster, but also of other members of the
      Bloomsbury Group." Focuses on two views of music as a nonmimetic
      and as a mimetic art form in Forster. Fry views music as purest art
      form: "A two-way pull between an interest in objective form and a
      concern for subjective responses is reminiscent of the struggle between
      classicism and romanticism, or perhaps between Aristotelian and
      Longinian impulses in critical thinking."

18   KENNY, SUSAN M., and EDWIN J. KENNEY, JR. "Virginia
      Woolf and the Art of Madness." *Massachusetts Review* 23, no. 1
      (Spring):161-185.
           Describes Woolf's relationship with Leonard and other
      Bloomsbury figures.

19   LEVY, PAUL. "Between the Books." *Times Literary Supplement*
      (London) (25 June):701.
           Review of *The Diary of Virginia Woolf*, Vol. 4, *1931-1935*, edited
      by Anne Olivier Bell and Andrew McNeille. Diaries do not show her

as "a monster of selfishness and snobbishness, or as a wilful creator of literary obscurity." Social life "occupied a third place in Virginia Woolf's hierarchy of concerns in this period." She lost several important friends, including Lytton Strachey, Roger Fry, and Francis Birrell. Claims the dairies also show she was more political aware than previously thought.

20 McDOWELL, FREDERICK P.W. *E.M. Forster.* Rev. ed. Boston: Twayne, 172 pp.
    Revised study originally published in 1969. The Cambridge milieu, in which Forster participated, "helped form the Bloomsbury ethos, and the values that it represented were ones that were also crucial to Forster." Flexibility, tolerance, and a disinterested "inquiry into ethical and philosophical issues were all aspects of the humanism that Forster cherished, as they were of the philosophy that his fellows in the Bloomsbury Group advocated."

21 _____. "'Fresh Woods, and Pastures New': Forster Criticism and Scholarship since 1975." In *E.M. Forster: Centenary Revaluations.* Edited by Judith Scherer Herz and Robert K. Martin. London: Macmillan; Toronto and Buffalo: University of Toronto Oress, pp. 311-29
    Comments on several studies that connect Forster to Bloomsbury.

22 McLAURIN, ALLEN. "Virginia Woolf and Unanimism." *Journal of Modern Literature* 9, no. 1 (1981-82):115-22.
    Virginia Woolf's fiction shows the prominence given social gatherings: "This interest in groups no doubt derives in part from her association with Bloomsbury." This idea leads to a consideration of connections between her work and the work of Jules Romains and the Unanimists. *The Waves* shows this connection best: "Romains thought that certain everyday situations contained the seeds of a unanime and that such a group needed only the consciousness of itself as a unanime in order to be fully developed."

23 MAHOOD, KENNETH. *The Secret Sketchbook of a Bloomsbury Lady.* Foreword by Michael Holroyd. New York: St. Martin's Press; London: Bodley Head, 64 pp.
    Humorous account of the Bloomsbury Group based upon the

fictitious diary of Maud Millicent Mahood. Includes many cartoons depicting Bloomsbury figures.

24   MARES, CHERYL JEAN. "Another Space of Time: The Dominion of Painting in Proust and Woolf." Ph.D. dissertation, Princeton University, 374 pp.

Evaluates connections between Proust and Woolf, especially in light of their views on the relationship between literature and painting: "Woolf's reading of Proust is highly ambivalent and in certain respects distorted," especially "in her effort to incorporate the painter's perspective into the novel while avoiding the extremes of formalism in Post-Impressionist theory and practice." See *Dissertation Abstracts International* 42:4821A.

25   MEYEROWITZ, SELMA S. *Leonard Woolf.* Boston: Twayne. 234 pp.

Biographical study that focuses on Woolf's published literary writings. Dies not interpret the "personal or literary relationship between Leonard and Virginia" or "Leonard's role and influence as a critic of Virginia's work." Deals somewhat with Leonard in relation to Bloomsbury: "Yet a study of Woolf's life and work reveals that he had a considerable influence on his society as an important writer, one whose literary and political work reflected the history of his times." Includes separate chapter, "Contributions to Journalism and the Hogarth Press."

26   NADEL, IRA BRUCE. "Moments in the Greenwood: *Maurice* in Context." In *E.M. Forster: Centenary Revaluations.* Edited by Judith Scherer Herz and Robert K. Martin. London: Macmillan; Toronto and Buffalo: University of Toronto Press, pp. 177-90.

Focuses on "two aspects of the homosexual experience presented in the novel: blackmail and working-class lovers." Connects these issues to the "island of sexual freedom amid the restrictive landscape of Edwardian England: Cambridge and, afterwards, Bloomsbury." Forster's own sexual development occurred independently of Bloomsbury.

27   POMEROY, ELIZABETH W. "Within Living Memory: Vita Sackville-West's Poems of Land and Garden." *Twentieth Century Literature* 28, no. 3 (Fall):269-89.

Critical consideration of Vita's poetry, which was the part of her creative work she valued most. Includes some minor references to her relationship with Virginia Woolf.

28   PUTT, S. GORLEY. "A Packet of Bloomsbury Letters: The
      Forgotten H.O. Meredith." *Encounter*, 59 (November):77-84.
         Commentary on and inclusion of various letters to H.O.
Meredith, who was an Apostle along with Lytton Strachey and others,
by various Bloomsbury figures. Includes letters from Virginia Woolf,
Roger Fry, and Lytton Strachey that were in the possession of S.
Gorley Putt.

29   ROCHE, PAUL. "Duncan Grant." *Transatlantic Review* 51
      (Spring):18-25.
         Personal account of Duncan Grant. Involves Grant's association
with Bloomsbury.

30   ____. *With Duncan Grant in Southern Turkey*. London: Honeyglen
      Publishing, 187 pp.
         Personal account of Grant by one of his dearest friends. Includes
commentary on Duncan Grant in and out of Bloomsbury.

31   ROSENBAUM, S.P. "*Aspects of the Novel* and Literary History." In
      E.M. Forster: Centenary Revaluations. Edited by Judith Scherer Herz
      and Robert K. Martin. London: Macmillan; Toronto and Buffalo:
      University of Toronto Press, pp. 55-83.
         Suggests that "the literary history of *Aspects of the Novel* begins
in Bloomsbury." Leonard Woolf had asked Forster to write a book on
psychology and fiction for the Hogarth Press, which may have
influenced Forster's selection of a topic for the Clark Lectureship at
Cambridge, which became *Aspects of the Novel*. This book displays a
"quintessential Bloomsbury characteristic--eclecticism."

32   ____. "The Intellectual Origins of the Bloomsbury Group." *Times
      Educational Supplement*(London) (29 October):14-15.
         Incorporated in *Victorian Bloomsbury*. (See 1987.27.)

33   ____. "Keynes, Lawrence, and Cambridge Revisited." *Cambridge
      Quarterly* 11, no. 1:252-64.
         The commentary by G.E. Moore on D.H. Lawrence's visit to
Cambridge offers new material to evaluate what has become part of
the mythology of literary history: "The most significant thing about

Moore's contemporary account and later recollection is their making
clear that if Lawrence was repelled by Cambridge rationalism and
cynicism, it was their embodiment in the personality and character of
John Maynard Keynes that really upset him."

34   SHONE, RICHARD. "Backgrounds for Being In." *Times Literary
      Supplement* (London) (30 April):494.
            Review of Isabelle Anscombe's *Omega and After*. The term
      "Bloomsbury art" is recent and "embodies a recognition of certain
      qualities and standards, in life as much as in work, which were shared
      by a small group of artists." Roger Fry, Vanessa Bell, and Duncan
      Grant were really the only "contenders," even though others were
      associated with the group. Feels that this book fails because of the
      mixture of biographical detail with a consideration of the works
      themselves.

35   SKIDELSKY, R.J. "Keynes and Bloomsbury." *Royal Society of
      Literature of the United Kingdom*, n.s. 42:15-27.
            "Although Keynes was a member of the Bloomsbury Group it is
      not immediately obvious why he should have been." He was a public
      figure, an economist: "In the world of affairs he was a man of
      Bloomsbury; in the world of Bloomsbury he was a man of affairs."
      Explains Keynes double nature: "Civilization for the minority; bread
      and circuses for the majority: this is not a bad description of Keynes's
      economic intentions."

36   STEWART, JACK F. "Impressionism in the Early Novels of
      Virginia Woolf." *Journal of Modern Literature* 9, no. 2 (May):237-66.
            Woolf conceived her fiction in visual scenes and stressed the
      close analogy between her art and that of the painter. Looks at
      impressionism rather than Post-impressionism. Suggests some
      connections between Woof's fiction and the work of Roger Fry's
      Omega workshops.

37   ____. "Spatial Form and Color in *The Waves*." *Twentieth Century
      Literature* 28, no. 1 (Spring):86-107.
            "Virginia Woolf's explorations of language and being made her
      acutely conscious of spatiality, and she conceived each of her novels,
      like a sculpture or painting, in terms of virtual space." Roger Fry
      serves as a major influence, although his criticism of Impressionism was
      not wholly accepted by Woolf.

38 TAYLOR, J.R. "Hated Him--Loved Her." *Art and Artists* 191 (August):23.
    Deals with the art of Vanessa Bell.

39 WHITEMAN, BRUCE. "Lawrence's War." *Russell* 2, no. 1 (June):78-80.
    Review of Paul Delaney's *D.H. Lawrence's Nightmare*. Describes Lawrence's life during the war in relation to his association with Russell through Lady Ottoline Morrell.

40 WILSON, C. "Illusion and Representation." *British Journal of Aesthetics* 22, no. 3 (June):218-19.
    Deals with Clive Bell and the aesthetics associated with Bloomsbury.

41 WOODESON, JOHN. *Mark Gertler*. London: Sidgwick & Jackson, 218 pp.
    Biographical study. Includes commentary on his relationship with Dora Carrington, Lytton Strachey, and other Bloomsbury figures.

42 WOOLF, VIRGINIA. *The Diary of Virginia Woolf*, Vol. 4, *1931-1935*. Edited by Anne Olivier Bell and Andrew McNeillie. London: Hogarth Press; New York: Harcourt Brace Jovanovich, 402 pp.
    Includes reference to and commentary on Bloomsbury and various Bloomsbury figures. The preface by Anne Olivier Bell states that Lytton had some years been "living in a circle of his own, whereas Riger remained much closer to what one might call the heart of Bloomsbury--if, that is, we think of Virginia Woolf and Vanessa Bell as the core of that elusive entity."

1983

1 ALEXANDER, PETER. "Roy Campbell, William Plomer, and the Bloomsbury Group." *Journal of Commonwealth Literature* 18, no. 1:120-27.
    Commentary on the relations of Roy Campbell and William Plomer, with remarks on Campbell's hatred of Bloomsbury. He stayed with Vita and Harold Nicolson in 1926 at which time Vita seduced Mary, Campbell's wife: "Campbell, when he learnt of their affair, which came close to destroying his marriage, was enraged and wrote

The Georgiad, his violent attack on Vita and members of the Bloomsbury Group, in revenge." Plomer had become friends with several people attacked by Campbell.

2   ANAND, MULK RAJ. "E.M. Forster: A Personal Recollection." *Journal of Commonwealth Literature* 18, no. 1:80-83.
      Personal account of Forster included in the special issue of this journal on Bloomsbury: "His stand for free speech and opinion also derived from his love of human beings and their instinctive truth."

3   ____. "In Conversation With H.G. Wells." *Journal of Commonwealth Literature* 18, no. 1:84-90.
      Briefly comments on Wells's outbursts against Virginia Woolf and the Bloomsbury sensibility: "In January 1932, Krishna Menon of the India League in London called a meeting of friends of India in the little Conway Hall in Red Lion Square, which was within the spiritual area of Bloomsbury, though geographically a little outside it."

4   BELL, QUENTIN. "Playing with Gender." *Vogue* 173 (November):435, 502.
      Commentary on Vita Sackville-West with considerable personal reflection: "Although Vita was an entirely amiable person and although she had a native and sympathetic modesty, she was also a person who could and did face the world majestically."

5   BELL, ROBERT H. "Bertrand Russell of the Eliots." *American Scholar* 52 (Summer):309-25.
      Clarifies the mystery of the relationship between Bertrand Russell, T.S. Eliot, and Eliot's wife, Vivien. Includes description of Lady Ottoline Morrell's move to Garsington and her connection with Russell and Eliot: "Besides Ottoline and Vivien, he [Russell] was flirting fairly seriously at this time with Katherine Mansfield." Also describes Leonard and Virginia Woolf's meeting Eliot in 1918. Concludes that "the triangle, then, was not as innocent as Russell wished us to believe nor as sordid as gossips imagined."

6   BURT, JOHN, and ELIZABETH INGLIS. "Special Collections Report." *English Literature in Transition* 26, no. 4:222-24.
      Describes two collections related to Leonard and Virginia Woolf at the University of Sussex Library. The Leonard Woolf Papers "record his personal and professional life over eighty years, from his

juvenile writings to his final diary entries." Includes letters from
Bloomsbury figures, as well as diaries related to the Bloomsbury years.
The Monks House Papers "comprise those documents used by
Professor Quentin Bell in writing the official biography of Virginia
Woolf."

7   CAIRNCROSS, ALEC. "The Apostle of Probability." *Times Literary
     Supplement* (London) (4 November):1209-10.
         Review of Robert Skidelsky's *John Maynard Keynes*, vol. 1,
     Hopes Betrayed, 1883-1920. Discusses the fact that Harrod's biography
     had "suppressed all reference to Keynes's homosexuality." Skidelshy's
     biography covers this material fully, especially his relationship with
     Duncan Grant. Also describes Keynes's early association with Lytton
     Strachey, the Cambridge Apostles, and G.E. Moore. Concludes by
     pointing out that "life in the treasury had a long-term influence on
     Keynes that was, in its way, as profound as that of life in Bloomsbury."

8   CALDER, ANGUS. "A Note on Parmenas Mockerie." *Journal of
     Commonwealth Literature* 18, no. 1:128-30.
         Leonard and Virginia Woolf's Hogarth Press published
     Mockerie's *An African Speaks for His People*. Describes the connection
     between this writer and Leonard Woolf.

9   *Commonwealth Literature and Bloomsbury: A Symposium. Journal of
     Commonwealth Literature* 18, no. 1:79-130.
         Special issue of "articles about the interaction of Bloomsbury and
     Commonwealth writers." The "point of the Symposium is the cross-
     fertilization between established English and struggling Commonwealth
     authors." The articles are described individually in this guide.

10   DAHL, CHRISTOPHER C. "Virginia Woolf's *Moments of Being*
     and the Autobiographical Tradition in the Stephen Family." *Journal
     of Modern Literature* 10, no. 2 (June):175-96.
         "Woolf's autobiographical works need to be seen not only as
     indicators of her development as a novelist, but also as products of a
     long tradition of autobiographical writing in the Stephen Family."
     Discusses autobiographic works delivered at gatherings of the Memoir
     Club: "Virginia Woolf's three surviving contributions--"22 Hyde Park
     Gate," "Old Bloomsbury," and "Am I a Snob?"--are written in a
     distinctive voice which combines the easy, conversational tone of her
     essays with the satiric bite of her letters." States that "though all the

Memoir Club contributions criticize the Victorian past in one way or another, they, like "Reminiscences," point directly back to various aspects of the Stephen family tradition in the nineteenth century."

11   DeSALVO, LOUISE A. "1897: Virginia Woolf at Fifteen." In *Virginia Woolf: A Feminist Slant*. Edited by Jane Marcus. Lincoln and London: University of Nebraska Press, pp. 78-108.

　　　　1897 was the year "in which one could catch a glimpse of the woman that the girl would become." Analyzes early signs of Woolf's illness, which Leonard had to contend with later. Also describes the early relationship with Vanessa.

12   DINNAGE, ROSEMARY. "The Madonna of Bloomsbury." *New York Review of Books* 30, no. 2 (22 December):43-44.

　　　　Review of Frances Spalding's *Vanessa Bell*. Gives overview of Vanessa Bell and other Bloomsbury figures associated with her. Comments on Bloomsbury's rationality, which also lead to the suppression of "unruliness" in Vanessa.

13   ＿＿＿. "Stumbling and Falling." *Times Literary Supplement* (London) (13 May):478.

　　　　Review of *Julia: A Portrait of Julia Strachey by Herself and Frances Partridge*. Julia only touched Bloomsbury tangentially: "She did less work than the Bloomsburyites, and she was much unhappier."

14   FORSTER, E.M. Selected Letters of *E.M. Forster*, vol. 1, *1879-1920*. Edited by Mary Lago and P.N. Furbank. Cambridge: Harvard University Press, 344 pp.

　　　　The introduction by Mary Lago states that "it is interesting, in the Letters, to observe the development of Forster's attitude to the war. It was a war for which, like many of his Bloomsbury friends, he refused, as it were, to take responsibility, for he felt it would bring out all that he most loathed--the conformism and hysteria--in English society." Letters from the Cambridge period reflect his association with the Apostles and many Bloomsbury figures he had met at that time.

15   FOX, ALICE. "Virginia Liked Elizabeth." In *Virginia Woolf: A Feminist Slant*. Edited by Jane Marcus. Lincoln and London: University of Nebraska Press, pp. 37-51.

　　　　Evaluates Woolf's interest in Queen Elizabeth, including her negative reaction to Lytton Strachey's *Elizabeth and Essex*.

16 GIDE, ANDRE, and DOROTHY BUSSY. *Selected Letters of André Gide and Dorothy Bussy.* Edited by Richard Tedeschi. Introduction by Jean Lambert. Oxford and New York: Oxford University Press, 316 pp.

Lambert's Introduction gives good background to the letters, with commentary on Gide's Bloomsbury connection and to the references to Bloomsbury figures in the various letters. Dorothy Bussy was "not a resident of Bloomsbury's enchanted world as fully as her sister Marjorie or her brothers Oliver, Lytton, and James."

17 GILLESPIE, DIANE FILBY. "'Oh to be a Painter!': Virginia Woolf as an Art Critic." *Studies in the Humanities* 10, no. 1 (June 1983):28-38.

Evaluates Woolf's various comments on the visual arts, particularly in relation to the influence of her sister Vanessa Bell. Gives history of Woolf's response to painting and looks at Vanessa Bell's aesthetic as manifest in her paintings: "Acknowledging both the formal and literary qualities of painting, Woolf ultimately is most concerned with what a writer can derive from works of visual art and most comfortable with the areas where the two media overlap."

18 GILLIE, CHRISTOPHER. *A Preface to E.M. Forster.* London and New York: Longmans, 196 pp.

Includes chapters on Forster and the Apostles, as well as Bloomsbury: "The most intelligible way to describe the Bloomsbury Group is perhaps to say that it is a climate of cultural opinion which had prestige in the first quarter of this century." The real importance of Bloomsbury "was the encouragement and stimulus it gave to the work of its individual members, and in the instance of Forster it seems plain that this fruitfulness derived more from his relationships within the circle than with the circle as a whole."

19 GOONERATNE, YASMINE. "A Novelist at Work: The Manuscript of Leonard Woolf's *The Village in the Jungle.*" *Journal of Commonwealth Literature* 18, no. 1:91-104.

Evaluation of Woolf's novel based upon a reading of the original manuscript. The process of composition involves Bloomsbury: "The novel was not begun in Ceylon, but in England during what Woolf later called 'the most exciting months of (his) life.' They were also the most decisive, since in the five months following his return to England from a visit to Europe in the middle of August 1911, 'Bloomsbury' really

came into existence and he fell in love with Virginia Stephen."
Discusses some revisions in relation to the Bloomsbury milieu.

20   GORDON, LYNDALL. "Our Silent Life: Virginia Woolf and T.S.
      Eliot." In *Virginia Woolf: New Critical Essays*. London: Vision
      Press; Totowa, N.J.: Barnes and Noble Books, pp. 77-95.
          Both writers "had definite ideas about the hidden essence and
      structure of lives which might serve, in turn, as guidelines for
      biographical studies of themselves." Involves some overlap in the
      Bloomsbury world. In part looks at Virginia Woolf "not so much as
      she appeared to others, to her family and Bloomsbury, but as she
      appeared to herself."

21   GRUNDY, ISOBEL. "'Words Without Meaning--Wonderful Words':
      Virginia Woolf's Choice of Names." In *Virginia Woolf: New Critical
      Essays*. London: Vision Press; Totowa, N.J.: Barnes and Noble
      Books, pp. 200-220.
          "General account of her habits and procedures in giving names,"
      which includes various sources in her Bloomsbury acquaintances.

22   GUNN, HELEN. "Bloomsbury Under the Downs." *Country Life*
      173 (27 January):240-41.
          Commentary on Monks House, Sussex. Describes the auction at
      which the Woolfs purchased the house: "It was the garden which first
      attracted them to the house." Various visitors came for long weekends:
      "A further incentive for the visitors to Monk's House was its proximity
      to Charleston, where Vanessa Bell lived with Duncan Grant and her
      three children." Includes photographs of the garden and some of the
      interior.

23   HAMILTON, ALAN. "Who's Afraid for Virginia Woolf?" *Times*
      (London) (16 May):9
          Commentary on Quentin Bell in relation to the Virginia Woolf
      and Bloomsbury "industry." Gives some negative reactions to feminist
      criticism of Woolf. Having been born in Bloomsbury, he is unable to
      completely "shuffle off the coil."

24   HANKIN, C.A. *Katherine Mansfield and Her Confessional Stories*.
      New York: St. Martin's Press, 271 pp.
          Includes a chapter, "Garsington as Fiction," which deals with
      Lady Ottoline Morrell and other Bloomsbury figures: "Whatever their

private disagreements, Katherine and Murry retained a sense of being outsiders in the literary circles of Garsington and Bloomsbury." She hated the "Bloomsbury element of life."

25 HEILBRUN, CAROLYN G. "Virginia Woolf in Her Fifties." In *Virginia Woolf: A Feminist Slant*. Edited by Jane Marcus. Lincoln and London: University of Nebraska Press, pp. 236-53.
    "Insofar as that is possible, Virginia Woolf became another person in her fifties." Suggests that her affair with Vita Sackville-West awakened her to the love of women and "to the possibilities embodied in *Mrs. Dalloway*." Also evaluates her relationship with Leonard during this period.

26 HOLLINGHURST, ALAN. "Parting with Respectability." *Times Literary Supplement* (London) (18 November):1267-268.
    Review of *Selected Letters of E.M. Forster*, edited by Mary Lago and P.N. Furbank. Includes minor reference to some Bloomsbury figures in relation to Forster.

27 HOLROYD, MICHAEL. "Married Alive." *Times Literary Supplement* (London) (30 September):1038.
    Review of Victoria Glendinning's *Vita: The Life of V. Sackville-West*. Vita's "most extraordinary incarnation is in Virginia Woolf's *Orlando*." Harold Nicolson described *Orlando* as "the longest and most charming love-letter in literature." Focuses on the marriage and questions, as did Virginia Woolf, whether it was a marriage at all.

28 HOLT, ESTELLE. "Another Window on Bloomsbury." *Manchester Guardian* (28 April):9.
    Interview with Frances Partridge in relation to *Julia Strachey by Herself and Frances Partridge*: "Julia Strachey was one of the more reticent of the set, but she left suitcases crammed with private papers which have now been turned into a book." Discusses her reticence and her marriage to Stephen Tomlin.

29 HYMAN, VIRGINIA R. "Reflections in the Looking Glass: Leslie Stephen and Virginia Woolf." *Journal of Modern Literature* 10, no. 2 (June):197-216.
    Evaluates the relationship of Virginia Woolf with her father, Leslie Stephen: "What was there in Leslie Stephen that made his memory so compelling and so threatening to the fifty-nine-year-old

woman thirty-seven years after his death?" Describes Leonard Woolf's
meeting of the Stephens through Thoby, as well as the early relation of
Vanessa and Virginia with their father. Final sections of the article
deal with the marriage of Leonard and Virginia, which "resembles more
and more that of her parents with the roles reversed."

30   JENKINS, WILLIAM D. "From Bloomsbury to Baker Street: Who's
      Afraid of Mrs. Turner?" *Baker Street Journal: An Irregular Quarterly
      of Sherlockiana*, n.s. 33, no. 3 (September):137-39.
          Brief commentary on Virginia Woolf's *Mrs. Dalloway* in relation
to allusions to Sherlock Holmes. Septimus Smith is a resident of
Bloomsbury and his doctor's name is Holmes.

31   KEYNES, MILO, ed. *Lydia Lopokova*. London: Weidenfeld &
      Nicolson, 218 pp.
          Collection of essays, articles, and commentaries on John
Maynard Keynes's wife. Includes extensive commentary on her various
assocaitions with Bloomsbury and Bloomsbury figures.

32   KIELY, ROBERT. "*Jacob's Room* and Roger Fry: Two Studies in
      Still Life." In *Modernism Reconsidered*, eEdited by Robert Kiely and
      John Hildebidle. London and Cambridge: Harvard University Press,
      pp. 147-66.
          Evaluates two works by Woolf, *Jacob's Room* and *Roger Fry*,
which have males as the central figure: "Both repeatedly assert the
impossibility of representing character accurately in words and thereby
undermine their apparent reason for being; both reveal an interest in
modern painting." Suggests that each is a still life. Discusses the
relationship between *Jacob's Room* and Thoby Stephen. The biography
of Fry "gives us, as she did more often in *Jacob's Room*, a formal
composition after her own heart, an effort, neither desperate nor
sentimental, to locate a center and make 'life stand still' there."

33   LAVIN, MAUD. "Roger Fry, Cézanne and Mysticism." *Arts
      Magazine* 58 (September):98-101.
          "In considering Roger Fry on Cézanne, it becomes apparent that
Fry's formalism is intertwined with his mysticism." Relates the shift on
Fry's critical beliefs to the organization of the two Post-impressionist
exhibitions.

34   LEWIS, THOMAS S.W. "Combining 'the advantages of fact and

fiction': Virginia Woolf's Biographies of Vita Sackville-West, Flush, and Roger Fry." In *Virginia Woolf: Centennial Essays.* Edited by Elaine K. Ginsberg and Laura Moss Gottlieb. Troy, N. Y.: Whitston, pp. 295-324.

Discusses Woolf's commentary on her Bloomsbury associates, Roger Fry and Vita Sackville-West.

35   McLAUGHLIN, ANN L. "An Uneasy Sisterhood: Virginia Woolf and Katherine Mansfield." *In Virginia Woolf: A Feminist Slant.* Edited by Jane Marcus. Lincoln and London: University of Nebraska Press, pp. 152-61.

The striking parallelism in Woolf's and Mansfield's work is important, not influence. The relations between these two writers developed in and around the Bloomsbury world.

36   McNEILLIE, ANDREW, ed. *An Annotated Critical Bibliography.* Totowa, N.J.: Barnes and Noble, 231 pp.

"Sections on Victorian patriarchal heritage, the philosophic and Apostolic Cambridge background, and the Bloomsbury Group are also provided." All relevant items from this text are described in this guide.

38   MARCUS, JANE. "Introduction: Virginia Woolf Aslant." In *Virginia Woolf: A Feminist Slant.* Edited by Jane Marcus. Lincoln and London: University of Nebraska Press, pp. 1-6.

Introduction to the volume, in which shes suggest that Woolf often found herself in the position of "Queen of Bloomsbury."

37   _____. "The Niece of a Nun: Virginia Woolf, Caroline Stephen, and the Cloistered Imagination." In *Virginia Woolf: A Feminist Slant.* Edited by Jane Marcus. Lincoln and London: University of Nebraska Press, pp. 7-36.

"Woolf's work, like her aunts, based religious and political stances on a celebration of celibacy and remade male repressive ideology into a feminist ideology of power." Describes Woolf's relationship with Caroline Stephen and her progress into the Bloomsbury world: "When Virginia Woolf left The Porch in 1904 for a new life in Bloomsbury, she was, in a sense, 'born again,' but not in the sense of her evangelical Clapham sect forebears--nor did she join the Quakers. She remained an agnostic, a rational mystic." Reprinted in *Virginia Woolf and the Languages of Patriarchy*, pp. 115-35. (See 1987.19.)

39   ____. "Virginia Woolf and Her Violin: Mothering, Madness, and
        Music." In *Virginia Woolf: Centennial Essays*. Edited by Elaine K.
        Ginsberg and Laura Moss Gottlieb. Troy, N. Y.: Whitston, pp. 27-
        49.
            Virginia Woolf perceived "very young that there were two modes
        of life for a Victorian girl of her class, to nurse or be nursed, to care
        for invalids or to be an invalid." Deals with Woolf's sense of her own
        illness and her relationship with her sister Vanessa, with Leonard
        Woolf, and with Vita Sackville-West. Reprinted in *Virginia Woolf and
        the Languages of Patriarchy*, pp. 96-114. (See 1987.19.)

40   NEVE, CHRISTOPHER. "France from Firle Becon: Vanessa Bell:
        Paintings 1910-20." *Country Life* 173 (19 May):1314-15.
            Brief discussion of Bell's early paintings: "Other members of
        Bloomsbury came to depend on her." States that "if she invented an
        unorthodox lifestyle, it was because she needed to get on with her
        work." The shifts in her work "reflected exactly in her feelings for
        Roger Fry and, three years later, Duncan Grant."

41   PELLAN, FRANÇOISE. "Virginia Woolf's Posthumous Poem."
        Modern Fiction Studies 29, no. 2 (Winter):695-700.
            Discusses the origin of a poem by Virginia Woolf, published by
        Vita Sackville-West and Harold Nicolson in their anthology, *Another
        World Than This*, which includes some discussion of the relationship
        among these figures.

42   ROSE, MICHAEL L. "Lawrence's Letters." *Russell* 3, no. 1
        (June):54-65.
            Deals specifically with the Lawrence-Russell letters in the
        Cambridge Edition of *The Letters of D.H. Lawrence*, vol. 2, *June 1913-
        October 1916*. Includes commentary on Lawrence and Lady Ottoline
        Morrell because of previously unpublished letters now included.
        Evaluates Lawrence's distrust of Cambridge- or Oxford-educated
        intellectuals.

43   ROSENBAUM, S.P. "An Educated Man's Daughter: Leslie
        Stephen, Virginia Woolf and the Bloomsbury Group." In *Virginia
        Woolf: New Critical Essays*. Edited by Patricia Clements and Isobel
        Grundy. London: Vision; Totowa, N. J.: Barnes & Noble, pp. 32-
        56.
            Evaluates "Virginia Woolf and the Bloomsbury Group from

some of the perspectives that Leslie Stephen's philosophical, historical, literary and biographical ideas offer." The "continuities and discontinuities that emerge from such a survey may also clarify developments from Victorian to modern English literature." Considers Stephen's agnosticism and liberalism, as well as his activities in literature and intellectual history, in relation to Bloomsbury. Incorporated in Rosenbaum's full-length study, *Victorian Bloomsbury*. (See 1987.27.)

44 ____. "Virginia Woolf and the Intellectual Origins of Bloomsbury." In *Virginia Woolf: Centennial Essays*. Edited by Elaine K. Ginsberg and Laura Moss Gottlieb. Troy, N.W.: Whitston, pp. 11-16.
Woolf's fiction was "shaped by a series of intellectual assumptions about reality, perception, morality, government, and art." The Bloomsbury Group "fostered Virginia Woolf's intellectual development and therefore their work provides extensive evidence for the description of that development." The members "display a family resemblance" among their intellectual assumptions that can be the basis for useful generalizations about the Group's and Woolf's intellectual origins. Suggests that Bloomsbury "was born and bred Victorian": "The literary history of Bloomsbury is, among other things, the story of how their writing transmuted Victorian beliefs into modern ones." Discusses Utilitarianism, aestheticism, liberalism, and Puritanism in relation to Bloomsbury.

45 RUSSELL, JOHN. "A Moon Among Shooting Stars." *Times Literary Supplement* (London) (16 September):986.
Review of Francis Spalding's *Vanessa Bell*. Vanessa's physical beauty and her presence were extraordinary. The biography gives Clive Bell credit for "the immense amount of spontaneous uncomplicated happiness that he gave so many people during his long life." The Bloomsbury group was famous for "its *franc-parler*, and nowhere more so than in sexual matters." Spalding deals well with the central part of Vanessa's life, "the first years of marriage to Clive Bell, her romance with Roger Fry, her long partnership in art with Duncan Grant, the death in Spain of her son Julian and her idiosyncratic but famously committed career as a mother."

46 SKIDELSKY, ROBERT. *John Maynard Keynes*, vol. 1, *Hopes Betrayed: 1883-1920*. New York: Viking, 447 pp.
First volume of a biography of Keynes that corrects many

limitations of Harrod's biography (see 1957.18). "I took the view that
Keynesian economics were robust enough to survive revelations about
Keynes's private life." Chapters of special interest: "The Cam,bridge
Undergraduate," "My Early Beliefs," "Lytton, Duncan, Maynard,"
"Private Lives," which includes a section on Bloomsbury, pp. 242-62.
Deals with early experiences at Cambridge, and with the Apostles,
including Strachey and Leonard Woolf. "At Cambridge Maynard
experienced a philosophic, aesthetic, and emotional awakening which
shifted his values." Comments on the development of the reputation of
the Group, from both defenders and admirers. Sees one primary
concern: "Members of Bloomsbury were uncommonly interested in the
question of what constitutes a good life, and their preoccupation with
this question shaped to an unusual extent the kind of lives they actually
led, and their valuation of people and activities." The cultural influence
of Bloomsbury was due in part to "the clarity of vision of its publicists
and the mutually supporting achievements of its members" but it was
also due to its relative financial independence and its power of
patronage." Deals candidly with the relationship between Keynes and
Duncan Grant.

47   SMITH, ANGELA. "Katherine Mansfield and Virginia Woolf:
      Prelude and *To The Light House*." *Journal of Commonwealth
      Literature* 18, no. 1:105-19.
         Discusses the relationship and the mutual influence of these two
writers: "Bloomsbury gossip hampered their relationship, as did
Katherine Mansfield's incisiveness as a critic and reviewer." Suggests
that in both "positive and negative ways, Katherine Mansfield's
relationship with Virginia Woolf seems to have clarified her view of
herself as a writer during her most productive years."

48   SPALDING, FRANCES. *Vanessa Bell: A Bloomsbury Portrait*. New
      York: Ticknor & Fields; London: Weidenfeld & Nicolson, 399 pp.
         Full-length biographical study of Vanessa Bell: "Vanessa Bell
lived at the very center of Bloomsbury and, though neither an
intellectual nor a writer, held sway with her acuity, integrity, maturity
and ironic sense of humor." Her work invites a biographical approach
because it is "so intimately associated with her family, friends and
surroundings." It is difficult to assess Bloomsbury with adequate
detachment: "When, however, its contribution to social history is finally
clarified, Vanessa Bell's personal achievement may appear the most
extreme, the most monumental."

49 SQUIER, SUSAN. "The London Scene: Gender and Class in
Virginia Woolf's London." *Twentieth Century Literature* 29
(Winter):488-500.
To Virginia Woolf, London was the focus for an "intense, often
ambivalent, lifelong scrutiny." Deals with the "London Scene" essays,
which show gender and class relations in the city. Relates somewhat to
her experiences "in the narrow streets of Kensington and then the
spacious squares of Bloomsbury."

50 STEINBERG, ERWIN R. "*Mrs Dalloway* and T. S. Eliot's Personal
Wasteland." *Journal of Modern Literature* 10, no. 2 (June):3-25.
Traces "the growing intimacy of Eliot and the Woolfs from
November 1918 through the period during which *Mrs. Dalloway* was
being written (August 1922 through 1925)" and "demonstrates in *Mrs.
Dalloway* echoes of Eliot's life and *The Waste Land*." The description
of the relationship involves various Bloomsbury figures, including
Ottoline Morrell, Clive Bell, and David Garnett. Suggests that there
are connections between Eliot's life and the life of Septimus Warren
Smith.

51 STRACHEY, JULIA. *Julia: A Portrait of Julia Strachey by Herself
and Frances Partridge*. New York: Little, Brown, 308 pp.
Autobiographical account of this Bloomsbury figure who is the
niece of Lytton Strachey and who married the artist Stephen Tomlin.
Taken from extracts of her papers, edited by Frances Partridge.
Includes her brief essay, "Carrington: A Study of a Modern Witch," in
which she states that "Carrington was by nature a lover of marvels, a
searcher for the emotionally magnificent life."

52 SUMMERS, CLAUDE J. *E.M. Forster*. New York: Frederick
Ungar, 406 pp.
Includes a biographical sketch describing Forster's association
with the Cambridge Apostles and, later, Bloomsbury: "Forster's belief
in individualism and the sanctity of personal relationships, his scorn for
conventionality and religion, his passion for truth and friendship, his
unaffected love for art and his intellectual romanticism all either sprang
from or were reinforced by his university experience."

53 TREVOR-ROPER, HUGH. "Acts of the Apostles." *New York
Review of Books* (31 March):3-7.
Review of *After Long Silence*, by Michael Straight, which

comments on Cambridge and the Apostles during the 1930s in the shadow of G.E. Moore, E.M. Forster, Maynard Keynes, and the origins of Bloomsbury.

54   WYKES-JOYCE, MAX. "Vanessa Bell: Paintings,.1910-1920." *Art and Artists* 200 (May):36.
    Review of Vanessa Bell exhibition held at the Royal Museum, Canterbury: "Vanessa Bell was the only major painter among the Bloomsbury Group (Edward Wolfe, much her superior, was only a marginal Bloomsbury; Grant followed where she led; and Fry was so beset by artistic theory that most of his efforts are no more than textbook exercises)."

55   ZYTARUK, GEORGE J. "Lectures on Immortality and Ethics: The Failed D.H. Lawrence-Bertrand Russell Collaboration." *Russell* 3, no. 1 (June):7-15.
    Evaluates the proposed collaboration between Lawrence and Russell on a series of lectures in opposition to World War I. Lady Ottoline Morrell served as intermediary. Lawrence objected to Russell's desire to speak directly on political issues.

1984

1   ACKROYD, PETER. *T.S. Eliot: A Life*. New York: Macmillan, 287 pp.
    Includes some commentary on T.S. Eliot's association with Bloomsbury. The Hogarth Press published his poetry, and Lady Ottoline Morrell often had him visit with other literary figures at Garsington, her country home outside of Oxford.

2   ADVANI, RUKUM. *E.M. Forster as Critic*. London: Dow Croom Helm, 255 pp.
    A study of Forster's criticism of society and literature. Focuses on four broad areas: the individual, society and politics, religion, and art. Describes the negative impact of novel as "significant form," which was central to the Bloomsbury aesthetic.

3   ALBRIGHT, DANIEL. "Virginia Woolf as Autobiographer." *Kenyon Review* 6, no. 4 (Fall):1-17.
    Twentieth-century novelists "have felt an immense pressure

toward the autobiographical." Woolf wrote diaries, "three papers which she wrote for the Memoir Club of Bloomsbury," and other autobiographical pieces. Woolf seems missing: "If it is not too far-fetched, then self-exclusion is one of the real purposes behind the whole project, and the diary is composed in order to omit Virginia Woolf." Evaluates Woolf's autobiographical writings, which relate to her world and the Bloomsbury Group, in terms of the banished soul: "The banished soul keeps returning in the costumes of friends and family."

4   AMAYA, MARIO. "Omega's Danby Doodles: The Bloomsbury Group and the Arts and Crafts." *Studio International* 196:33-35.
        Commentary on the Bloomsbury craze in relation to the sale of many Bloomsbury artifacts: "Bloomsbury art was nothing more than a local, actually a provincial, manifestation of continental Post-impressionism and decorative Cubism, totally misunderstood, naively applied, poorly executed, but still with a great deal of fervent good wishes and pleasant charm."

5   ANNAN, NOEL. *Leslie Stephen: The Godless Victorian.* New York: Random House, 432 pp.
        Biographical study with various references to Bloomsbury, including three important sections, "From Clapham to Bloomsbury" (pp. 152-62), "Stephen's Reputation" (pp. 322-28), and "The Other Side of the Coin" (pp. 328-38). Suggests that Bloomsbury, like Clapham, was a coterie: "It was exclusive and clannish. It regarded outsiders as unconverted" and was contemptuous of good form. Compares the two in terms of religious revolt. The reputation of Leslie Stephen at one point centered on Desmond MacCarthy's comment that Stephen was the last aesthetic critic. The Leavises then entered the battle developing the ideal of seriousness in opposition to Bloomsbury.

6   _____. "Portrait of a Genius as a Young Man." *New York Review of Books* (12 July):35-39.
        Review of several books on Keynes, including *Lydia Lopokova* edited, by Milo Keynes; *John Maynard Keynes,* by Charles Hession; and *John Maynard Keynes: Hopes Betrayed,* by Robert Skidelsky. Comments on Keynes in relation to G.E. Moore and suggests that Skidelsky "shows beyond doubt how loyal Keynes remained all his life to the beliefs he formed and friends he made at King's and in the Apostles."

7   BANKS, JOANNE TRAUTMANN. "Some New Woolf Letters."
     Modern Fiction Studies 30, no. 2 (Summer):175-202.
         Includes introduction and several new letters, edited by Banks:
"they range in time from shortly after Woolf's marriage in 1912 to
about a year before her death, aged fifty-nine, in 1941." The
Bloomsbury "pastime, the mildly vulgar flirtation, which Woolf was as
likely to address to Ethel Smyth as to Lytton Strachey, is here seen in
the letters to Duncan Grant." Includes a number of letters to Julian
Bell, who was teaching in Wuhan, China, as well as one each to Molly
MacCarthy and Vanessa Bell. Most include many references to
Bloomsbury figures and activities.

8   BAYLEY, JOHN. "Diminishment of Consciousness: A Paradox in
     the Art of Virginia Woolf." In *Virginia Woolf: A Centenary
     Perspective*. Edited by Eric Warner. New York: St. Martin's Press,
     pp. 69-82.
         The Voyage Out portrays directly the Morrells, Bells, Stephens,
and Stracheys. Deals with other novels. The meditation on the works
is inspired by two small landscapes by Roger Fry in a public room in
Somerville College, Oxford.

9   BELL, QUENTIN. "A 'Radiant' Friendship." *Critical Inquiry* 10, no.
     4 (June):557-66.
         Article written to correct various Woolf misconceptions,
especially in relation to Jane Marcus's statement that due to Caroline
Emelia Stephen's, Violet Dickinson's, and Madge Vaughan's influence
Woolf became a mystic and a Marxist. Suggests that Janet Case and
Margaret Llewelyn Davies "are much stronger candidates," but he even
doubts that they were Marxists. Discusses Woolf's association with the
Woman's Cooperative Guild. Uses documents at Monks house to
make his point that Marcus overstates the case.

10   CAMPBELL, ROY. "Wyndham Lewis." In *Blast 3*. Edited by
     Seamus Coony. Santa Barbara: Black Sparrow Press, pp. 15-38.
         Previously unpublished essay by Campbell which was to appear
through Chatto & Windus in 1931. Comments on Lytton Strachey,
Bloomsbury and attacks on figures of the past. Would not attack "the
smaller fry of their same species--since it is not in the nature of the
Bloomsbury to make an attack (unless collectively) on any outstanding
man who is capable of defending himself while he is alive."

11   COLLINS, JUDITH. "The 'Fearfully Expensive' Omega Illustrated
      Books." *Antique Collector* 55 (February):54-57.
          Describes the Omega Workshops' involvement in book design.

12   ____. *The Omega Workshops*. Preface by Quentin Bell. Chicago:
      University of Chicago Press; London: Secker and Warburg, 310 pp.
          Gives the full history of the Omega Workshops, which Fry
      established just prior to World War I. Describes in influence of Post-
      impressionism on the art of Vanessa Bell, Duncan Grant, and others.

13   ____. "Roger Fry and Omega Pottery." *Ceramic Review* 86
      (March-April):29-31.
          Gives overview of the pottery of the Omega Workshops and its
      Post-impressionist origins. Deals with the primitive quality of the work
      and Fry's interest in design rather than craft.

14   CORK, RICHARD. "The Omega Workshops: Alliance and Enmity
      in English Art 1911-1920. Anthony d'Offay Gallery; The Omega
      Workshops 1913-1919: Decorative Arts of Bloomsbury, Crafts
      Council Gallery." *Artforum* 22 (May):94-95.
          Commentary on exhibition dealing with the Omega Workshops.
      Discusses Bloomsbury.

15   DeSALVO, LOUISE. "Every Woman Is an Island: Vita Sackville-
      West, the Image of the City, and the Pastoral Idyll." In *Women
      Writers and the City: Essays in Feminist Literary Criticism*. Edited by
      Susan Merrill Squier. Knoxville: University of Tennessee Press, pp.
      97-113.
          Evaluates Vita Sackville-West in relation to her notion of the
      city, "that social, political, and economic fortress erected by man to
      enable him to carry out his work while banishing all things natural,
      including human affection, and where he incarcerates the woman he
      has chosen to live his life with him, beside him, while he devotes
      himself to the task of building the British Empire." Deals with her
      relationship with Virginia Woolf and the image Woolf projects of
      Sackville-West in *Orlando*.

16   DIAMAND, PAMELA. "Recollections of the Omega." In *The
      Omega Workshops: Alliance and Enmity in English Art, 1911-1920*.
      Exhibition Catalog. London: Anthony d'Offay Gallery, pp. 8-10.
          Recollections by Roger Fry's daughter. Fry had commissioned

Duncan Grant and Henri Doucet to paint her portrait sitting by the pond in their garden at Guildford. Grant could not afford the car fare. This event lead to the forming of the Omega Workshops to help employ artists who otherwise had few prospects of selling their art. Comments of Doucet's painting a dress for Lady Diana Manners, the Ideal Home Exhibition, Lady Ottoline Morrell, and Wyndham Lewis. Fry felt good about what Omega had accomplished. "What changed this mood I do not know but in 1916 Roger Fry wrote from Paris that Picasso and all the other artists were thinking of Seurat more than Cézanne." Catalog also includes chronology by Judith Collins, pp. 11-23.

17   D'OFFAY, ANTHONY. Preface to *The Omega Workshops: Alliance and Enmity in English Art 1911-1920*. Exhibition Catalog. London: Anthony d'Offay Gallery, pp. 5-7.
        Same catalog as 1984.16. Includes chronology by Judith Collins, pp. 11-23. Preface describes aspects of quarrel between Roger Fry and Wyndham Lewis. "The joy in decoration for its own sake, the unworried insouciance of the less revolutionary and economically hard-pressed Bloomsbury, clearly got the goat of the radically idealistic Vorticists-to-be--in particular Wyndham Lewis and Gaudier-Brzeska." Compares to Arts and Crafts Movement and William Morris. Importance was that Omega "attacked bourgeois preconceptions about decorative art and furnishings." Exhibition designed to complement *Abstract Art in England, 1913-1915*, held in 1969 by this gallery.

18   EDGAR, SUZANNE. "Bloomsbury: Vita Sackville-West." *Quadrant* 28, no. 3 (March):76-78.
        Review of Victoria Glendinning's *Vita: The Life of Vita Sackville-West*. This book will not help critics to assess Vita's position in Bloomsbury: "Glendinning explores the connection very little." Most of the group "deplored Vita's artistic ordinariness and lack of literary judgement." Describes qualities that attracted Woolf to Vita and vice versa.

19   ELLMANN, LUCY. "Fearfully Exciting." *Times Literary Supplement* (London) (27 January):86.
        Commentary on the Crafts Council exhibition, *The Omega Workshops, 1913-1919: Decorative Arts of Bloomsbury*, and the Anthony d'Offay Gallery exhibition, *The Omega Workshops: Alliance and Enmity in English Art, 1911-1920*. Also comments on Judith Collins's *The*

Omega Workshops (see 1984.12). Gives overview of artists involved, including Wyndham Lewis's objections to Fry.

20   FROST, ALAN. "Omega Anonymous." *Crafts* 66 (January-
        February):40-44.
            Discussion of the Omega Workshops and Bloomsbury. Focuses
on Roger Fry's belief that the crafts work should remain anonymous.

21   GALBRAITH, JOHN KENNETH. "General Keynes." *New York
        Review of Books* (22 November):10-14.
            Review of *The Collected Writings of John Maynard Keynes*.
Comments briefly on the relevance of his association with Bloomsbury.

22   GARNETT, ANGELICA. *Deceived with Kindness: A Bloomsbury
        Childhood*. London: Chatto & Windus; Hogarth Press, 181 pp.
            Memoir by Angelica Bell Garnett, daughter of Vanessa Bell and
Duncan Grant, about her childhood in Charleston, the farmhouse-home
Vanessa set up with Clive Bell and Duncan Grant, her relationship with
various Bloomsbury figures, her marriage to David Garnett, and, finally,
her mother's death. Feels it is necessary to come to terms with her
image of her mother and father "in a place where I had spent a large
part of my childhood and which I had always thought of as home."
Gives background to Vanessa and her relationships with Clive Bell and
Duncan Grant. In response to the deception as to her true father
during her childhood she says, "given the freedom that Bloomsbury
supposed it had won for itself, it is, on the contrary, the conventionality
of deception that is surprising." Feels at the end that, in order to
separate herself from her past, she may have "painted Vanessa in
darker colours than she merited, having no doubt distorted her for my
own purposes."

23   GERZINA, GRETCHEN HOLBROOK. "Carrington: Another
        Look at Bloomsbury." Ph.D. dissertation, Stanford University, 247
        pp.
            "My intention has been to use Carrington as a window on
Bloomsbury. Windows are two-directional, so this means that while she
is provides 'another look at Bloomsbury,' Bloomsbury also provides
another look at Carrington." Deals with Carrington's life, her work in
relation to Bloomsbury, and with fictional works by Aldous Huxley,
Gilbert Cannan and D.H. Lawrence "in which Carrington and

Bloomsbury appear as characters." See *Dissertation Abstracts International* 45:1758A.

24   GILBERT, SANDRA. "The Battle of the Books/The Battle of the Sexes: Virginia Woolf's *Vita Nuova*." *Michigan Quarterly Review* 23 (Spring):171-95.
        Deals with the impact of Oxbridge, Woolf's Cambridge-educated brothers and their friends, on Woolf's consciousness and work in relation to the humanistic tradition. Deals also with Woolf's relationship with Vita Sackville-West.

25   GLENDINNING, VICTORIA. *Vita: The Life of Vita Sackville-West*. London: Weidenfield & Nicholson, 487 pp.
        Biographical study, which includes considerable material on Vita Sackville-West's relationship with Virginia Woolf and Bloomsbury, which began around 1920.

26   GLOVERSMITH, FRANK. "Autonomy Theory: Ortega, Roger Fry, Virginia Woolf." In *The Theory of Reading*. Edited by Frank Gloversmith. Brighton, Sussex: Harvester; Totowa, N.J.: Barnes & Noble, pp. 147-198.
        Compares the aesthetic ideas of Ortega to those of Fry and Woolf. Fry's "conception of the novel as 'a single perfectly organic aesthetic whole,' and his readiness to center this within the comprehensive theory of Significant Form and the nature of perception itself gave Woolf the confidence to convert it all to her own artistic purposes." Fry brings together "in a radically new synthesis" theories from many areas of art and culture. Sees McTaggart as source of Fry's thought. Discusses Woolf's *Mrs. Dalloway* in relation to Fry's theories and evaluates "popular" novelist's reliance on realism: "The experimental fiction is a rebuttal of realism, whose unquestioning 'materialism' overloads the novel with fact, appearances, stolid characterization and labyrinthine plots. The answering structure can only be evoked in images, sensory, tactile, predominantly visual and painterly."

27   GORDON, LYNDALL. *Virginia Woolf: A Writer's Life*. New York: W.W. Norton; Oxford: Oxford University Press, 350 pp.
        Virginia Woolf's "imagination was shaped first by a natural scene, the Cornwall shore, then by a social scene, Victorian London, and then, as she grew, she began to perceive the originality of her

father and mother." Includes various references to Bloomsbury and its influence on Woolf's aesthetic: "It was not the intellects of Thoby's friends that so delighted the Stephen sisters; it was the freedom of speech which would have been unremarkable on the staircase of Trinity College, Cambridge, but to which these women were totally unaccustomed in the presence of young men." The original Bloomsbury group "was an extension of the Stephen family and retained a domestic character."

28   GRIFFIN, NICHOLAS. "Bertrand Russell's Crisis of Faith." *Russell* 4, no. 1 (Summer):101-22.
       "Russell's intellectual response to his crisis of faith developed in two stages during the years before the First World War. The first response, roughly contemporaneous with the early years of the break-up of his marriage, was the bleak existentialism of 'The Free Man's Worship.' The second, coinciding with his relationship with Lady Ottoline Morrell, was an attempt to find some mystical faith by which this bleakness could be overcome."

29   HALPERN, BARBARA STRACHEY. "The Life of Julia Strachey." *Russell* 3, no. 2 (Winter 1983-1984):177-79.
       Review of *Julia: A Portrait of Julia Strachey*, by her half-sister: "To know Julia was at once alarming, delightful and maddening, and all these qualities appear most clearly in this book, together with the tragedy which increasingly overtook her."

30   HANLEY, LYNNE T. "Virginia Woolf and the Romance of Oxbridge." *Massachusetts Review* 25, no. 3 (Autumn):421-36.
       Woolf's attitude toward Oxbridge changed throughout her life: "Her progress is reluctant because she adores patriarchal English culture, she loves her father, husband, brothers, and she is extremely fond of several Oxbridge men, but war (in retrospect and in prospect) forces her to painful conclusions." Deals with the nature of Oxbridge culture which was so integral to Bloomsbury.

31   HEINE, ELIZABETH. Introduction to *The Longest Journey*. The Abinger Edition. Edited by Elizabeth Heine. London: Edward Arnold, pp. vii-lxv.
       Evaluates the connection between *The Longest Journey* and Forster's association with the Apostles, which also connects the novel to the Bloomsbury milieu: "The effect of the development of Moore's

ethical arguments on the younger Apostles is recorded not only in *The Longest Journey* but in several Bloomsbury memoirs."

32   HEPBURN, JAMES G. "Ottoline the Terrible." In *Critic into Anti-Critic*. Columbia, S.C.: Camden House Studies in English and American Literature, pp. 109-14.
         Commentary on Lady Ottoline Morrell and the world of Garsington Manor. She wanted to do more than inspire creative people, such as D.H. Lawrence and Bertrand Russell. Relies heavily on the two volumes of her *Memoirs* for material on her life.

33   HESSION, CHARLES H. *John Maynard Keynes: A Personal Biography of the Man who Revolutionized Capitalism and the Way We Live*. New York: Macmillan; London: Collier Macmillan, 400 pp.
         Biographical study focusing on Keynes's creativity which includes several chapters relevant to Bloomsbury: "The King's Scholar at Cambridge" (pp. 37-51), and "Bloomsbury and Its Influence on Keynes's Creativity" (pp. 94-114). Keynes's activities in the Apostles was formative: "By the fall of 1904, Lytton and Maynard were the main figures in the society, Moore's influence being on the wan." Discusses androgyny in relation to Keynes. Suggests that Bloomsbury "sensed and expressed the 'double nature' of the intellectual process," masculine and feminine.

34   HIGNETT, SEAN. *Brett: From Bloomsbury to New Mexico: A Biography*. London and Toronto: Hodder and Stoughton, 233 pp.
         Biographical study of Dorothy Brett. Deals with her family background and her life with D.H. Lawrence in Taos, New Mexico. Several Chapters deal with her relationship to Bloomsbury and Bloomsbury figures, "The Slade," "Ottoline," "Garsington and Hampstead" in particular. Describes Brett's meeting with Dora Carrington at the Slade School of Art. Deals extensively with her associations through Lady Ottoline Morrell. "From Ottoline's point of view, Brett was the first intimate friend of the same sex that she felt she could treat as an equal, at least as far as matters other than sex were concerned." Includes only minor commentary on the work of the various artists and writers in Bloomsbury.

35 HOPWOOD, ALISON. "No, No, Ladies Are Quite Impossible:
The Anti-Feminist Society around Virginia Woolf." *Room of One's
Own: A Feminist Journal of Literature and Criticism* 9, no. 1
(February):38-45.
Deals with the society which evolved out of the male-dominated
world of Cambridge, as well as the general anti-feminist trend. The
male-dominated society of Cambridge was central to Bloomsbury's
development.

36 HUTCHEON, LINDA. *Formalism and the Freudian Aesthetic: The
Example of Charles Mauron.* Cambridge: Cambridge University
Press, 263 pp.
Deals with the formalism that Roger Fry promoted with the two
Post-impressionist exhibitions.

37 KLEIN, JURGEN. "Die Avantgarde von Bloomsbury--Kunst und
Literatur des englishen Post-Impressionismus." *Universitas: Zeitschrift
für Wissenschaft, Kunst und Literatur* 39:1333-44.
Not seen.

38 KRAMER, HILTON. "Bloomsbury Idols." *The New Criterion* 2, no.
5 (January):1-9.
Discusses the revival of interest in Bloomsbury due to the
publication 17 years ago of Michael Holroyd's *Lytton Strachey*. Points
out that it was "not criticism but *biography* [that] was to be the
foundation on which this revival would be based." Our times are
interested in the "life-style' of these figures. Describes some
characteristics of Bloomsbury, such as its candor: "The more one looks
into the Bloomsbury revival, the more convinced one is that
Bloomsbury, despite the immense number of books, articles, and
reviews already devoted to it, is a subject which has not yet found its
writer, and that the writer is unwilling to be a specialist in biography."

39 LAMBERT, ELIZABETH. "Gardens: Genius Among the Flowers."
Architectural Digest 41 (March):140-45.
Visits Lady Ottoline Morrell's Garsington Manor and reviews the
beauty and literary history associated with this location, including many
Bloomsbury figures who spent weekends at Garsington.

40 LEE, HERMIONE. "Dear Bubbling Desmond." *Times Literary Supplement* (London) (8 June):628.

Review of *Desmond MacCarthy: The Man and His Writings*, edited by David Cecil. Describes MacCarthy's mixed career, including his inability to live up to his early promise as a literary figure: "But for all his bubbling inconclusiveness, and his disappointment in his own career (touchingly displayed here in a rueful letter written at fifty-four, in 1931, to his younger self), the literary journalism that came out of his years as literary editor (the 'Affable Hawk') of the *New Statesman*, editor of *Life and Letters* and literary critic of the Sunday *Times* is rich and impressive."

41 ____. "With Towser and Patto." *Times Literary Supplement* (London) (21 December):1480.

Review of *The Letters of Vita Sackville-West to Virginia Woolf*, edited by DeSalvo and Leaska, and *Virginia Woolf: A Writer's Life*, by Lyndall Gordon. The relationship between Sackville-West and Woolf is interesting because it "links two slices of English society between the wars--the landowning political patriotic aristocracy, and the intellectual, artistic, pacifist puritans of Bloomsbury." Gordon suggests that the relationship between Woolf and Katherine Mansfield was more serious.

42 LEVINE, JUNE PERRY. "The Tame in Pursuit of the Savage: The Posthumous Fiction of E.M. Forster." *PMLA* 99, no. 1 (January):72-88.

Forster's homosexual fiction "indicates a marked impulse in his work: the tame in pursuit of the savage, oscillation within a field of attraction and repulsion." Includes some commentary on Lytton Strachey's reaction to the drafts of *Maurice*.

43 LIVELY, PENELOPE. "Bloomsbury Women." *Encounter* 62 (February):40-43.

Review of Victoria Glendinning's *Vita: The Life of Vita Sackville-West* and Francis Spalding's *Vanessa Bell*: "In both instances, it is the life that seizes the attention rather than the work." Both biographies "are chronicles of sexual ambivalence--or rather, of the way in which compassionate love can transcend sexual inclination." Describes Vanessa as "the linchpin of Bloomsbury."

44   LOVE, JEAN O. "Portraying and Explaining Lives: The Case of
     Virginia Woolf." *Michigan Quarterly Review* 23, no. 4 (Fall):529-42.
          Discusses the delicate balance between biographer and
     psychologist she tries to maintain in her writing on Virginia Woolf.
     Alludes to figures in Woolf's life drawn from her Bloomsbury
     association, including Vita Sackville-West, and Thoby Stephen. Article
     followed by discussion questions.

45   MacCARTHY, DESMOND. *Desmond MacCarthy: The Man and
     His Writings*. Edited with an introduction by David Cecil. London:
     Constable, 313 pp.
          A collection of articles by MacCarthy taken from various texts,
     including *Portraits, Criticism, Memories, Humanities*, and *Experience*.
     Cecil's introduction (pp. 13-35) gives an overview of MacCarthy,
     including his association with Bloomsbury and Bloomsbury aesthetics:
     "At Cambridge he had made some lifelong friends who were later to
     found the nucleus of the so-called Bloomsbury Circle. Desmond is
     sometimes spoken of as belonging to it. This was not so. As he
     himself said, 'Bloomsbury has never been a spiritual home for me.'"

46   MacCARTHY, FIONA. "Roger Fry and the Omega Idea." In *The
     Omega Workshops, 1913-19: Decorative Arts of Bloomsbury*.
     Exhibition Catalog. London: Arts Council Gallery, pp. 9-23.
          History of the Omega Workshops, which self-consciously lacked
     "the Ruskin-based philosophy, concern with workmen's souls and social
     message." We have to see the enterprise in the context of a part of
     Bloomsbury, "as a *jeu d'esprit*. . . , a gesture of defiance against the
     inhabitants of Bird's Custard Island, as Fry so despairingly described his
     country." Fry had turned to continental movements in the applied arts,
     such as the Martine, for inspiration. Admired the spontaneity and lack
     of pomp in decorative style. Also shows how Fry's ideas derive from
     Fauve painters and the great Italian masters' style of mosaic.
     Bloomsbury's insistence on freedom of expression was central to the
     scheme. "And it was from Bloomsbury circles that the Omega acquired
     its most regular clients."

47   McLAURIN, ALLEN. "Consciousness and Group Consciousness in
     Virginia Woolf." In *Virginia Woolf: A Centenary Perspective*. Edited
     by Eric Warner. New York: St. Martin's Press, pp. 28-40.
          One of the ideas presented by Woolf "as a network of images
     and suggestions is the notion of a group mind." Ideas about the "group

mind" and about group psychology were very much in vogue during the
time she began writing: "Virginia Woolf was aware of other works on
group psychology and crowd theory which were written in the first
decades of the century, and which were discussed with great interest by
members of the Bloomsbury Group."

48   MANSFIELD, KATHERINE. *The Collected Letters of Katherine
     Mansfield*, vol. 1, *1903-1917*. Edited by Vincent O'Sullivan and
     Margaret Scott. Oxford: Clarendon Press, 376 pp.
        Includes letters to and about various Bloomsbury figures.
Editorial commentary also describes her association with the Group:
"She was drawn into Bloomsbury through her growing acquaintance
with Lytton Strachey, and her brief but intense friendship with Bertrand
Russell."

49   MARQUAND, DAVID. "Life-Size Portraits of Two Giants: Ernest
     Bevin and J.M. Keynes." *Encounter* 62 (April):43-47.
        Review of Robert Skidelsky's *John Maynard Keynes, 1883-1920:
Hopes Betrayed*: "Skidelsky has uncovered huge floods of evidence
about his subject's private life. In places he has allowed it to
overwhelm him; but it is easy to see why." Harrod's official biography
concealed Keynes's homosexuality, wjich played a crucial role in his
values. Briefly discusses his evolution through Cambridge to
Bloomsbury.

50   MATRO, THOMAS G. "Only Relations: Vision and Achievement
     in *To The Lighthouse*." *PMLA* 99, no. 2 (March):212-24.
        Redefines Woolf's *To the Lighthouse* in relation to Roger Fry's
theories of art: "I propose a rereading of the novel that acknowledges
the role of Fry's aesthetic but redefines Woolf's achievement." Woolf
uses the Post-impressionist "concern with form, pattern, balance, and
significant design" metaphorically rather than "a quietly applied method
or aesthetic that would require more explanation than the novel itself
supplies." Woolf transforms "the making of Post-impressionist art into
a metaphor for the common conditions of seeing and loving that the
characters, the artist, and the reader must always share."

51   MOOREHEAD, CAROLINE. "Exorcising the Ghosts of
     Bloomsbury." *Times* (London) (1 August):8.
        Commentary on Angelica Garnett's *Deceived With Kindness*,
which is "like a very hard session with a tough psychoanalyst."

52 MORAN, MARGARET. "Experiment in Biography." In *Biography: Fiction, Fact, and Form*. New York: St. Martin's Press, pp. 183-205.

Evaluates the development of biographical form, including references to Virginia Woolf and Lytton Strachey. Also deals with group biography in relation to Leon Edel's *Bloomsbury: A House of Lions*: "Dealing with the fashionable subject of Bloomsbury, however, poses dangers to any biographer, not the least being the overshadowing of one figure by another, a worry in any group biography."

53 MORROW, BRADFORD. "History of an Unapologetic Apologia: Roy Campbell's Wyndham Lewis." In *Blast 3*. Edited by Seamus Coony. Santa Barbara: Black Sparrow Press, pp. 11-14.

Campbell's book on Lewis made "Chatto & Windus's shell-shocked libel lawyers quiver." Relates to the belief that Bloomsbury dominated the artistic world and to the claims Campbell made about Strachey.

54 OATES, QUENTIN. "Critics Crowner: *Desmond MacCarthy: The Man and His Writings*, edited by David Cecil." *Bookseller* (9 June):2368-69.

Review which comments on MacCarthy's work as a critic and on the connection between MacCarthy and Bloomsbury.

55 RICE, THOMAS JACKSON. *Virginia Woolf: A Research Guide*. New York: Garland Press, 258 pp.

Annotated listing of criticism on Virginia Woolf. Includes commentary on various items that relate to Woolf's Bloomsbury connections. Useful for further reading in Woolf not directly related to her Bloomsbury activities.

56 ROSENBAUM, S.P. "Bertrand Russell in Bloomsbury." *Russell* 4, no. 1 (Summer):11-30.

Considers the complexity of Russell's relationship with Bloomsbury: "In trying to understand the particular nature of Russell's relevance to Bloomsbury, it is helpful to follow these distinctions he made between his life and his technical and non-technical philosophy, beginning with a short account of his place among the Apostles and then going on to a brief consideration of his Edwardian work in logic and epistemology before turning to the ethical and social philosophy that influenced Bloomsbury mainly during the First World War and

then concluding with a look at Russell's criticism of Bloomsbury, which
will take us back to the Apostles again."

57   _____. "The First Book of Bloomsbury." *Twentieth Century
      Literature* 30, no. 4 (Winter):388-403.
            Discusses history of *Euphrosyne*, an anonymous book of poems
      which appeared in 1905, which includes poems by Clive Bell, Leonard
      Woolf, Lytton Strachey, and Saxon Sydney-Turner: "The unique
      character of *Euphrosyne* along with the responses it evoked and
      provoked among the Group also made it, in another sense, the last
      book of Bloomsbury. Never again did members of the Group publish a
      joint literary work." Gives contents, authorship, and evaluation of the
      work in this volume: "The verses of Clive Bell and Saxon Sydney-
      Turner that make up most of *Euphrosyne* differ from each other most
      in their tones." Suggests that this is Bloomsbury's most decadent work:
      "The influences of *fin-de-siécle* English and French poets are
      unmistakable."

58   SACKVILLE-WEST, VITA. *The Letters of Vita Sackville-West to
      Virginia Woolf*. Edited by Louise DeSalvo and Mitchell A. Leaska.
      London: Hutchinson. Reprint. New York: William Morrow, 1985,
      474 pp.
            Introduction by Leaska (pp. 9-46) gives an overview of the
      relationship that produced these letters: "The letters which follow
      chronicle the story of two extraordinary women--Vita Sackville-West,
      who quested for glory, and Virginia Woolf, who sought her love and
      affection." Includes commentary on Vita's affair with Mary Campbell,
      Roy Campbell's wife, during the period Virginia was writing *Orlando*.

59   SCOTT, P.J.M.   *E.M. Forster: Our Permanent Contemporary*.
      London: Vision. New York: Barnes & Noble, pp. 215.
            Focuses on Forster's "narrative attitude." Includes commentary
      on Forster's *Commonplace Book* and Bloomsbury.

60   SHERMAN, MURRAY H. "Lytton and James Strachey: Biography
      and Psychoanalysis." In *Blood Brothers: Siblings as Writers*. Edited by
      Normand Kiell. New York: International University Press, pp. 329-
      364.
            Deals with the relationships in the Strachey family, especially
      between Lytton Strachey and his brother, James, who was to become
      actively involved in the publication of Sigmund Freud's collected works

through the Hogarth Press. Deals with the Bloomsbury milieu in which much of the mature relationship between these tow figures took place.

61 SHONE, RICHARD. "*The Charleston Artists*: Vanessa Bell, Duncan Grant, and Their Friends." In *The Charleston Artists: Vanessa Bell, Duncan Grant and Their Friends*. Exhibition Catalog. Dallas, Tex.: Meadows Museum and Gallery, pp. 8-10.

Interest in these painters has be prompted by interest in Bloomsbury. It has become difficult, because of the cries "Not those Bloomsberries *again!*", to persuade people "that here are good pictures by interesting artists, work well worth looking at on its own terms." The importance of their home, Charleston, cannot be over estimated, "both as an inspiration of their work and a unique 'document' of a way of life." The catalog includes commentary on individual works.

62 ____. "Omega Workshops: Review of Exhibition." *Burlington Magazine* 126 (June):374-77.

Commentary on two London exhibitions related to the Omega Workshops, one at the Crafts Council Gallery and one at the Anthony d'Offay Gallery: "Both exhibitions demonstrated the great range of imagery at the Omega, when its artists were working with representational motifs--from Lewis's risqué scenes of a procuress and her client to Grant's lily pond on a table-top or the panels of a screen." Also comments on Judith Collins's *The Omega Workshops 1913-19: Decorative Arts in Bloomsbury*.

63 SPADONI, CARL. "Bertrand Russell on Aesthetics." *Russell* 4, no. 1 (Summer):49-82.

Discusses the various influences on Russell's thinking on aesthetics, including his association with G.E. Moore and other Cambridge Apostles, as well as Lady Ottoline Morrell: "Though aware of Ottoline's sponsorship of the post-Impressionism of Roger Fry and her interest in the artistic members of Bloomsbury, Russell could not identify with her endeavors in this direction and he felt very much an outsider."

64 SQUIER, SUSAN MERRILL. "Tradition and Revision: The Classic City Novel and Virginia Woolf's *Night and Day*." In *Women Writers and the City: Essays in Feminist Literary Criticism*. Edited by Susan

Merrill Squier. Knoxville: University of Tennessee Press, pp. 114-33.
  Commentary on *Night and Day*, which involves Woolf's move from Kensington and residence in Bloomsbury. Also deals with connection between E.M. Forster and Virginia Woolf in relation to the novel of the city: "She had moved, upon her father's death, from the restrictions of Kensington to the spacious squares of Bloomsbury, only to retreat after her marriage to the calm of suburban Richmond. So she turned to the classic city novel to explore an issue which was intimately related to her own response to the city in 1915: a woman's struggle to do her own work."

65   STIMPSON, CATHARINE R. "The Female Sociograph: The Theater of Virginia Woolf's Letters." *New York Literary Forum* 12-13:193-203.
  Woolf's letters form "an autobiography of the self with others, a citizen/denizen of relationships." Describes the nature of her relationship with various figures based upon the content of these letters: "Two strong, linked lines in Woolf's letters are witty, incisive, acerbic comments about other people and apologies for having made trouble; for having been indiscreet or acerbic; for having been too little of the angel in the them." Includes comments on her relationship with Bloomsbury figures.

66   STRAWSON, GALEN. "The Ups and the Downs." *Times Literary Supplement* (London) (7 September):986.
  Review of *The Diary of Virginia Woolf*, vol. 5, *1936-1941*, edited by Anne Olivier Bell and Andrew McNeillie. States that in her diary the life outside of her work remains in the background: "But even the death of her nephew Julian Bell, killed in Spain in July 1937, takes second place to her relationship with her work." Mentions briefly the strain of writing the biography of Fry: "She struggled unaccustomed with the constraints of facts."

67   TAYLOR, JOHN RUSSELL. "Roger Fry's Amazing Time-Capsule." *Times* (London) (24 January):7
  Review of two exhibitions, "The Omega Workshops 1913-19," Crafts Council Gallery, and "The Omega Workshops," Anthony d'Offay Galleries. Roger Fry "emerges as the hero of the shows." Suggests that the Omega Workshops represented the confluence of two very different

elements: the Arts and Crafts Movement and the "dangerous forces of international modernism."

68   TOMLIN, E.W.F. "Wyndham Lewis the Emancipator." In *Blast 3*. Edited by Seamus Coony. Santa Barbara: Black Sparrow Press, pp. 109-13.
        Lewis believed "in society, the society of men of intellect, the Republic of Letters. And he spent much time trying to encourage the formation of such a society in the London of his day." In doing so he was fighting against Bloomsbury.

69   TURNER, RALPH. Preface to *The Omega Workshops 1913-19: Decorative Arts of Bloomsbury*. Exhibition Catalog. London: Arts Council Gallery, p. 7.
        Brief note by the Head of Exhibitions, which comments on value of the Omega Workshops to current craftspeople.

70   WOOLF, VIRGINIA. *The Diary of Virginia Woolf*, vol. 5, *1936-1941*. Edited by Anne Olivier Bell and Andrew McNeillie. London: Hogarth Press; New York: Harcourt Brace Jovanovich, 402 pp.
        Preface by Anne Olivier Bell. Various entries deal with Bloomsbury and many Bloomsbury figures. The preface says about these years, "privately she had much to suffer: illness--her own, and more agitating because less expected, her husband's; deaths--sudden and lingering, of friends; violent and devastating, of her nephew; overdue, of her mother-in-law; the tangible dangers and destruction of war; the intangible but nevertheless disabling effects of her own vulnerable nature."

71   WRIGHT, SARAH BIRD. "Staying at Monks House: Echoes of the Woolfs." *Journal of Modern Literature* 11, no. 1 (March):125-42.
        Describes research stay at Monks house, which the author visited in January: "The cheer and laughter of Bloomsbury were absent." Gives history of the house to the present ownership by the National Trust. Prior to this it was let to scholars by the University of Sussex: "The house seemed lonely without a visitor in the garden, often writing about Bloomsbury subjects near the two busts of Virginia and Leonard." Includes photographs of the interior: "Our surroundings were enriched by the paintings, watercolours, and painted tiles of Duncan Grant, Vanessa Bell, Quentin Bell, Roger Fry, and others."

1985

1   ANNAN, NOEL. "Earlier Stracheys." *Listener* (21 November):26-27.

Deals with the Strachey family, with some commentary on the family's association with Bloomsbury.

2   ANSCOMBE, ISABELLE. "Charleston: 'An Imperious Urge to Decorate.'" *Antiques* 127 (June):1360-67.

Charleston is more than the house where Vanessa Bell and Duncan Grant lived. It is a record of "some of the major examples and developments in British decorative arts from 1910 until the 1930s." Gives brief history of Bloomsbury decorative arts, including Omega and developments up to Duncan Grant's death.

3   BAIZER, MARY MARTHA. "The Bloomsbury Chekhov." Ph.D. dissertation, Washington University, 238 pp.

Studies the "role of Bloomsbury in promoting English familiarity with and appreciation for Chekhov's work." Chapter 2, almost half of the dissertation, deals with Bloomsbury writer's contribution to the 1920s enthusiasm for Chekhov. Also evaluates the Hogarth Press's work. Covers figures associated with as well as in Bloomsbury. See *Dissertation Abstracts International* 46: 2286A.

4   BANKS, JOANNE TRAUTMANN. "Virginia Woolf and Katherine Mansfield." In *The English Short Story, 1880-1945: A Critical History.* Edited by Joseph M. Flora. Boston: Twayne, pp. 57-82.

Deals with the inter-relationship of these two figures. They met through Bloomsbury connections.

5   BELL, QUENTIN. "A Cézanne in the Hedge." *Southwest Review* 70 (Spring):154-59.

Describes John Maynard Keynes's "picture coup" in which he purchased various paintings for the nation. A Cézanne still life, *Pommel,* ended up in the hedges outside Charleston. On his return to Charleston from Paris, "he had more luggage than he could easily manage on the walk up to Charleston and that's how the Cézanne got into the hedge."

6   CASHDAN, SONYA HANNAH. "'A Hint of the Fang': Virginia Woolf's Personal Portraits of Women." Ph.D. dissertation, Texas

A&M University, 301 pp.
    Woolf never trusted men and looked to woman for emotional
sustenance: "Their portraits in her private writing reveal the quality of
Woolf's perceptions." Deals with relationship with Vita Sackville-West
and other figures: At the periphery of Woolf's life were strangers,
casual friends, less favored relatives; the outer circle included closer
friends and more favored relatives. Maternal women and 'sweethearts'
comprised the inner circle; at the center of her life was Vita Sackville-
West, her only lover." See *Dissertation Abstracts International* 46:3172A.

7   CLEMENTS, KEITH. *Henry Lamb: The Artist and His Friends*.
     Bristol: Redcliffe Press, 226 pp.
    Lamb at one point had asked Virginia Woolf to marry him and
was actively involved in various Bloomsbury get-togethers when the
Stephen children moved to Bloomsbury.

8   COLEMAN, ALEXANDER. "Bloomsbury in Aracataca: The
     Ghost of Virginia Woolf." *World Literature Today* 59, no. 4
     (Autumn):543-49.
    Questions what texts of Virginia Woolf "have any bearing on the
making of the New Novel in Spanish America," particularly in relation
to Gabriel Garcia Marquez: "The distance between Bloomsbury and
Aracataca is not that great--through the medium of literature, she
spoke to him in ways he never forgot, and of which we have some
record."

9   CORK, RICHARD. *Art Beyond the Gallery in Early 20th Century
     England*. New Haven and London: Yale University Press, pp. 117-
     76.
    Chapter 3, "Omega Interiors," gives an analytical history of
Roger Fry's work on the Omega Workshops, which included work by
Duncan Grant and Vanessa Bell. Ruskin, who exposed "the terrible
wastefulness of a society which prevented so many of its members from
fulfilling their creative selves," is the progenitor. Fry's interest in
"extending his work to the architectural sphere coincided with Fry's
wholehearted commitment to Post-Impressionism." Describes the Ideal
Home Exhibition, "The Post-Impressionist Room," which "broke so
defiantly with the interior design conventions of the day."

10   DEACON, RICHARD. *The Cambridge Apostles: A History of
     Cambridge University's Elite Intellectual Secret Society*. London:

Robert Royce. Reprint. New York: Farrar, Strauss & Giroux, 1986, 214 pp.

History of the secret society that included many Bloomsbury figures among its membership, including Saxon Sydney-Turner, E.M. Forster, Lytton and James Strachey, Leonard Woolf, Henry Norton, Maynard Keynes, and Roger Fry. Suggests that "after Lytton Strachey probably the dominant influence in the Society for many years was John Maynard Keynes." Various chapters deal with Bloomsbury related issues, such as "The Higher Sodomy," which describes "the distinct undercurrents of homosexuality in the Society" that were to carry over to Bloomsbury, and "After Armageddon," which covers the pacifist activities of members during World War I.

11   DOWLING, DAVID. *Bloomsbury Aesthetics and the Novels of Forster and Woolf.* New York: St. Martin's Press; London: Macmillan, 249 pp.

Extensive study of the inter-relation of the arts that emerged as a result of Bloomsbury associations: "I believe that aspects of the ideas of Bell and Fry--significant form, psychological volume, rhythm, the aesthetic emotion--inform, in different ways, the novels of Woolf and Forster." The opening chapters deal with the relation of painting and writing and with an overview of Bloomsbury aesthetics. Charles Mauron and Goldsworthy Lowes Dickinson are next identified as convenient personal and theoretical loci for the literary theories of the Bloomsbury figures. Definitions of literature and painting emerged over the years in spatial and temporal terms. The relation between art and life also becomes crucial. "The difference between Bell and Forster's aesthetics lies in the different emphases placed on space and time. For Bell, Beauty is spatial and exists out of time; for Forster it is intimately connected with time." Evaluates Forster's and Woolf's novels, as well as their critical dialogue, in relation to these issues. Woolf's exposure to Fry's ideas influenced her work significantly: "Woolf found the enterprise and product of painters a useful sounding-board for the development of her own ideas about the novel." Finally, Woolf and Forster exemplify two artistic responses to G.E. Moore's influence on Bloomsbury: "Now, to put it crudely, Forster's novels are studies of friendship, and the essential element in the business of fiction for him is the friendship between the writer and reader; Woolf's novels are studies of how to contemplate (aesthetically) the world, and the essential element in the business of fiction for her is the novel as a beautiful object."

12   FORSTER, E.M. *Selected Letters of E.M. Forster*, vol. 2, *1921-1970*.
      Edited by Mary Lago and P.N. Furbank. Cambridge: Harvard
      University Press, 365 pp.
          Includes letters to and about Bloomsbury and Bloomsbury
      figures: "Oh the Bells, the Woolves--or rather Virginia, for I do like
      Leonard! Oh how I do agree, and if to become anti-Bloomsbury were
      not to become Bloomsbury, how I would become it."

13   FROMM, HAROLD. "Recycled Lives: Portraits of the Woolfs as
      Sitting Ducks." *Virginia Quarterly Review* 61, no. 3 (Summer):396-
      417.
          The lives, more than the writings, of Leonard and Virginia
      Woolf are suffering "from the ills of hyperpoliticization." Uses Cynthia
      Ozick's review of Quentin Bell's biography of Virginia Woolf and
      Elaine Showalter's *A Literature of Their Own* as emblematic of the
      assault on their lives: "Ozick's assault on Leonard Woolf, more
      demeaning to herself than to him, exhibits the all-too-familiar way in
      which political positions develop as emanations of private psychological
      needs and then are projected as binding morality upon a resisting
      outside world." Relates this discussion to the Bloomsbury milieu.

14   FURBANK, P.N. "Forster, Eliot, and the Literary Life." *Twentieth
      Century Literature* 31, nos. 2-3 (Summer):170-75.
          Lessons that emerge from the "tenuous, but actually rather
      friendly, relationship" between T.S. Eliot and Forster "concern, first, the
      potentialities of humanism as a way of looking at literature, and,
      secondly, the rewards of good style in the leading of the literary life."
      Involves some overlap with the Bloomsbury milieu.

15   GARNETT, ANGELICA. "Life at Charleston." *Southwest Review*
      70, no. 2 (Spring):160-72.
          Personal commentary on the history and life of Charleston, the
      farmhouse Vanessa Bell set up with Clive Bell and Duncan Grant.
      Describes the early years when Virginia Woolf and David Garnett were
      also in residence: "Perhaps the most characteristic thing about our
      lives there was the way they fell into halves: on the one hand the
      painters, on the other Clive and his friends, mostly literary."

16   GILLESPIE, DIANE F. "Bloomsbury, Forster and Woolf." *English
      Literature in Transition* 28, no. 3:312-15.
          Review of David Dowling's *Bloomsbury Aesthetics and the Novels*

of Forster and Woolf. Focuses on two ways paintings and novels relate:
the temporal form of the novel, "within which references to paintings
can appear in the narrative to aid in character development," and the
novel as painting, "the sense that a novel should be *appreciated* in the
same way as a painting."

17   GRANT, DUNCAN. "A Letter to Michael Holroyd." *Southwest
     Review* 85, no. 2 (Spring)70:149-53.
         Shows Grant's reactions to Michael Holroyd's biography of
Lytton Strachey. Introductory note by Richard Shone states that "it was
interesting to see Grant making his contribution to the emancipation
climate of the Sixties just as he had participated in a similar movement
a half century before."

18   HALLS, MICHAEL. "The Forster Collections at King's: A Survey."
     Twentieth Century Literature 31 (Summer-Fall):147-69.
         Survey of E.M. Forster's papers bequeathed to his College,
which includes memoirs written for the Bloomsbury's Memoir Club:
"Other memoirs written for the Memoir Club are known as *Bloomsbury*
(a brilliant and witty account of Forster's first contacts with Roger Fry
and the Bloomsbury world; this may be the contribution to the Club
that Virginia Woolf admired, given on 17th November 1920), and an
abstract, well-crafted meditation beginning 'How can I write a memoir
when I have lost my memory?'"

19   HARRIS, MARTHA JOHNSON. "Clive Bell's Formalism in
     Historical Perspective." Ph.D. dissertation, University of Georgia,
     231 pp.
         "In the early part of the twentieth century, the ideas espoused by
Bell's Bloomsbury friends such as Roger Fry, and the philosopher G. E.
Moore's theory of value, played an important role in the formulation of
his hypotheses in *Art*." Deals with Bell's concept of "significant form"
and "aesthetic emotion" in relation to Fry, Post-impressionists, and
German aesthetics. See *Dissertation Abstracts International* 46:2469A-
70A.

20   HIMMELFARB, GERTRUDE. "From Clapham to Bloomsbury: A
     Geneology of Morals." *Commentary* 79 (February):36-45.
         Gives history and connections between the Clapham Sect and
the Bloomsbury Group: "Bloomsbury was, in fact, as much a group (or
circle or coterie) as Clapham was a sect. And it performed something

of the same function, setting the tone and agenda for the cultural 'vangard' of the nation. Where Clapham had inspired a moral and spiritual reformation, Bloomsbury sought to effect a moral and spiritual liberation--a liberation from Clapham itself and from those vestiges of Evangelicalism and Victorianism that still persisted in the early 20th century." States that if Bloomsbury had any philosophy it was this: "a total commitment to 'personal affections' and 'aesthetic enjoyments.'" Similar article published in 1985 (1986.17). Reprinted in *Marriage and Morals Among the Victorians and Other Essays*.

21   HOLROYD, MICHAEL. "A Visit with Duncan Grant." *Southwest Review* 70, no. 2 (Spring):148-49.
        Personal account of his visit with Duncan Grant during the period he was writing his biography of Lytton Strachey: "My day at Charleston taught me something about Bloomsbury that I could never have picked up in so vital a way from paperwork," the quality of the virtues of private life that Grant embodied.

22   LEWIS, THOMAS S.W. "Virginia Woolf's Sense of the Past." *Salmagundi* 68 (Fall-Winter 1985-86):186-205.
        Evaluates Woolf's sense of the past as shown in her various writings, including letters, diaries, biographies, novels: "For Woolf historical facts are not enough to convey history; indeed, they count for very little when not acted upon by a vital imagination." Her move to Bloomsbury "enabled Virginia Woolf to enter a new world, to shuck temporarily the past of her parents and all they stood for, and to create a new order." Describes the Sackville's past as emblematic as well.

23   MEESON, PHILIP. "In Search of Child Art." *British Journal of Aesthetics* 25 (August):362-71.
        "The idea of child art and modern art go hand and hand." In Britain, Clive Bell and Roger Fry were involved in "broad critical support for child art." Shows connection between Fry and Maurice Denis.

24   MEISEL, PERRY, and WALTER KENDRICK. Introduction and Epilogue. *Bloomsbury-Freud: The Letters of James and Alix Strachey*. New York: Basic Books, pp. 3-49, 305-34.
        The introduction gives intellectual and social context of the psychoanalytic revolution for letters in this volume. Also gives the

biographical background of Alix Sargent-Florence and James Strachey, who was the brother of Lytton. Alix took up residency in Bloomsbury, where she became "friendly with the group that would define her social world for many years. It included Carrington, the Olivier sisters, and several of the Stracheys, along with economist John Maynard Keynes and mathematician Harry Norton." James's activities included association with the 1917 Club: "If Bloomsbury had an official headquarters, it was the 1917 Club, founded in that year (taking its name from the Russian revolution) by Leonard [Woolf] and Oliver Strachey, with premises in Garrard Street, Soho." The "Epilogue" describes the aftermath of the separation that produced these letters: "Though by the late twenties the close connection between Bloomsbury and psychoanalysis had been confirmed, Virginia, alone among her circle, was entirely hostile to the idea of being analyzed."

25   MITTAL, S.P. *The Aesthetic Venture: Virginia Woolf's Politics of the Novel*. Delhi: Ajanta Publishers, 169 pp.
      Chapter Two, "The Shaping Influences" (pp. 13-35) deals with Bloomsbury. The foundation of Virginia Woolf's "catholic literary taste was laid by her father," but the period of rigorous training occurred after her father's death and she moved to Bloomsbury. Evaluates the influence of G.E. Moore and Roger Fry, who became "the aesthetic mentor of Bloomsbury" and exercised the greatest influence on Woolf. He changed the perspective of Bloomsbury to French literature and art.

26   MORAN, MARGARET. "'The World as It Can Be Made': Bertrand Russell's Protest against the First World War." *Prose Studies* 8, no. 3 (December):51-68.
      Russell "sincerely believed that his stand" against the war "could make a difference to the fate of the world." The perilous state he felt Western culture was in was communicated to Lady Ottoline Morrell, with whom he was having an affair. Letters to Ottoline show his private attitude about individuals.

27   NATHANSON, CAROL A. "The American Reaction to London's First Grafton Show." *Archives of American Art Journal* 25, no. 3:2-10.
      Examines how modernism passed from Europe to America, with the American reaction to the first Post-impressionist exhibition as more central than the Armory Show of 1913. Describes fully the American press's reaction to the exhibition, as well as many contemporary accounts published in British periodicals and in books.

28 PAPADOPOULOS, V.D. "Virginia Woolf and G.E. Moore: The Importance of Moore's Personal and Aesthetic Ideas in Selected Works by Virginia Woolf." M.A. thesis, Exeter University, 156 pp.

Evaluates Wool's intellectual background, including "the education she received and her relation to the young intellectuals who were later to form the Bloomsbury Group." Gives an account of the central ideas of Moore's philosophy in relation to Bloomsbury. See *Index to Theses* 35, no. 3:1088.

29 PARTRIDGE, FRANCIS. *Everything to Lose: Diaries, 1945-1960.* London: Victor Gollancz, 383 pp.

Diaries by a Bloomsbury figure which deals with the activities of many Bloomsbury figures, first and second generation, who survived into the post-World War II world. Also includes commentary on past activities and figures of Bloomsbury: "The Bloomsbury philosophy of sex, surrounded by which Ralph and I have lived for twenty years, disregards conventions but certainly not human feelings, nor does it sanction causing unnecessary pain. G.E. Moore's *Principia Ethica* set personal relations on a pinnacle for Bloomsbury, yet I think they are less promiscuous than their image in the eyes of the more conventional."

30 QUICK, JONATHAN R. "Virginia Woolf, Roger Fry and Post-Impressionism." *Massachusetts Review* 26, no. 4 (Winter):547-70.

Describes the evolution of the connection between Virginia Woolf's aesthetic and the influence of Roger Fry and Post-impressionism: "Fry's influence did not blossom suddenly in the writing of *Mrs. Dalloway* and *To the Lighthouse*, but was the result of the gradual and complex growth of their relationship, which was as deeply personal as it was intellectual and professional."

31 RHEIN, DONNA E. *The Handprinted Books of Leonard and Virginia Woolf at the Hogarth Press, 1917-1932.* Ann Arbor: UMI Research Press, 166 pp.

Attempts to "show through the handprinted books the rich and fascinating contribution made by the Woolfs to British literature and their place in the tradition of book arts." Deals with the connections between Bloomsbury, the Bloomsbury Artists, the Omega Workshops and the handprinted books produced by the Hogarth Press. Separate chapters deal with "The Press in the Lives of the Woolfs" and "Books by Friends." Cambridge and the Apostles tie many of these authors to the Woolfs.

32 ROSENBAUM, S.P. "Towards a Literary History of Monteriano." *Twentieth Century Literature* 31 (Summer-Fall):189-98.

The generic and thematic relations of Forster's fiction and essays to "that of his predecessors, contemporaries, or followers have still to be studies in any comprehensive way." Looks at his first novel: "To a certain degree the focus will be on the interrelations of *Where Angels Fear to Tread* [which Forster wanted to call *Monteriano*] and Forster's Cambridge milieu, which included various members of what was to become the Bloomsbury Group." Relates the novel to Bloomsbury values as they evolved out of the Cambridge world.

33 SPENCE, MARTIN. "Inspired Clutter." *Art and Artists* 223 (April):8-11.

The Subtitle reads: "Martin Spence tells the story of Charleston, the farmhouse home near Berwick in Sussex of the Bloomsbury painters Duncan Grant and Vanessa Bell, now being restored and opened to the public." Describes the impulsive nature of these figures as manifest in the decorative work, the clutter, of Charleston. Includes a discussion of the Omega Workshops. Includes photographs.

34 SQUIER, SUSAN MERRILL. *Virginia Woolf and London: The Sexual Politics of the City*. Chapel Hill: University of North Carolina Press, 220 pp.

Argues that Virginia Woolf "used the city in her works to explore the cultural sources and significance of her experience as a woman in a patriarchal society." Woolf's treatment of the city "reveals not only her personal history but also her developing understanding of the political and psychological implications of gender and class distinction." The characteristics of Bloomsbury often figure in the argument.

35 STEEL, D.A. "Escape and Aftermath: Gide in Cambridge." *Yearbook of English Studies* 15:125-59.

Describes Gide's visit to England and his relationship with several Bloomsbury figures associated with Cambridge: "Lady Strachey, a widow since 1980, had rented 27 Grange Road for the summer. Around this formidable lady was gathered the equally formidable Strachey family, several of whom Gide was to come to know." Also discusses his association with Roger Fry, Lady Ottoline Morrell, Lytton Strachey, and Dorothy Bussy.

36 STEWART, JACK F. "Color in *To the Lighthouse*." *Twentieth Century Literature* 31, no. 4 (Winter):438-58.
　　In *To The Lighthouse* "Woolf's search for spiritual essences is expressed in light and color." Shows connection between Woolf and Fry in the connection between the novel and painting, particularity in relation to Cézanne and the Post-impressionists.

37 ____. "Cubist Elements in *Between the Acts*." *Mosaic* 18, no. 2 (Spring):65-69.
　　Picasso hand "made a personal impact on Bloomsbury in 1919, when he and Olga came to London with Diaghilev's *Ballets Russes*; Picasso made some drawings of Lydia Lopokova (later Mrs Maynard Keynes), dined with Clive Bell (an old acquaintance) and Fry, and visited the Omega." The creative consciousness "behind Cubism finds an echo in Virginia Woolf," especially in *Between the Acts*. Shows influence of Fry on Woolf as well.

38 SUTTON, DENYS. "Duncan Grant: A Centenary Tribute." *Apollo* 121 (April):218-19.
　　In recent history there have been several approaches to painting; significant form, which excludes the human; the social and personal, which places the artist on the analyst's couch; and now we have the nostalgic: "Nostalgia has done much to promote the images of the Bloomsbury set, and excessive praise, some may think, has been lavished on Virginia Woolf." Duncan Grant was a part of this work and is caught up in the nostalgia.

39 ____. "Herbert Horne: A Pioneer Historian of Early Italian Art." *Apollo* 122 (August):130-35.
　　Deals with the relationship between Roger Fry and Herbert Horne in light of their interest in early Italian art. Covers the period prior to Fry's association with Bloomsbury. Deals briefly with Fry's attitudes that led up to the Post-impressionist exhibition of 1910.

40 TILBY, MICHAEL. "André Gide, E.M. Forster, and G. Lowes Dickinson." *Modern Language Review* 80, no. 4 (October):817-32.
　　Forster never knew Gide well, but there is "more to say about the connections between the two men than existing biographies

suggest." Includes some overlap into the Bloomsbury world Gide
became associated with during his 1918 visit to England, especially his
relationship with Dorothy Bussy.

41   TORGOVNICK, MARIANNA. *The Visual Arts, Pictorialism, and the*
      Novel: James, Lawrence, and Woolf. Princeton: Princeton
      University Press, 267 pp.
            Includes two relevant sections, chapters Three, "The Sisters'
      Arts: Virginia Woolf and Vanessa Bell" (pp. 107-23) and Four, "Art,
      Ideologies, and Ideals in Fiction: The Contrasting Cases of Virginia
      Woolf and D.H. Lawrence" (pp. 124-156). Chapter Three explores
      some of the roles that Vanessa played "in Virginia's attitudes toward
      her own work, toward the visual arts that constituted her sister's arena,
      and especially the connections between the two." Chapter Four deals
      with Woolf's admiration for modern art and Lawrence's distrust of it.
      Early sections of this study comment on the association James and
      Lawrence had with Bloomsbury.

42   TOTAH, M.F. "Consciousness Versus Authority: A Study of the
      Critical Debate Between the Bloomsbury Group and the Men of
      1914, 1910-1930." D.Phil. dissertation, Oxford University, 315 pp.
            Investigates the critical debate between Bloomsbury and the
      Men of 1914 (Ezra Pound, Wyndham Lewis, T.S. Eliot, and James
      Joyce). Evaluates aesthetic concepts and doctrines of these two groups:
      "activism and passivism; classicism and romanticism; anti-humanism and
      liberal humanism; the non-vital; the image of art and life as amorphous
      and fluid, and an art of fixity and stasis." See *Index to Theses* 35, no.
      2:550.

43   VELICU, ADRIAN. *Unifying Strategies in Virginia Woolf's*
      Experimental Fiction. Uppsala: Uppsala University, 120 pp.
            Includes some commentary on Woolf's experimental fiction and
      Bloomsbury, as well as connections with Post-impressionist aesthetics.

1986

1   "An Afternoon at Charleston." *Crafts* 80 (May-June):11-12.
            Brief commentary on the opening of Charleston, the farmhouse
      where Vanessa Bell and Duncan Grant lived, to the public. Quotes
      Quentin Bell on the environment as art: "Vanessa Bell and Duncan

Grant had already come to the conclusion that a painting might escape from the picture frame."

2   ARCHER, JANE. "The Characterization of Gender-Malaise: Gazing up at the Windows of *Jacob's Room*." In *Gender Studies: New Directions in Feminist Criticism*. Edited by Judith Spector. Bowling Green, Ohio: Bowling Green University Press, pp. 30-42.
    Analytical essay on *Jacob's Room* which involves a discussion of Virginia Woolf's relationship with her brother, Thoby. Evaluates her role in this society: "After Leslie Stephen's death, when the young Stephens set up house together in Bloomsbury, Woolf had a chance to enter this romanticized world of intellectual communion." This world raises gender problems: "Gender-based power structures and gender-inspired hostilities appear on nearly every page" of *Jacob's Room*.

3   BERGONZI, BERNARD. "The Bloomsbury Pastoral." In *The Myth of Modernism and Twentieth Century Literature*. New York: St. Martin's Press, pp. 1-11.
    Reprinted from *New Review* (November 1974):50-54. (See 1974.7.)

4   BHARUCHA, RUSTOM. "Forster's Friends." *Raritan* 5, no. 4 (Spring):105-122.
    Commentary on Forester's various friendships, including some of his Bloomsbury associates. Gives sense of the influence the Group had on his work.

5   CHEW, SHIRLEY. "Leonard Woolf's Exemplary Tale 'Pearls and Swine.'" *Journal of Commonwealth Literature* 13, no. 1: 44-49.
    Analytical article on Woolf's story. Deals briefly with his Bloomsbury association.

6   COMPTON, SUSAN. *British Art in the 20th Century: The Modern Movement*. Exhibition Catalog. London: Royal Academy of Arts, 457 pp.
    Includes several articles relevant to Bloomsbury: Frederick Gore, Introduction; Andrew Causey, "Formalism and the Figurative Tradition in British Painting"; Charles Harrison, "Critical Theories and the Practice of Art." Also includes reproductions and commentary on various Bloomsbury artists and related figures: Frederick Gore and Judith Collins, "Camden Town and Bloomsbury"; Richard Core, "The

Cave of the Golden Calf"; Richard Cork, "The Vorticist Circle,
Bomberg and the First World War"; Frederick Gore, "The Resilient
Figure: Mark Gertler and Matthew Smith." The introduction describes
Fry's impact through the Post-impressionist exhibitions and the Omega
Workshops. "Formalism and the Figurative Tradition in British
Painting" deals specifically with Vanessa Bell and Duncan Grant.
"Critical Theories and the Practice of Art" describes the aesthetic
ground of modern art as staked out by Roger Fry and Clive Bell.

7   EDEL, LEON. "Leonard Woolf and His Wise Virgins." In *Essaying
     Biography: A Celebration of Leon Edel*. Edited by Gloria G. Fromm.
     Honolulu: University of Hawaii Press, pp. 10-17.
         Study of Leonard Woolf's novel from the perspective of what it
tells us about Woolf at this time and his reaction to Bloomsbury. He
later tried to destroy all copies of the book: "Woolf had good reasons
for his attempts to push his novel out of sight. It was an indiscretion of
his early maturity. He had exhibited too much impatience with his
Bloomsbury friends; he had not disguised Virginia's emotional
difficulties; he had satirized his brother-in-law, Clive Bell; and in
general had shown himself highly irritable--as Quentin Bell remarks--
with 'a certain amount of brittle talk' in Bloomsbury." Edel calls for a
reprinting because of what it tells us of the Group.

8   FIELDING, XAN, ed. *Best of Friends: The Brenan-Partridge Letters*.
     London: Chatto & Windus, 252 pp.
         Various letters by these two Bloomsbury associates who met in
the army during the First World War relate to other Bloomsbury
figures, Dora Carrington, Lytton Strachey, and Virginia Woolf in
particular. Many letters deal with the relationship between Carrington,
Strachey, Partridge, and Brennen. Includes some commentary by the
editor.

9   FLINT, KATE. "Virginia Woolf and the General Strike." *Essays in
     Criticism* 36, no. 4 (October):319-34.
         States that "Virginia and Leonard Woolf's friends and associates
were not easy to define in political terms." Their personal politics were
radical, and "their sense of liberation from conventions of social
behavior spread into other areas." The involvement of "the Bloomsbury
Group in issues of social reform was strong."

10   FORBES, PETER. "Art Unfettered: Charleston Restored." *Country Life* (28 August):609-11.

Commentary on the restoration of Charleston, the farmhouse home of Vanessa Bell, Duncan Grant, and Clive Bell. Includes photographs.

11   FROMM, GLORIA G. "Re-Inscribing the Years: Virginia Woolf, Rose Macaulay, and the Critics." *Journal of Modern Literature* 13, no. 2 (July):289-306.

Based upon earlier drafts, various critics are recasting *The Years*: "As a result, the emphasis--and the preference--began to shift from the public version of *The Years* to the raw materials that went into shaping it, for from these sources could be constructed the views of an angry militant feminist." Deals with her relationship with Rose Macaulay, a lesser-known contemporary, which includes a discussion of other figures such as Vita Sackville-West.

12   FROMM, HAROLD. "Leonard Woolf and His Wise Virgins." *Hudson Review* 38, no. 4 (Winter):551-69.

Characterizations Leonard Woolf's psychological make up, which is also expressed in his novels: "Woolf's fatalism and its by-product, the protestation that nothing matters, are demonstrated with relentless and depressing intensity in his novels." Raises a problem with *The Wise Virgins*, his most autobiographical novel. Deals with the relationship between the biographical elements and the structure of the novel as Bildungsroman.

13   GARNETT, ANGELICA. "Charleston Remembered." *Antique Collector* 57, 5 (May):66-71.

Autobiographical account of Vanessa Bell's daughter of her early life in the farmhouse where her mother and natural father, Duncan Grant, lived, on the occasion of the restoration of Charleston Farmhouse. Gives sense of Bloomsbury from second-generation point of view. Describes the partnership of Duncan Grant and Vanessa Bell in the decoration of the house. Recounts the activities during World War I, when David Garnett and Duncan Grant did farm work as conscientious objectors to the war: "After 1918 Charleston was used mainly for holidays and not always then. Little decoration was done until with the acquisition of a car the house became more easily accessible from London and owing to renewal of the lease it was worth spending something on."

14   GLENDINNING, VICTORIA. "Analysis Envy." *Times Literary
     Supplement* (London) (28 March):334.
          Review of *Bloomsbury/Freud* edited by Perry Meisel and Walter
     Kendrick. The relationship between James and Alix Strachey was
     tenuous: "Both were sexually ambivalent and a perfect match." They
     did manage to "love one another, in an uncosy Bloomsbury way."
     Gives overview of the letters in relation to the translation of Freud's
     work, which took twenty-one years for the Stracheys to complete.

15   GOLDSTEIN, MALCOLM. "Review of Angelica Garnett's
     Deceived with Kindness: A Bloomsbury Childhood." *Sewanee Review*
     94 (Summer):1xi-1xii.
          Questions the world of Bloomsbury's candor based upon
     Garnett's more cynical view.

16   GROSSKURTH, PHILLIS. "Review of James and Alix Strachey,
     Bloomsbury/Freud." *University of Toronto Quarterly* 55 (Spring):306-
     10.
          Stresses the importance of the Hogarth Press and the
     introduction of the English translation of Freud in Britian. Bloomsbury
     was central to this accomplishment.

17   HIMMELFARB, GERTRUDE. "From Clapham to Bloomsbury."
     Quadrant 30, nos. 1-2 (January-February):19-28.
          Commentary on the intellectual development from the Clapham
     Sect to the Bloomsbury Group: "If Bloomsbury had any philosophy it
     was this: a total commitment to 'personal affections' and 'aesthetic
     enjoyments.'" See 1985.20.

18   HODGKINSA, LIZ. "No Longer Afraid of Virginia." *Times*
     (London) (24 October):15.
          Subtitle reads, "Henrietta Garnett, a scion of the Bloomsbury
     group, wants her first novel to be judged on its own merits." Gives
     overview of Henrietta's life, with comments on her famous relations.
     Her novel is *Family Skeletons*, published by Gollanez.

19   HOOKER, DENISE. *Nina Hamnett: Queen of Bohemia.* London:
     Constable, 325 pp.
          Biographical account of Hamnett, a figure related to
     Bloomsbury. Deals with her artistic development and with her

relationship with Bloomsbury, particularly with Roger Fry and the Omega Workshops.

20   HOWARD, RICHARD. "Stanzas in Bloomsbury." *Paris Review* 28 (Summer-Fall):187-88.
     Poem with Bloomsbury theme, subtitled, "Mrs. Woolf entertains the notion of a novel about Lord Byron."

21   HUXLEY, JULIETTE. *Leaves of the Tulip Tree: Autobiography.* London: John Murry, 248 pp.
     Autobiography of Juliette Baillot, who served as governess to Julian Morrell and later married the elder brother of Aldous Huxley, Julian. Includes a chapter on the world of Garsington during World War I, "Life at Garsington," in which she describes various Bloomsbury figures and activities: "The religion of Bloomsbury was above all anti-bore. To be a bore was a Crime, the horror of horrors which put one beyond the pale; to avoid such a calamity, gossip took wing and malice sharpened every telling."

22   KNOX, BERNARD. "Forster's Later Years." *Grand Street* 5, no. 4 (Summer):120-36.
     Commentary on Forster in the 1930s and his public work: "His Bloomsbury friends in fact did not take his role as a public figure seriously."

23   LEE, HERMONIE. "Introduction." In *The Hogarth Letters.* Athens: University of Georgia Press, vii-xxviii.
     Gives background to the collection of letters which the Hogarth Press began to publish in 1931. The idea was Virginia Woolf's: "You may write the letter to anyone, dead or alive, real or imaginary, on any subject." The letters were written by various Bloomsbury figures and associates. Lee shows how the letters refelct much of the Cambridge/Bloomsbury milieu: "This is the language of rational liberal optimism, of Cambridge and Bloomsbury; it expresses belief in the possibility of maintaining a free civilization in the jungle of the modern political world."

24   LEVEY, MICHAEL. "The Earliest Years of the Burlington Magazine: A Brief Retrospective." *Burlington* 128 (July):474-78.
     Comments on Roger Fry's association with this magazine, including a sense of the artistic world during the early part of the

twentieth century which was important in relation to Fry's involvement in the Post-impressionist exhibitions and Bloomsbury.

25 McCORD, FRUS PHYLLIS. "'Little Corks that Mark a Sunken Net': Virginia Woolf's 'Sketch of the Past' as a Fictional Memoir." *Modern Language Studies* 16, no. 3 (Summer):247-54.
     Question critical response in relation to works by Woolf: "The autobiography of even such a figure as Virginia Woolf, who died in 1941, cannot be subjected to verification by our knowledge of the reality of the author and her Bloomsbury surroundings: the historical character of Virginia Woolf (née Stephen) is herself a construction of the evidence provided to most of us by literary means only--biographies, her own works, and so on."

26 McNEILLIE, ANDREW. Introduction to *Essays of Virginia Woolf*, vol. 1, *1904-1912*. London: Hogarth Press. pp. ix-xvii.
     Gives the early history of Woolf's essay writing, which is distinct from the "Great Tradition" of F.R. Leavis and the high culture of T.S. Eliot. By 1909 she is less preoccupied with reviewing: "In 1910 she volunteered to work for Women's Suffrage and took part in the *Dreadnought* hoax. Roger Fry that year organized the first Post-impressionist exhibition and became a part of Bloomsbury."

27 MORAN, MARGARET. "More or Less in Love." *Russell* 5, no. 2 (Winter 1985-86):175-83.
     Review of several texts, including *Brett: From Bloomsbury to New Mexico* by Sean Hignett. Involves commentary by Lady Ottoline Morrell on various figures, as well as some remarks about Brett and Russell.

28 NOJIMA, HIDEKATSU. "Bloomsbury no Naka kara." *Eigo Seinen* 131:556-58.
     In Japnese. Not seen.

29 PLATT, SUSAN NOYES. "Formalism and American Art Criticism in the 1920s." *Art Criticism* 2, no. 2:69-84.
     Describes the link between Clement Greenberg's formalistic criticism and the aesthetics of Clive Bell and Roger Fry. Gives overview of the formalism of Bell and Fry: "While Bell was a successful popularizer, although with a solid intellectual foundation, Roger Fry was a systematic analyzer."

30   RUDIKOFF, SONYA. "Virginia Woolf in Sweden and Finland."
     Virginia Woolf Miscellany 27 (Fall):3.
         Comments on the enthusiasm for Woolf's work. Irma
     Rantavaara's work on Woolf and Bloomsbury has created a special
     climate of interest in Finland.

31   SCHNEIDER, DANIEL J. *The Consciousness of D.H. Lawrence:
     An Intellectual Biography.* Lawrence: University of Kansas Press,
     207 pp.
         Deals somewhat with Lawrence's relationship with Lady
     Ottoline Morrell and the Garsington crowd, as well as with the
     Cambridge figures associated with Bloomsbury, whom Lawrence met
     through David Garnett and Bertrand Russell.

32   SHUSTERMAN, RICHARD. *British Journal of Aesthetics* 26
     (Winter):87-88.
         Review of David Dowling's *Bloomsbury Aesthetics and the Novels
     of Forster and Woolf.* Bloomsbury aesthetics needs and should reward
     serious study: "The fascinating and unconventional lives and loves of
     the Bloomsburies have understandably though regrettably claimed far
     more attention and study than their interesting and influential aesthetic,
     literary, and cultural theories."

33   SPALDING, FRANCIS. *British Art since 1900.* London: Thames
     and Hudson, 252 pp.
         Chapter Two, "Post-Impressionism: Its Impact and Legacy" (pp.
     37-89), describes the change in consciousness that resulted from these
     exhibitions and their relations to Bloomsbury artists and writers.
     Relates this event to other artistic movements, such as Futurism and
     Vorticism. Deals also with Frank Dobson, a sculptor admired by Clive
     Bell, Fry, and Raymond Mortimer. "He was invited to join the
     Bloomsbury-dominated London Artists' Association." It was Stephen
     Tomlin, however, "who made busts of key figures within Bloomsbury, of
     Lytton Strachey, Duncan Grant, David Garnett and Virginia Woolf."

34   ____. "Roger Fry and His Critics in a Post-Modernist Age."
     Burlington Magazine 128 (July):489-92.
         Focuses on Fry's artistic theory, especially his notion of
     formalism, in relation to other critics, including Clive Bell: "It is
     important to distinguish not only between the formalism of Fry and

Bell, but also between Fry's thought and the more dogmatic formalism promoted by Clement Greenberg."

35   SQUIER, SUSAN M. "Tradition and Revision in Woolf's *Orlando*: Defoe and 'The Jessamy Brides.'" *Women's Studies* 12, no. 2 (February):167-77.

Deals with Woolf in relation to the patriarchal tradition of her father and Defoe. *Orlando* was a challenge to this tradition. The relationship and the novel were sexually liberating. The original title of the novel, "The Jessamy Brides," reinforces "Woolf's own defiance of social conventions in her love affair with Vita Sackville-West."

36   TRAUB, EILEEN. "The Early Years of the Hogarth Press." *American Book Collector* 7, no. 10 (October):32-36.

Describes the establishment of the Hogarth Press and many of the early works and authors associated with the press, including T.S. Eliot's *The Wasteland*: "The Woolfs no only printed many of the early Hogarth Press titles themselves, they scrupulously supervised any title done outside. The making of their books was always important to them."

37   WATNEY, SIMON. "Charleston Revisited." *Art and Antiques* (October):86-91, 108.

The subtitle for this article is, "a friend of Duncan Grant's recalls the country house [Charleston] where the principles of the Omega Workshops came home to roost." Spontaneity was central to their work. Describes Grant and Vanessa Bell.

38   ZWERDLING, ALEX. *Virginia Woolf and the Real World*. Berkeley and London: University of California Press, 374 pp.

Includes commentary on Woolf and her association with Bloomsbury. Deals also with the relationship between the real world and Post-impressionist disregard for representational art.

1987

1   ALLISON, SUE, and ANN BAYER. "Bloomsbury Revisited: Descendants and Intimates Recall a Legendary Circle of English Intellectuals." *Life* 10, no. 3 (March):76-79.

Brief commentary, including photographs by Alen MacWeeney,

by the various surviving descendants of the Bloomsbury Group on the original members. Includes Quentin Bell, Julian Bell, George Rylands, Francis Partridge, Henrietta Garnett, Anthony Fry, Nigel Nicolson, and John Lehmann.

2   BAYLEY, JOHN. "Fun While It Lasted." *New York Review of Books* (17 December):32-35.
      Review of *The Neo-Pagans: Rupert Brooke and the Ordeal of Youth,* by Paul Delany. Comments on the relation of the Neo-Pagans to Bloomsbury: "The term 'Neo-Pagans' was coined by Virginia Woolf. Standing with one foot in Bloomsbury, with its more sophisticated and metropolitan atmosphere, she gave a quizzical glance at the young men and women, many from Cambridge like her brother and friends, who preferred a more bracing and open-air existence."

3   BELL, QUENTIN. "Some Memories of Sickert." *Burlington Magazine* 129 (April):226-31.
      Discusses Sickert's reaction to the Post-impressionist exhibition. Also describes Sickert's various activities in the Bloomsbury Group, including his relationship with Clive Bell and Maynard Keynes.

4   BELL, QUENTIN, ANGELICA GARNETT, HENRIETTA GARNETT, and RICHARD SHONE. *Charleston: Past and Present.* London: Hogarth Press, 176 pp.
      Guide to Charleston, the farmhouse in Sussex which served as the country retreat for the Bloomsbury circle. Includes various essays, "Official Guide to the House and Garden" by Richard Shone, "Charleston Garden: A Memory of Childhood" and "Charleston Preserved" by Quentin Bell, "The Earthly Paradise" by Angelica Garnett, and "Visits to Charleston: Vanessa" by Henrietta Garnett. Also includes a section on the rooms and contents of the house, as well as a section of extracts from various letters and memoirs that relate to Charleston. The essays cover the history of the house, its use by Bloomsbury figures, as well as a description of the attempts to save it.

5   BROUGHTON, PANTHEA REID. "Impudence and Iconoclasm: The Early *Granta* and an Unknown Roger Fry Essay." *English Literature in Transition* 30, no. 1:69-79.
      An essay of Fry's formed part of a coup against Oscar Browning, Fellow of King's, in *Granta*, a Cambridge undergraduate magazine: "This 1889 *Granta* essay exhibits, even as it expresses his immaturity,

what would become Fry's mature questioning of formula and cant." He became the quintessential modernist and an iconoclast, especially in 1910 with the Post-impressionist exhibition.

6   CEVASCO, G.A. *The Sitwells: Edith, Osbert, and Sachevenall.*
     Twayne: Boston, 165 pp.
     Group critical study, with an opening chapter of primarily biographical information: "Beyond the first chapter, biography plays at best a supportive role; for thereafter the focus is analytical and critical." Biographical material leads up to this group's involvement with Bloomsbury figures.

7   CHASE, KATHLEEN. "Legend and Legacy: Some Bloomsbury
     Diaries." *World Literature Today* 61 (Spring):230-33.
     Looks at Bloomsbury through various diaries, including those of Virginia Woolf, Evelyn Waugh, Katherine Mansfield, Frances Partridge, Vita Sackville-West. Gives general picture of Bloomsbury attitudes and opinions as expressed in these documents: "What one looks for in a good diary are improvisation, spontaneity, reasonable truthfulness, a trustworthy picture of the period in which it is written, and a good idea of the character of the writer."

8   CONNETT, MAUREEN. "Carrington." *Bedfordshire Magazine* 21
     (Autumn):69-74.
     Deals with the artistic accomplishment of Dora Carrington and her commitment to Lytton Strachey. Comments generally on Carrington's involvement in Bloomsbury through Strachey, as well as her relationship with Ralph Partridge.

9   DELANY, PAUL. *The Neo-Pagans: Rupert Brooke and the Ordeal
     of Youth.* New York: Free Press, 270 pp.
     Several chapters deal with the Neo-Pagans in relation to the Bloomsbury Group: "What might be called a collective 'affair' between Bloomsbury and the Neo-pagans began near the end of January 1911, when Virginia Stephen met Ka Cox at Bertrand Russell's house near Oxford." Virginia saw the Neo-pagans as "capable of a clean start, free from the Victorian gloom and debility that had shadowed the youth of herself and her friends." The Neo-pagans, in the long run, had less to build on than the Bloomsbury Group: "Part of their fragility as a group derived from a simple inferiority of character and talent, compared with Bloomsbury."

10 FORSTER, E.M. *Forster in Egypt: A Graeco-Alexandrian Encounter: E.M. Forster's First Interview.* Edited by Hilda D. Spear and Abdel Monein Aly. London: Cecil Woolf, 64 pp.

Introduction mentions Bloomsbury. Forster in his interview talks about the Bloomsbury Group.

11 GLENDINNING, VICTORIA. *Rebecca West: A Life.* London: Weidenfeld & Nicolson, 288 pp.

The relationship between West and Virginia Woolf began in 1928, but West "did not fit into Bloomsbury, or want to. She found the whole group 'physically peculiar.'" She made friends with Raymond Mortimer and Clive Bell and thought Vanessa Bell's painted plates were "not good enough to feed a dog off."

12 HAMPSHIRE, STUART. "Liberator, Up to A Point." *New York Review of Books* (26 March):37-39.

Review of Regan's *Bloomsbury's Prophet: G.E. Moore and the Development of His Moral Philosophy* (1987.26). Believes that Regan has succeeded somewhat in "supplementing the conventional picture of Moore." Feels that more has to be made of Moore's "peculiar personality, the impression made by his physical appearance and manners in any gathering, before his civilizing and genial influence can be fully understood."

13 HENDERSON, L.D. "Mysticism and the 'Tie that Binds': The Case of Edward Carpenter and Modernism." *Art Journal* 46 (Spring):24-37.

Describes, in part, Carpenter's importance to the English literary and cultural avant garde, including Roger Fry: "Carpenter's mystical philosophy must have struck a responsive cord in Fry, since a similar outlook infuses Fry's writings on art."

14 HOBERMAN, RUTH. "Feminism and Biography: *Orlando* and *Flush*, Virginia Woolf's 'Jokes.'" In *Modernizing Lives: Experiments in English Biography, 1918-1939.* Carbondale: Southern Illinois University Press, pp. 133-60.

Makes some connections between Woolf's interest in biography, Bloomsbury, and the Memoir Club. Suggests that biography mattered to Woolf because she experimented with it as a means of "redefining her relationship to her father and, on a larger scale, the relation of women to history." Describes some of the influence of Lytton Strachey on Woolf's biographical writing: "To a large extent, Woolf is in agreement with Strachey about what a biography should do, and *Orlando* and *Flush* can be easily read as novelistic biography taken to its logical extreme."

15   McCAIL, RONALD C. "A Family Matter: *Night and Day* and Old Kensington." *Review of English Studies* 38 (February):23-39.
      Describes the connection between Woolf's novel and the intellectual world of her father and old Kensington. Deals also with the movemebt toward the intellectual world of Bloomsbury.

16   McNEILLIE, ANDREW. Introduction to *Essays of Virginia Woolf*, vol. 2, *1912-1918*. London: Hogarth Press, pp. ix - xvii
      Overview of marriage between Virginia Stephen and Leonard Woolf, her mental breakdowns from 1912-1918, and the establishment of the Hogarth Press: "The War, and in particular the introduction of conscription in the spring of 1916, brought certain members of Bloomsbury into the public arena." Briefly describes Bloomsbury's connection to the second Post-impressionist exhibition in 1912 and the Omega Workshops, which followed in July of that year.

17   MANSFIELD, KATHERINE. *The Collected Letters of Katherine Mansfield*, vol. 2, *1918-1919*. Edited by Vincent O'Sullivan and Margaret Scott. Oxford: Clarendon Press, 365 pp.
      Includes letters to and about various Bloomsbury figures, especially Virginia Woolf, Lady Ottoline Morrell, and Dorothy Brett. Comments on her relationship with the figures who attended Ottoline's weekends at Garsington.

18   MARCUS, JANE, ed. *Virginia Woolf and Bloomsbury: A Centenary Celebration*. Bloomington: Indiana University Press, 307 pp.
      Collection of essays on Woolf which originated in the Virginia Woolf Centenary Lectures at the University of Texas. Includes many contributions that deal directly with Bloomsbury, while several other essays deal more specifically with Woolf. In "Bloomsbury: Myth and Reality" Nigel Nicolson states that "Bloomsbury was a reality. It did exist. It is identifiable with named individuals about whom we can now know a great deal. Separately they achieved much in different fields, and collectively they expressed an attitude to life of which each of us is unconsciously an inheritor." Noel Annan, in "Bloomsbury and the Leavises," states that "no one can make sense of the dispute between

Bloomsbury and their bitter critics the Leavises if he does not recognize
that Bloomsbury wrote in the service of an artistic revolution in whose
shadow we still live--of atonalist music; the painting of Picasso and
Matisse; the post-Symbolist poets; and the experimental novel; perhaps,
above all, a new skepticism about authority and tradition." Michael
Holroyd, in "Bloomsbury and the Fabians," uses Lytton Strachey and
Bernard Shaw as representatives of the Bloomsbury Group and the
Fabian Society to describe distinctions between these two groups.
Bloomsbury, unlike the Fabians, "wanted to develop their own emotions
and talent first, and to influence society indirectly, by example more
than precept. It was a renewal of eighteenth-century culture in place
of Victorian values." Angela Ingram, in "'The Sacred Endices': Virginia
Woolf and Some of the Sons of Culture," comments on Woolf's attitude
toward Cambridge: "The buildings of Cambridge, most especially
King's College Chapel, did not merely represent men's 'psychic space,'
but were actual spaces enclosed by actual walls with stones smoothed
and validated, often, by the 'six hundred years' which spelled the
existence of the fictitious St Katherine's College, Oxford, one of the
settings for *The Years*." Jane Marcus, in "'Taking the Bull by the
Udders': Sexual Difference in Virginia Woolf--A Conspiracy Theory,"
states that "it is my contention that what is called 'feminisation' is really
another form of patriarchal power--a homosexual hegemony over
British culture derived from the values of the Cambridge Apostles and
King's College and anti-feminist with a difference--scorpions, not whips."
In "The War between the Woolfs" Laura Moss Gottlieb argues that
most scholars have not "compared Virginia's and Leonard's political
writings," and those that have "ignored the conflict between their views."
Such a comparison sheds "light on the way Leonard and Virginia
communicated with each other."

19   ____. *Virginia Woolf and the Languages of Patriarchy*. Bloomington:
        Indiana University Press, 219 pp.
        Includes "Sapphistry: Narration as Lesbian Seduction" (pp. 163-
87), which comments on Woolf's reaction to "Oxbridge": "But what
concerns me here is that for women like Virginia Woolf, the
homosexual men of Cambridge and Bloomsbury appeared to be, not
the suffering victims of heterosexual social prejudice, but the
intellectual itself, an elite with virtual hegemony over British culture."
Also includes various essays discussed elsewhere in this guide.

20   MEISEL, PERRY. *The Myth of the Modern*. New Haven and
      London: Yale University Press, 288 pp.
           Chapter on "Bloomsbury Novel" deals with Bloomsbury as
      compromise between extremes in modernism: "It is no less than the
      canonical texts of Bloomsbury that provide the middle, saving ground,
      forming as they do a uniformly balanced kind of discourse that
      negotiates the will to modernity." Bloomsbury wishes to return to
      origins, and, simultaneously, calls the reality of such ideals into question
      by exposing the belated means of their literary production. Discusses
      Howard's End, To the Lighthouse, Eminent Victorians, and various other
      works by Strachey: "Strachey is likely Bloomsbury's consummate
      achievement."

21   OAKLAND, JOHN. "Virginia Woolf's Kew Gardens." *English
      Studies* 68 (June):264-73.
           Includes commentary on the visual aspects of Woolf's work and
      the Post-impressionist aesthetic of Roger Fry: "Woolf was initially
      attracted to Post-impressionist thinking, in spite of later changing views,
      since she had reacted to the Edwardian literary concentration upon the
      alien and the external, opposed the arbitrary and limiting conventions
      of Naturalism."

22   PALMER, ALAN, and VERONICA PALMER. *Who's Who in
      Bloomsbury*. Sussex: Haverton Press, 215 pp.
           Alphabetical listing of information relevant to the Bloomsbury
      Group and to the Bloomsbury area of London. The Preface gives a
      brief history of the area and the group: "So varied were the interests,
      achievements and disappointments of this gifted circle that it has
      seemed worthwhile to us to collect summary biographies of them in the
      present book. We have added entries for men and women never at
      the heart of affairs but associated with the group, both before the
      coming of the war and later, when Bloomsbury expanded and conclaves
      would gather, as often as not, in Sussex or Wiltshire and sometimes in
      France."

23   PANKEN, SHIRLEY. *Virginia Woolf and the "Lust of Creation."*
      Albany: State University of New York Press, 336 pp.
           Deals with psyche of Virginia Woolf somewhat in relation to her
      Bloomsbury world.

24 PARKE, MARGARET. "Back in Bloom: The Garden Bloomsbury Made Famous." *Connoisseur* 217 (June):104-7.

Commentary on the Charleston farmhouse garden, which has been restored: "From the start, the garden at Charleston figured in the domestic routine and the idiosyncratic creativity that gave its character to the place." Includes photographs and commentary on the art that also populates the garden along with flowers and shrubs.

25 PAUL, JANIS M. *The Victorian Heritage of Virginia Woolf.* New York: Pilgrim Books, 225 pp.

Deals with the connection between Woolf and the Victorian world out of which she developed her own mode of expression. Gives good sense of background to the Bloomsbury world of which she became the center.

26 REGAN, TOM. *Bloomsbury's Prophet: G.E. Moore and the Development of His Moral Philosophy.* Philadelphia: Temple University Press, 307 pp.

Feels that Moore's importance has waned because he has been misinterpreted. Must consider the early moral and metaphysical doubts and despairs which lead to *Principia Ethica.* Bloomsbury figures are the way into Moore's work, "recall him through Bloomsbury's eyes." Deals with Moore as a liberating force in relation to Victorianism. Includes accounts of conversations and correspondence of Moore and other Bloomsbury figures, drawing extensively on unpublished material. The majority of the text deals with the development of Moore's philosophy using Bloomsbury as a focus.

27 ROSENBAUM, S.P. *Victorian Bloomsbury: The Early Literary History of the Bloomsbury Group*, vol 1. New York: St. Martin's Press, 298 pp.

Not much that has been written about Bloomsbury deals with the texts, which should be our primary concern. This study "describes a historical sequence of Bloomsbury's early interconnected texts in order to interpret them analytically and comparatively." Overall, this work deals with the "intellectual, family, and Cambridge origins of the Group, often as these are reflected in the Group's autobiographical and undergraduate writings." Separate chapters deal with the intellectual origins, including commentary on Leslie Stephen, the Cambridge literary education, the Cambridge philosophical education, and some commentary on early writings, including Apostle papers: "What makes

the Bloomsbury Group more than simply a collection of affinities is the
work they achieved. Their lives are best understood, finally, as they are
enacted in and through their work."

28   SPALDING, FRANCES. "Simon Watney and His Friends in a Post-
     Modernist Age: A Reply." *Burlington Magazine* 129 (April):251-52.
        Reply to Watney in relation to the discussion of Fry's formalistic
     theory of art. Comments briefly on Fry's theory of Post-impressionists
     and on the Omega Workshops.

29   TURNBAUGH, DOUGLAS BLAIR. *Duncan Grant and the
     Bloomsbury Group*. Secaucus, N. J.: Lyle Stuart; A Mario Sartori
     Book, 216 pp.
        Biographical study which includes "Duncan Grant: A Memory"
     by the Duke of Devonshire, Andrew Devonshire, and "Duncan Grant"
     by Kenneth Clark, which serves as an epilogue. Describes his life when
     part of the Bloomsbury Group, as well as the last thirty years of his life
     when his fame had declined. Separate chapters are devoted to
     Bloomsbury, which includes biographical sketches of the various
     participants, the move to Charleston, and Omega Workshops.

30   TWITCHELL, BEVERLY H. *Cézanne and Formalism in
     Bloomsbury*. Ann Arbor, Mich.: UMI Research Press, 315 pp.
        The twentieth century might be called the "Age of Analysis."
     Part of this notion comes from Clive Bell and Roger Fry, whose
     formalist criticism usurped the authority of John Ruskin and Walter
     Pater: "Formalist criticism was born in England in 1910, when Roger
     Fry, with Clive Bell and others in Bloomsbury, assembled and
     catalogued for exhibition a group of French works to demonstrate
     Manet's liberating influence on painting and the ultimate triumph of
     form over content." Includes separate chapters: "Cézanne and the
     Beginnings of Formalism," "Roger Fry's Formalism," "Clive Bell's
     Significant Form," "Cézanne and Formalism in Bloomsbury," "The
     Critics," "Cézanne and Formalism in Bloomsbury: The Artists," and
     "Beyond Bloomsbury."

31   WATNEY, SIMON. "Roger Fry and His Friends in a Post-
     Modernist Age: A Reply to Dr. Frances Spalding." *Burlington
     Magazine* 129 (April):150-51.
        Reply to Spalding's article above in relation to Fry's formalism.
     Also deals with Fry and Post-impressionism.

32 WILSON, JEAN MOORCROFT. *Virginia Woolf: Life and London: A Biography of Place.* London: Cecil Woolf, 256 pp.
    London stimulated Woolf's imagination and "exhausted her with its too abundant 'life.'" This biography looks at Woolf's life, "in particular her response to the various houses in which she lived and worked." In relation to Bloomsbury, for example, Moorcraft suggests that "her feelings of claustrophobia about her Kensington birthplace gave way to a sense of enormous liberation when she moved with her sister and two brothers, after the death of their father, to Bloomsbury." The discussion is organized into separate sections on the various homes, including 46 Gordon Square, which Woolf felt was "her personal center of the universe."

1988

1 FERNS, JOHN. *Lytton Strachey.* Boston: Twayne, 133 pp.
    Study which suggests that Strachey's "more important biographical work grew out of his earlier creative and critical work." Includes some commentary on his relationship with Dora Carrington, Lady Ottoline Morrell, Virginia Woolf, and other Bloomsbury figures. Need more critical work on Strachey: "One can foresee a complete letters and eventually a complete works with supporting or related critical studies that consider such questions as Strachey's role in the new biography, his place in the Bloomsbury group or in the tradition of anti-Victorianism."

2 GILLESPIE, DIANE FILBY. *The Sisters' Arts: The Writing and Painting of Virginia Woolf and Vanessa Bell.* Syracuse: Syracuse University Press, 376 pp.
    Evaluates the inter-relation of creative theory and expression in works of these two sisters: "The sisters shared many assumptions. Most important was their conviction that art is valuable, that the activity of those who are sincere in communicating their perceptions is worthwhile in itself and necessary to generate the few geniuses each age produces." The relationship was complex and supportive: "Competitors and raiders of each other's artistic territories, as well as collaborators and inspirers of each others art works, Virginia Woolf and Vanessa Bell were, above all, productive professional artists whose relationship as

such illuminates the tension and encouragement that exists in the
families of both society and the arts."

3   HERZ, JUDITH SCHERER. *The Short Narratives of E.M. Forster*.
     London: Macmillan, 168 pp.
         Includes a section on E.M. Forster and Virginia Woolf (pp. 140-
147). Relates Forster's use of this genre to Bloomsbury and "the
intensely verbal world they lived in."

1989

1   "Bloomsbury." In *Oxford English Dictionary*. 2 ed. Vol. 2. Oxford:
     Clarendon Press, p. 311.
         Gives definitions of Bloomsbury and Bloomsburian, with various
uses of these words that cover the period of Bloomsbury and before.

Index